THE SHAPING OF WESTERN SOCIETY
An Inquiry Approach

HOLT SOCIAL STUDIES CURRICULUM
General Editor   Edwin Fenton

THE SHAPING OF WESTERN SOCIETY

An Inquiry Approach

EDWIN FENTON
Professor of History
Director, Social Studies Curriculum Center
Carnegie-Mellon University
Pittsburgh, Pennsylvania

JOHN M. GOOD
Formerly, Co-Director of Social Studies Curriculum Center
Carnegie-Mellon University
Pittsburgh, Pennsylvania

HOLT, RINEHART AND WINSTON, INC.
New York / Toronto / London / Sydney

Copyright acknowledgments appear with the materials quoted.
Art acknowledgments appear on pages 394-395.

Cover design: Marvin Goldman
Maps and chart illustrations: William Plummer

CONTENTS

Chapter 2   Medieval Society

Chapter 3   The Renaissance

Chapter 6   The Anatomy of Absolutism

Chapter 7   The Birth of Modern Science

Chapter 8　Economic Growth in a Market Economy

Chapter 9   The French Revolution

Chapter 10   The Movement for Equality and Full Citizenship

Chapter 11   Nationalism

Chapter 12   War and Peace

Chapter 13   Authoritarianism in Russia

Chapter 14   Nazism in Germany

Chapter 15   The West Since World War II

Maps

Charts and Graphs

TO THE STUDENT

This is a new kind of textbook. Most social studies texts you have used in the past probably contained information about one subject, such as civics or geography. The textbooks were usually written by one or two authors who organized material into chapters, each with an important theme. The authors illustrated these books with pictures, graphs, and charts, each with a caption beneath it to explain what the illustration showed. You read or examined this material to learn the facts and generalizations it contained.

Instead of twenty or thirty chapters written by one or two authors, this textbook has sixty-five readings arranged in sixteen chapters. Each reading contains one or more articles or pieces of source material taken from a newspaper, magazine, book, government document or other publication, or written especially for this volume. An introduction which connects one reading to another and study questions which will help guide your search for information precede each selection. A question for thought follows each reading. It is intended to help you reflect on the connections among the readings. The essays link the historical periods and summarize information contained in the readings. In addition, most readings contain two value clarification questions, identified by the mark ▶. These questions are designed to help you consider how changes or new developments cause value dilemmas for individuals. They may cause value dilemmas for you too.

Numerous illustrations designed, like the written materials, to provoke careful thought appear throughout the book. In addition, the Classroom Support Unit which accompanies the course contains a number of silent filmstrips, sound filmstrips, recordings, picture cards, transparencies, tests, and dittoed handouts. Your teacher will use these materials from time to time. He or she will also probably encourage you to work individually or as a member of a small group on special materials designed for individual and group activities.

All these materials have been chosen or written with great care. Instead of merely memorizing facts or generalizations, you will be asked to use them to identify problems, develop hypotheses or tentative answers to questions, gather information, and come to your own conclusions. Throughout this course, you will be challenged to think for yourself and to make up your own mind.

Most teachers assign one reading from this book for each night's homework. Because most classes meet from seventy-five to eighty-five times a semester and there are only sixty-five readings in the book, there will be days when no readings from the book are assigned. There are many ways to use the extra days. Some teachers prefer to move quickly through the readings. They then develop separate activities for the remaining weeks in the semester. Others prefer to build a variety of related activities into each chapter. They assign supplementary readings, study current events, hold individual conferences with students, give tests, or encourage you to do individualized projects from the Individual and Group Activity Component.

During the last century, the influence of western society has touched the entire world. American and Canadian civilization grew from the cultures that Europeans brought to this continent. Even tiny villages in Africa and Asia feel the impact of ideas, institutions, and technology developed in the West. No one can hope to understand what is happening in the world today without having a knowledge of the history that shaped western society and, hence, so much of the modern world. But Europe's history alone spans twenty-four centuries, beginning with the humanist tradition that flowered in ancient Athens. Therefore, instead of trying to mention everything that happened during these centuries, the readings in this book concentrate on the most important elements in western history. The historical essays and the time lines provide essential chronological links.

Edwin Fenton
General Editor
Holt Social Sciences Curriculum

HOW TO USE THIS BOOK

The text of *The Shaping of Western Society* consists of sixty-five readings which have been edited from published works or written especially for this course. Each reading follows a common pattern:

1. *The introduction.* Each introduction relates a reading to other readings in the course and supplies the essential background information.
2. *Study questions.* A few study questions call your attention to the most important points of the reading so that you can think about them in preparation for class discussion.
3. *The article or source material.* Each reading contains one or more documents, newspaper accounts, articles from magazines, or other forms of written material.
4. *A thought question.* One question designed to provoke thought about the meaning of a reading appears at the end of each lesson.

You are expected to read each day's lesson and to take notes on it before you come to class. Since your teacher will distribute dittoed material from time to time, you ought to get a three-ring looseleaf notebook which can hold both the material to be distributed and your homework and classroom notes.

Note-taking is a vital skill. We suggest that you read and take notes (using ink so that notes will be legible at final examination time) on the readings in the following manner:

1. *Write the reading number and title at the top of a piece of notebook paper.*
2. *Skim the entire reading.* Read the first sentence in each paragraph of the introduction. Next read the study questions and get them fixed in your mind. Finally, read the first sentence in each paragraph of the article or source material. When you have finished, try to state in your own words what the lesson for the day is all about. Skimming such as this should never take longer than a few minutes.
3. *Read the introduction and take running notes.* Do *not* read first and then read again for notes. Do *not* underline or mark the textbook in any way. Write down the major ideas from the introduction and any supporting evidence that seems

particularly important. You need not use complete sentences, but remember that you may wish to study from the notes later, so take down enough information to make notes meaningful.

4. *Read the article or source material carefully and take running notes.* Do *not* read first and then read again for notes. Do *not* underline or mark the textbook in any way. Take the same sort of notes you took for the introduction. Put any conclusions you draw in parentheses to show that they are your own ideas.

5. *Go over your notes, underlining key ideas or words.* This procedure is the best way to begin learning the information in the lesson.

6. *Try to answer the question found at the end of the reading.* When you have finished studying your notes, try to answer the question that follows the reading. This question will always require you to think independently about the subject you have been studying. Do not write out the answers to this thought question. Think it through so that you will be prepared to discuss it in class.

Two additional study techniques will be useful. First, keep a vocabulary list in which to enter all new words and their definitions. In many cases, vocabulary words have been defined in the textbook in the marginal notes. Second, keep your class notes and your reading notes on a lesson together in your notebook so that you can review for tests without flipping through a mass of paper to find material on the same subject.

Your teacher will help you if you have trouble with this note-taking technique. He or she may occasionally spend time in class to demonstrate good note-taking techniques and will criticize your notes in an individual conference if you request one. Do not hesitate to ask for help.

INDIVIDUAL AND GROUP ACTIVITIES

At the end of each chapter, you will find brief descriptions of activities designed for individual or small group study. If your school has purchased The Shaping of Western Society Support Unit, your teacher will find an Individual and Group Activity Component inside it. This component may also be purchased separately. Your teacher will tell you how to find detailed instructions for each activity in the *Student Book of Activities and Readings* contained in the Individual and Group Activity Component. He or she will also explain procedures for using this material. From time to time, teachers may also make supplementary assignments of their own, independent of the Individual and Group Activity Component.

An Introduction
to the Study of History

STATING THE ISSUE

What image pops into your head when you hear the word *history?* Some people see great leaders or glamorous men and women from the past. Others see a dull collection of facts and generalizations bound into a textbook. Still others see events in the lives of ordinary men and women.

What is history? Here are three quite different definitions:

—a chronological record of events, particularly of the development of a people, country, or institution;

—one person's interpretation of the past;

—a pack of tricks we play on the dead.

As you study this chapter, try to develop your own idea of what history is. Not everyone will arrive at the same definition. Historians often disagree with each other about the nature of history. They have written thousands of books in an attempt to work out a definition of history that would be accepted by all historians. So far no one has succeeded.

You should not expect to understand the nature of history at the end of one week's study. The five assignments in this Introduction merely open the topic. They give you an opportunity to begin to develop some ideas about the nature of historical investigations.

This chapter's examination of the nature of history concentrates on a few key issues. For example, it analyzes how historians decide what is fact and how they classify facts into groups of related events. And it examines ways in which historians develop and support hypotheses. Your ideas about such issues will mature as you continue to study and write history yourself. Only by using the tools of a historian can you fully understand what history means. This chapter marks the beginning point in your study.

1 HOW A HISTORIAN CLASSIFIES INFORMATION

Historians usually begin an investigation by asking a question, such as "What caused the French Revolution?" Historians answer such questions in books or articles and give evidence to support their answers. They collect information by taking notes from many sources. Then they arrange this evidence so that the facts support a conclusion. But what determines the facts that a historian will note in the first place? Will all historians using the same sources and trying to answer the same question take the same notes? And how does a historian decide how to arrange the evidence that he or she has collected? Without careful structuring, this evidence would have little or no meaning.

Your study of history begins with the problems of selecting and arranging data. In order to concentrate on these problems without becoming involved in a true historical subject, we have chosen evidence that would usually not appear in a history course. In class, however, you will be able to examine the meaning of this evidence for the study of history.

A list of eighteen terms follows. Classify them into groups of terms that seem to belong together for some reason. For example, if you had been given the words *tiger, pine tree,* and *iron ore,* you might classify them as animal, vegetable, and mineral. Or you might classify them as living and non-living. You can probably think of a number of additional ways to classify these words.

Think of as many ways to classify the following eighteen terms as you can. Come to class prepared to discuss your classification system.

shark	tuna	pike
turkey	condor	eagle
rabbit	ostrich	sheep
cat	lion	pheasant
grouse	black bass	collie dog
rainbow trout	elephant	barracuda

2 HOW A HISTORIAN INQUIRES INTO THE PAST

Many high school students believe that history tells a dull story about dead men. Historians would not agree. Many of them define history as inquiry—the systematic examination of alternative solutions to problems. But what problems do historians choose to examine? And how do they examine these problems systematically?

The problems that historians choose to examine come from their frames of reference. Their personal experiences, their concern for the problems of society, their position in the social scale, and their knowledge all help to shape the questions they ask. A historian who worked her way through college might ask questions about how poor people were educated in colonial times. Another historian who has felt the effects of racial discrimination might investigate slavery in the United States in the early nineteenth century. Still another historian who comes from a family of lawyers and who has studied the history of France might investigate the role of lawyers and judges during the time of the French Revolution.

In addition to historians, anyone who reads magazines or books often identifies historical problems. A study of history always begins with a problem to investigate. As Reading 1 showed, historical problems come out of the frame of reference of the investigator. For this reason, different people will often see different problems in the same body of evidence.

Historians often phrase their problems in the form of questions, such as "What caused the fall of the Roman Empire?" or "How did people govern themselves in ancient Athens?" To begin their investigations, they develop hypotheses—tentative answers to their original questions. Then they gather evidence to see whether or not their hypotheses are right.

Reading 2 gives you an opportunity to identify a historical problem of your own and to develop hypotheses about it. Following are a selection of pictures showing eighteenth-century Great Britain. These pictures show events in the daily lives of the people. Your teacher will probably divide the class into groups to look at these pictures. As you examine them, try to follow these steps:

1. Identify one or more historical problems suggested by the pictures.
2. Write down these problems in the form of questions.
3. Develop hypotheses about these questions.

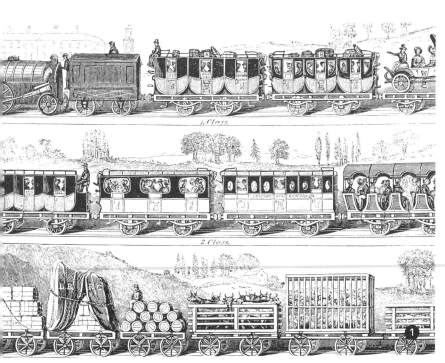

An English city scene

Housing in an English city

Coal-mining in 1750

4

A spinning mill

Steam engines transporting coal

5

3 HOW A HISTORIAN DECIDES WHAT IS FACT

Identify a problem; develop hypotheses; search for valid evidence which relates to these hypotheses. All historians are familiar with these steps in the inquiry process. But how do historians know that the evidence they find is accurate? Sometimes scholars can find only one account of an event, and they must then decide whether or not to believe it. Sometimes two or more sources disagree about what happened. Historians must then decide which account, if any, to accept.

This reading will give you an opportunity to decide which facts can be accepted when two authors disagree about many details. Suppose that civilization on earth has long since been destroyed by hydrogen bombs. You have just landed from Mars. (We won't speculate about what you look like or how you got here.) You are able to read both English and Russian because your midget computer makes instant translations into Martian.

In a time capsule buried on the site of ancient New York, you discover a yellowed magazine containing an account of a revolution in a place called Hungary. In another time capsule on the site of ancient Moscow, you discover a fading radio script describing the same event. The two accounts are all the information you have. As a historian, Martian variety, it is your task to decide what the facts are. As you read these two articles (one from *Time* magazine and the other an actual broadcast from Radio Moscow), think about the questions that follow:

1. Do the two accounts agree about some things? If so, are you willing to accept those things as fact? Why or why not?
2. What are some of the issues on which the accounts differ?

Hungary: The Five Days of Freedom

"Hungary: The Five Days of Freedom," **Time,** November 12, 1956, p. 40, copyright © 1956 by Time, Inc. Reprinted by permission.

For five frantic days Hungary was free.

From . . . Budapest on Tuesday [October 30, 1956] the news flashed that the Soviet tanks were pulling out. Shouted the jubilant announcer:

"For long years past this radio had been an instrument of lies. It lied day and night. It lied on all wavelengths. . . . From this moment those who mouthed the lies are no longer. . . . We who are now facing the microphone are new men." It was the voice of the people of Hungary in that hour: a great burden had been cast off.

The first to see the unfamiliar face of freedom were the young rebels. Their weapons at the ready, their faces filthy with the grime of battle, their clothes often blood-caked, they stood along the arteries of battle leading out of the battered city, happily jeering the departing Soviet tanks as they rumbled sullenly by.

TANK SMASHING

Only a few hours before, desperate battles had been fought at the Maria Theresa barracks, at the Communist Party headquarters, and at the steel mills at Csepel Island. With their heavy 76-mm. guns, the Soviet tanks had attempted to blast the rebels out of their hiding places, but the "incredible youngsters" had evolved their own technique for dealing with the mighty 26-ton tanks. First they would fire on the tanks from upper-story windows, then as the big T-34s rumbled up, their great guns elevated, a small boy would leap out of a doorway, fling a pail of gasoline over the tank's engine compartment, and leap back to shelter. As the tank took fire and its crew scrambled out of the turret, the young Tommy-gunner firing from the windows above would mow them down. An alternate system was to slosh a bucket of gasoline across a street and throw a match in it just as a Soviet tank plunged past.

FREEDOM FIGHTERS

Now, as they began to realize what had happened and what they had done, the faces of the rebels were lit with a kind of ecstasy. There were vigorous blond students and tough-looking workers among them, but many seemed pitifully young. A correspondent noted a boy who could not have been more than ten years old holding himself at the ready with a rifle as tall as himself. Beside him was a 15-year-old girl with a submachine gun and a forage cap on her head. Gray with the fatigue of four days' ceaseless fighting, almost falling from exhaustion, they solemnly welcomed the foreigners: "We greet you in the name of the Hungarian Freedom Fighters!" Some carried machine-gun ammunition belts slung around their shoulders, and out of almost every pocket and above every inch of belt protruded hand grenades.

Premier Nagy had disowned the city's 10,000-man Communist security-police force, and the Russians had pulled out leaving the hated AVH men to their fate. Most of them had found temporary ratholes. In a huge concrete bunker below Communist Party headquarters, some 200 were said to be hiding out with political prisoners as hostages. Scores hung from trees and lampposts. . . .

The AVH were the secret police.

DEMOCRACY'S RETURN

What had come over Hungary, without anyone quite realizing it, was democracy.

To continue holding down the premiership, new Premier Nagy was forced to yield to the pressures of the new parties, to promise free elections, to acclaim neutrality, and, above all, to insist that the Russian troops be withdrawn, not only from Budapest, but from Hungary.

From the moment the U.S. correspondents had begun coming into free Budapest the rebels had never ceased to ask, "When are the Americans coming?" During the middle of the fighting a Hungarian had lifted up his son so that a child might touch a U.S. flag on a correspondent's car. Again and again, innocent of world affairs, they had asked if arms would come soon from America. Said one: "If the Russians come back, we can't hold out forever."

The Russians were coming back, and many Americans were leaving Budapest. Sadly the Hungarians watched them go. They had no stake in the revolution; they were at peace with the mighty Soviet Union and hoped to remain so—Hungary's bloodshed was only a drop of what the world would suffer in a total war.

A Soviet Tourist in Budapest

Moscow

E. M. Bazarina, as quoted in Richard Lettis and William F. Morris, "The Hungarian Revolt," in **The Hungarian Revolt,** Melvin J. Lasky, ed., pp. 126-127, copyright© 1957 by Melvin J. Lasky. Reprinted by permission.

We arrived in Hungary on 19 October with other Soviet tourists. We spent four days touring this beautiful country and were everywhere given a most cordial and hearty welcome. On Tuesday, 23 October, on our way to a theatre we saw crowds of people in the streets of Budapest. They were lined up in ranks and carried placards, many of which bore the inscription "Long live Hungary!". . . The students were demanding the redress [correction] of errors . . . committed by the Hungarian Government. They were legitimate demands. . . .

On that first evening I saw from the hotel in which we were staying a man with a rifle appear in the deserted street. He took up a position in one of the drives and, taking careful aim, began shooting out the street lamps. The lamps went out one by one and darkness enveloped the street. What prompted the marksman to do this? Just hooliganism? Hardly. I think he was one of the bright sparks of the reactionary underground who wanted to create confusion and chaos in the city. Quite soon afterwards there were flashes of gunfire and sounds of battle and we saw wrecked and burning buildings in the streets of Budapest, overturned tram-cars and other vehicles. Firing would die down and then flare up again. Hostile elements were aiming at paralyzing the city's life but the workers of Budapest were repelling the rebels. Detachments of armed workers tried to restore order in the streets and prevent looting. In many places, including the area around our hotel, workers' patrols were posted. . . .

One member of our hotel staff, a middle-aged man with grey hair, told us: "Our workers cannot have had a hand in this looting and rioting. It is fascism raising its head." And that is what it was. The counterrevolutionary underground was in action in Budapest. Fascist reactionary elements had arrived there from abroad. The hostile venture was gathering momentum and the Hungarian Government asked the USSR Government for aid. In response to this request Soviet military units in Hungary under the Warsaw Treaty entered Budapest in order to help to restore order. The overwhelming majority of Hungarians welcomed this move in the hope that life in the city would quickly return to normal. I myself saw in one street how the people were welcoming the Soviet tanks. . . .

When Soviet troops began withdrawing from Budapest, an unbridled White Terror started in the Hungarian capital. We Soviet tourists recall this time with horror. It is difficult to describe the chaos which reigned in the city where public buildings were destroyed, shops looted, and where crowds of armed bandits, obviously fascists, walked along the streets committing bestial [brutal] murders in broad daylight. I shall never forget what I saw with my own eyes. I think it was on 30 or 31 October. A man in a sports suit walked along the Lenin Boulevard. He might have been one of those who tried to restore order in the city. Several armed ruffians wearing counterrevolutionary tricolours ran up to him. A horrible inhuman cry was heard. A whole crowd of bandits appeared from somewhere. I was unable to see what they were doing with their victim, but in a few minutes he was hanging on a nearby tree with an eye gouged out and his face slashed with knives.

Some time ago I read how the fascists in Germany burnt progressive literature on bonfires. We saw similar things. . . . A group of some hooligans looted and set fire to the House of Books. Thousands and thousands of books were smouldering in the muddy street. We were there, witnesses of this barbarity. The works of Chekhov, Shakespeare, Tolstoi, Pushkin, and other famous authors were lying in the mud, black

Fascism is a form of government based on feelings of nationalism and anti-Semitism. Fascists claim to be the promoters of law, order, Christian morality, and the rights of the educated class. Being very class-based, fascism is in direct opposition to Communism.

The Warsaw Treaty, signed in 1955, was a twenty-year pact that set up a unified military command for the Soviet satellite nations and provided for the maintenance of Soviet troops in these territories.

White Terror was a counter-revolutionary movement that took place during the French Revolution.

smoke rising. We saw an old man who lifted a few books, then carefully wiped the mud with his sleeve, pressed them to his breast and walked slowly away. Many people did the same. . . .

More than once we were witnesses to acts which manifested [showed] the friendly attitude of the Hungarians towards the Soviet people. This friendly attitude was felt by us Soviet people, when we were leaving Budapest. . . . In small groups of two or three people we made our way along the devastated streets towards the Danube in order to board a Red Cross steamer. We were accompanied by a worker . . . a young girl. She led us from one crossroad to another, fearlessly seeking the safest way. At the pier we heartily embraced her. She said: "Someone in the West wants us to pull their chestnuts out of the fire. Don't believe them, dear friends. We Hungarians are for socialism and we are with you." When we were in Czechoslovakia on our way home, we learned that the counterrevolution in Hungary was routed and that life was becoming normal in the country. Now we are at home in Moscow. We shall not forget that Hungarian girl who said that the Hungarians were for socialism and that they were with us. . . .

FOR THOUGHT:

What standards should you use to decide whether a statement of fact in an account is correct?

Dog meat has been eaten in every major German crisis at least since the time of Frederick the Great, and is commonly referred to as "blockade mutton." It is

4 WHAT IS HISTORY?

Students often think of history as a chronological account of facts about past events. But actually the history that appears in history textbooks consists mainly of generalizations rather than facts. For example, examine the following two paragraphs from a well-known American history textbook:

Slavery was further weakened by the fall of the Roman Empire and the rise of a new way of life (feudalism) in western Europe. Though there were still slaves in Europe during the Middle Ages, the average person was a serf. He had to obey his master, work for him, and give him a large share of all he produced. But a serf was much better off than a slave. He could not be sold away from his land and his family. He could keep what was left of his produce after he paid his dues to his lord.

As conditions in Europe improved, the serfs and slaves gradually obtained their freedom. In the seventeenth century, when the English colonies in America were founded, both serfdom and slavery were disappearing in western Europe. . . . Strangely enough, this evil practice got a fresh start in the New World just when it was ending in the old one.

Sidney Schwartz and John R. O'Connor, **Exploring Our Nation's History** (New York: Globe Book Co., 1969), p. 288.

tough, gamy, strong-flavored.
—*Time, November 25th.*

Look up the word *fact* in your dictionary. Then look up the words *generalization* and *generalize*. Reread the two paragraphs above with these definitions in mind. Examine each sentence independently to see whether it contains facts or generalizations.

Even if historians wanted to, they could not give a complete and unbiased account of the past in a textbook. In the first place, only a tiny proportion of one percent of all the events that happened in one place during any period of time—say France during the eighteenth century—were ever recorded. Most events either went unnoticed by writers or did not seem important enough to record. For this reason, no one can make statistically accurate statements about how people in France felt about their rulers. Hence, a history of France during the eighteenth century can record only a tiny proportion of all the recorded events.

In a lifetime, no person could study all the first-hand accounts of life in France during the eighteenth century. Imagine the task. You would have to read all the newspapers written in France and abroad, work through all the relevant government documents of a dozen nations, examine the collections of family papers, check the diaries, and visit the museums, the picture collections, and the buildings that remain from the period. A historian who spent his or her entire life studying eighteenth-century France could examine only a small part of the events that had been recorded.

History textbook writers who have not specialized in the study of eighteenth-century France will read a number of books and articles about it before they write a textbook. Perhaps they might read fifty during their scholarly lifetime. But they cannot possibly read the remaining thousands of books and articles, and they have no good reason to do so anyway. They could not use most of the information they would learn from this reading. So textbook writers know only part of what specialists in a subject know; the specialists in turn have examined only part of what was recorded; and the recorded materials cover only a small part of what actually happened.

Then the authors of a conventional text decide to give twenty pages in their book to an analysis of eighteenth-century France, focusing their materials on the causes of the French Revolution. They must decide what to include and what to leave out. Often they will look at what other authors have written as a rough guide to what is important. But they can include only a small part of what they know about the eighteenth century in the twenty pages they write. Their account represents a part of what they know, learned from reading a part of what specialists know, written from studying a part of the records, which represent only a tiny fraction of one percent of all the events that happened.

"*Tell it like it was, man!*"

Can the writer really "tell it like it was"?

Why should you learn the facts and generalizations in these twenty pages?

History is a kind of research or inquiry. It is organized around asking and trying to answer questions. These questions concern something the investigator does not know for certain.

Historians work by interpreting remains from the past, such as documents, buildings, paintings, or recordings. Historians read and look and listen, selecting the evidence that seems important and arranging it according to established logical rules.

History is useful to study because it can encourage reflective thinking leading to self-knowledge. A person should know himself or herself. A person should know what distinguishes him or her from other persons and should know the nature of humankind. A clue to what humans are and to what each individual can become lies in what humankind has already done.

Rather than memorize generalizations and facts in a history course, students should learn how to make their own interpretations. All of us must interpret evidence all of our lives. The modern world changes more rapidly than it has ever changed before. The total amount of knowledge now doubles every ten years. This knowledge explosion means that people must be able to learn independently after they leave school.

Studying history as inquiry can help people to become independent thinkers prepared to cope with the knowledge explosion. Readings 1-3 introduced you to parts of a historical method of inquiry. All of the steps in this process appear in the following chart. Examine it carefully. It is the basic method that you will be using in your study of historical problems in the weeks to come.

Steps in a Method of Inquiry for History

1. Recognizing a problem from data
2. Formulating hypotheses
    Asking analytical questions
    Stating hypotheses
    Remaining aware of the tentative nature of hypotheses
3. Recognizing the logical implications of hypotheses
4. Gathering data
    Deciding what data will be needed
    Selecting or rejecting sources on the basis of their relevance
        to hypotheses
5. Analyzing, evaluating, and interpreting data
    Selecting relevant data from the sources
    Evaluating the sources
        Determining the frame of reference of the author of a source
        Determining the accuracy of statements of fact
    Interpreting the data
6. Evaluating the hypotheses in light of the data
    Modifying the hypotheses, if necessary
        Rejecting a logical implication unsupported by data
        Restating the hypotheses
    Stating generalizations

5 SUMMARY EXERCISE

In this chapter, you have been studying the way in which historians investigate the past. As you read and discussed the readings in class, you should have begun to develop your own interpretation of the nature of historical investigations and your own preliminary definition of history.

For the next class, select a historical problem that you would like to examine. For example, you might choose to study the causes of the Russian Revolution of 1917. Then write a paper of no more than three hundred words, in which you analyze how you would investigate this historical problem using the inquiry method.

The Classical Heritage

STATING THE ISSUE

The shaping of western society began more than four thousand years ago on the shores of the Mediterranean Sea. There, three ancient peoples developed values that endure today throughout the West. These values helped to shape the goals and ideals of western economic, political, and social systems. They underlie the western belief in the dignity of man. Therefore, the study of western society often begins with an inquiry into its classical foundations.

Western values have grown primarily from the Judeo-Christian heritage and the ideas of the Greeks and the Romans. Each of these great peoples contributed a number of valuable insights into the nature of man. Great thinkers from each society tried to answer questions that philosophers are still debating: What is a good person? What is a good life? What is a good society?

The heritage from these three cultures eventually came together in western Europe. From the Hebrews and Christians came many of the moral principles that still influence western men and women today. The ancient Greeks gave the West humanism, a philosophy that stressed the dignity and worth of the individual. And the Romans added a legal system that became the cornerstone of many western governments.

Although the people from these cultures started with different ideas about the nature of truth and the origins of man, they developed many of the same values. Chapter 1 explores these values and their meaning. It also discusses ways in which classical values were passed on to the modern world.

15

c. 2000 B.C.	Abraham lays foundation for Hebrew religion.
c. 1225 B.C.	Moses leads Hebrews out of Egypt.
c. 930 B.C.	Palestine is divided into Israel and Judah.
c. 500 B.C.-322 B.C.	Athens flourishes during Golden Age.
461 B.C.-429 B.C.	Pericles serves as leader of Athens.
c. 450 B.C.	Twelve Tables become fundamental laws of Rome.
431 B.C.-404 B.C.	Peloponnesian War ends in ruin for Athens.
390 B.C.-264 B.C.	Rome conquers Italian peninsula.
338 B.C.	Philip of Macedonia conquers Greece.
117 A.D.	Roman Empire reaches greatest extent.
63 B.C.	Palestine falls to Rome.
4 B.C.-29 A.D.	Jesus lives and preaches in Palestine.
476	Barbarians depose last western emperor.
527-565	Justinian rules eastern empire and produces Justinian Code.

6 THE JUDEO-CHRISTIAN HERITAGE

According to that part of the Hebrew Scriptures that Christians call the Old Testament, the Jews are descended from the Hebrews who were led by Abraham during their early wanderings in Arabia. The Hebrews believed in Yahweh, a god who would look after them and protect them as long as they remained faithful to Him. This belief sustained them as they slowly moved westward. Some settled in northern Palestine. Later, others entered Egypt where they prospered, free to practice their religion for many years. But gradually the pharoahs, or Egyptian rulers, enslaved the Hebrews.

After many years, a great leader, Moses, arose among the Hebrews in Egypt. Moses convinced the Hebrews to revolt, and they fled Egypt. They roamed the Sinai Peninsula for forty years. There, according to the Old Testament, God gave Moses the laws He wanted the Hebrews to obey. United by these laws and inspired by Moses, the Hebrews crossed the border of Palestine. In time, the Hebrews dominated the region with powerful kings and judges.

16

About 930 B.C. Palestine was divided into the northern kingdom of Israel and the southern kingdom of Judah. Civil disruption and poor rulers weakened the kingdoms. Eventually other countries won control over them. Only in the years between 168 and 63 B.C. did the Jews regain political control of Palestine but these years ended in internal strife, and Rome easily conquered Palestine.

During the years that Rome ruled Palestine, the Jews were divided among themselves. Their leaders argued about the rituals of Judaism and how to interpret its laws. Many Jews came to believe that God would send a Messiah, a leader, to restore their kingdom. In 4 B.C. Jesus of Nazareth, a Jew and the son of a poor carpenter, was born. When Jesus began his religious ministry, many Jews believed he was the Messiah. But Jesus also made many enemies during his ministry, and in 29 A.D. he was arrested and condemned for his teachings. The court handed him over to the Roman governor, who sentenced him to death. But the teachings of Jesus continued to spread throughout the Mediterranean world.

The Judeo-Christian heritage is largely a legacy of oppressed people subjugated by foreign rulers. Unable to express their values in other ways, the Jews and Christians expressed them in their religions. Their traditions survived in their homes and in their synagogues and churches. Reading 6 contains excerpts from the sacred writings of the Jews and Christians. As you study them, think about the following questions:

1. What moral principles were given in the Jewish laws? How do they define the good person?
2. What moral principles did Jesus preach? How did he define the good person?
3. Compare the teachings of the Jewish laws and Jesus. How do they differ? How are they similar?

God Gives His Laws to the Jews

The first five books of the Hebrew Scriptures—Genesis, Exodus, Leviticus, Numbers, and Deuteronomy—are called the Books of Moses. Moses was said to have written them during the years he led the Hebrews from Egypt to Palestine. According to the Scriptures, God made himself known to Moses in the desert. During these visits God dictated the laws that He wanted His people to obey. Primary among these laws were the Ten Commandments. According to the Scriptures, God called Moses to the top of Mount Sinai to receive the commandments. The following selection includes a modern translation of the Ten Commandments and of other Jewish laws.

CHAPTER 20

The Holy Bible, Revised Version, The Book of Exodus (New York: Division of Christian Education of the National Council of Churches of Christ in the United States of America, 1952).

2 "I am the Lord your God, who brought you out of the land of Egypt, out of the house of bondage.

3 "You shall have no other gods before me.

4 "You shall not make yourself a carved image, or any likeness of anything that is in heaven above, or that is in the earth beneath, or that is in the water under the earth; ⁵you shall not bow down to them or serve them; for I the Lord your God am a jealous God, visiting the wickedness of the fathers upon the children to the third and fourth generation of those who hate me, ⁶but showing steadfast love to those who love me and keep my commandments.

7 "You shall not take the name of the Lord your God in vain; for the Lord will not hold him guiltless who takes his name in vain.

8 "Remember the sabbath day, to keep it holy. ⁹Six days you shall labor, and do all your work; ¹⁰ but the seventh day is a sabbath to the Lord your God; in it you shall not do any work, you, or your son, or your daughter, your manservant, or your maidservant, or your cattle, or the traveler who is within your gates;

12 "Honor your father and your mother, that your days may be long in the land which the Lord your God gives you.

13 "You shall not kill.

14 "You shall not commit adultery.

15 "You shall not steal.

16 "You shall not bear false witness against your neighbor.

17 "You shall not covet [wish for] your neighbor's house; you shall not covet your neighbor's wife, or his manservant, or his maidservant, or his ox, or his ass, or anything that is your neighbor's."

CHAPTER 21

"Now these are the ordinances which you shall set before them. ²When you buy a Hebrew slave, he shall serve six years, and in the seventh he shall go out free, for nothing.

20 "When a man strikes his slave, male or female, with a rod and the slave dies under his hand, he shall be punished. ²¹But if the slave survives a day or two, he is not to be punished; for the slave is his money.

22 "When men strive together, and hurt a woman with child, so that there is a miscarriage, and yet no harm follows, the one who hurt her shall be fined, according as the woman's husband shall lay upon him; and he shall pay as the judges determine. ²³If any harm follows, then you shall give life for life, ²⁴eye for eye, tooth for tooth, hand for hand, foot for foot, ²⁵burn for burn, wound for wound, stripe for stripe.

▶Do you think a person who breaks the law should be sent to prison to be punished, to be rehabilitated, or both?

18

25 "If you lend money to any of my people who is poor, you shall not be to him as a creditor, and you shall not exact interest from him."

Jesus Preaches His Message

The following selection includes the Sermon on the Mount, containing many of Jesus' teachings. Jesus challenged the old interpretations of Jewish law and added his own commandments. He described a new way of life.

CHAPTER 5

Seeing the crowds, he went up on the mountain, and when he sat down his disciples came to him. ²And he opened his mouth and taught them, saying:

3 "Blessed are the poor in spirit, for theirs is the kingdom of heaven.

4 "Blessed are those who mourn, for they shall be comforted.

5 "Blessed are the meek, for they shall inherit the earth.

6 "Blessed are those who hunger and thirst for righteousness, for they shall be satisfied.

7 "Blessed are the merciful, for they shall obtain mercy.

8 "Blessed are the pure in heart, for they shall see God.

9 "Blessed are the peacemakers, for they shall be called sons of God.

10 "Blessed are those who are persecuted for righteousness' sake, for theirs is the kingdom of heaven.

11 "Blessed are you when men abuse you and persecute you and utter all kinds of evil against you falsely on my account. ¹²Rejoice and be glad, for your reward is great in heaven, for so men persecuted the prophets who were before you.

21 "You have heard that it was said to the men of old, 'You shall not kill; and whoever kills shall be liable to judgment.' ²²But I say to you that every one who is angry with his brother shall be liable to judgment; whoever insults his brother shall be liable to the council, and whoever says, 'You fool!' shall be liable to the hell of fire.

38 "You have heard that it was said, 'An eye for an eye and a tooth for a tooth.' ³⁹But I say to you, Do not resist one who is evil. But if anyone strikes you on the right cheek, turn to him the other also; ⁴⁰and if anyone would sue you and take your coat, let him have your cloak as well, ⁴¹and if anyone forces you to go one mile, go with him two miles. ⁴²Give to him who begs from you, and do not refuse him who would borrow from you.

The Holy Bible, Revised Standard Version, The Gospel According to St. Matthew (New York: Division of Christian Education of the National Council of Churches of Christ in the United States of America, 1946).

►What two or three words would you use to characterize the teachings of the Ten Commandments? What words would you use to characterize the teachings of Jesus? How does your choice of words indicate your values?

43 "You have heard that it was said, 'You shall love your neighbor and hate your enemy.' [44]But I say to you, Love your enemies and pray for those who persecute you, [45]so that you may be sons of your Father who is in heaven; for he makes his sun rise on the evil and on the good, and sends rain on the just and on the unjust. [46]For if you love those who love you, what reward have you? Do not even the tax collectors do the same? [47]And if you salute only your brethren, what more are you doing than others?"

CHAPTER 6

24 "No one can serve two masters; for either he will hate the one and love the other, or he will be devoted to the one and despise the other. You cannot serve God and mammon [material wealth].

25 "Therefore I tell you, do not be anxious about your life, what you shall eat or what you shall drink, nor about your body, what you shall put on. Is not life more than food, and the body more than

20

clothing? [31]Therefore do not be anxious, saying, 'What shall we eat?' or 'What shall we drink?' or 'What shall we wear?' [32]For your heavenly Father knows that you need them all. [33]But seek first his kingdom and his righteousness, and all these things shall be yours as well."

FOR THOUGHT:

How do the religious values that Jesus preached influence modern life? How were these values passed on to the modern world?

7 ATHENS IN THE GOLDEN AGE

Beginning about 500 B.C. the people of Athens produced some of the most remarkable art, literature, history, and philosophy of all time. During the next 150 years, Athenians built the Acropolis temples. They produced great philosophers such as Plato, Aristotle, and Socrates, as well as great playwrights, poets, and historians. Perhaps most important, they developed values and concepts of humanism, a philosophy directed at making people master of themselves and of their world.

What sort of people were these Athenians? They were city dwellers and farmers who took pride in Athens. They were able soldiers who took up sword and shield willingly to protect their city-state. Finally, they were active citizens. All native-born Athenian males who owned property participated in political decision-making through the Assembly, the representative body in which legislative power lay. However, women, slaves, and foreigners were barred from government affairs.

Ancient Greece was not one unified nation, but a collection of independent city-states, each jealous of its independence. By 500 B.C. Athens had emerged as the most powerful of the city-states. To avoid being taken over by Athens, many city-states appealed to Sparta, the great military city-state on the Peloponnesus, the southern part of Greece. Although Athens was a superior naval power, Sparta had a far better army. The two powers engaged in a series of conflicts ending with the Peloponnesian War. After nearly thirty years of fighting,

Athens' defeat in 404 B.C. ended its political and economic supremacy. But Athens continued as the cultural center of the Mediterranean world for nearly another century.

To most, the age of Pericles expresses the democracy and culture of Athens at its peak. Pericles ruled from 461 to 429 B.C., when he fell victim to the plague that swept Athens in the early years of the Peloponnesian War. The Athenian historian Thucydides, who recorded the events of the war, included an account of a speech given by Pericles shortly before his death. Reading 7 is a modern translation of the speech. As you study it, think about the following questions:

1. According to Pericles, what are the characteristics of the good person?
2. What advantages did Pericles think that the political and social systems of Athens had over others?
3. How do Athenian values differ from Judeo-Christian values? How are they similar?

Pericles in Praise of Athens

At the end of 431 B.C., after a year of the Peloponnesian War, Pericles spoke at a ceremony honoring those who had fallen in battle. Recent victories over invading Spartan armies had boosted the confidence of the Athenians, and Pericles reflected this mood. He praised the values fundamental to all Athenians and rallied the citizens to the defense of their city.

Thucydides, **History of the Peloponnesian War,** Benjamin Jowett, trans. (Oxford, England: Clarendon Press, 1881), Vol. 1, pp. 36-41. Language simplified.

Before I praise the dead, I should like to point out those principles which had guided our rise to power and describe the institutions and way of life which have made our empire great. For I believe such thoughts are appropriate to the occasion and the citizens and foreigners gathered here may profit from them.

No other form of government rivals our own institutions. We have not copied the governments of our neighbors, but rather, have set an example for them. We are called a democracy because the power to make laws is given to many rather than a few. But while the law gives equal justice to everyone, it does not fail to reward excellence. While every citizen has an equal opportunity to serve the public, we reward our most distinguished citizens by asking them to make our political decisions. Nor do we discriminate against the poor. A man

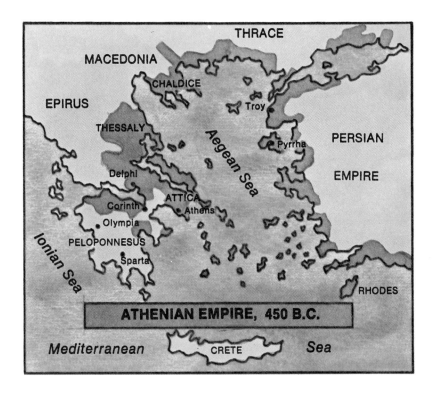

ATHENIAN EMPIRE, 450 B.C.

may serve his country no matter how low his position. We do not allow secrecy in our public affairs, and in our private relations we are not suspicious of one another. We do not become angry with our neighbor if he does what he likes. While we are tolerant of how our neighbor acts, we approach our public duties with reverence. We are prevented from doing wrong out of respect for the authorities and the laws, particularly the laws that protect those who have been injured.

Our military policy is also superior to that of our enemies. Our city is thrown open to the world. We have never expelled a foreigner nor prevented him from seeing or learning anything he could use against us as our enemy. We do not control the lives of our citizens and trick our neighboring cities to assure victory. Instead, we depend on the patriotism of our hearts and the skills of our hands. And in the matter of education, while the Spartans force their youth into lives of hardship and labor to make them brave, we live an easy life. Yet, we are equally ready to face the perils of battle. And here is the proof: The Spartans come to Athens not by themselves, but with all their allies. At the same time we seldom have difficulty defeating them in their own territory, where they are fighting for their homes. Our enemies have never faced our entire military force. We have had to divide our men

23

among our navy and several armies. But when our enemies defeat a part of our force, they are as proud as if they had defeated us all, and when they are defeated, they pretend that our entire force defeated them.

If we prefer to prepare for danger with a light heart rather than with laborious training, and if we gain our courage by force of habit rather than by force of law, do we not gain much? We do not devote our entire attention to getting ready for war, but when the hour comes we are as brave as those who never stop preparing for battle.

▶ If what Pericles said was true, would you agree with him that Athens was "an excellent place to live?"

Our city is an excellent place to live. We are lovers of the beautiful, yet we have simple tastes. We cultivate the mind without losing our manliness. We use our wealth for our needs, not for show. To be poor is no disgrace; the true disgrace is in doing nothing to avoid poverty.

An Athenian citizen does not put his private affairs before affairs of the state; even our merchants and businessmen know something about politics. We alone believe that a man who takes no interest in public affairs is more than harmless—he is useless. And if few of us have the imagination to develop new policies, we all are sound judges of the policies proposed by others. Our enemies believe that discussing a policy prevents action, but we believe that the greatest barrier to wise action is not understanding an issue. Athenians have that particular ability to think before they act, but we do not allow thinking to interfere with acting. Other men either act without thinking or hesitate to act if they think.

We are also unlike other cities when it comes to doing good. We make our friends by doing favors, not by receiving them. He who does a favor is the better friend. We do good to our neighbors not because we want them to repay us in our own time of need but because we are men of good will.

In short, I say that Athens is the school for all Greece. The individual Athenian is able to adapt to all types of conditions and to undertake any project with grace. Our city shall always be remembered. Mighty monuments of our power are the wonders of our own age and will be the wonders of ages to come. We shall not need any poet to praise us, for we have compelled every land and every sea to yield to our valor. Everywhere we have left memorials of friendship and our hostility. Such is the city for whose sake these men nobly fought and died. Everyone of us who survives should, like them, gladly suffer for Athens.

▶ Pericles' speech could be classified as propaganda. He praises the political, military, and cultural life of the Athenians to arouse their patriotism. What place, if any, does propaganda have in politics today? Should it have any place?

The sacrifice which they made has been repaid to each of them, for each has received our praise, and each has been given the noblest of sepulchers [tombs]. I do not speak of those sepulchers in which their bones are laid, but of those in which their glory survives and is proclaimed always and on every fitting occasion in word and deed. For the whole earth is the sepulcher of famous men.

IN THIS TEMPLE
AS IN THE HEARTS OF THE PEOPLE
FOR WHOM HE SAVED THE UNION
THE MEMORY OF ABRAHAM LINCOLN
IS ENSHRINED FOREVER

▶ If, as Pericles says, "the whole earth is the sepulcher of famous men," why do so many modern societies build memorials for their dead leaders? Are there other ways in which you would prefer to spend the money, such as building a concert hall or giving to charity.

FOR THOUGHT:

To what extent are the values in this speech similar to those of modern Americans? How could these values have been passed on to the modern world?

8 LAW AND THE ROMAN EMPIRE

In the seventh century B.C., Rome was a farming village on the Tiber River. Then strong invaders from the north conquered Rome and the area around it. They ruled there for a century and a half, building Rome and its surrounding villages into a powerful

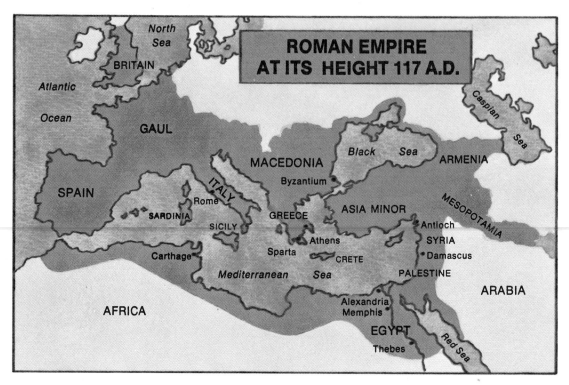

ROMAN EMPIRE AT ITS HEIGHT 117 A.D.

city-state. By 264 B.C. the Romans had overwhelmed their neighbors in Italy and dominated the entire peninsula. By 146 B.C. they had conquered Greece. During the next 250 years, Rome absorbed the peoples of the eastern Mediterranean. By 117 A.D. the Roman Empire reached its greatest extent, covering an area of nearly 4 million square miles. (See map, this page.)

The Romans were more than conquering armies. They displayed a quality that was to temper their rule for hundreds of years. Rome gave Roman citizenship with all its privileges to many of its conquered subjects. It also gave the provinces the right to govern themselves in local matters. In return, the provinces willingly provided Rome with tax revenues, trade, and soldiers for its armies.

In addition, the Romans were agents of civilization, carrying with them not only their own culture but also the culture of Greece. They modeled conquered cities after Rome and built schools and great libraries in them. They constructed highways and built fleets to carry products and armies throughout the empire. Water flowed to the cities through massive aqueducts, and public works were a source of pride. But most importantly, the Romans established rule by law in all the lands they conquered. They administered government that was both just and efficient, and they brought peace to their empire.

26

Roman law evolved from the Twelve Tables, a code of laws that dates from about 450 B.C. As Rome absorbed the areas around it, then the lands bordering the Mediterranean, and finally much of western Europe, the laws were expanded into two separate codes. The *ius civile*, or civil law, governed the Roman citizens, and the *ius gentium*, or law of the peoples, governed all subjects. Gradually, however, Rome granted citizenship to more of its subjects, and the *ius civile* became the basic law.

Roman law was expanded in two ways. First, Roman authorities added to the laws by edicts and decrees. Second, the opinions of judges were added. Roman laws eventually became a hopeless tangle. Attempts were made to collect and interpret them. This task was finally completed under Justinian, emperor of the eastern part of the Roman Empire from 527 to 565 A.D. By the time of Justinian's rule, the western part of the empire had collapsed from economic pressures, civil war, and the attacks of barbarian tribes.

Justinian ordered his lawyers to put Roman law into one legal code, the *Corpus Juris Civilis*. As you study the following excerpts from the code, ask yourself these questions:

1. What rights did Roman citizens have? What procedures protected those accused of crimes? How were disputes decided?
2. What is the Roman definition of justice? How did the laws make it possible for Romans to get justice?

The Justinian Code

In the kingdoms carved out of the western empire, the Germanic rulers adopted much of the old Roman law. After the twelfth century, when western Europe reestablished contact with the Byzantine Empire, much of the Justinian Code worked its way into the laws of European countries. In this way, Roman legal principles survived into modern western society.

GENERAL RULES OF LAW

That which was wrong in the beginning does not become right as time goes on.

Anyone who has the power to condemn a man also has the power to acquit him.

Any privilege or right that is not given to the defendant should not be given to the plaintiff.

Anyone who knows about a crime that is to be committed but cannot stop it from being committed cannot be blamed for the crime.

Corpus Juris Civilis of Justinian. Language simplified.

The plaintiff is the party who sues in a lawsuit.

27

THE CONSTITUTION of the UNITED STATES

Article 1

Section 9

Clause 3

No bill of attainder or ex post facto law shall be passed.

▶Do you agree with this principle of the Constitution? Or should society be able to punish people for doing something that was not a crime when they did it?

No one may be forcibly removed from his own house.

In a case in which the claims of the two parties appear to be equal in merit, the person who has the object in dispute ought to be considered to have the stronger claim.

The seriousness of an offense never increases *ex post facto.*

Anyone who orders an injury to be inflicted is guilty of having inflicted it; but the person who obeyed the order is not guilty.

When a court judges that a man must pay to the extent of his ability, it should take care that the convicted man is not reduced to complete poverty and want.

It is not right under natural law that one should increase his wealth by harming or injuring another person.

No one must suffer a penalty because of what he thinks.

CRIMINAL LAW

The Emperor Trajan ruled that no one was to be convicted merely because he was suspected of committing a crime. He said that it was better for the crime of a guilty person to go unpunished than for an innocent person to be condemned.

In the case of a major offense it makes a difference if the crime was committed accidentally or on purpose. Those who accidentally commit a crime ought to be moderately punished. Those who purposely commit a crime should be dealt with more severely.

The guilt or punishment of a father should not be carried over to his son. Everyone must be judged for his own actions.

When a punishment is prescribed by the court, the age and inexperience of the guilty party must be taken into account.

RULES OF EVIDENCE

The Acts of the Apostles. Chapter 25:16, refers to this principle of Roman law: "It is not the Roman custom to condemn any man until he has met his accusers face to face and has had opportunity to defend himself against their charges."

▶How would you evaluate a person's honorableness, honesty, and objectivity? For example, should a person's social class be used to judge him?

The person who accuses someone must prove that his charge is true. This is not the obligation of the person denying the charge.

The reliability of witnesses should always be carefully considered. Therefore, attention should first be paid to finding out what rank a witness has—whether he is upper class or lower class. The court should find out whether he has led an honorable life. It should find out if the witness is rich or poor in order to discover whether or not he might be likely to falsify his testimony for a bribe. The court should find out if the witness is hostile or friendly to the person against whom he is giving testimony. A man's testimony may be admitted in the court if he is free from suspicion of being dishonorable, free of being motivated by economic gain, and free from influence resulting from friendship or hostility to the accused.

FOR THOUGHT:

How are the legal principles of Rome similar to those of the United States? How might these principles have come to this country?

9 THE CLASSICAL HERITAGE OF WESTERN SOCIETY

A HISTORICAL ESSAY

The values of western society grow from a unique mixture of the traditions of several ancient peoples: the Jews and Christians, the Greeks, and the Romans. The West derived the ideal of brotherhood from the basic Judeo-Christian ethic "Love thy neighbor." From the Greek humanists, the West learned to value liberty. From Rome came the concept that men should be ruled by law. In addition, each of these ancient cultures contributed to the western belief in the dignity of man.

▶What do you consider the most valuable part of your own personal heritage?

The early Hebrews believed that their God, Yahweh, would protect them from earthly harm. In return, they thought that He demanded faithful obedience to His laws. According to the book of Exodus, Yahweh chose Moses to lead the enslaved Hebrews from Egypt and He destroyed the pursuing Egyptian army. When the wandering Hebrews faced starvation in the desert, Yahweh sent them food. He gave Moses the Ten Commandments and the other laws that were to form the body of Judaic belief. At last, Yahweh led the Hebrews to Palestine—the Promised Land. They joined with other tribes of Hebrews already there to overthrow the Canaanites and found their own nation. Weakened by disunity, however, they later became easy victims to conquering armies.

The Jews suffered oppression and misery. Prophets among them said that the Jews had brought misery down upon themselves, for they had violated God's commandments. That is why God sent locusts to devour crops and foreign rulers to subdue the Jews and force them to pay tribute.

The prophets reexamined Jewish religious ideas. Some began to teach the doctrine of salvation after death. A day would come, they said, when God would judge all men, granting everlasting life to the souls of those who had kept His commandments and everlasting torment to the souls of those who had sinned against Him. For many Jews,

29

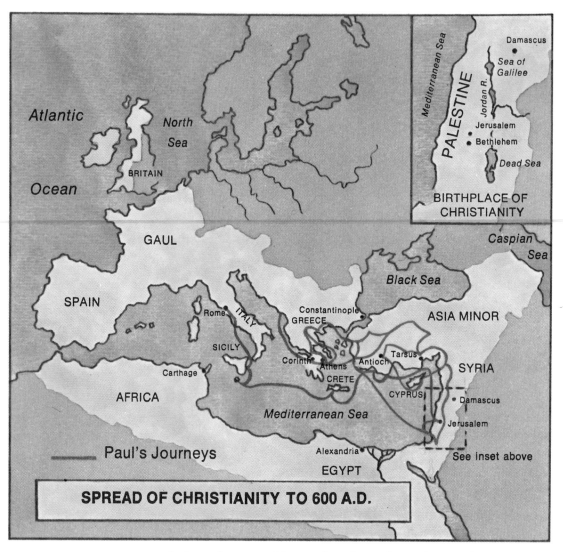

Paul's Journeys

SPREAD OF CHRISTIANITY TO 600 A.D.

the hope for an earthly paradise changed into the belief that salvation lay in eternity.

One prophet, Isaiah, held out hope for a glorious age on earth. He spoke of a Messiah whom God would send to end the suffering of the Jews. He would reunite the Jews to form their own nation once again, and they would spread the word of God's righteousness. An age of universal brotherhood would begin. In the dark years of captivity, such an age seemed very distant to the Jews. But when Jesus appeared in Galilee, many accepted him as the Messiah of Isaiah's prophecy.

30

Jesus proclaimed that he came to uphold the Jewish law and that his God was the Jewish God of salvation. He fulfilled the prediction of the prophets by promising eternal life to those who followed God's law. But Jesus preached that the people must go beyond the letter of the law to its spirit.

As expressed by Jesus, the spirit of God's law can be found in the expression "Love thy neighbor." Yet western history has been as much a history of hatred as one of love. For example, although Jesus was welcomed by many people, he also won the hatred of others and made some powerful enemies. He was arrested, tried, and found guilty of blasphemy. Pontius Pilate, the Roman governor of Palestine, ordered his death, hoping to snuff out a troublesome disturbance in a distant outpost. Yet 350 years later, Christianity had become the official religion of the Roman Empire.

Blasphemy means showing contempt for God by an act or in speech or writing.

The Romans had the ability to adapt new knowledge. Long before they encountered the Christians, they had absorbed the culture of another people—the Greeks. Rome owed much of its grandeur to Greece, particularly to Athens.

The ancient Greeks were the first humanists, the first people to believe in individual dignity and achievement. Athenian citizens were free men, able to live their lives to the fullest. However, the Greeks denied political rights to women and refused to accept them as men's equals. In addition, non-citizens made up more than half of the population. Some were aliens with limited rights. Many others were slaves who were considered property. Greek citizens were able to enjoy their city partly because slaves supported them. Slave labor gave citizens the leisure and the economic means to pursue philosophy, government, and the fine arts.

The Athenians idealized man. They marveled at man's capacity to reason, to create beauty, and to perform feats of physical daring with skill and grace. Their monuments and public buildings, their sculpture and paintings, and their literature and drama all glorified man.

In part Greek religion explains the Athenian view of man. Most ancient peoples regarded their gods as punishers, whose spirits lived in the natural world around them. The Greeks worshiped gods who resembled humans. But the gods were more beautiful, more skillful, and more intelligent than human beings, and they had great powers over man and nature. Their gods were ideals to which the Greeks could aspire. They could hope to be as beautiful as Aphrodite, as athletic as Hermes, and as wise as Pallas Athena.

Aphrodite was the goddess of love and beauty. Hermes was primarily the messenger of the gods. Pallas Athena was the goddess of wisdom.

The military history of Greece also explains its high regard for man. In earlier civilizations landowners did much of the fighting. Only wealthy nobles could afford the armor, chariots, and horses required to take part in battles. But the Greeks fought with foot soldiers, not cavalry.

When faced with a faster moving and more heavily armed cavalry, an army of foot soldiers formed a **phalanx.** They marched shoulder to shoulder, their shields overlapping, making it difficult for the cavalry to penetrate their ranks.

Any farmer or artisan could afford the spear, sword, and shield of the foot soldier. As more of these ordinary citizens began to serve in the armies, Greek cities granted them a greater voice in government. Ordinary citizens enjoyed more economic prosperity and higher status in the social system.

At the top of Athenian society were the aristocrats who traced their power and wealth back to the early Greek kingdoms. At the bottom were poor people and slaves. But most of Athenian society was made up of independent farmers, artisans, and traders. Free to serve his own interests, the average Athenian was much better off than other people of the Mediterranean world. Farmers, for example, did not try to grow grain in their rocky soil, but grew olives and grapes instead. Both cities and overseas markets demanded olive oil and wines. Farmers exchanged them for manufactured goods and for much more grain than they could have produced themselves.

Such was Athens at its height. But Athens slowly lost power after defeat by Sparta in the Peloponnesian War in 404 B.C. Then, in 338 B.C. while still at its cultural height, Athens and all of Greece were conquered by Philip of Macedonia. Alexander the Great succeeded to the throne of Macedonia ten years later. During the next thirteen years, Alexander conquered most of the known world. An ardent admirer of Greek culture, Alexander carried it throughout his empire. Merging with the cultures of the East, Greek culture became known as Hellenism. This was the culture the Romans found when they marched into Greece in the second century B.C. Hellenism provided the bridge from Greek to Roman culture.

The Romans borrowed generously from Greek culture. But the Romans also produced a distinctive art and literature of their own. In science they stressed practical application rather than theory. They were brilliant engineers and architects. But Rome's major contribution to western society grew from its tradition of law. Rome replaced government by men with government by laws that were flexible and just.

As farmers, Romans had to understand the laws of nature. As soldiers, they had to devise laws to regulate the power of some men over others. Roman religion also stressed laws and obedience to authority. In their temples, the Romans created gods to symbolize all the forces that ruled man's life. There were house gods who watched over family and home and nature gods to bring good harvests. When Rome became a city, the Romans created civic gods. All these gods possessed the power to help man, but only if he served them. Obedience to the laws of the gods prepared the Romans to obey the laws of the state.

The early Romans did not separate religion from civic affairs. Their priests became political officials who conducted public sacrifices and

These two pictures show the Parthenon, an Athenian temple built in the fifth century B.C., and the Virginia State Capitol, built in 1792. Why do you think an Athenian building was chosen as a model for a building in the United States?

offered prayers to the gods. But as Rome grew from village to empire, the practical responsibilities of the state took more and more of the magistrates' time. A separate class of priests, trained in special schools, assumed the duties of public worship. They also served as advisers to the rulers, interpreting the will of the gods for them.

Although the Romans grew more and more powerful, they kept their conviction that law comes from an authority greater than man. Nevertheless, the authority of the state gradually replaced that of the gods. Roman law demanded obedience, but for the most part it was applied equally to all. The magistrates and courts could not violate the legal code when acting against a Roman citizen. Laws and customs protected the accused from false charges and prejudiced witnesses. A defendant could not be convicted on hearsay evidence, and the courts assumed that he was innocent until evidence proved him guilty. The law usually governed everyone alike, and therefore it provided justice.

More than any other ancient power, Rome was qualified to administer an empire of many diverse peoples and cultures. Roman law respected the differences among people. The Romans tolerated other religions, they gave their provinces a large measure of self-government, and they extended citizenship to a growing number of subjects. For more than two hundred years, the empire enjoyed the *Pax Romana*—the Peace of Rome. Roman law kept order and administered justice to nearly 100 million people spread over nearly 4 million square miles.

Gradually internal decay and attacks from barbarian tribes destroyed the empire. By 476 A.D. Rome itself was in the hands of the barbarian armies, and the Roman Empire of the West had collapsed. The fall of Rome, however, did not destroy the values and institutions it had carried into the fifth century. These values had been widely diffused throughout the empire. Conquest had played its part. Commerce had been a means of trading ideas as well as products. The remarkable spread of Christianity was the work of dedicated missionaries led by Peter, Paul, and John.

Christianity filled the gap left by the decline of Roman authority. Greek humanism lived on in the schools and libraries built by the Greek colonists. Later, Alexander and then the Romans spread Greek culture. And Roman law outlived the imperial city. The people who struck the fatal blow to the Roman Empire were willing learners. They assimilated much of Rome's culture. They adopted Christianity with zeal. And when the Crusaders in the Middle Ages discovered Greek culture preserved in the Middle East, they again looked to Greece as the center of learning. Western society emerged from the Middle Ages with deep convictions born in ancient times about the good person, the good life, and the good society.

▶What is your definition of law? What limitations, if any, do you think should be put on the law?

Diffusion is the process by which the ideas, institutions, and technological developments of one culture are spread to other cultures.

This missionary spirit in time carried Christianity to all parts of the world.

The Crusades began in 1095 when Pope Urban II urged his followers to march against the Muslims who controlled Jerusalem. The Crusades continued until the end of the thirteenth century.

For full descriptions of these activities, turn to the **Student Book of Activities and Readings** included among the materials for individual and group activities.

Activity 1A: Interview and essay on contemporary conceptions of the dignity of the individual (individual)

Interview three people whose professions bring them into close contact with many different people. In a short essay discuss their conceptions of the dignity of the individual and compare their ideas to the classical view.

Activity 1B: Pictorial illustration of the influence of Greek architecture on contemporary architecture (individual or group)

This activity consists of a group of pictures showing Greek architecture. Examine them carefully. Then photograph examples of Greek architecture in your community or cut out appropriate pictures from magazines. Prepare a photo display, montage, or filmstrip to demonstrate your evidence.

Medieval Society

CHAPTER

2

The strong central government of Rome kept peace and unity in the Mediterranean world and much of Europe for nearly five hundred years. Trade thrived, spreading the values and institutions of the ancient world far and wide. Greek humanism, the moral ideas of Judaism and Christianity, and the Roman tradition of law and government became part of western culture.

Toward the end of the fourth century A.D., Roman control began to weaken. The emperors struggled in vain to put down local revolts and to rid the seas of pirates. Barbarian German tribes from the north pressed against the frontiers of the empire. Some Germans had already filtered in either as recruits for the army or in search of land. But during the fourth century, large bands came to plunder. By 476 the Roman armies were no longer able to hold back the barbarians, and the last Roman emperor in the West was over-thrown by them.

The fall of western Rome created three pressing problems in Europe. First, the people had to find some way to protect and govern themselves. They needed to create a new political system to replace that of Rome. Second, the end of the peace which Rome had maintained brought an end to most trade. Europeans had to find new ways to make a living. They needed to create a new economic system. Third, the resulting changes in both political and economic life affected the social structure. For this reason, Europeans had to develop a new system of social classes.

A society's political, economic, and social systems usually have characteristics in common. For example, the United States has a democratic government, an economic system which offers most people a chance to get ahead, and a flexible system of social classes. The political, economic, and social systems of the Middle Ages also had characteristics in common. These characteristics differed from those in earlier societies. Chapter 2 focuses on these three systems within medieval society. Your study of this chapter should help you see why the political, economic, and social systems of this period had so much in common.

476	The western Roman Empire falls to barbarians.
496	Clovis converts to Christianity.
635-732	Muslims conquer Middle East, North Africa, and Spain.
732	Charles Martel defeats Muslims at Tours.
752	Pepin the Short is crowned king of Franks.
768-814	Charlemagne expands Frankish empire.
800	Pope crowns Charlemagne emperor of West.
843	Charlemagne's three grandsons divide his empire.
c. 843-1300	Feudal nobles gain power.
1066	Normans under William I conquer England.
1095-1291	Crusades fail to capture Holy Land.
1254-1273	St. Thomas Aquinas writes philosophical works.
1337-1453	England and France fight Hundred Years' War.
1347	Hatters' Guild establishes regulations.
1348	Black Plague kills one fourth of Europe's population.

10 MEDIEVAL GOVERNMENT

Charlemagne, who ruled from 768 to 814, established many institutions typical of all medieval political systems. His empire blended German, Roman, and Christian traditions. It solved many of its political problems in ways imitated by later medieval governments.

Charlemagne's government differed from other medieval governments in one major way. He ruled far more territory than any of his successors. His heirs lost power to the landholding nobles and churchmen. Since military and economic power in medieval times depended on landholding, the nobles and churchmen gradually assumed more and more control. Consequently, a century after Charlemagne's death, Europe had broken up into thousands of small political units, each ruled by one of these landowners.

Charlemagne's government faced some of the problems that all governments face. People in eighth-century Europe, for example, had to develop a method of choosing leaders. These leaders had to make decisions and protect their power from those who wished to take it from them. Political institutions had to be set up to pass laws, administer the government, and provide justice. Citizens had to define their roles in the new governments. Finally, the entire system had to be consistent with the political beliefs and values (the political culture) of the society.

People have solved their political problems by developing three basic types of political systems. In traditional societies, people follow rules handed down from the past. In authoritarian countries, a few people solve the political problems for everyone. In democracies, citizens have a significant voice in the solution of political problems.

Reading 10 contains selections from a biography of Charlemagne, written shortly after his death, and an excerpt from Charlemagne's laws. By using analytical questions derived from the social science concepts of decision-makers, decision-making, institutions, citizenship, and political culture, you can analyze past political systems from documents such as these. The following questions will help you as you read:

1. How were political leaders (kings, mayors of the palace, and nobles) recruited in the time of Charlemagne? How did these leaders hold on to their power?
2. How were laws made and enforced under Charlemagne? What role did citizens play in the process?
3. What beliefs and values governed political life?

The Life of Charlemagne

Einhard, one of Charlemagne's closest advisers, wrote The Life of Charlemagne *some time between 817 and 830. In his preface, Einhard stated, "I have condensed the biography into as brief a form as possible. I have been careful not to omit any facts that could come to my knowledge.... No man can write with more accuracy than I of events that I witnessed.... I became one of Charlemagne's closest friends after I took up residence at the court." Remember this frame of reference as you read this selection.*

Einhard, **The Life of Charlemagne,** Samuel Epes Turner, trans. (New York: American Book Co., 1880). Language simplified.

Einhard refers to Charlemagne as Charles. Charlemagne means Charles the Great.

Aquitaine was ruled by rebellious dukes.

The Merovingian family, from which the Franks used to choose their kings, lasted until the time of Childeric. But though the reign of the Merovingians appeared to end with Childeric, the family had lost its strength long before. The real power and authority in the kingdom had fallen into the hands of the chief officer of the court, the so-called mayor of the palace.

When Childeric was deposed, Pepin, the father of King Charles, was mayor of the palace. Pepin was raised from mayor of the palace to king by decree of the pope. He ruled over the Franks for fifteen years or more, dying of dropsy in Paris at the close of the war with Aquitaine. By the grace of God, the right to rule was passed on to his two sons, Charles and Carloman.

38

The Franks, in a general assembly of the people, made them both kings, dividing the whole kingdom equally between them. Carloman died after ruling two years. At his death, Charles was unanimously elected king of the Franks.

Charles's first military undertaking was the Aquitainian War which his father had begun but not finished. Once the campaign began, Charles conducted it with great vigor. He compelled the duke of Aquitaine, Hunold, to leave his country and flee to Gascony. The king threatened to take Hunold by force unless Lupus, duke of Gascony, promptly gave him up. Lupus chose the wiser course. He surrendered Hunold and submitted himself and his province to the king's rule.

Gascony, located in southwestern France bordering Aquitaine, was conquered by the Franks in the sixth century. However, Frankish control was never absolute.

Charles enlarged the Frank kingdom, which was already great and strong when he received it at his father's hands. He more than doubled its former territory.

Charles showed himself to be great not only in extending his empire, but also in carrying out many works to benefit his kingdom. Among these were the cathedral at Aix-la-Chapelle and a bridge over the Rhine River at Mainz. Above all, Charles concerned himself with the churches and cathedrals of the kingdom. He commanded the priests and monks who were in charge of them to keep them in good repair.

Often, while Charles was dressing and putting on his shoes, he would hear requests from his officials. If the count of the palace told him of a legal dispute, he would hear both parties and give his decision. This was not the only business he took care of at this time. He attended to any matter of the day.

Charles had a deep faith in the principles of the Christian religion. He always worshiped at the cathedral at Aix-la-Chapelle as long as his health permitted. He was very careful to see that the services were always conducted in the proper manner.

Charles made his last journey to Rome to help Pope Leo. At that time the pope decided to confer the title of emperor on the king. Charles did not want the title, and even planned to stay away from church on the day that the honor was to be given. However, the pope wished to reward the king who had done so much for him. He arranged to have the king crowned on Christmas Day, when Charles would be sure to attend church.

Leo III was pope from 795 to 816. Leo, who had never been well liked by the people of Rome, was imprisoned in a monastery in 799.

After he received the title of emperor, Charles decided to reform the laws of the empire which were in great disorder. The Franks had two sets of laws which differed in many ways. Charles decided to add new laws, to eliminate conflicting laws, and to correct what was wrong. However, he added only a few laws, and they were imperfect. But he did have the unwritten laws of all the tribes gathered into one set of written laws.

Toward the close of his life, suffering from ill health and old age, Charles summoned his son, Louis, king of Aquitaine. He gathered together all of the chief men of the kingdom in a solemn assembly. He appointed Louis, with the unanimous consent of the Frankish chiefs, to become joint ruler of the entire empire, and to rule it after he died. After sending his son back to Aquitaine, he set out on a hunt. When he returned he was taken ill with a high fever and took to his bed. He died January twenty-eighth at nine o'clock in the morning, after taking holy communion, in the seventy-second year of his age and the forty-seventh of his reign.

Group of peasants paying their respects to their lord, ready to do work on his land

Vassal swearing allegiance to his lord

These pictures show scenes from medieval political life. What sort of ties held the political system together? How do these ties differ from the ones that cement modern political life?

Medieval soldiers going off to war

Charlemagne's Government

Charlemagne had to depend on the Frankish nobility to provide the army for his wars. However, he could not pay the nobles to fight for him because he received little tax money. With frequent wars and the reduction of trade, the use of money had declined. But Charlemagne did own vast tracts of land which he gave to the nobles in exchange for the use of their armies. The following excerpt from Charlemagne's laws reveals the feudal aspect of his government.

James Harvey Robinson, **Readings in European History** (Boston: Ginn and Co., 1904), Vol. 1, pp. 135, 140-141. Language simplified.

A **mansus** contained about 135 acres.

Every freeman who owns a manor containing four *mansi* shall equip himself and go to the army with his lord. He who owns a manor containing three *mansi* shall be joined to a man who owns one *mansus*. The owner of the three *mansi* shall serve for both of them, but will be aided by the owner of the one *mansus*. He who owns only two *mansi* shall be joined to another who also owns two *mansi*, and one of them shall go to the army, and the other will aid him. He who owns only one *mansus* shall be joined to three others who also own but one *mansus*. One of the four shall serve in the army, and the other three will remain at home to aid him.

▶Do you believe that military service is the duty of every citizen?

No one shall refuse to serve when summoned to war by the lord emperor. And none of the lords will dare to excuse from service any of those who own land and are therefore required to perform military service.

FOR THOUGHT:

Was Charlemagne's government mainly traditional, authoritarian, or democratic?

11 THE MEDIEVAL ECONOMY

When the Roman Empire collapsed in the West, the commerce that had carried goods to all parts of the empire dwindled away. Barbarian invasions, pirates and highwaymen, feudal warfare, and the decline of towns shattered the economy of Europe. As a result, each area had to rely on its own land and people to produce nearly all its goods and services. Europe split into thousands of self-sufficient agricultural units called manors. Historians generally call the medieval economic system manorialism.

Like all people everywhere, the people of medieval Europe had to solve the central economic problem of scarcity. Resources—natural, human, and capital—have always been scarce when compared with people's needs and wants. Therefore, people must make three basic economic decisions. First, they must decide what goods and services to produce—whether they will use their iron to make swords or kettles, for example. Second, they must decide how to produce these goods and services—whether they will weave cloth in their homes or make it in shops. Finally, people must decide to whom these goods and services will be distributed—whether they will go to the workers who produced them, to the owners of the equipment and raw materials with which they were made, or to the government as taxes.

Economists have identified three models or types of economic systems—traditional, market, and command economies. In practice, no pure traditional, market, or command economies exist. Every economic system contains elements of all three. But by comparing an economy with the models, you can identify its characteristics.

People in traditional economies rely on the customs and ways of the past to guide their decisions. They produce the same goods and services every year, using about the same combinations of natural, human, and capital resources. They distribute goods and services among their members according to time-honored patterns.

In market economies, the demands of the consumers control these decisions. If customers prefer one style of shoe, producers make more of that style and discontinue unpopular ones. To make the shoes, the producers use natural, human, and capital resources as efficiently as possible, in order to make a maximum profit. The benefits of their production, in the form of wages, rents, profits, and taxes, are distributed among workers, owners, and the government in varying proportions.

In command economies, a group of planners make all three basic economic decisions. They decide what goods and services to produce and assign the necessary natural, human, and capital resources. They also decide to whom to distribute the goods and services.

Reading 11 illustrates how medieval people answered the three basic economic questions. During the Middle Ages, most economic decisions were made on manors or in guilds, two terms that are explained later in this reading. The excerpts in Reading 11 focus on economic decision-making in these two institutions. As you read, think about the following questions:

1. What goods and services were produced on the manors? How did the manors combine natural, human, and capital resources to produce these goods and services? How were these goods and services distributed among workers, owners, and government?

2. What goods and services were produced by the guilds? How did the guilds combine natural, human, and capital resources to produce these goods and services? How were these goods and services distributed among workers, owners, and government?

Natural resources are raw materials, such as land, minerals, and timber. Capital resources are tools and equipment used to produce goods and services. Human resources are workers and their skills.

A Contract
Between a Villein
and His Lord, 1307

Custumals of Battle Abbey,
S. R. Scargill-Bird, ed. (The
Camden Society, 1887), pp.
19-23. Language simplified.

Michaelmas is the feast of
the archangel Michael,
celebrated on September 29.

Shillings are no longer in
circulation since England
changed to the decimal
money system. In modern
times, a shilling was worth
about twelve cents in
American money. But it was
worth many times that
amount during the Middle
Ages.

A bailiff was appointed by a
lord as general overseer of
the manor.

During the Middle Ages, economic life centered on the manor. Lords received manors from kings and other lords in return for military service. A manor consisted of the lord's house; cottages for his tenants; a church, mill, and workshops; and woodlands, fields, and pastures. Most of the tenants were serfs bound to the manor for life. Other tenants, called villeins, were legally free but subject to the authority of the lord.

Each villein had a contract with his lord spelling out his rights and duties. Eventually lords wrote these contracts down in account books so that everyone would know what the villein's duties were. An example of such an account book follows.

John of Cayworth [villein] holds from his lord one house and thirty acres of land. For his right to this land, he must pay the lord two shillings a year at Easter and Michaelmas. At Christmas he must give the lord one cock and two hens worth four shillings.

He must harrow [cultivate] the lord's land for two days during Lent at sowing time with his own horse and harrow. He receives from the lord each day that he harrows three meals.

He must carry the manure of the lord's animals for two days using his own two oxen. He receives from the lord three meals each day that he carries the manure.

He must carry wood from the lord's forest to the manor house for two days in summer. He receives from the lord three meals each day that he carries wood.

John of Cayworth may not allow his daughters to marry without the consent of the lord or the lord's bailiff. Neither may he permit his sons to enter the clergy without the lord's consent. He may not cut the timber growing on his land without the consent of his lord or the bailiff, and then only for the purpose of building.

After his death, his survivors will pay to the lord the best animal that he had, unless he has no living beast, and then the lord will receive no payment.

And if his sons or daughters wish to continue holding his house and thirty acres after his death, they must make a payment to the lord equal to the entire rent for one year, and continue paying the rent as set down in this contract.

44

A medieval manor

Traveling merchant

Tradesmen paying toll on barrels of wine

The pictures on this page show some economic activities of the Middle Ages. How did different classes of medieval people supply their economic needs? On which group did the burden of production fall? According to the text, what did this group receive in turn from the other classes?

How to Run a Manor

The following selection comes from a book written by Walter of Henley in the thirteenth century. The book advises noblemen on how best to manage their estates.

Walter of Henley's Husbandry, Elizabeth Lamond, trans. (New York: Longman's Green & Co., 1890), pp. 3-15. Language simplified.

Husbandry, here, refers to the management of a manor.

This is the book on husbandry written by Sir Walter of Henley. He wrote it to teach those who have lands and tenants. If those who are ignorant will pay attention to these teachings, great wealth may come to them.

The father, having become old, said to his son, "Dear Son, always be careful in your relationships to God and to the world. With regard to God, think often of the crucifixion and death that Jesus Christ suffered for us, and love Him above all things, fear Him, and keep His commandments. With regard to the world, remember that sometimes a man may be lucky and little by little accumulate wealth and become prosperous. But then by mishap he falls little by little into poverty and finally into wretchedness. I warn you, therefore, live within the income which your lands can provide you each year. If, after improving your

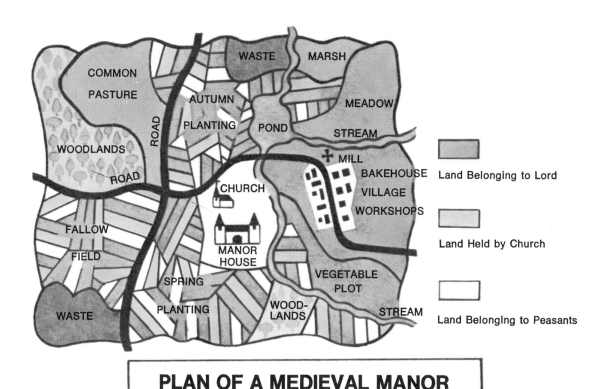

PLAN OF A MEDIEVAL MANOR

lands, you have a surplus, put the extra into savings so that if you harvest a bad corn crop, or your cattle die, or if a fire burns your crop, or some other mishap should happen, then you will have something to help you.

"An old proverb says, 'He who provides for the future enjoys himself in the present.' You will see men who have great lands and many tenants, and yet they are always in debt. That is because they spend their surplus, and when bad times fall upon them, they must borrow. He who borrows, robs himself. Those men live without rule or thought of the future. They spend and waste more than their lands can give them in a year. Then they can only live from hand to mouth and they are always in want. Furthermore, they can make no bargains that will serve their interests. Dear Son, be careful in your doings and be on your guard against the world which is so wicked and deceitful."

▶What values does this excerpt reveal? How do these values compare to your own?

Guild Rules

During the eleventh century, trade and the use of money increased, and town life revived. As town craftsmen began to manufacture more goods, they organized into guilds, or craft associations. Each town established separate guilds for merchants and for members of each craft such as weavers, hat makers, or glove makers. Gradually the rules of the guilds began to regulate economic affairs in the towns. The following regulations come from two medieval guilds.

The Merchant Guild
of Lynn Regis

Charles Gross, The Gild Merchant (Oxford, England: Clarendon Press, 1890), Vol. II, pp. 160-162. Language simplified.

Lynn Regis, or King's Lynn, had one of the main ports and busiest fairgrounds of medieval England.

Alderman, here, refers to the leader of the guild.

If any stranger wishes to enter the Merchant Guild of Lynn Regis, he must pay the alderman one hundred shillings.

If any member of the guild has a son or sons who wish to enter the guild, each one ought to pay the guild four shillings for his entrance.

If any of the members of the guild tell any stranger the plans or the decisions of the guild, without the permission of the alderman, they shall pay a fine of thirty-two pence.

If any of the members should fall into poverty or misery, all the members of the guild are to assist him out of the treasury of the guild or out of their own pockets.

If any member should fall asleep because of too much drink at a general meeting or at the feasts of the guild, he must pay a fine of four pence.

The Hatters' Guild of London

H.T. Riley, **Memorials of London and London Life in the XIII, XIV, and XV Centuries** (London: Longman's Green & Co., 1868), pp. 239-240. Language simplified.

A master was usually the owner of a shop. A journeyman worked for a master.

The most experienced and best hat makers shall rule the guild as wardens. They shall watch all members of the guild to see that the regulations are kept.

No one shall make or sell hats in London unless he is a citizen and a member of the guild.

Only men who take an apprenticeship under one of the masters of the guild may enter the hatters' trade. An apprentice must serve a term of at least seven years before he may become a journeyman.

Because some of the members of the guild have made hats that do not meet the standards of the guild, no workman in the trade shall work at night. All workmen in the trade shall make hats in the daytime so that the wardens may inspect their work.

St. Thomas Aquinas on Values

St. Thomas Aquinas, **Summa Theologica**. Language simplified.

A society's values affect its economic decisions as much as they affect all other aspects of its conduct. Medieval values came primarily from the teachings of Christianity. In the thirteenth century, one of the Church's great religious thinkers, St. Thomas Aquinas, explained how the good Christian should conduct himself in economic affairs. His ideas were based on both Aristotle's work and the moral teachings of the Church.

▶Do you think charging interest for lending money is morally acceptable? If so, how do you think interest rates should be decided?

If a man buys something, he may lawfully sell it at a profit if he has made the thing better or if he has had to meet the expenses of transporting it from one place to another.

But to take interest for lending money is unjust. Money was invented chiefly to make exchange easy. In itself, it does not fill a need of life. Money only represents the goods that can be acquired with it. Hence, to take interest for money lent means to take a payment for something that does not satisfy a natural need. Rather, the payment is taken to satisfy greed.

FOR THOUGHT:

Was the medieval economy primarily traditional, market, or command?

12 THE MEDIEVAL SOCIAL SYSTEM

A new social structure grew up on the manors and in the towns and cities during the Middle Ages. Modern social scientists have developed four concepts that they use to analyze social structure—role, status, norms, and social class. A student must know what these concepts mean in order to use them as analytical tools.

Role refers to the activities that a society expects of someone. For example, a female adult in the United States today may play many roles, such as lawyer, mother, community worker, and church member. The kinds of roles given to men and women of different social classes reveal a great deal about the values of a society.

Status refers to ranking roles in relationship to one another. People in roles with high status enjoy more prestige, wealth, freedom, and power than people in roles with low status. For example, successful businessmen have high status in modern American society. They receive good incomes. Social scientists try to find out which roles in a society have high status and which ones have low status. They try to find out what privileges high status brings. This information helps them analyze the society.

Norms are the standards of behavior that society expects of people. Depending on his role and status, each individual is expected to act according to certain norms. Norms help to determine with whom a person associates, and how he or she raises children, uses leisure time, or treats individuals of different status. When analyzing a social structure, social scientists examine the norms that regulate behavior.

A social class is a broad group of people who share the same general roles, status, and social position. Social scientists look for information that gives clues about a person's social class—for example, education, wealth, family connections, and occupation. In some societies, social classes are widely separated from one another. Members of one social class rarely associate with members of another. In such societies individuals find it difficult to move from a lower social class to a higher one. Both the standards for membership in social classes and the relative ease of movement from one class to another reveal much about a social system.

The selections in Reading 12 cast light on the social system of the Middle Ages. Many of the documents in the two preceding readings have also touched on this subject. As you analyze medieval society, keep in mind the following questions:

1. In theory, what were the social classes of the Middle Ages? How accurately did the actual class structure of the period follow the theory? What characteristics determined a person's class?
2. What roles did the people in the following readings fill? What status was given to each of these roles? What norms guided the relationships between people of different roles and status?

The Orders of Society

This selection from the early eleventh century describes a bishop's view of the organization of French medieval society. It was written by Adalberon, a bishop and adviser to Hugh Capet, king of France from 987 to 996.

Adalberon, **Carmen ad Rothertum Regem,** as quoted in Robert Boutruche, **Seigneurie et Feodalite** (Paris: Aubier, 1959), pp. 371-372. Translated by John M. Good.

▶Do you believe that free people cannot exist without unfree people to work for them?

The clergy forms one order in society. It is governed by church law. Two other orders are governed by civil laws. They are the noble and the nonnoble.

The nobles are the warriors and the protectors of the churches. They defend all people, rich and poor. As a matter of fact, they even protect themselves.

The nonnoble class does not enjoy the freedom of the noble class. This unfortunate group obtains nothing without suffering. It provides food, clothing, and other supplies for everyone in the society. No free man can live without unfree men.

A Medieval Diocese

Adalberon stated that the clergy made up one order of society. The following account provides evidence about the lives of clergymen in the twelfth century.

A diocese was the administrative unit of the Church. It was divided into parishes.

Benefice, here, refers to the property or fixed income attached to high Church offices.

The bishop and his aides conducted the affairs of the Church from the administrative center of the diocese. The administrative center was always the city where the bishop's cathedral was built. Among the bishop's aides were the chancellor of the diocese who supervised the cathedral school, the treasurer who looked after the financial affairs of the diocese, and the archdeacon who presided over the Church court. Priests and deacons assisted these officials.

The donations of the nobles, the offerings of the peasants either in money or produce, and the income from the bishop's benefice permitted the bishop and his most important officials to live very comfortably. They were able to buy fine robes, ornaments, and other luxuries. The bishop also supported a number of charitable causes in his diocese. Many bishops devoted more than half of their income to maintaining cathedral schools, building parish churches, and supporting the poor.

In addition to administering Church affairs, the bishop also assisted the nobles of his diocese. He advised them on government policies, settled differences between competing nobles, and served as an ambassador to the courts of other noblemen.

The boundaries of a parish were usually the same as the boundaries of a manor. The parish was supervised by a priest selected by the lord of the manor with the approval of the bishop. He was generally drawn from the ranks of the local peasantry. Most parish priests attended the cathedral school only long enough to learn to read the Scriptures and the mass. They could not afford the extensive education that noblemen received to become bishops. The priests performed the services in the manor church and spent much of their time ministering to the needs of the peasants. They often acted as family doctors and lawyers as well.

As you have just read in the excerpt from Adalberon, society in the early Middle Ages contained three classes: the clergy, the nobles, and everyone else. How might the economic developments shown on pages 51-53 have affected this class structure?

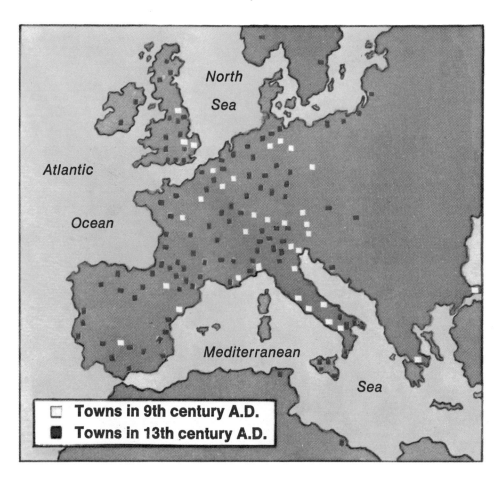

North Sea

Atlantic

Ocean

Mediterranean

Sea

☐ **Towns in 9th century A.D.**
■ **Towns in 13th century A.D.**

A medieval market

A moneychanger

Cloth dyers

Medieval merchants loading a ship

The Life of a Nobleman

Froissart's Chronicles of England, France, Spain and the Adjoining Countries, Thomas Johnes, trans. (New York: Leavitt & Allen, 1858). Vol. I, pp. 94-95. Language simplified.

Knights were the armed and mounted warriors of the nobility. Often, they were given land for their military service.

The nobility was another order of society mentioned by Adalberon. The following selection describes a French nobleman of the fourteenth century. It was written by Jean Froissart, a French chronicler of that period.

Count Gaston Phoebus de Foix was, at the time I visited him, fifty-nine years old. I must say that although I have seen very many knights, kings, princes and others, I have never seen any other so handsome. He was a prudent knight, full of enterprise and wisdom. He never associated with men of bad character. He was constant in his devotion to God.

A squire was a knight's attendant.

A minstrel was a musical entertainer.

In such manner did the Count de Foix live. When he went for his supper at midnight, twelve servants carried large torches before him, and they placed them near his table when he ate. The hall was full of knights and squires. No one spoke to him at his table unless the count himself began the conversation. He had great pleasure in hearing minstrels, and made his secretaries sing songs and ballads. He remained at supper for about two hours and was always pleased when fancy dishes were served to him. After he had inspected each dish, he had portions of it served to his knights and squires.

In short, I was never at a court which pleased me more than that of the Count de Foix.

A Peasant Family's Day

Eileen Power, **Medieval People** (London: Methuen & Co., Ltd., 1954), pp. 20-22. Reprinted by permission.

A steward was in charge of the administration of a manor.

▶ Do you think it is sometimes right to take a bribe? to give a bribe?

The peasants were part of the nonnoble class mentioned by Adalberon. In the following selection, a twentieth-century English historian reconstructs a day in the life of a ninth-century Frankish peasant.

Let us try and imagine a day in Bodo's life. On a fine spring morning towards the end of Charlemagne's reign Bodo gets up early, because it is his day to go and work on the monks' farm, and he does not dare to be late, for fear of the steward. To be sure, he has probably given the steward a present of eggs and vegetables the week before, to keep him in a good temper; but the monks will not allow their stewards to take big bribes (as is sometimes done on other estates), and Bodo knows that he will not be allowed to go late to work. It is his day to plough, so he takes his big ox with him and little Wido [his son] to run by its side . . . .

Let us go back and see what Bodo's wife, Ermentrude, is doing. She is busy too; it is the day on which the chicken-rent is due—a fat pullet

54

[hen] and five eggs in all. She leaves her second son, aged nine, to look after the baby Hildegard and calls on one of her neighbors, who has to go up to the big house too. The neighbor is a serf and she has to take the steward a piece of woolen cloth, which will be sent away . . . to make a habit for a monk. Her husband is working all day in the lord's vineyards, for on this estate the serfs generally tend the vines, while the freemen do most of the ploughing. Ermentrude and the serf's wife go together up to the house . . . .

Ermentrude finds the steward, bobs her curtsy to him, and gives up her fowl and eggs, and then she hurries off to the women's part of the house . . . .

A habit, here, refers to a monk's robe.

The Wife of a Medieval Businessman

As trade revived and the population of the towns increased in the last half of the Middle Ages, businessmen emerged as a new class. Called the bourgeoisie, or middle class, they lived in the cities and acquired substantial wealth from commerce and finance. The medieval businessman fell outside of Adalberon's classification. Technically he could be considered a member of the nonnoble class. But the businessman's life differed from the peasant's as much as the peasant's life differed from the noble's. The following selection focuses on the wife of a medieval businessman in fifteenth-century Paris.

In the morning [the young wife] rises . . . . After Mass, and perhaps confession, back again to see if the servants are doing their work, and have swept and dusted the hall and the rooms, beaten the cushions and coverlets on the forms and tidied everything, and afterwards to . . . order dinner and supper. Then she sends Dame Agnes to see to the pet dogs and birds . . . . Then, if she be in her country house, she must take thought for the farm animals and Dame Agnes must superintend those who have charge of them . . . . If she be in her town house she and her maids take out her dresses and furs from their great chests and spread them in the sun in the garden or courtyard to air, beating them with little rods, shaking them in the breeze, taking out spots and stains . . . .

After this comes dinner, the serious meal of the day, eaten . . . about 10 a.m. After dinner she sees that the servants are set to dine, and then the busy housewife may become the lady of leisure and amuse herself. If in the country she may ride out hawking with a gay party of neighbours; if in town, on a winter's day, she may romp and play with other married ladies of her tender years, exchange riddles or tell stories

Eillen Power, *Medieval People,* pp. 122-123.

Hawking is the use of trained hawks to hunt birds.

55

round the fire. When she tires of this, the busy one gathers together Dame Agnes and her maids, and they sit under the carved beams of the hall mending his mastership's doublet, embroidering a vestment for the priest . . . or a tapestry hanging for the bed-chamber. Or perhaps they simply spin . . . .

At last it is evening, and back comes the lord and master. What a bustle and a pother [fuss] this homecoming meant . . . . Such a running and fetching of bowls of warm water to wash his feet, and comfortable shoes to ease him; such a hanging on his words and admiring of his labors. Then comes supper, with a bevy [crowd] of guests, or themselves all alone . . . . Afterwards an hour of twilight, when she tells him how she has passed the day . . . .

FOR THOUGHT:

How was the medieval social system related to the medieval economic and political systems?

13 MEDIEVAL SOCIETY

A HISTORICAL ESSAY

The end of Roman authority changed the political, economic, and social forces that had shaped western European society. Feudalism, a system of small semi-independent local governments based on personal contracts between lords and vassals, replaced Roman law and government. The broad commercial economy of the Roman Empire was replaced by manorialism, an economic system based on farm communities called manors. Manors supplied most of the goods and services the people living on them needed. The vibrant urban life that Roman commerce had supported nearly disappeared, cutting off the exchange of ideas and institutions between Europe and the Middle East.

The western Roman Empire had collapsed under its own weight as well as from barbarian invasions. It had become too large and costly to maintain. Communication was slow, and the emperors could not react quickly to changing conditions. The expense of keeping standing armies on the frontiers strained the treasury, and self-seeking provincial governors often took public money for their own use. In addition, Roman citizens became increasingly unwilling to serve as soldiers and public

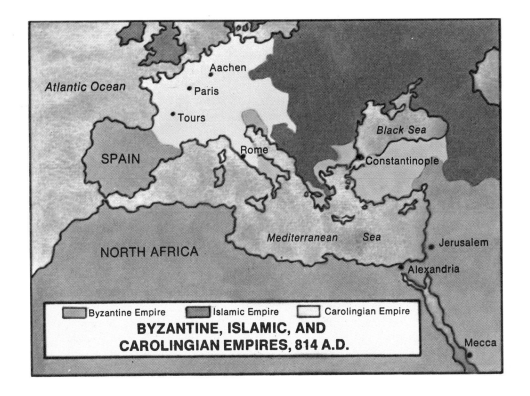

Byzantine Empire | Islamic Empire | Carolingian Empire

**BYZANTINE, ISLAMIC, AND
CAROLINGIAN EMPIRES, 814 A.D.**

servants, and the wealthy indulged themselves in pleasure. Finally, thousands who had become Christians were more interested in serving God than Rome.

The lands once controlled by the Roman Empire split into three major divisions: the Byzantine Empire, the Islamic Empire, and the Carolingian (or Charlemagne's) Empire. (See map, this page.) The Byzantine Empire, also known as Byzantium, was the eastern part of the Roman Empire. It survived until 1453, when it fell to the Ottoman Turks. In the seventh century, the Arab Muslims, followers of Islam, waged holy wars in the former Roman lands in the Middle East and North Africa. They believed that they should win converts by force, and many of the conquered peoples did become Muslims. By the eighth century, the Muslims had also conquered Spain, and they threatened the rest of Christian Europe. There they came in contact with Charlemagne's empire, which included Rome's former provinces in western Europe.

Medieval Europe inherited many Roman traditions and institutions. German tribal chieftains imitated Roman emperors and wealthy landowners. They settled on estates farmed by serfs who were not allowed to leave the land. In 800, on Christmas day, Charlemagne, king of the

The Ottomans were a new group of Muslim Turks who appeared around 1300. They were very successful as a military power.

Mohammed (570?-632) was the founder of the religion of Islam. The followers of Islam are called Muslims.

▶Followers of many religions have waged wars to win converts. Should believers in a religion force others to join them? Why or why not?

57

Franks, was given the Roman title of emperor by Pope Leo III. He united under his rule most of the western Roman Empire and some lands that had not been in the empire.

The kings of western Europe needed the allegiance of the nobles if they were to stay on their thrones. The nobles enforced the laws and manned the armies that protected the kingdoms against invaders. Even Charlemagne depended on the noble landowners to see that churches were maintained, roads kept up, and the laws enforced. Through the institution of feudalism, the Frankish nobility supported Charlemagne. For their continued oaths of loyalty and obedience, Charlemagne gave his vassals grants of land. In return, they came equipped to do battle whenever he called.

Charlemagne's ability to govern was not inherited by his successors. At his death in 814, his son Louis I became emperor. However, Louis and his sons quarreled about dividing the empire. Their struggle permitted ambitious nobles to war among themselves and to increase their landholdings and power. They granted land to their followers, often requiring the vassal to supply armed men. The vassal, in turn, gave his followers portions of his land in exchange for their allegiance.

From the ninth century until the thirteenth, most of Europe was thus divided into hundreds of small feudal holdings. No monarch emerged, such as Charlemagne, powerful enough to rule over a large territory. For hundreds of years, the feudal governments provided Europe with adequate local administration and defense against invaders.

The Church, also inherited from Rome, played a major role in the feudal system. Christianity had become the dominant religion of the Roman Empire by the fourth century. After the crucifixion of Jesus, his followers had carried his message to all parts of the empire. They had created a permanent church to preserve and spread Christianity. Each Christian community was placed under a priest who preached the teachings of Jesus and administered the sacraments, or church rituals such as baptism. Each priest was appointed by the bishop in charge of his diocese. Eventually, the bishop of Rome dominated all other bishops and became the pope, the supreme authority of the Christian Church.

By 476 when the last western Roman emperor was deposed, the Church had become one of the most important institutions in western Europe. As the Church's power grew, the kings and nobles of Europe set aside large tracts of land to support its bishops and monasteries. But if the kings and nobles made the Church powerful, the reverse was also true. Kings and nobles relied on the Church to help them keep the support of the peasants and, more importantly, of the warrior-vassals.

The popes called upon the kings and nobles to go to war on behalf of the Church. Beginning in 1095 and continuing for two hundred years, the popes called for Crusades to recapture Palestine, the Holy Land of Jesus' birth, from the Muslims. Armies of Europeans went to Palestine. Although the Crusaders failed to take Jerusalem, those who returned to Europe brought with them a desire for the products of the East and curiosity about the rest of the world.

The Church served still another need during the Middle Ages. At a time when most people were occupied with satisfying their needs and fighting local wars, the Church carried on the intellectual traditions of the ancient world. The clergy ran the schools. Monks copied and illustrated the few books of the times. Churchmen continued to study Greek and Roman writings so that they were not forgotten. Religion was the subject of most medieval art and drama. Without the medieval Church, much that is fundamental to western culture would have disappeared.

At the same time that feudalism developed and the Church's influence increased, Europe's political unity was destroyed. Commerce was disrupted as thieves and the wars between nobles made trade dangerous. Tolls collected by each noble at the border of his territory made transporting goods expensive. Pirates on the Mediterranean Sea ended almost all trade between western Europe and the Middle East for hundreds of years. Europeans had to produce their own goods and services.

Most medieval Europeans were peasants who farmed the manor lands. Their contracts with the manor lords gave them protection and the right to cultivate a part of the land in return for dues and services. Most of these peasants were serfs who were not free to leave the manor. Those who were freemen could leave. But without much hope of finding a better life in the towns, they usually remained on the manors.

A small number of people continued to live in the towns during the Middle Ages. The medieval towns were the administrative centers of the Church. In addition, they housed a few small craft industries. Beginning late in the eleventh century, trade and the use of money revived. The population of the towns began to increase. As the merchants and craftsmen found a greater demand for their products, they organized into guilds.

Manors and guilds were responsible for most of the economic decisions during the Middle Ages. They decided what goods and services would be produced with the available resources. The manor lords selected the crops that would be grown and the items that would be made in the manor workshops according to long-standing traditions. In the towns, each guild regulated the production of a particular item. Manors and guilds also decided how resources would be used. Contracts with the lord of a manor stated when the peasants would work for the lord and when they would work for themselves. Guild regulations specified what capital and natural resources would be used to make

Crusaders praying before going off to fight

each article. Finally, manors and guilds decided how goods and services would be distributed. Contracts also stated what portion of the peasants' crops and labor went to the lord. Guild rules listed prices craftsmen could charge for their articles and how much of the profits went to the guild masters.

The manors and guilds also regulated the roles and status of medieval men and women, and they established the norms of behavior. In addition to stating the peasant's economic duties, a manorial contract specified whom his daughters could marry, what his sons would do when they were grown, and what would become of his wife after he died. The contract of a serf gave him less status on the manor than the contract of a freeman. On the whole, role and status were inherited. The son of a serf grew up to be a serf; the son of a freeman grew up to be a freeman. Likewise, the oldest son of the manor lord inherited his father's role and status.

Inheritance played a smaller part in controlling role and status in the towns, but they were still largely inherited. Guild rules often barred

Using the pictures on these two pages, in what nonreligious activities did the medieval Church play a part? How did these activities affect the Church's importance in medieval life?

School run by the Church

Monks tilling the monastery fields

►What organizations, if any, do you feel have the right to dictate the roles, norms, and status of their members?

Gregory VII, known as Hildebrand before his election as pope, was educated in a Roman monastery. He became a monk and then progressed steadily within the Church hierarchy until he became pope in 1073.

►Some people in the United States live in small traditional communities. Often these communities were founded by religious or national groups. Do you think these communities should be left as they are or should they be brought into the mainstream of American culture?

from the trade anyone who was not the son of a member. And fathers expected their sons to practice their crafts. Guilds also concerned themselves with norms of behavior. Guild regulations had provisions about drunkenness, thievery, and piety. Moreover, the guild determined the status of its members according to their rank as craftsmen—apprentice, journeyman, or master.

Status in the medieval Church also often depended on one's father. Bishops and other high Church officials were generally selected from the nobility. Parish priests were usually the sons of peasants. On the other hand, the talented son of a peasant might become a bishop or even a pope, as did Gregory VII, son of an Italian peasant. A serf's son could become an administrative officer of a diocese. Within the monastic communities, men of humble origins sometimes worked their way up.

The political, economic, and social systems of the Middle Ages restricted change. Besieged by invaders and divided into small political units, medieval Europeans followed the ways of custom and tradition. Political power, wealth, role, and status were generally inherited. The same families often owned and ruled their land for many years.

Yet many of the political, economic, and social forces that later shaped modern western society took root in the Middle Ages. The following chapters explore some of these forces as they contributed to the Renaissance and the Reformation. They show the development of national states and parliamentary and absolutist governments. Finally, they investigate the beginnings of modern science and the growth of market economies.

Individual and Group Activities for Chapter 2

For full descriptions of these activities, turn to the **Student Book of Activities and Readings** included among the materials for individual and group activities.

Activity 2A: Comparison of the architecture and music of the medieval cathedral with the modern Roman Catholic Church (individual)
This activity shows pictures of a medieval cathedral and a modern Roman Catholic Church and also examples of medieval and modern Church music. After examining this material, write an essay about their similarities and differences.

Activity 2B: Interview and comparison of modern unions and medieval guilds (individual)
This activity contains a description of the medieval guild system. After reading the selection carefully, interview a union leader in your community. Then write a short essay summarizing the guild system and explaining how the modern union differs from it.

The Renaissance

STATING THE ISSUE

A medieval traveler, coming to Chartres or Reims, would be drawn to the cathedral that played such an important role in town life. He might write to his friends to tell them how the building glorified God with its splendid altars, stained glass windows, sculpture, and spires towering toward heaven. He might describe how insignificant he felt before the majestic structure and how his thoughts turned to God.

In 1432 Aeneas Silvius Piccolomini, who became Pope Pius II later, visited Genoa. In a letter to a friend he described the magnificent palaces of Genoa's wealthy citizens and told about the shops filled with luxury goods. Instead of being overcome by religious fervor, he was filled with the delights of this world. He was not a medieval man on a pilgrimage; he was a Renaissance man on vacation.

Renaissance means rebirth and refers to the period in European history from about 1300 to about 1600. No one event marks the end of the Middle Ages and the beginning of the Renaissance. Instead, a number of changes took place over the centuries that gradually brought about a change in focus. Medieval Europe focused on God; Renaissance Europe focused on people. For people living during the Renaissance, life on earth was not something to be endured while waiting for the better life of the next world. It was to be enjoyed in its own right.

Although medieval and Renaissance people held many values in common, new values began to emerge during the Renaissance period. These new values reflected fundamental changes in society. Chapter 3 examines the values of the people living during the Renaissance. It also presents evidence to help you see how new Renaissance values reflected changes in the political, economic, and social systems.

63

c. 1300-c. 1600	The period of history called the Renaissance takes place.
c. 1300	Florence, Genoa, Pisa, Milan, and Venice flourish as trading centers.
1321	Dante Alighieri completes **The Divine Comedy.**
1326-1374	Francesco Petrarch writes poetry.
1348	Giovanni Boccaccio writes **The Decameron.**
1429	Medicis begin a three-century domination of Florence and Tuscany.
1485	Sandro Botticelli paints **The Birth of Venus.**
1498	Leonardo da Vinci finishes the **Last Supper.**
1509-1511	Raphael paints **The School of Athens.**
1528	Baldassare Castiglione publishes **The Courtier.**
1534-1541	Michelangelo Buonarroti paints **The Last Judgment** in the Sistine Chapel.
1558	Benvenuto Cellini begins his **Autobiography.**

14 THE EMERGENCE OF THE RENAISSANCE IN ITALY

Medieval political, economic, and social systems had never taken strong hold in Italy. Feudalism, a political power structure based on control of land, was imported into Italy from the north, but it never sank deep roots there. While northern Europe became mainly rural, Italian commerce continued to support an urban society. Moreover, manorial life in Italy never became as self-sufficient as it did in France, England, and Germany. Nor did the social classes created by feudalism and manorialism become firmly established in Italy.

Like ancient Greece, medieval Italy developed around city-states such as Genoa, Milan, Pisa, Florence, Venice, and Naples. Their political power grew from a firm economic base dominated by merchants and bankers. They outfitted the Crusaders and transported them on Italian ships. These ships came back filled with the products of the East, much in demand all over Europe.

The Renaissance emerged in these Italian cities. As new forces developed and combined, they changed the nature of society in the Italian cities. Then these forces reached into the surrounding areas and, in time, spread northward into all of western Europe.

64

What were these forces? Reading 14 contains excerpts from the writings of three Renaissance Italians. Using these documents, you should be able to develop and test hypotheses to explain why Italy developed a new type of society. Eventually this new society influenced most of the western world.

The frame of reference of the authors of this book influenced their choice of documents. Your frame of reference will color your interpretation of these documents. At the same time, your knowledge of inquiry skills should help you to ask good analytical questions and to be aware of bias. As you read, think about the following questions:

1. What characteristics of Italian cities did Piccolomini and Villani describe? Why do you think they chose these characteristics?
2. Which of Cosimo de Medici's characteristics did this biographer describe? Why do you think he chose those characteristics?

Genoa in 1432

The following selection is an excerpt translated from the letter Piccolomini wrote in 1432 while visiting Genoa.

Would you were with me! You would see a city which has no equal anywhere on earth. It lies upon a hill over which rude mountains tower, while the lower city is washed by the waves of the sea. The harbor is bow-shaped so that storms cannot do the ships any harm. And what a coming and going there is! You may see daily people of the most different sort with unimaginable rough manners and customs and traders with every conceivable ware. Right at the shore arise the most magnificent palaces, heaven-scaling, built of marble, decorated with columns and often too with sculptures. Under them runs an arcade for the length of a thousand steps where every conceivable object is for sale. The rest of the city winds upward along the side of the hill. In this section the houses are so large and distinguished that a king or a prince might be content with any one of them. The churches, beautiful as they are, do not seem to me to be worthy of such a city. However, they are not without splendor and boast some handsome tombs.

Now as to the life and customs of the population. The men are substantial, well grown, and impressive, carry themselves proudly and are in fact proud. They are a gifted folk, not likely to be found inferior to any other people in the quality of their mind. Strenuous labors they bear easily. Their deeds of bravery at sea are incredible. The advantages that come with profits and riches offer compensation for hardships.

They dress nobly and elegantly. They are not afflicted with thirst for education, though they learn languages as they need them. For other elements of the liberal arts they have little use, except as a possible relief

Der Briefwechsel des E. S. Piccolomini, herausgegeben von R. Wolkan. Fontes Rerum Austricarum, II Abtheilung, LXI, 7. Translated by Edwin Fenton.

▶ What hardships, if any, do you think are worth "profits and riches"?

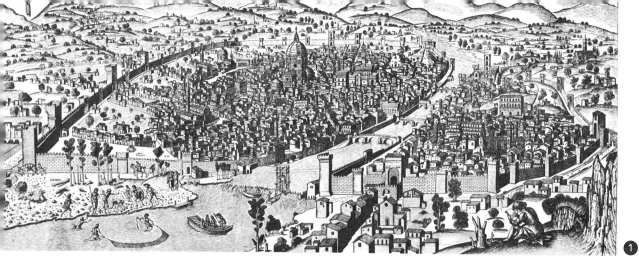

Florence in the 1400's

A navigational instrument

Detail from Stories of the Antichrist *by Luca Signorelli, who has painted himself into the picture. He appears at left.*

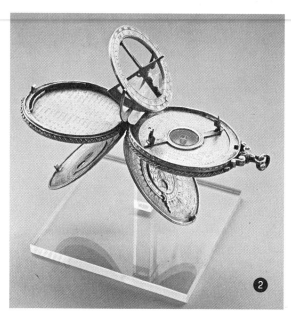

The woolworkers' guild sign

The pictures on these two pages show a number of Renaissance scenes. What were some of the characteristics of the Renaissance?

A fresco painted by Michelangelo on the ceiling of the Sistine Chapel

from business. The women of this city enjoy great freedom; indeed it would not be an exaggeration to designate Genoa as the paradise of women. Their dresses are luxurious, loaded with gold and silver trimmings and with jewels. On their fingers sparkle emeralds and diamonds supplied by India and Persia. They bother neither about the household nor about needle and dishes, for every house enjoys abundant service.

The Chronicle of
Giovanni Villani

Of all Renaissance Italian cities, Florence had one of the most remarkable histories, particularly from the mid-fourteenth century to the late fifteenth century. The following selection is from The Chronicle of Giovanni Villani. *Villani (c. 1275-1348) was a Florentine historian and city official during the early fourteenth century.*

La Cronaca di Giovanni Villani (Veneza Plampato: 1833). Translated by Edwin Fenton.

An abacus is a wooden frame with beads strung on wires. It is used to solve arithmetic problems.

A florin was a gold coin first minted in Florence.

An entrepreneur organizes, controls, and manages a business.

A denier was a small silver coin.

A close look at the figures of this period show that about 25,000 men in the 15 to 70 age bracket lived in Florence. The city's bread consumption indicated that some 90,000 mouths, including those of men, women, and children, must be filled. At this time about 1,500 foreigners, transients, and soldiers, not counting the clerics and cloistered monks and nuns, already lived in Florence. The total number of men in the territory and district of Florence in the period was estimated at 80,000. The rector's ceremony as he baptized infants—depositing a black bean for male infants and a white bean for female infants baptized in the church of San Giovanni—showed a yearly total of from 5,500 to 6,000 baptisms per year. The black beans outnumbered the white by some 300 to 500. The number of children learning to read ranged from 8,000 to 10,000; those learning the abacus and algorism [arithmetic], from 1,000 to 1,200; and those learning grammar and logic from 550 to 600.

The workshops of the guild of wool merchants, the *Arte Della Lana*, numbered over 200 and produced some 70,000 to 80,000 pieces of cloth worth more than 1,200,000 gold florins. After deducting the profit of the entrepreneurs, over a third of this amount remained in the land as a reward for labor, and more than 30,000 people lived on this money. Thirty years before this, many more workshops—some 300—had produced more than 100,000 pieces of cloth; but the cloths at that time were coarser and much less valuable since English wool was not imported then nor did laborers know the techniques of working it.

Every year in Florence some eighty banks of money-changers produced about 350,000 to 400,000 gold florins and about 20,000 pounds of deniers worth four pennies each.

Merchants and artisans, including shoemakers, slipper makers, wooden shoemakers, stone and carpentry masters, and masters in many other crafts, were so numerous that some 300 left the city to do business. Florence also had 146 bakeries. Information furnished by the bakers and a look at the tax on grinding show that 140 bushels of grain were needed every day.

Cosimo de Medici: Renaissance Despot

The Medici of Florence were one of the most important families of Europe. Beginning in the fourteenth century, they made their fortune in trade, manufacturing, and banking. Cosimo de Medici inherited the family fortune in 1429 and added to it by making loans to popes and kings. For thirty years he was the dominant political figure of Florence. The following excerpt is a description of Cosimo taken from the writings of Vespasiano da Bisticci, who lived from 1421 to 1498.

Vespasiano da Bisticci, Vite di Uomini Illustri del Secolo XV; Stampate la Prima Volta da Angelo Mai Nuova Mente da Adolfo Bartoli (Florence: Barbera Bianchi e chomp, 1859). Translated by Edwin Fenton.

Tuscany is located in central Italy, and Florence is its chief city.

Cosimo di Giovanni de Medici was descended from one of the most honorable families in Florence. He was a very prominent citizen and had great influence in the Republic of Tuscany.

As a leading citizen, Cosimo devoted much attention to the affairs of the city. He associated with other men of high station who gave their time to serious business. He had a great liking for learned men.

Cosimo considered how he could best gather together a company of worthy and learned men to live in his house. First, he decided to collect a large number of books. One day, when I was with him, he said, "What plan can you suggest for the formation of this library?" I replied that the books could not be bought because copies were unavailable, I said it would be necessary to have the books copied from others, whereupon he wanted to know if I would undertake the task. I said that I would. He was anxious that I complete the task as quickly as possible, and since there was no lack of money, I hired forty-five scribes who completed two hundred volumes in twenty-two months.

Cosimo knew how difficult it was to rule a state, since he had ruled Florence despite opposition from influential citizens who had rated themselves his equals. In order to safeguard himself, he acted with great discretion in private matters. Whenever he started a new project, he made it appear that someone else had started it in order to escape envy.

He was attracted to all musicians, and he delighted greatly in their art. He had dealings with painters and sculptors and had a number of the works of several masters in his house.

FOR THOUGHT:

What relationships do you see between life in Renaissance cities and the values of the people who lived there?

15 AN ARTIST OF THE RENAISSANCE

Benvenuto Cellini—goldsmith, sculptor, lover, braggart, and writer—left a vivid account of Renaissance culture and the life of Renaissance artists. He spent time with popes, dukes, and other leaders of European society. But more important, he filled his lively *Autobiography* with observations and criticisms of Renaissance art.

Raphael's The School of Athens

Titian's Assumption

What is your opinion of these examples of Renaissance art? Which do you like best? Which do you like least? Would you admit disliking a work of art that others consider great?

Detail from Botticelli's
The Birth of Venus

Cellini lived from 1500 to 1571. During this time, the cultural achievements of the Italian Renaissance reached their peak. This was the period of writers and artists such as Boccaccio, Leonardo da Vinci, Michelangelo, and Raphael. In their work, Renaissance individualism reached its artistic peak, ending a hundred years of experimentation with new techniques, materials, and subjects.

But the political conditions under which the Renaissance had flourished were changing. Many Renaissance leaders took measures to assure that their sons would inherit their power. This development severely limited the social mobility that was so much a part of the Renaissance. It prevented men of lower class origin from climbing the political, economic, and social ladders. Furthermore, French and Spanish invasions had ended the independence of Naples, Milan, and other Italian city-states.

Reading 15 contains passages from Cellini's *Autobiography*. In these excerpts, Cellini describes his work and the work of other artists for two of his patrons. As you read, try to answer the following questions:

1. Who were Cellini's patrons? What interested them?
2. What standards did Cellini use to criticize Bandinello's statue?

The Autobiography of Benvenuto Cellini

The Autobiography of Benvenuto Cellini, George Bull, trans. (Baltimore: Penguin Books Ltd., 1956), pp. 87-90, 335-338. Copyright © 1956 by George Bull. Reprinted by permission.

Traiano was the pope's head attendant.

Michele and Pompeo were jewelers and rivals of Cellini.

Michele had obtained designs for the pope's button from a number of draftsmen.

"I [Pope Clement VII] shall employ you on a very important work . . . the button for my cope [cloak] . . . . The design is to be a figure of God the Father, in half relief, and in the middle I want you to set that big, beautifully cut diamond, as well as a large number of other priceless gems . . . ."

Within a few days I had put the last touches to the model, and one morning I took it along to show the Pope. Traiano made me wait while he hurriedly sent for Michele and Pompeo, telling them to bring their designs with them. When they arrived, we were shown inside, and they immediately began to hold out their designs for the Pope to see. As it turned out, the draughtsmen [draftsmen] not being jewellers, had no idea how to set the gems, and the jewellers had not given them any instructions (and a jeweller must when he is introducing figures among his gems know how to draw; otherwise his work will be worthless). And so in all their designs, that marvellous diamond had been placed in the middle of God the Father's breast.

72

The Pope, whose judgement was very sound, saw what had happened and thought they were without merit. After he had inspected about ten of them, he threw the rest on the floor, turned to me, who was standing on one side, and said:

"Let me have a glance at your model, Benvenuto, so that I can see if you've made the same mistake as they have."

I came forward and opened a little round box; the Pope's eyes seemed to light up, and he cried out:

"You wouldn't have done it in any other way, even if you were my very self. The others couldn't have thought up a better way of disgracing themselves."

Then a great number of important noblemen flocked round, and the Pope pointed out to them the difference between my model and the other designs. He praised it to the skies, with those two [Michele and Pompeo] standing terrified and dumfounded in front of him, and then he turned to me and said:

"I can only see one snag, Benvenuto, but it's very important. It's easy to work in wax; the real test comes when one has to work in gold."

I answered him eagerly: "Holy Father, if it isn't ten times better than my model, we'll agree that I won't be paid for it . . . ."

What I had done was to place the diamond exactly in the centre of the whole work, with the figure of God the Father, gracefully turning to one side, seated above it, and so the design was beautifully balanced, and the figure did not detract from the jewel. With His right hand raised, God the Father was giving a blessing; and beneath the jewel I had placed three cherubs, supporting the diamond with raised arms; the middle one was in full, and the other two in half relief. Round about I had designed a crowd of cherubs, beautifully arranged with the other gems. God the Father was draped in a flowing mantle, from which the other cherubs peeped out; and there were many other exquisite adornments . . . .

One feast day or other I went along to the [Duke's] palace . . . . The Duke [greeted] me pleasantly:

"You're welcome! Look at that little chest that the lord Stefano of Palestrina has sent me as a present: open it and let's see what it is."

I opened it at once and said to the Duke: "My lord, it's a statue in Greek marble, and it's a splendid piece of work: I don't remember ever having seen such a beautiful antique statue of a little boy, so beautifully fashioned. Let me make an offer to your Most Illustrious Excellency to restore it—the head and the arms and the feet. I'll add an eagle so that we can christen it Ganymede. And although it's not for me to patch up statues—the sort of work done by botchers, who still make a bad job of it—the craftsmanship of this great artist calls me to serve him . . . ."

While I was entertaining the Duke in this agreeable way . . . . Bandinello came in . . . . [He said:]

▶Giovanni Pico della Mirandola (1463-1494), an Italian humanist, wrote that God, in creating man, said to him: "I have set you in the center of the world." How would you agree or disagree with that opinion?

Cellini now describes his work for Cosimo 1 de Medici, duke of Florence and nephew of Cosimo de Medici, whom you read about earlier.

In Greek mythology Ganymede was cupbearer for the gods.

Baccio Bandinello was a Florentine sculptor and painter who lived from about 1493 to 1560.

"My lord, here you have one of those things I have so often mentioned to you. You see, those ancients knew nothing about anatomy, and as a result their works are full of errors."

I remained silent, taking no notice of anything he was saying; in fact I had turned my back on him. As soon as the beast had finished his disagreeable babbling, the Duke said:

"But Benvenuto, this completely contradicts what you have just been proving with so many beautiful arguments. Let's hear you defend the statue a little."

In reply to this noble little speech of the Duke's, so pleasantly made, I said:

"My lord, your Most Illustrious Excellency must understand that Baccio Bandinello is thoroughly evil, and always has been. So no matter what he looks at, as soon as his disagreeable eyes catch sight of it, even though it's of superlative quality it is at once turned to absolute evil. But for myself, being only drawn to what is good, I see things in a more wholesome way. So what I told your Illustrious Excellency about this extremely beautiful statue is the unblemished truth; and what Bandinello said about it reflects only the badness of his own nature." . . .

Then Bandinello began to gabble. "My lord," he said, "when I uncovered my Hercules and Cacus I am sure that more than a hundred wretched sonnets were written about me, containing the worst abuse one could possibly imagine this rabble capable of."

Replying to this, I said: "My lord, when our Michelangelo Buonarroti revealed his Sacristy, where there are so many fine statues to be seen, our splendid talented Florentine artists, the friends of truth and excellence, wrote more than a hundred sonnets, every man competing to give the highest praise. As Bandinello's work deserved all the abuse that he says was thrown at it, so Buonarroti's deserved all the good that was said of it."

Bandinello grew so angry that he nearly burst: he turned to me and said: "And what faults can you point out?"

"I shall tell you if you've the patience to listen." . . .

"The expert school of Florence says that if Hercules' hair were shaven off there wouldn't be enough of his pate [head] to hold in his brain; and that one can't be sure whether his face is that of a man or a cross between a lion and an ox; that it's not looking the right way; and that it's badly joined to the neck, so clumsily and unskilfully that nothing worse has ever been seen; . . . that his . . . muscles aren't based on a man's but are copied from a great sack full of melons, set upright against a wall . . . . As for the legs, it's impossible to understand how they're attached to the sorry-looking trunk; it's impossible to see on which leg he's standing, or on which he's balancing, and he certainly doesn't seem to be resting his weight on both, as is the case with some of the work

Hercules was a Greco-Roman god most famous for 12 labors he performed to atone for crimes he committed while insane. Cacus was a fire-breathing Roman god. He stole giant cattle from Hercules, who then killed him.

A sacristy is a room in a church where sacred utensils and vestments are kept.

done by those artists who know something . . . . As for the arms, it's said that they both stick out awkwardly, that they're so inelegant that it seems you've never set eyes on a live nude; that the right leg of Hercules is joined to that of Cacus in the middle in such a way that if one of the two were removed both of them—not merely one—would be without a calf . . . .

Suddenly the fellow cried out: "Oh, you wicked slanderer, what about my design?"

I replied that anyone who was good at designing would never make a bad statue, therefore I judged that his design was the same quality as his work . . . .

FOR THOUGHT:

What relationships do you see between Cellini's values and the type of society in which he lived?

▶What standards do you apply in judging art? Would you use Cellini's or different ones?

16 THREE RENAISSANCE WRITERS

Renaissance artists gradually developed a new style in painting and sculpture. Medieval paintings and sculpture usually decorated churches. Renaissance paintings and sculpture adorned the mansions of wealthy businessmen, as well as churches. Medieval painters rarely signed their work. Renaissance artists signed theirs in bold letters. Some even painted their own faces into crowd scenes. Medieval art centered on religious subjects and man's relation to God. While they did not abandon religious themes, Renaissance painters and sculptors also represented classical myths and scenes from everyday life. Their great contribution was the use of perspective.

In literature, Renaissance people also departed from tradition. They wrote in their native tongues as well as in Latin, the language of the educated. The Florentine Dante Alighieri (1265-1321), known best for the *Divine Comedy*, was the first great writer to use Italian. Moreover, in the *Divine Comedy* Dante gave the major role of guide to Virgil, the Roman poet, rather than to a religious figure.

The Renaissance writers studied the styles used by the ancient Romans and tried to imitate them. But more important, the ideas they expressed were far different from those of medieval writers. They attempted to portray people and the world they lived in. Reading 16 contains excerpts from three Renaissance writers. As you study these selections, keep the following questions in mind:

1. What is Petrarch's attitude toward women? What is the point of Boccaccio's tale? What is Castiglione's ideal of the well-rounded man?
2. How does Castiglione's courtier compare to Cosimo de Medici? to Benvenuto Cellini?

A Sonnet by Petrarch

Francesco Petrarch (1304-1374) is often referred to as the "father of humanism." He was one of the earliest scholars to study the classical writings of ancient Rome and to write poetry in Italian. The following selection is one of Petrarch's many sonnets to Laura, the woman he loved.

The Sonnets, Triumphs, and Other Poems of Petrarch, translated by various hands (London: George Bell and Sons, Ltd., 1879), pp. 88-89.

Loose to the breeze her golden tresses flow'd
Wildly in thousand mazy ringlets blown,
And from her eyes unconquer'd glances shone,
Those glances now so sparingly bestow'd
And true or false, meseem'd some signs she show'd
As o'er her cheek soft pity's hue was thrown;
I, whose whole breast with love's soft food was sown,
What wonder if at once my bosom glow'd?
Graceful she moved, with more than mortal mien,
In form an angel: and her accents won
Upon the ear with more than human sound.
A spirit heavenly pure, a living sun,
Was what I saw; and if no more 'twere seen,
T' unbend the bow will never heal the wound.

Mien refers to a person's air or appearance.

The *Decameron*

Giovanni Boccaccio (1313-1375) is best known for the Decameron, *written about 1348. One of the earliest prose works in Italian, it is a collection of tales supposedly told by a group of people who are staying at a country estate when the Black Plague has struck the city. To pass the time, they take turns telling tales.*

THE SIXTH DAY, THE FOURTH TALE

Currado Gianfigliazzi was always a noble citizen of our city, liberal and magnificent, leading a gentleman's life, continually delighting in dogs and hawks, and allowing his more serious affairs to slide. One day . . . his falcon brought down a crane, and finding it to be plump and

Giovanni Boccaccio, **The Decameron,** trans. by Richard Aldington (New York: Doubleday & Company, Inc., 1930). Copyright, © 1930 by Mme. Catherine Guillaume. Reprinted by permission of Doubleday.

young he sent it to his excellent cook, a Venetian named Chichibio, telling him to roast it for supper and see that it was well done.

Chichibio, who was a bit of a fool, prepared the crane, set it before the fire, and began to cook it carefully. When it was nearly done and giving off a most savory odor, there came into the kitchen a young peasant woman, named Brunetta, with whom Chichibio was very much in love. Smelling the odor of the bird and seeing it, she begged Chichibio to give her a leg of it. But he replied with a snatch of song:

"You won't get it from me, Donna Brunetta, you won't get it from me."

This made Donna Brunetta angry, and . . . they had high words together. In the end Chichibio, not wanting to anger his lady-love, took off one of the crane's legs, and gave it to her. A little later the one-legged crane was served before Currado and his guests. Currado was astonished at the sight, sent for Chichibio, and asked him what had happened to the other leg of the crane. The lying Venetian replied:

"Sir, cranes only have one leg and one foot."

"What the devil d'you mean," said Currado angrily, "by saying they have only one leg and foot? Did I never see a crane before?"

"It's as I say, Sir," Chichibio persisted, "and I'll show it you in living birds whenever you wish."

Currado would not bandy [exchange] further words from respect to his guests, but said:

"Since you promise to show me in living birds something I never saw or heard of, I shall be glad to see it tomorrow morning. But . . . if it turns out otherwise I'll have you tanned in such a way that you'll remember my name as long as you live."

When day appeared next morning, Currado, who had not been able to sleep for rage all night, got up still furious, and ordered his horses to be brought. He made Chichibio mount a pad [horse], and took him in the direction of a river where cranes could always be seen at that time of day, saying:

"We'll soon see whether you were lying or not last night."

Chichibio, seeing that Currado was still angry and that he must try to prove his lie, which he had not the least idea how to do, rode alongside Currado in a state of consternation, and would willingly have fled if he had known how. But as he couldn't do that, he kept gazing round him and thought everything he saw was a crane with two legs. But when they came to the river, he happened to be the first to see a dozen cranes on the bank, all standing on one leg as they do when they are asleep. He quickly pointed them out to Currado, saying:

"Messer, you can see that what I said last evening is true, that cranes have only one leg and one foot; you have only to look at them over there."

Donna is an Italian term of address used with the Christian name of a woman.

St. Peter's Church in Rome which Michelangelo helped to design

►These four pictures show four great artistic achievements of the Renaissance. Each artist received support from patrons who, in turn, got money from taxes, gifts to the Church, or banking, manufacturing, or trade. Many of the workers who produced these goods and services lived in or near poverty. Do you think society can be justified in producing great works of art if they can be done only by using slaves or poorly paid workers?

Haffi nel priuilegio,& nella gratia ottenuta dalla Illuftriffima
Signoria che in quefta,ne in niun'altra Citta del fuo
dominio fi poffa imprimere, ne altroue
impreffo uendere quefto libro
del Cortegiano per·x· anni
fotto le pene in effo
contenute ·

Cover of The Book of the Courtier by Castiglione

Portrait of Cardinal Dovizi *by Raphael*

Hercules and Cacus *by Bandinello*

79

"Wait," said Currado, "I'll show you they have two."

And going up closer to them, he shouted: "Ho! Ho!" And at this the cranes put down their other legs and, after running a few steps, took to flight. Currado then turned to Chichibio, saying:

"Now, you glutton, what of it? D'you think they have two?"

In his dismay Chichibio, not knowing how the words came to him, replied:

"Yes, messer, but you didn't shout 'ho! ho!' to the bird last night. If you had shouted, it would have put out the other leg and foot, as those did."

Currado was so pleased with this answer that all his anger was converted into merriment and laughter, and he said:

"Chichibio, you're right; I ought to have done so."

So with this quick and amusing answer Chichibio escaped punishment, and made his peace with his master.

The Ideal of the Well-Rounded Man

The ancient Greeks believed a man should be well-rounded and that he should develop every aspect of his personality. Count Baldassare Castiglione, a sixteenth-century Italian diplomat, combined this ideal with a Renaissance outlook in a book called The Courtier. *As the title implies, Castiglione was writing for the nobility, not the merchants and craftsmen.*

Baldassare Castiglione, **The Book of the Courtier,** Leonard E. Opdycke, trans. (New York: Charles Scribner's Sons, 1903). Language simplified.

For this evening's game, let us select someone to portray a perfect courtier. He should explain all of the conditions and special qualities that a courtier must have.

I would have our courtier sometimes take part in quiet and peaceful exercises. If he is to escape envy and appear agreeable to everyone, the courtier should join others in what they are doing. Yet he must use good judgment to see that he never appears foolish. Let him laugh, joke, banter, frolic, and dance, yet in such a way that he shall always appear genial and discreet. And in whatever he does or says, let him do it with grace.

I would have the courtier know literature, in particular those studies known as the humanities. He should be able to speak not only Latin but Greek, as well. Let him read and know the Roman and Greek poets, orators, and historians. Let him be proficient in writing verse and prose, particularly in our own language. Even if he does not become perfect in the art of writing verse and prose, he should still practice it so that he will at least be able to judge the work of others.

My lords, you must know that I am not content with the courtier unless he is also a musician. Besides being able to read and understand music, he must be able to play the different instruments. Music is the best relaxation or medicine for a troubled man. Moreover, it is a most becoming and praiseworthy pastime during leisure hours, especially in the court, where it relieves the boredom and pleases the ladies.

Our courtier should know how to draw and paint. Do not be surprised that I believe the courtier should know this art, which today seems to be practiced only by artisans and not by gentlemen. I remember having read that the ancients, especially in Greece, had the boys of noble birth study painting in school. They believed it was an honorable and necessary thing, and it was recognized as the first of the liberal arts. At the same time they forbade slaves to practice art. Among the Romans, too, it was held in highest honor.

And truly one who does not honor this art seems unreasonable to me. This universe that we see—the vast heaven so richly adorned with shining stars, the earth circled by seas, varied with mountains, valleys, and rivers and decorated with so many different trees, beautiful flowers, and grasses—is a great and noble picture, painted by the hand of nature and of God. Whoever is capable of copying the picture seems to me to deserve great praise.

▶Are any of your values the same as those of Petrarch, Boccaccio, or Castiglione? Do you have similar ideas about the nature of man?

FOR THOUGHT:

To what degree do the values of Petrarch, Boccaccio, and Castiglione reflect the society in which they wrote?

17 THE RENAISSANCE

A HISTORICAL ESSAY

Eternal salvation, protection from enemies, and sufficient food and shelter were the chief concerns of medieval man. Bound to the soil he tilled, the medieval peasant looked to his lord to save him from enemies and to his priest to save him from eternal damnation. The warrior-noble, charged with protecting and governing his society, depended on his land to feed his body and on his church to feed his soul. The priest, watching over the spiritual needs of his people, relied on the sword of the noble and the hoe of the peasant to meet his earthly needs.

At least in theory, every man had a place in medieval society, doing his duty to God and to his fellow men. But gradually changes began to take place. Toward the end of the tenth century, enemy invasions subsided. At the end of the eleventh century, Europeans marched off to the Middle East on the Crusades. Trade with the East, from which many Italian cities profited, extended into northern Europe, making the French and Germans less dependent on their own resources. No longer tied to the manors economically, medieval men began to move to the cities. There a new social structure gradually evolved.

The changes that transformed Europe started in Italy's cities—Venice, Florence, Genoa, Pisa, Milan, and Naples. (See map, p. 83.) Unlike other cities in Europe, they had not declined much during the Middle Ages. Many nobles had moved from their rural manors into the cities at the earliest opportunity. Serfs were not as large a proportion of Italy's lower class as they were elsewhere in Europe. Commerce grew rapidly in the cities and created the dynamic urban life that in turn helped to create the Renaissance. Seaports, particularly Venice and Genoa, served as transfer points between Europe and the East. The Crusades increased the flow of people, trade, and ideas through the Italian seaports.

Italian manufacturing developed in the wake of the trading vessels. Needing goods to exchange for the spices, jewels, and silk of the East, merchants invested in cloth and leather industries and in shipbuilding. They imported raw wool and skins, and their ships carried finished cloth and leather goods to other ports. They used their profits to hire more workers and buy more tools. As the merchants gained control of manufacturing, they broke the monopoly of the guilds over urban economic decisions.

The merchants also invested in banking. With the increase in trade came a demand for more money. Clothmakers, for instance, might need to buy large quantities of wool before they had enough money available. Many merchants lent their extra money to such men to finance their enterprises. In return, the borrowers paid a certain percentage of interest on the loans. Lending money proved so profitable that many business-men gave up their other activities to devote their entire financial re-sources to banking.

As trade, manufacturing, and banking increased, prices began to rise. Many nobles who owned land outside the cities could not pay all their debts, and they found it necessary to mortgage or sell their land to the merchants and bankers. As the urban businessmen became landowners, the cities gained political control of the countryside.

During the Middle Ages, wealth had gone to those who had political power. During the Renaissance, political power went to those who had wealth. In the tenth century, many Italian cities had become part of the Holy Roman Empire, which was ruled by German emperors. These

MONTFERRAT

Milan

MILAN

SAVOY

Genoa

GENOA

Verona   Venice

Mantua

MANTUA   Ferrara

FERRARA

REPUBLIC OF VENICE

Bologna

MODENA

LUCCA   Florence

Pisa   FLORENCE

Siena

SIENA

Urbino

PAPAL

STATES

Adriatic

Sea

Mediterranean Sea

CORSICA

Rome

KINGDOM

OF NAPLES

Naples

Tyrrhenian

Sea

SARDINIA

Palermo

RENAISSANCE
ITALY

SICILY

Syracuse

emperors were continually involved in political struggles with the German nobles and the Italian popes. As a result, they could not watch over the growing cities, and the businessmen were able to win political control.

At first, the great merchant and banking families vied with each other for control of the cities. They bought votes in the municipal elections and hired mercenary, or paid, armies. Eventually, one family, such as the Visconti and Sforzas of Milan or the Medici of Florence, acquired enough power to become powerful rulers. Their mercenary armies

83

Churchmen are selling indulgences, which were pardons for sins. Originally, indulgences were given only to a person who had performed some good work. But Renaissance popes began to give out indulgences in return for money.

Detail from a portrait of Pope Leo X by Raphael showing the wealth of the upper clergy.

These pictures show conditions within parts of the Church during the Renaissance. How had the Church changed since the medieval period? Do you think any of these changes might become problems for the Church? If so, how?

This illustration shows Rome as a widow dressed in rags, forsaken by the popes who have moved to Avignon during the period known as the Babylonian Captivity.

85

crushed threats to their power. But always they had to be on guard against popular rebellions and other ambitious families.

Money and credit replaced land as the means of acquiring goods. Renaissance men also took interest in New World explorations and in the discoveries of science. With the expansion of commerce and the rise of a wealthy, politically powerful urban class, the city became the focus of life in Italy and the source of the development of Renaissance values.

Renaissance interest in worldly affairs resulted in part from a decline in the authority of the Roman Catholic Church. Much of medieval life had been guided by the doctrines of the Church. The Church participated in political decisions and often forced kings and nobles to change their policies in the interest of the Church. But such interference eventually brought the Church into conflict with political rulers. As the European monarchs gained more power, they defied the rulings of the Church. In fact, the French king was able to influence the selection of the pope. The new pope then moved to Avignon in southern France.

The popes resided in Avignon until 1378. Petrarch named this period the "Babylonian Captivity," an allusion to the captivity of the ancient Jews in Babylonia. The Babylonian Captivity is discussed further in Chapter 4.

Along with these developments, the moral authority of the Church also declined. Although the popes at Avignon were no longer able to dictate to the monarchs, the papal court was one of the grandest in Europe. The magnificent palace was adorned with many of the finest works of art. Bishops imitated the papal splendor. This interest in earthly concerns caused many people to question the spiritual authority of the Church. Reformers began to question its doctrines with greater frequency. In the fourteenth and fifteenth centuries, John Wycliffe and John Huss attacked the worldliness of the Church and tried unsuccessfully to reform it. But in the early sixteenth century, this movement led to the Protestant Reformation and to reform within the Roman Catholic Church itself.

John Wycliffe and John Huss were forerunners of the Reformation. They will be discussed further in Chapter 4.

The worldliness of the Italians also made the Church more secular, or interested in earthly affairs. As Renaissance values took hold, men with a more secular outlook joined the ranks of the clergy. Aeneas Silvius Piccolomini who became Pope Pius II in 1458 carried his values with him to the papacy. (See p. 65.) Julius II, pope from 1503 to 1513, commissioned Michelangelo to paint the ceiling of the Sistine Chapel.

The Sistine Chapel is a private chapel of the popes in the Vatican.

The clergy, the despots, the merchants, and the bankers all promoted Renaissance values through their patronage of the arts. In medieval times, the greatest market for artistic works was the Church. Painters contributed altarpieces, sculptors fashioned statues, and musicians composed and performed music for the Church. But the Renaissance leaders, eager to display their wealth, commissioned paintings, sculpture, and music for their personal enjoyment. The Medici employed Michelangelo to carve statues for their town house in Florence. Popes and bishops also were interested in glorification through art. Such patronage gave Leonardo da Vinci, Michelangelo, Cellini, Bandinello, Petrarch, and many others the means to create one of the most magnificent cultural achievements in the history of the world.

What was this burst of cultural activity like? What values were expressed? These questions can be answered by looking first at the art of the Renaissance and second at its literature. The artists' subjects reflected the earthly concerns of their patrons. Although much of Renaissance art was devoted to religious themes—Michelangelo's *David* or Leonardo's *Last Supper,* for example—the artists handled these subjects in a worldly manner. Raphael's portrait of Pope Julius II and Ghirlandaio's portrait of Count Sassetti reflected the interest of these leaders in their personal glory. Classical subjects offered still another theme, of which Botticelli's *The Birth of Venus* and Raphael's *The School of Athens* are examples.

▶ Do you think that the wealthy should support artists? Should the government? Or do you think that struggling is important to artistic development?

Unlike medieval art, Renaissance art was intended to glorify its artists. Like their patrons, Renaissance painters and sculptors wanted to be remembered for their personal contributions. They competed to find new ways to express themselves on canvas, in stone, or with precious metals. Individualism, a characteristic of humanism, was the mood in art. Each artist developed a personal style.

Raphael, who lived from 1483 to 1520, was one of the major artists of the Italian Renaissance. Ghirlandaio was a fifteenth-century Florentine artist. Botticelli, a Florentine artist and favorite of the Medici, lived from about 1444 to 1510.

Renaissance artists tried to represent the world as it actually existed. They studied anatomy so they could paint the human form more accurately. They developed perspective, making distant objects smaller than those in the foreground, thus giving depth to canvas instead of just height and width.

The secular concerns of the Renaissance also dominated its literature. Medieval writers had worried about the relationship of the state to the Church and about the individual's obligations to God. But Petrarch's sonnets focused on woman's beauty. Boccaccio described the values and life-styles of Renaissance life. Castiglione instructed courtiers to delight in beauty and gracious living. And the great political scientist of the time, Niccolo Machiavelli, advised princes about how to stay in power instead of discussing the role of religion in government.

As Renaissance people developed secular values, they rediscovered the classical world and the humanism of the Greeks. Remnants of Greek sculpture and literature had always been present in Europe, but Renaissance people found new meaning in them. They rediscovered the writings of Homer, Plato, and Cicero. The ancient civilizations seemed to justify their new attitudes toward the individual and the world when their religion could not.

Cicero (106-43 B.C.) was a Roman orator and philosopher.

The Renaissance was a rediscovery of the delights and beauty of this world. Sometimes using examples from ancient times and sometimes not, Renaissance man changed the direction of European history. Never again would western men be so occupied with the next world that they would ignore this one.

▶ Do you prefer the values of the Middle Ages or those of the Renaissance? Why?

87

For full descriptions of these activities, turn to the **Student Book of Activities and Readings** included among the materials for individual and group activities.

Activity 3A: Illustrations of Renaissance rules for living (individual)

This activity contains a collection of rules for living taken from the diary of a Renaissance statesman. After reading it, illustrate several of these rules with cartoons, drawings, or magazine pictures.

Activity 3B: Essay on Leonardo da Vinci based on evidence from his notebooks (individual)

This activity is made up of material from the notebooks of Leonardo da Vinci. Examine his drawings carefully. Write an essay to answer the question: What sort of person was Leonardo da Vinci?

The Reformation

On October 31, 1517, Martin Luther, a professor of theology at the University of Wittenberg in Germany, posted ninety-five theses, or propositions, criticizing Church practices. Luther meant only to invite other theologians to debate the points he had raised. Yet, without meaning to, he had challenged the authority of the Church. He soon found himself at the center of a revolt, called the Reformation, that divided western Christendom. Within a quarter of a century, the Reformation destroyed the religious monopoly of the Roman Catholic Church in the West.

Why did the Reformation take place? For centuries Christians had complained about a number of Church practices. They had charged that Church officials were corrupt or that Church doctrines could not be supported in the Bible. European rulers had long opposed the secular power which popes and bishops had won because they controlled land. Yet the attempts of reformers to change the Church had frequently failed in the past.

Beginning students of history often look for a single major cause for developments such as the Reformation. They look for one new ingredient to explain the change, such as the influence of a man like Martin Luther. Historians use the term single causation to describe explanations of this kind. These explanations occur frequently when people praise or blame a single powerful individual, such as a President, for a major change in society.

Chapter 4 examines the Protestant Reformation that took place during the early part of the sixteenth century. The first three readings focus on the causes of the Reformation. They raise the issue of whether a single event or several related events were responsible for this major change in the religious life of the West. The last reading in the chapter summarizes the argument about causation and traces the development of the Protestant revolt.

CHAPTER

4

1198-1216	Pope Innocent III brings papacy to its greatest power.
1305-1378	Popes reside in Avignon during Babylonian Captivity.
1376	John Wycliffe attacks Church doctrines and abuses.
1378-1417	During Great Schism, popes in Avignon and Rome vie for power.
1415	Council of Constance condemns John Huss, and he is burned for heresy.
1509	Desiderius Erasmus writes **The Praise of Folly.**
1517	Martin Luther publicizes Ninety-Five Theses attacking indulgences.
1519	Luther repudiates divine authority of Church.
1521	Pope excommunicates Luther.
1525	Luther opposes peasant uprising of 1524.
1534	English Act of Supremacy makes king head of Church of England.
1536	John Calvin publishes **Institutes of the Christian Religion.**
1545-1563	Council of Trent clarifies Catholic doctrines and censures Church abuses.
1598	Henry IV of France signs Edict of Nantes protecting French Protestants.
1618-1648	Thirty Years' War between German Protestants and Catholics soon involves most of Europe.

18 CRITIQUES OF THE MEDIEVAL CHURCH

The medieval Church believed that salvation was given to man by the grace of God, and that the Church alone had the keys to that grace. These keys were the seven sacraments: baptism, confirmation, penance, the Eucharist, marriage, extreme unction, and holy orders. The sacraments had to be administered by the clergy. This power over the souls of people gave the Church great authority in medieval Europe.

The Church did not limit this authority to its religious role. Throughout the Middle Ages, it was actively involved in non-religious affairs. By the early thirteenth century, the Church was the single largest landholder in Europe, and the pope, Innocent III, was the most powerful man of his time. The popes ruled a vast area, collecting taxes and waging war with their feudal vassals. Their calls for Crusades sent Christian rulers and many of their subjects to fight the Muslims in the Holy Land.

Many of the clergy became so involved in worldly pursuits that they ignored their religious vows. Some were self-seeking men who had bought their religious offices. Sometimes they held several at a time. Churchmen began to try to reform the Church and its practices. John Wycliffe, a fourteenth-century churchman and Oxford professor, believed that the Church had no right to own property. According to Wycliffe, the true Church was made up of ordinary people who found the means to salvation by reading the Bible. His views influenced the priest and scholar, John Huss of Bohemia. (See map, p. 112.) Huss challenged the pope openly, calling Christ the only head of the Church. He attacked Church beliefs and spoke out against its rituals and worldly wealth. Both men were condemned as heretics, people who denied the truth of Church beliefs. But Wycliffe was finally permitted to retire to private life while Huss was burned at the stake in 1415.

By the sixteenth century more voices were raised against abuses in the Church. Most notable among them were Martin Luther and Desiderius Erasmus. Erasmus was a Catholic priest in Rotterdam and a leader of the humanist movement in northern Europe. The selections in Reading 18 are excerpts from each of their protests. As you read, keep the following questions in mind:

1. What religious practices did Erasmus ridicule? What did he reveal about medieval Christians and the Church?
2. What was Luther protesting in his Ninety-Five Theses? What reasons did he give?

Erasmus: *The Praise of Folly*

Erasmus was the most famous scholar of his day and a great admirer of the Greek and Roman civilizations. Alarmed by conditions within the Church, Erasmus prepared his own Greek and Latin translations of the New Testament by going back to the original texts. He hoped to remove the errors made in earlier translations and force the Church to reexamine some of its beliefs. In The Praise of Folly, *Erasmus used his sharp wit to ridicule some of the religious practices of sixteenth-century Europeans.*

To the class of fools who listens to ghost stories and tales of miracles belong those people who believe in the silly but pleasing notion that if they look at a picture of St. Christopher, they will not die that day. This group also includes those who believe that if they offer a greeting to an image of St. Barbara they will return safely from battle. These fools have found a new Hercules in St. George. They seem to adore

Desiderius Erasmus, The Praise of Folly, as quoted in James Harvey Robinson, Readings in European History (Boston: Ginn and Co., 1906), Vol. II, pp. 41–44. Language simplified.

even his horse, which is decked out in gorgeous trappings. They make additional offerings in the hope of gaining new favors. One would think that his bronze helmet was half divine, the way people swear by it.

And what should I say about those who delude themselves with the comfort that comes from imaginary pardons for their sins when they pay for indulgences? They have taken to measuring their time in purgatory by years, months, days, and hours, calculating how much they subtract from their time there with each payment. There are plenty of those who rely on certain little magical certificates and prayers to win riches, honor, future happiness, health, perpetual prosperity, long life, a lusty old age—even, in the end, a seat at the right hand of Christ in heaven. But they are not anxious for the end to come. They will content themselves with the joy of heaven only after they must finally surrender the pleasures of this world, to which they so lovingly cling.

The trader, the soldier, and the judge think that they can clean up the sins of a lifetime by donating a single ill-gotten coin. They flatter themselves into believing that all sorts of dishonesty, drunkenness, quarrels, bloodshed, evil, and treason can be taken care of with a contract in which they pay a particular price to obtain salvation.

These various forms of foolishness are so worked into the lives of Christians that even the priests in the Church do not object to them. In fact, they foster these beliefs because they are smart enough to realize what tidy little sums of money come to them because of these follies.

As for the theologians, perhaps the less said the better, since they become quite irritable unless they can force you to give up those beliefs that you worked out through honest reason and scholarship. And if you do not give them up, they brand you as a heretic, for it is their custom to use all manner of thunderings to terrify those whom they dislike.

According to Church doctrine, people whose sins had been forgiven at confession had to spend time in purgatory before going to heaven when they died. The Church began to pardon some sins when people donated large sums of money. This practice was called indulgence.

▶Among the "follies" Erasmus criticized was superstition. What do you think of superstition? Does it influence you in any way?

Luther: The Ninety-Five Theses

In 1517 Johann Tetzel, a Dominican friar, was authorized by the pope to distribute indulgences in the German principality of Saxony. Half the money he received was to go to Rome to help build St. Peter's Church. The other half was to go to the German prince of Saxony who owed great sums to the papacy and to a private banking house. Tetzel reportedly encouraged sales by proclaiming, "When the coin in the coffer rings, the soul from purgatory springs." To Luther, who had long agonized over the means to his own salvation, indulgences corrupted the very meaning of Christianity. His Ninety-Five Theses attacked the sale of indulgences, although the Church denied selling them.

It insisted that it only granted them. A selection of Luther's theses appears below.

1. When our Lord and Master Jesus Christ said "Repent ye," he intended that the whole life of believers ought to be one of penance.

2. This kind of penance is not the same as sacramental penance in which the believer performs the ritual of confessing and atoning for his sins under the ministry of a priest.

3. At the same time, penance does not mean only an inner feeling of regret. This feeling of regret must also make the believer want to perform certain acts to atone for having done wrong.

5. The pope does not have the power to remove a man's obligation to pay a penalty for committing a sin except for those penalties which the pope himself has imposed.

21. The preachers of indulgences, who say that buying a certificate of indulgence from the pope or his representative frees a man from all punishment, are wrong.

27. Those who preach that the soul flies out of purgatory as soon as the money rattles in the chest preach man's values, not God's.

28. It is certain that when the money rattles in the chest, greed and gain may be increased, but the forgiveness of sins can come from God alone.

43. Christians should be taught that he who gives to a poor man or lends to a needy man does better than if he used the money to buy an indulgence.

44. By works of charity, a man's charitable nature increases, but in buying an indulgence the man does not become better—only freer of punishment from the Church.

50. Christians should be taught that if the pope knew of the money his indulgences have taken from poor people, he would prefer that St. Peter's Church be burned to ashes rather than have it built with the flesh, bones, and skin of his people.

86. Why does not the pope, who has enormous riches, build St. Peter's with his own money rather than the money of poor believers?

91. If those who preach the sale of indulgences in Germany would preach them in the spirit that I believe the pope intended them to be preached, all of these questions would be answered with ease. In fact, they would not even be asked.

Martin Luther, Ninety-Five Theses, as quoted in Robinson, **Readings in European History,** Vol. II, pp. 58-61. Language simplified.

►Should people build elaborate and expensive churches, or should they build simple ones and use the savings for charity or some other worthy purpose?

FOR THOUGHT:

Suppose someone told you that Martin Luther caused the Reformation. How would you respond?

These three pictures show Martin Luther in different lights. How does each artist portray Luther? How can you explain the similarities and differences in these portrayals?

19 THE APPEAL OF THE PROTESTANT REVOLT

Only a hundred years before Luther, John Huss had made similar charges against the Church. Huss was burned at the stake, but Luther died of natural causes. Huss did not destroy the religious unity of Europe, but Luther divided it into Protestant and Catholic camps. What had happened during those hundred years to make Luther successful where Huss had failed?

Part of the explanation can be found in the weakening of Church authority. Late in the thirteenth century, kings and princes began to resist papal interference in their political and economic activities. Some rulers were able to gain control of the Church in their territories. At the same time, the clergy was growing increasingly worldly and fond of luxury. Many Europeans began to question their Church. They became less willing to recognize its divine right to dictate their moral values.

However, some of Luther's success resulted from the popularity of his ideas and those of other Protestant reformers. The landowning nobility, for example, resented the Church's vast holdings within their territories. And the reformers had all attacked the right of the Church to own property. Some had gone so far as to say that the Church should be under the control of the state. Thus, the nobility saw the possibility of taking the Church's land if the Church were successfully challenged. The middle class wanted freedom from the restrictions the Church put upon their commercial interests. And the peasants, oppressed by taxes and debts, wanted the chance for dignity that Luther, himself a peasant, seemed to offer. These groups defended the reformers and assured their success. From the evidence in Reading 19, you should be able to develop some hypotheses about the appeal of Protestantism in the sixteenth century. Keep the following questions in mind as you examine the evidence in the readings.

1. For what reasons did Luther appeal to the German nobles? How did his ideas reflect recent political changes in Europe?
2. What were the major complaints of the peasants? Why were they attracted to Protestant ideas?
3. To what class would Calvin's ideas most appeal? On what do you base your answer?

Luther's *Address to the German Nobility*

Luther's protest against indulgences became a protest against the Church. When Luther defended his views publicly in 1519, he stated that the laws of the Church were not necessarily God's laws. The Bible alone contained the proper guides for Christians. In 1520 Luther published three pamphlets, including his Address to the German Nobility. *In 1521 he was excommunicated.*

It is not out of mere arrogance and stubbornness that I, one poor and insignificant man, have decided to appeal to your lordships. The distress and misery which oppress all the ranks of Christendom, especially in Germany, have made not only me but everybody cry aloud for help.

Those who support the authority of the pope have built three "walls" of belief to protect the Church from reform. In the first place, when kings and princes have asked them to reform, they have stated that the secular rulers have no power over the spiritual rulers—that, on the contrary, the spiritual power is above the secular rulers. Secondly, when some have used the Holy Scriptures to call for reform, they said "No one but the pope can interpret the Scriptures." And thirdly, when a council of the Church has called for reform, they invented the idea that no one but the pope can call a council.

Let us, then, attack the first wall.

The defenders of the Church maintain that the pope, bishops, priests, and monks should be called "the spiritual class," while princes, lords, artisans, and peasants make up the "temporal class." Then they affirm that spiritual authorities are superior to temporal authorities. But do not be afraid of this claim. All Christians are truly members of the spiritual class, and there is no difference between us, except for the office we hold. As St. Paul says, in Corinthians I, Chapter 12, we are all one body in Christ. Each of us has a particular task to perform as the various parts of the body perform particular functions.

Therefore, a priest should be nothing in Christendom but a man with a particular function. We see, then, that all those we call churchmen, be they priests, bishops, or popes, are not different from or higher than other Christians, except insofar as they have the responsibility and the honor of preaching the word of God and giving man the sacraments.

Now let us look at the doctrine that states the temporal authorities have no power over the spiritual. That is like saying that the hand shall do nothing to help the eye, despite the fact that it is severely injured. I say that since God has given the temporal power the responsibility

Luther, Address to the German Nobility, as quoted in Robinson, Readings in European History, Vol. II, pp. 74-77, 79-80. Language simplified.

Many reformers believed that councils of churchmen and representatives of the European rulers could best rid the Church of abuses. Several such councils were held during the first half of the fifteenth century. The councils and the papacy were in conflict, since each insisted on its superiority.

to punish the wicked and protect the good, we must let it perform its task regardless of whether or not it must punish popes, bishops, priests, monks, nuns, or whatever.

What is the use of those who are called "cardinals"? I will tell you. In Italy and Germany there are many rich convents, endowments, and tracts of land belonging to the Church. The best way of getting these into the hands of the pope in Rome is to create cardinals and give them these rich holdings. That is why Italy is almost a desert now: The convents are destroyed, the Church lands consumed, the revenues of all the churches drawn to Rome. Why? Because the cardinals must have all the wealth.

Now that Italy is sucked dry, they come to Germany. We shall soon see Germany in the same state as Italy. Now this devilish state of things is not only open robbery and deceit, but it is destroying the very life and soul of Christianity. Therefore, we must use all of our diligence to ward off this destruction. Let us begin with the pope and cardinals—we cannot find worse ones. If we rightly hang thieves and behead robbers, why do we leave the greed of Rome unpunished? Rome is the greatest thief and robber that has ever appeared on earth or ever will; and all in the holy name of the Church.

The College of Cardinals, established in 1059, elects the pope.

The Declaration of the Peasants

The peasants of sixteenth-century Germany, though in many cases no longer serfs, were still heavily taxed and deprived of their common pastures and woods. When a peasants' war broke out in Germany in 1524, the peasants drew up a declaration of grievances. Excerpts from that declaration follow.

The Declaration of the Peasants, as quoted in Robinson, **Readings in European History**, Vol. II, pp. 95-98. Language simplified.

First, it is our humble desire that in the future we, the peasants, should have the power to choose and appoint the pastor of our own community, and that we should have the right to depose him if he should conduct himself improperly. The pastor we choose should teach us the gospel pure and simple, without adding any doctrine or ordinance made by man.

Second, as a just tithe is called for in both the Old and New Testaments, we are ready and willing to pay a fair tithe in grain. From this tithe will come the salary of the pastor which the community will establish. What remains should be given to care for the poor.

In medieval times, a tithe was a Church tax amounting to one-tenth of a person's income.

The peasants are referring to nobles, princes, and lords of the Church, such as bishops, who had serfs.

Third, it has been the custom until now for men to hold us as if we were their own property, which is pitiable enough since Christ has delivered and redeemed us all, lowly as well as great. Accordingly, it is consistent with the Scriptures that we should be free. Not that we

From this picture, how would you describe the lives of the German peasants in Luther's time? What do you think these people might have wanted from the Protestant revolt?

wish to be absolutely free under no authority. God teaches us that we should not lead a disorderly life. But He has not commanded us to obey the authorities except as we should obey the word of God; that is, we should be humble toward everyone, powerful or not. We are thus ready to obey our authorities in all things becoming to a Christian. But we take it for granted that you will release us from serfdom as true Christians, unless it can be shown in the gospel that we are serfs.

Our sixth complaint is in regard to the excessive services which are demanded of us and which are increased from day to day. We ask that

99

this matter be properly looked into so that we shall not continue to be oppressed in this way.

Seventh, the lord should no longer try to force more services on the peasant than are provided for in the contract between peasant and lord, unless the lord will make an additional payment.

In the eighth place, we are greatly burdened by small holdings which cannot support the rent that is due from them. We ask that the lords fix a just rent, so that the peasant shall not work for nothing.

▶Do you take for granted many of the rights the German peasants requested 450 years ago? Can you think of any dangers in taking such rights for granted?

Calvin: *Institutes of the Christian Religion*

Calvin was a French theologian who had accepted many of Luther's teachings. When he openly denounced the Church and papal authority, he was threatened with persecution and so he fled to Switzerland. There, Calvin established a church-run state, a theocracy. The following excerpts from the Institutes of the Christian Religion *present Calvin's views on economic practices.*

John Calvin, **Institutes of the Christian Religion,** John Allen, ed. (Philadelphia: Philip H. Nicklin & Hezekiah Howe, 1816), Vol. II, pp. 196-202. Language simplified.

The Scriptures teach us about how we should use our earthly blessings. There are two kinds of goods which God has given us. The first are those necessities we must have to live on earth before passing to our heavenly reward. Second, in addition to the goods we must have in order to live, we obtain goods which we use primarily for our own pleasure. Whether the goods we obtain are for necessities or for pleasure, we must use them in moderation. This the Lord teaches us in the Scriptures when He states that life on earth is like a pilgrimage. Christians travel through this life on their way to God's heavenly kingdom. If we are only passing through life on earth to eternal life in heaven, we ought to make use of earth's blessings to assist us in our journey.

We state the principle, then, that we ought to use God's earthly gifts, so long as we use them for the same purposes for which God created them. After all, He created them for our benefit and not for our injury. Moreover, He has provided these gifts for more than existence; He has created them for our pleasure and delight, as well.

▶What would you include among "those things that are necessary in order to live"?

Let us discard that inhuman philosophy which states that we should use God's gifts for only those things that are necessary in order to live. In the first place, this philosophy deprives us of the lawful enjoyment of the Divine gifts. Secondly, this philosophy turns man into a senseless block. We should, therefore, use goods for pleasure, but we must oppose extravagant use of these goods to satisfy the pleasures of the flesh.

100

Lastly, the Lord commands everyone of us to take his work seriously. He has appointed each of us to particular duties, or callings. Every individual's occupation, therefore, is a post assigned to him by God. Hence, no work is so lowly that it is not important and respectable in the sight of God.

FOR THOUGHT:

The three documents in Reading 19 all criticize practices of the Roman Catholic Church. Would you therefore conclude that Church abuses were the sole cause of the Reformation?

20 THE CHURCH REFORMED: PROTESTANT AND CATHOLIC

When Luther posted his Ninety-Five Theses in 1517, he had no thought of establishing a separate church. Rather he hoped only to force the Church to reform its doctrines concerning penance and indulgences. Luther had suffered grave anxiety over the destiny of his own soul. Searching in the New Testament for some guide to God's grace, Luther had found the words of St. Paul, "The just shall live by faith." (Romans Ch. 1:17) For Luther, thereafter faith alone provided the means to salvation. But this belief contradicted the Church teachings that salvation required faith in Jesus, participation in the sacraments, and the performance of good works.

Luther continued to challenge the Church's emphasis on good works and the sacraments. Luther claimed that the doctrine of indulgences made a farce of true repentance. Penance and other sacraments encouraged empty participation in religious ritual. Luther further argued that salvation was God's gift to man and that the only means of achieving it was by following the Scriptures and having faith in Jesus.

Luther was very much a man of his times. It was not unusual for a European of the late Middle Ages to be preoccupied with his soul and salvation. And people were questioning the morals, philosophies, and values of medieval Europe as well. When Church theology failed to answer these questions, many reformers left the church and developed Protestant theologies.

Some religious reformers, such as Erasmus, did not leave the Church. And by the mid-sixteenth century the Church had begun its own counterreformation. Paul III, the first reforming pope, revived the Church council movement begun in the previous century. The council he called met in the northern Italian city of Trent periodically between 1545 and 1563 to reexamine and clarify Church beliefs. It reasserted the supreme position of the pope and took strong measures to end immoral practices among the clergy. The material in Reading 20 shows some of the charges leveled against the Church and how the Church responded. As you study the selections, consider the following questions:

1. What was Luther's interpretation of the Eucharist? How did it differ from that of the Council of Trent?
2. According to Luther, how is man saved? How did the Council of Trent respond to this belief?
3. How did the Council of Trent reform the Church? What did it not change?

Luther: The Sacrament of the Eucharist

The Catholic sacrament of the Eucharist, or the mass, cele-brates the Last Supper of Jesus. Jesus had taken bread and wine and called them his body and blood. Then he had told his disciples to repeat

Lutherans receiving wine

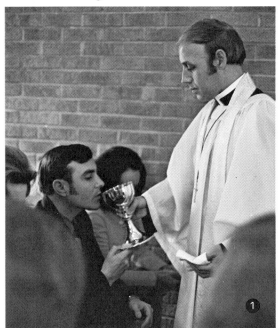

Catholic priest drinking wine

102

The pictures on these two pages show two scenes from a Catholic mass and two parallel scenes from a Lutheran communion. What similarities and differences do you see? Why do you think the question of the proper type of Eucharist is no longer very controversial?

Lutherans receiving bread

Catholic child receiving bread

what he had done in remembrance of his death on the cross. Roman Catholic Church doctrine holds that Christians who take bread and wine during the mass renew Jesus' sacrifice for man's sins and receive God's mercy.

The medieval Church held to the doctrine of transubstantiation—the transformation of the bread and wine into the body and blood of Jesus. In the medieval mass, the priest repeated Jesus' words, offered only the bread to the congregation, and then drank the wine himself. Luther took issue with the Church's definition and administration of the Eucharist in On the Babylonian Captivity of the Church, *one of the three pamphlets he wrote in 1520.*

Luther, **On the Babylonian Captivity of the Church,** as quoted in **Luther's Primary Works,** Henry Wace and C.A. Buchheim, eds. and trans. (London: Hodder and Stoughton, 1896), pp. 302-313. Language simplified.

Matthew, Mark, and Luke agree that Christ gave both the bread and the wine to all of his disciples. No one has denied that Paul gave both to the early Christians. According to Matthew and Mark, Christ did not say concerning the bread, "Eat ye all of this," but did say concerning the cup, "Drink ye all of this." Each writer points out that the disciples drank the wine.

Priests who refuse to give both the bread and wine to members of their congregation commit a sin. The priests are at fault, not the laity [nonpriests]. The sacrament does not belong to the priests, but to all believers. The priests are not lords. They are servants whose duty it is to give both the bread and the wine to those who seek them.

We should interpret the Scriptures accurately. We should read God's words in their simplest meaning. In this case, the early fathers of the Church wrote that Christ took bread and blessed it. The Book of Acts and the Apostle Paul also call it bread. We must understand that the bread and wine of the mass are real bread and real wine. It is not necessary to believe that the bread and wine are transubstantiated by Divine power. This belief is mere opinion. The idea that the bread and wine are changed into the body and blood of Christ is not supported by Scripture or by reason.

Luther: Justification by Faith Alone

According to Luther, man could not earn his salvation; he could only receive it from God. God granted salvation to those who accepted the true meaning of the sacrifice of His son, Jesus. Luther spelled out this doctrine of "justification (salvation) by faith" in A Treatise on Christian Liberty, *the third pamphlet he published in 1520.*

Man is composed of two elements, a spiritual element and a bodily element. The spiritual nature, which we call the soul, may be thought of as the inward man. The bodily nature, which we call the flesh, is the outward man. And, though our outward flesh may perish, the inward soul will have everlasting life if it is renewed in Jesus Christ.

So it will bring no profit to a man if his body is adorned with sacred vestments such as the priests wear, or live in sacred places like the monks, or hold sacred office like a bishop, or pray, fast, and abstain from certain foods. Any person whose inward soul has not been justified by faith in Christ could do any one of these things. On the other hand, the soul will not be injured if the outward body is clothed in ordinary dress, if it should live in ordinary places, or should eat and drink in an ordinary fashion.

One thing, and one thing alone, is necessary for justification of the soul and Christian liberty, and that is the most holy word of God, the Gospel of Christ. As He says: "I am the resurrection and the life; he that believeth in me shall not die, but live eternally." The soul can do without everything except the word of God, without which none of its wants are provided for. The Christian is free from doing good works to gain his salvation. He must strengthen his faith.

One who has faith in Christ believes that Christ had died for him. He believes that Christ intercedes with God for his salvation. Not only does Christ pray for us, but he teaches us through his spiritual presence in all of us. Praying for us and teaching us are supposedly the functions of an earthly priest. But since Christ has done these, everyone who believes in him is his own priest.

Here you will ask, "If all who are in the Church are priests, how are those whom we call priests different from the laymen?" I reply that an injustice has been done in giving special powers to a few, when according to the Scriptures thay belong to all. Those who are now boastfully called popes, bishops, and priests are called ministers, servants, and stewards in the Bible, for they serve the rest of us by teaching us to have faith in Christ.

Although, as I have said, inward faith in Christ is enough for salvation, still the outward man, or the man of the flesh, lives a mortal life in which he comes into contact with other men. Here then, good works begin. The outward man will perform good works if faith and Christ's spirit have become part of the inward man, or the soul. When he follows the instructions of his inner self, he comes into conflict with the will of his flesh, which is to seek gratification. But the spirit of faith will not let the outward man do this. Using this principle of letting the inward faith dictate the actions of the outward man, every man can easily decide for himself how he ought to behave. But those who pretend to gain salvation by doing good works are only fooling themselves. Truly good works do not make a man good, but a good man will do good works.

Luther, A Treatise on Christian Liberty, as quoted in Luther's Primary Works, Wace and Buchheim, eds. and trans., pp. 81-87. Language simplified.

▶Are you concerned about your spiritual life? What, if anything, has replaced the importance of religion in your life?

▶Should people do good in the hopes of some reward either on earth or in an afterlife, or should they do good for its own sake?

The Catholic Reformation: The Council of Trent

Church authorities consider the Council of Trent the most important council in the modern history of the Roman Catholic Church. The following passages are taken from the council's decrees.

The Canons and Decrees of the Council of Trent. Language simplified.

Let the following be cursed: anyone who says that the New Testament does not provide for a distinct priesthood; anyone who says that priests do not have the power of bringing about the transubstantiation of the bread and wine into the body and blood of Christ; anyone who preaches that priests do not have the power of forgiving or not forgiving; and anyone who says on the other hand that a priest is merely a minister whose only duty is to preach the gospel.

If anyone says that a man can be justified before God by doing good works without also having the divine grace of Jesus Christ, let him be cursed.

If anyone says that a sinner is justified by faith alone, meaning that it is not necessary for him to receive sacraments to prepare for grace, let him be cursed.

If anyone says that a man's justification before God is not increased by his good works, let him be cursed.

In order that Christians may receive the sacraments with greater devotion, this holy council commands that bishops and priests should first explain the purpose and use of the sacraments in a way that the congregation can understand, using the native tongue of the people if it is necessary.

It is to be desired that all who become bishops should understand what portion of their income should be devoted to their own maintenance, and to comprehend that they are called to the office of bishop not for riches or luxury, but to the labors and cares for the glory of God.

FOR THOUGHT:

For which of the hypotheses that you developed at the beginning of this chapter have you been able to find supporting evidence? What do you think now about the issue of single causation vs. multiple causation?

A HISTORICAL ESSAY

For a thousand years, the western Church was directed from Rome. The capital city of the empire changed from the political center of western Europe to the religious center. Long before 1054, when the Christian Church officially divided into Roman Catholic and Eastern Orthodox, Rome was the unquestioned authority for Christianity in the West.

The Roman Catholic Church rose to great influence in medieval Europe. By the tenth century, most of the people in and around the old Roman Empire had converted to Christianity. After Charlemagne's empire broke up, the Church struggled against corruption within its ranks and attacks against its beliefs. But it rose to these challenges. It controlled abuses among the clergy. It developed its doctrines into a large body of Roman Catholic law. And it branded as heretics those who did not hold the doctrines it endorsed.

The Roman Catholic Church derived its enormous power from the role it played in the lives of all medieval Europeans, the poor, the wealthy, and the powerful alike. Salvation was everyone's major concern. And the Church taught that it alone could prepare people to receive salvation through the sacraments it administered. The sacraments put the cycle of human life—birth, maturity, marriage, and death —into a religious context. They included the Eucharist, penance, and holy orders, thus making the Church the intermediary between God and man.

The Church, however, used its authority over the wealthy and the powerful to further its own economic and political interests. The clergy acquired valuable landholdings and were among Europe's richest men. Popes advised rulers and sometimes were powerful enough to make kings and princes their feudal vassals.

The Church was also the single major source of learning in medieval Europe. Until printing became available in the fifteenth century, the clergy provided nearly all of Europe's books. The Church produced the great scholars of the period. Schools and universities developed from the Church, and the clergy were the teachers.

Until the late Middle Ages, the Church's scholars and teachers had defended it against those who had questioned its doctrines. But eventually the universities became the center for the changes that were to end the Roman Catholic monopoly in western Europe. The Church had condemned John Wycliffe and John Huss for heresy in the centuries before Luther. They had both taught at major universities, Wycliffe at Oxford and Huss at the University of Prague. Their ideas were known to Martin Luther, a teacher at the new University of Wittenberg.

On October 31, 1517, Luther posted his Ninety-Five Theses challenging Church doctrine on indulgences and triggered the Protestant Reformation. His protest was successful not because people of his time were unconcerned with salvation, but because many had come to believe that the Church could not provide it. Political rivalry, economic changes, and Renaissance worldliness had affected churchmen as well as laymen. The Church had grown rigid in its struggle to preserve its power and wealth. Churchmen patronized the arts and the royal courts at the expense of their spiritual responsibilities. The bishops themselves often were not men of religion but political appointees controlled by kings and nobles.

Pope Urban II had first granted indulgences to the knights who went on the First Crusade. Later popes also granted indulgences to Crusaders and to those who made pilgrimages or performed other good works. By the early fourteenth century, however, Boniface VIII made indulgences obtainable for money. Boniface declared that a truly penitent person who confessed his sins and received the blessing of his priest might earn an indulgence by donating a fixed sum to the Church.

Like many others, Luther felt that indulgences were another example of how the Church had corrupted Christian doctrines until they little resembled the teachings of Jesus and his disciples. Luther knew that indulgence money was often shared with princes, spent on lavish palaces, and put to other nonreligious uses. Yet before October 1517, Luther had shown little sign that he would lead a revolt against the Church.

Luther had begun his long inner struggle over the fate of his soul while studying law. His tormented search for personal salvation led him to enter a monastery. But he found that prayer, contemplation, and ritual did not answer his questions nor assure him of salvation. Luther moved to Wittenberg to continue his studies and teach. There Luther found what he was seeking in St. Paul's letter to the Romans (Ch. 1:17) which said, "The just shall live by faith." To Luther this passage meant that faith in Jesus and his redemption of man's sins led to salvation. There was no need for sacraments and good works.

However, Luther made no move to challenge the Church until Tetzel's peddling of indulgences aroused him to protest. When the pope ordered Luther to accept the traditional doctrine on indulgences, he refused. In 1519 he defended his stand against one of the Church's strongest spokesmen, John Eck. During the debate, Luther declared that it was possible for popes and Church councils to be wrong and that the only true authority was the Bible.

108

Erasmus and other reformers urged a compromise between Luther and the Church, but compromise became increasingly difficult. Luther denied the role of the priest, stating that each person must deal with God directly. He denied most of the sacraments and the right of the Church to interpret the Scriptures. In effect, Luther rejected the Church itself by denying the very reasons for its existence. He was excommunicated in 1521 for heresy and might have been put to death had not Frederick the Wise, Prince of Saxony, protected him.

But one man does not make a new church. Luther needed followers, and he found many. Why did Luther succeed where earlier men had failed? In the years between Wycliffe and Luther, the forces of change had gathered strength. Politically, feudal holdings were being combined under strong monarchs, so that the Church lost much of its influence. Economic patterns changed as trade and industry expanded in the cities and money came into use. Social practices were adjusting to the demands of the commercial middle class. These changes created a sympathetic climate for Luther's revolt against the medieval Church.

Beginning in the tenth century, the popes had asserted the right of the Church to interfere in secular affairs. But at the same time, many European monarchs schemed to free themselves of Church domination. Throughout the twelfth century, this power struggle was generally weighted in favor of the Church. Europe was still divided into warring feudal holdings. Kings and nobles each sought Church support in their fight to hold their power. The political fortunes of the Church continued to rise well into the next century.

But by the late thirteenth and early fourteenth centuries, the weight of political power shifted sharply from popes to kings. Early in the fourteenth century, the French king, Philip IV, demanded the right to tax the clergy in his kingdom and to try them in the courts of France. When the pope opposed him, Philip sent his soldiers to Rome to capture him. But the aged pope died three days after they arrived. Philip then forced the election of a French pope who set up his papal court in Avignon, in southern France. Thus began the Babylonian Captivity, during which the popes were under the control of the French king. The Babylonian Captivity ended in 1378, but later popes never enjoyed the political power of earlier centuries.

The fortunes of the Church suffered in still another way. The Church had always been one of the great landowners of the Middle Ages. As long as the people of Europe depended on land to support them, the Church had great economic power. But as trade and industry grew, money became the medium of exchange. The Church had to develop ways of raising money. One method they used was the distribution of indulgences.

The nobles, whose wealth also lay in land, had the same economic problems as the Church. They found themselves competing with city merchants, manufacturers, and financiers for the control of the money in Europe. They passed their economic burdens onto their serfs and freeholders. They forced them to plant the common lands to produce surplus goods to trade for money. They required payment of feudal dues in cash rather than in goods and services. They reinstated old dues and created many new taxes.

But neither the Church nor the nobility could compete with the kings. The kings already had the power to tax their vassal nobles. Gradually they won the right to tax the clergy. And by supporting and financing commercial ventures, they received a growing tax revenue as well as political support from the commercial class. The kings used their great supplies of money against their ambitious vassals—both bishops and lords—and hired mercenary armies to put down their rebellions.

John Huss at the stake

▶ The three people pictured on these two pages gave their lives for the religions in which they believed. Would you die for your religious beliefs? for any other belief?

110

A heretic being tortured during the Inquisition, a period in which the Church tried to convert or eliminate all heretics

Joan of Arc at the stake

In addition to losing its political and economic power, the Church faced other problems. There was great corruption among the clergy. Church offices were bought and sold. Some clergy held several offices at one time and used Church income for their own pleasures. Such practices led many Europeans to question the moral authority of the Church. Among them were powerful rulers like Frederick the Wise who protected Luther. These rulers resented papal taxes and considered papal interference to be foreign intervention.

Thus in the sixteenth century, Luther found many people ready to defy the pope with him. He appealed successfully to many German

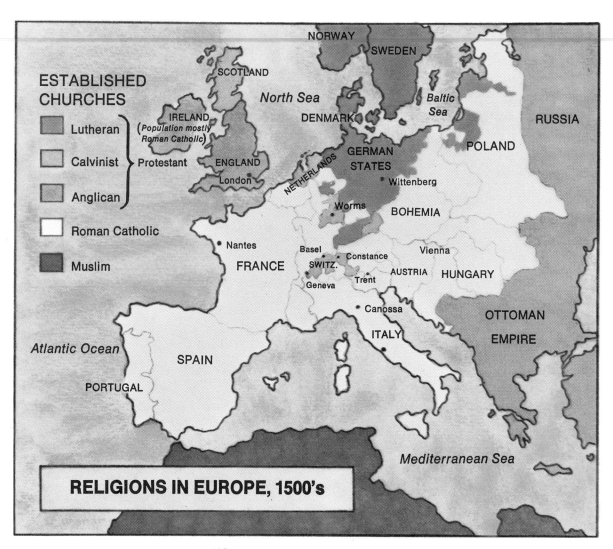

ESTABLISHED CHURCHES

- Lutheran
- Calvinist ⎫
- Anglican ⎬ Protestant
- Roman Catholic
- Muslim

IRELAND (Population mostly Roman Catholic)

RELIGIONS IN EUROPE, 1500's

princes by asking why a foreign pope should drain them of their wealth or control religion in their states. As a result, the Church could not rely on the nobles to suppress the Lutheran revolt. Charles V, then the Holy Roman emperor, was caught in a dilemma. If he allowed Luther to continue, he would lose the support of those princes still loyal to the Church. If he sided with the pope, he would lose the support of those who had converted to the new religion. Charles finally did side with the Church, but he never intervened directly to stop the Lutherans.

The urban middle class and most of the peasants outside Germany also supported the Protestant revolt. Catholic doctrines had prohibited many moneymaking practices necessary to a growing commercial economy. Moreover, the middle class resented the Church's large landholdings and the money it collected. They felt that these resources should be used for their economic growth, not sent to Rome and Avignon to adorn the papal courts. The peasants, the largest social class in Germany, thought that Luther supported their claims to social justice. However, Luther turned against the German peasants for using his teachings as the basis for their violent uprisings, and he lost most of their following. But peasants in the adjoining countries continued to fill the growing Lutheran congregation.

Technology also contributed to the Protestant movement. The invention of the printing press quickened the communication of ideas among Europe's educated classes. Therefore, Luther's ideas were far more publicized than those of Wycliffe and Huss. Soon other Protestant reformers had established churches in many parts of Europe. Among them was John Calvin, the second major figure of the Reformation.

Calvin followed Luther in rejecting the authority of the pope. He also scorned the Church's emphasis on ritual. But he differed with Luther on what took place during the mass. And he stressed the doctrine of predestination, saying that God had predestined, or determined beforehand each man's eternal fate.

Calvin established his church in Geneva after he fled from his native France. Geneva under Calvin was a stern theocracy where all worldly pleasures were forbidden. Calvin's followers carried his teachings into northwestern Europe. Protestants in France and the Netherlands followed the religious beliefs of Calvin rather than Luther. Calvinists became numerous in England, where they were called Puritans, and many of them crossed the Atlantic to colonize North America.

A theocracy is a government ruled by a clergy claiming God's authority.

Despite the rapid growth in popularity of Protestantism, most of southern Europe remained Roman Catholic. And the Reformation forced the Church to make some reforms of its own. Pope Paul III was persuaded to call a Church council which began meeting in Trent in 1545. The council called for reforms in the behavior and education of the clergy. It outlawed the selling of indulgences, but it restated the

113

doctrine of indulgences and how to grant them. Other doctrines also concerning the sacraments and good works were clarified so that the Church's teachings could not be misunderstood.

The division of western Christendom into Catholicism and Protestantism brought war, rebellion, and persecution. The Catholic monarch of Spain tried to remove all Protestants from his kingdom. The French Protestants warred against their Catholic kings until they were granted protection by the Edict of Nantes in 1598. In Germany, Protestant and Catholic princes struggled for power in the Thirty Years' War which involved nearly all Europe between 1618 and 1648. And in England, persecution of Catholics alternated with persecution of Protestants for nearly two hundred years.

The Edict of Nantes and the Thirty Years' War will be discussed further in Chapter 6.

Such turmoil resulted from the revolutionary character of the Protestant Reformation. The reformers had denied the centuries-old belief that salvation came from the Church. They claimed that faith alone was all God required of people for their salvation. In effect, they replaced the authority of the Church with the authority of each individual's own conscience.

Individual and Group Activities for Chapter 4

For full descriptions of these activities, turn to the **Student Book of Activities and Readings** included among the materials for individual and group activities.

Activity 4A: Interviews and panel discussion or essay on contemporary views of the causes of the Reformation (individual or group)
Interview one Protestant minister and one Catholic priest on the causes of the Reformation. In either a panel discussion or a written essay, explain how their accounts differ.

Activity 4B: Investigation of hymns as an expression of Reformation ideas (individual)
Borrow a hymnal from a Lutheran church in your community. Look for hymns written during the sixteenth century and see what they say about the Reformation. Then summarize your conclusions in a short paper.

The Growth of Parliament

STATING THE ISSUE

Every autumn the oldest representative lawmaking body in the world, the Parliament of Great Britain, meets in the House of Lords to hear the queen open its annual meeting. The queen's government, the majority party in Parliament, sits to her right. To her left sits her loyal opposition, the minority party, ready to govern should the voters elect its members to the most seats.

Political changes come about either by revolution or evolution. Revolution involves a sudden and usually violent overthrow of an existing government by its opponents. Evolution takes place more slowly. It involves a large number of small changes, often over many years. Yet added together, evolutionary changes can shift power from one person or group to another, or even to the elected representatives of all the citizens.

News about revolutions fills modern newspapers and magazines. Throughout the developing nations in Asia, Africa, and Latin America, citizens have risen in revolt. Some of them have fought to throw out colonial governments set up by foreign lands. Others have tried to replace autocratic governments with more democratic ones or to substitute one group of rulers for another. However, few of these revolutions have successfully installed democratic governments.

Chapter 5 examines the evolution of the Parliament of Great Britain. Parliament developed slowly over many centuries. On several occasions, the English rose in armed revolt against their rulers. But when these revolts ended successfully, the English kept many of the governmental institutions they had known rather than start totally new ones. Most governmental change in Great Britain came through an evolutionary process in which small changes taking place over centuries shaped new ways to rule. Chapter 5 focuses on the ways in which Great Britain's government has blended continuity with change.

1215	King John signs Magna Carta.
1265	Simon de Montfort calls first Parliament.
1295	Edward I summons Model Parliament.
1642-1646	Civil war erupts between Parliament and Charles I.
1649	Charles I is executed.
1649-1658	Oliver Cromwell heads Commonwealth.
1660-1685	Charles II's rule restores monarchy.
1685-1688	James II rules as a Catholic.
1701	Act of Settlement gives Parliament legislative supremacy.
1832	First Reform Bill makes representation in Commons reflect population distribution.
1872	Voting is held by secret ballot.
1884-1885	Reform Bill gives vote to most adult males.
1911	Parliament Act gives Commons power to override vetoes of Lords.
1918	Parliament grants the vote to men at twenty-one and women at thirty.
1928	Parliament grants the vote to women at twenty-one.

22 A CONSTITUTIONAL MILESTONE

The earliest move toward parliamentary government in England appeared to be a move backward—a move to reaffirm the feudal rights of the nobility. In 1066 William, duke of Normandy, defeated Harold, the Anglo-Saxon king, at Hastings and won the throne of England. William the Conqueror and his successors accumulated great power by reducing the political strength of their feudal nobles. William forced all the nobles to swear direct loyalty to him. In addition, he destroyed the fortresses of the nobility so that they could not resist.

William the Conqueror's great-great-grandson, John, continued these policies. John was a vassal of the King of France because English kings had acquired lands on the continent through conquest or marriage. John fought with Philip Augustus of France over these feudal holdings. To support these wars, John imposed heavy taxes on the nobles without consulting them. He demanded long military service, and he even used foreign soldiers against nobles who refused his demands. These deeds violated longstanding feudal codes. The great barons reacted to John's tyranny by rebelling. Stephen Langton, Archbishop of Canterbury and the most important of England's clergy, supported them. On June 15, 1215, the barons forced John to accept Magna Carta.

Magna Carta is a feudal document demanding that John restore the rights and privileges of his noble vassals. It also demanded an end to the illegal means John and his ancestors had used to increase the royal income. In addition, Magna Carta gave the barons several new political powers. Reading 22 contains two parts: a chronological chart showing the major events of John's reign, and excerpts from Magna Carta. Study both parts of the reading and try to answer the following questions:

1. What clues does the chronological chart give to show why the barons forced John to accept Magna Carta?
2. How did Magna Carta limit the power of the king? What rights did it guarantee to the nobility? to the freemen?

A Chronology of John's Reign

RELATIONS WITH FRANCE	DOMESTIC EVENTS	CHURCH AFFAIRS
	1199 John becomes king.	
1200 John accepts Philip Augustus of France as overlord of England's territory on the European continent.	**1200** John offends the English barons by divorcing Isabella of Gloucester.	
1202 John marries Isabella of Angoulême, betrothed to a French vassal. John's French vassals appeal to Philip Augustus.		
Philip calls John to France to answer the charge. John refuses. Philip claims John has forfeited his possessions on the continent.		
1202-1204 Philip enforces the forfeiture and invades Normandy. Maine, Anjou, and Brittany transfer to Philip.	**1203** John's nephew Arthur disappears. John is suspected of his murder.	

RELATIONS WITH FRANCE	DOMESTIC EVENTS	CHURCH AFFAIRS
1204 Philip gains Normandy.		
1204-1206 John loses Touraine and Poitou to Philip.	**1205** John assesses a duty of 1/15 on exports and imports.	**1205** The monks choose one Archbishop of Canterbury, John another. Pope Innocent III refuses to recognize either.
	1207 John levies a special tax of 1/13 on all movable property.	**1207** John assesses a special tax on the Church. Pope Innocent III names Stephen Langton Archbishop of Canterbury. John refuses to accept him.
		1208 Innocent places England under an interdict. John seizes the Church revenues.
		1209 John is excommunicated by the pope.
	1210 Jews are taxed 44,000 pounds.	
		1213 Innocent asks Philip Augustus to invade England. Under this threat John submits to the pope and accepts him as feudal lord of England. John also recognizes Langton who then proposes some reforms to check royal despotism.
1214 John's attempt to recapture his French territories fails.	**1214** John levies a heavy scutage to pay for his French expedition.	

▶ What influence, if any, do you think a government should have over church affairs?

Movable property consisted of all possessions except real estate. The tax applied mainly to money, farm produce, and manufactured goods.

Under an interdict, no English subject was allowed to take the sacraments.

Scutage was a tax levied by the king upon his vassals. Usually a noble paid scutage as a substitute for serving in the army.

Magna Carta

On June 15, 1215, King John met with the rebellious barons at Runnymede, a meadow in southern England. They forced him to sign a list of demands known as Magna Carta. Some of these demands follow.

John, by the grace of God king of England, lord of Ireland, duke of Normandy and of Aquitaine, count of Anjou, make this proclamation to our archbishops, bishops, abbots, earls, barons, justices, foresters, sheriffs, ministers, bailiffs, and faithful men.

2. If any one of our earls or barons or other men who hold land in a grant from the king should die, and if his heir owes us relief, he will be given his inheritance provided he pays the ancient relief. The relief shall be 100 pounds for an earl, 100 pounds for a baron, and 100 shillings for a knight.

12. Scutage or aid shall be paid in our kingdom only after the common counsel has approved it, except when a ransom must be paid for returning us safe after capture, when our eldest son is knighted, and when our eldest daughter is married. At these times, only a reasonable aid shall be taken. The same provision shall hold with regard to the aids collected from the city of London.

13. And the city of London shall have all its ancient liberties and be allowed to collect its own customs, both by land and by water. Besides, we grant that all the other cities, boroughs, towns, and ports shall have all their liberties and be allowed to collect their own customs.

14. And in order to have a common counsel of the kingdom meet to determine the aid or the scutage which must be paid in all cases other than the three instances mentioned in Article 12, we will invite the archbishops, bishops, abbots, earls, and greater barons in letters sent to each individually. In addition, we will invite through a general proclamation to the sheriffs and bailiffs, all those who hold land in a grant from us. Our invitation will specify a certain day, at least forty days from the time the invitation was sent, and a certain place for the meeting of the common counsel. In all such invitations we shall state why we wish to call the common counsel together.

17. Civil lawsuits shall not have to be held in our court, but shall be held in some fixed place.

20. A peasant who is not a serf shall be fined for a small offense only according to the degree of the offense, and for a serious offense he shall be fined according to the seriousness of the offense, except that the fine shall not deprive him of all his land. And a merchant shall be fined in the same way, except that his merchandise will not be taken. A villein shall be fined in the same way, except that his

The Charters of England Complete; also Magna Carta and the Bill of Rights, John Luffman, ed. (London: T. Evans, 1793), pp. 374-397. Language simplified.

When kings refer to themselves, they commonly use "we" or "our."

Relief was the sum a vassal paid to his lord when he took possession of his father's estate.

Aid, here, means a tribute paid by a vassal to his lord.

By this time in England, the distinction between villein and serf had practically disappeared, and the words were used interchangeably.

119

Congress in the United States

The pictures on these two pages show modern American and early British political and legal institutions. What similarities do you see? What do these similarities tell you about the influence of British institutions on America?

British Parliament in the 1200's

A jury trial in the United States

A British jury trial of the 1800's

farm implements will not be taken away. And none of the fines shall be imposed unless good men from the neighborhood swear that the individual committed the offense.

A constable, here, means the warden of a royal household.

28.   No constable or other bailiff appointed by us shall take grain or other possessions away from anyone unless he pays for them with money, unless the seller is willing to postpone payment.

39.   No freeman shall be captured, imprisoned, dispossessed of his land, declared an outlaw, exiled, or in any way destroyed except after he has been judged guilty by his peers or by the law of the land.

40.   We will not sell, deny, or delay justice to anyone.

51.   Immediately after peace has been restored, we will send out of the kingdom all foreign knights, crossbowmen, and sergeants, who have caused great injury to the kingdom.

61.   Since we have granted all these liberties for the love of God and for the improvement of our kingdom, and to bring to an end the conflict that has arisen between us and our barons, we have granted the following security to back up our pledge. Namely, we have granted that the barons shall elect any twenty-five barons they please who will observe, and see that we observe, the peace and liberties that we have granted to them and confirmed by this charter. Specifically, if we, the man who rules in our place when we are out of the kingdom, or any of the bailiffs we have appointed shall break any of the articles of this charter, our offense shall be reported to at least four of the twenty-five elected barons. Those four barons shall come to us, or to the man who rules in our place when we are out of the kingdom, and explain to us the wrong we have committed, and ask that we correct it. If we, or the man who rules in our place, do not correct the wrong within forty days from the time we are notified, the four barons will refer the case to the rest of the twenty-five. Those twenty-five, together with the rest of the country, shall injure us in all ways possible—namely, by capturing our castles, land, and possessions—until they are satisfied that the offense we have committed is fully repaid. However, they must not injure our body and the body of the queen and our children. And once they are satisfied, they will be obedient to us as they were before. And neither will we, nor ourselves working through others, take away these concessions and liberties.

▶Which clauses in Magna Carta do you consider most important? Why?

63.   And we wish and order that the English Church shall be free, and that the men in our kingdom shall have all the liberties, rights, and grants mentioned in this charter for themselves and for their heirs, and that our heirs will abide by them in all things and in all places.

FOR THOUGHT:

To what degree does Magna Carta represent continuity in English government? To what degree does it represent change? How did it combine these two trends?

Magna Carta began the centuries-long movement that changed England's monarchy into a representative democracy based on parliamentary institutions. John and his son, Henry III, ignored Magna Carta when they felt the barons did not have the military strength to resist them. But when Henry tried to regain England's lost territories on the continent, he forced several unpopular policies on the barons. Starting in 1258, the barons again attempted to put controls on the power of the monarch. Henry renounced these controls, and civil war broke out in 1263.

In 1264 Simon de Montfort, Henry's brother-in-law, emerged as the leader of the rebellious barons, other nobles, and influential commoners. De Montfort defeated and captured Henry. De Montfort then called a parliament to demand that Henry abide by the feudal rights of his vassals. The Parliament included not only the barons and the clergy, but two knights from each shire (county) and representatives from the boroughs and towns. For the first time, all the influential groups in England participated in the government's decision-making. But in 1265 Henry's son, Edward, led the king's loyal barons against de Montfort. De Montfort's troops were defeated and he was killed. Henry III returned to power and ruled until his death in 1272.

Although he had supported his father against de Montfort, Edward had learned a valuable lesson from the rebellion: a king against the nation was less powerful than a king who had the support of the nation through its representatives. Accordingly, as King Edward I, he called many sessions of Parliament. During his thirty-five year reign, Parliament became a permanent institution in England's government.

The following selections from the official records of Edward's parliaments reveal much about early developments in the rise of Parliament. As you read them, consider one way political scientists analyze the powers of a government. They divide government powers into extractive, regulative, and distributive. The extractive power of a government is its ability to obtain income and services—taxes and military service, for example—from its citizens. Its regulative power is its ability to control the behavior of its subjects—to force them to act in certain ways and to punish them for not doing so. The distributive power of a government is its ability to make available to its subjects goods, services, opportunities, and rewards. As you study the documents, ask questions to help you decide what extractive, regulative, and distributive powers the king had and which ones Parliament was gaining. The following questions will guide you:

1. Who called the parliaments? Who was invited to attend?
2. Why did the king call the parliaments? Did the members of Parliament have different goals from those of the king?

Parliamentary Summons

The following excerpts come from Edward's summons to the parliaments of 1275, 1283, and 1295. The Parliament of 1295 is called the Model Parliament because it included representatives of all classes, an example followed by most later parliaments.

All three documents from **Parliaments and Councils of England Chronologically Arranged from the Reign of William I to the Revolution of 1688,** Charles Parry, ed. (London: John Murray, 1839), pp. 49-57. Language simplified.

PARLIAMENT OF 1275

Edward, by the grace of God king of England to the sheriff of Middlesex, greeting. Whereas we have suspended our Parliament at London until the morning of the Sunday after Easter, we command you to summon four knights from your county to meet at the same place on

What extractive, regulative, and distributive powers of the United States government do these pictures show?

Burgesses were citizens of boroughs who could vote for members to Parliament. Generally, they represented commercial interests.

Llewelyn, prince of Wales, had joined de Montfort's opposition. In 1282 he renewed war with the English. Edward I defeated him and conquered Wales.

▶ Do you think that the amount of property a person owns should have any effect on how much he is permitted to participate in government?

Westminster Abbey, in London, was once the church of a Benedictine monastery. Its construction was begun in the eleventh century. Changes and additions continued into the eighteenth century. All English monarchs since William I have been crowned in Westminster.

the same day. And likewise summon six or four citizens, burgesses, or other good men from each of the cities, boroughs, and trading towns. Along with the magnates [people of high rank] of the kingdom they will consider the affairs of the kingdom.

PARLIAMENT OF 1283

The king to the sheriff of Norfolk and Suffolk, greeting. Whereas Llewelyn and the other Welshmen, who are our enemies, have so often disturbed the peace of our kingdom, we command you to summon to Northampton all men in your territory who are able to bear arms, who have land worth £20, and who are not with us on this Welsh expedition. Also summon four knights from each of your two counties who will have authority to act on behalf of the communities in those counties; and summon two men from each city, borough, or trading town who likewise will have power to act for their communities, in order that they all will hear and do what we explain to them.

The king to John, Archbishop of Canterbury, greeting. Whereas Llewelyn and the other Welshmen, who as our enemies, have so often disturbed the peace of our kingdom, we command you to summon to Northampton all your bishops, abbots, priors, and other heads of religious houses. And you are to be present on the same day at the same place to hear and do what we shall explain to you, and also to give us your advice and assistance.

PARLIAMENT OF 1295

The king to Robert, Archbishop of Canterbury, greeting. Whereas we are unwilling to settle certain difficult affairs touching upon us and our kingdom without your presence and the presence of the other prelates [high-ranking churchmen], we wish to hold our Parliament and to have a conference with you concerning these matters. Therefore, we command you to join us at Westminster on the first day of August to consider these difficult affairs and to give us your counsel.

The king to the sheriff of Northampton, greeting. Whereas we wish to have a conference with the earls, barons, and other nobles of our realm concerning measures we can take to remedy the dangers that threaten our kingdom, we have ordered them to come to Westminster to consider and take whatever action may be necessary. We command you to send two knights elected from your county and two citizens from each city and two burgesses from each borough to Westminster. The knights and citizens and burgesses will have the authority to do whatever is decided by common counsel.

The king to his beloved and faithful kinsman, Edmund, Earl of Cornwall, greeting. Whereas we wish to have a conference with you and the other magnates of the kingdom to find ways to meet the dangers

126

that threaten our entire kingdom, we command you to be present at Westminster to consider and decide, together with us, the prelates, the rest of the magnates, and with other inhabitants of our kingdom how such dangers can be prevented.

Parliamentary Records

The following documents describe actions taken by Edward following the parliaments.

PARLIAMENTARY SUBSIDY, 1283

The king to the mayor, sheriffs, and all the people of London, greeting. We are exceedingly grateful to you for having granted us a subsidy of one thirtieth of all your movable goods for our expedition in Wales, on the condition that the magnates of the kingdom would grant the same amount. And we wish you to know that, at our request, the magnates have agreed to grant the subsidy. And since we greatly need the money for the sake of our expedition in Wales, we have assigned three collectors to assess the tax and collect it.

CONFIRMATION OF THE CHARTERS, 1297

Edward, by the grace of God king of England to all who may see or hear these letters, greeting. Whereas some people of our kingdom fear that we will routinely expect to collect the aids and taxes which they have specially granted us for our wars and other needs, we have granted for us and our heirs that we will not make these taxes permanent in the future. And we have also granted that on no account will we collect such aids and taxes except by the common assent of the whole kingdom and for the common benefit of the whole kingdom.

A PARLIAMENTARY BILL, 1301

Bill of the prelates and nobles delivered to the lord king on behalf of the whole community in the parliament of Lincoln in the year 1301.

If it pleases our lord king, the community is of the opinion that the charter of liberties and the charter of the forest shall be observed in all particulars from now on. [The king's response:] It expressly pleases the king.

And statutes that conflict with these charters shall be declared null and void. [The king's response:] It expressly pleases the king.

And the areas that have been surveyed according to the provisions of the charter shall be promptly disforested according to the boundaries determined by the surveyors. [The king's response:] It expressly pleases the king.

All three documents from Parliaments and Councils of England Chronologically Arranged from the Reign of William I to the Revolution of 1688, Parry, ed., pp. 51-64. Language simplified.

▶For what purposes, if any, do you think a government has the right to tax its subjects?

The Charter of Liberties means Magna Carta. The Charter of the Forest, signed by Henry III in 1217, concerned land reserved to the king for hunting. The charter restored many forest lands to "free" status. Henry III and Edward I had taken back many of these lands.

On the condition that these matters are carried out and accomplished, the people of the realm grant the king a fifteenth [6.7%] of their movable goods rather than a twentieth [5%], which they had already granted. [The king's response:] It expressly pleases the king.

FOR THOUGHT:

How were continuity and change blended in the reforms described in these documents? How did these reforms contribute to the development of freedom in England?

24 PARLIAMENT IN THE SEVENTEENTH CENTURY

Magna Carta made the monarchs of England subject to the law. Rather than anger influential groups in the kingdom, most rulers obeyed the law and observed the main provisions of the charter. Like Edward I, they frequently called Parliament to share in decision-making. In particular the Tudor monarchs, Henry VIII and his daughter Elizabeth I, saw that working through Parliament often served their purposes.

Still, some kings ignored Parliament when they could. The first Stuart kings, James I and Charles I, tried to live within their royal incomes so that they would not have to call on Parliament to raise money. In fact at one point Charles ruled for eleven years without once calling Parliament. Nonetheless, Parliament and the rule of law never fell into disuse in England as it did in France.

During the rule of the early Stuarts, the political allegiance of much of Parliament began to shift away from the crown. The wealthy middle class of England, many of them Puritans who had left the Anglican Church, had begun to accumulate political power. Finally in 1640 Charles became involved in a war with the Scots. In dire need of money to fight the war, Charles was forced to call Parliament into session to approve new tax measures. Nobility and commoners alike acted together in Parliament to impeach and later execute Charles's most trusted advisers, the Earl of Strafford and William Laud, Archbishop of Canterbury. Then they passed a number of bills designed to make the king almost wholly dependent on Parliament.

Charles's attempt to rule England as an absolute monarch resulted in his losing first his throne and then his life. Charles and his supporters resisted the demands of Parliament, and in 1642 a civil war began. The war ended four years later in victory for Parliament and its supporters. In 1649 a special court convicted Charles of treason for waging war against Parliament. Charles was beheaded, and Parliament established a republic under Oliver Cromwell.

Cromwell, the leader of the Puritan faction in Parliament, was a major figure in the civil war and also in the execution of Charles I. In 1653 he was made lord protector of the republic and ruled as such until his death. The republic ended in 1660, shortly after Cromwell died, and the Stuart heir, Charles II, was restored to the throne. On his death in 1685, Charles was succeeded by his brother, James II, a Catholic, who ruled only three years.

During the Restoration, the period during which Charles II and James II ruled, there was much political and religious strife. The Anglican Church placed strict controls over the Puritans and other dissenters from the Anglican Church. Some of them were not allowed to participate in government. Then, too, because Charles and James stayed out of war, they seldom needed to call on Parliament for extra income. And James II's ambition to return England to the Roman Catholic Church further inflamed the English people. The Restoration period ended in 1688 when Parliament set out to limit England's monarchy once and for all. To do so, it had to gain control over the treasury, over the making of laws, and over the army.

Reading 24 contains several documents that concern some of the events of 1688 to 1694. Using these documents, try to reconstruct these events. Then try to determine what new extractive, regulative, and distributive powers Parliament won. Let the following questions help you:

1. What happened from 1688 to 1694? Why did it happen?
2. What new powers did Parliament acquire during this period? Why were these powers important?

An Invitation to William of Orange

June 30, 1688

To the Dutch stadholder [viceroy] William:

We are very pleased to learn from our special agent that your Highness is ready and willing to give us assistance. We have great reason to believe that every day our condition will get worse than it is, and we will be less able to defend ourselves, unless you will help us find a remedy. But though we want you to help us, we do not wish to misguide you in this matter. The best advice we can give you is to inform

Parliaments and Councils of England Chronologically Arranged from the Reign of William I to the Revolution of 1688, Parry, ed., pp. 600-601. Language simplified.

► These people are marching in support of a revolution against the British government. Yet the police are not arresting them. Should a government permit its citizens to urge revolt?

130

your Highness of the true state of affairs in England at this time and of the difficulties we see before us. The people are very dissatisfied with the present conduct of James II's government. The king has invaded their religion, liberties, and properties, and they expect worse day by day. Your Highness may be assured that nineteen out of every twenty Englishmen desire a change. We believe, therefore, that the majority will support you against the present government if you land here with sufficient troops to protect them until a new government can be organized and matters set in order. We further believe that the king's army will not be able to offer you great resistance, because, in all likelihood, the officers and men will be divided among themselves. Since the soldiers fight only for subsistence, and since they are greatly repelled by the popish [Catholic] religion which the present king has adopted, we believe that great numbers will desert. Besides all this the king has called a Parliament which has been packed with his own supporters so that only forty of the members are against the present trend.

William of Orange was the husband of Mary, the Protestant daughter of James II.

Declaration of William

September 30, 1688

The public peace and happiness of any state or kingdom cannot be preserved when the laws, liberties, and customs established by the lawful authority are openly violated. To our great regret, we see that the king and his counselors have overturned the religion, laws, and liberties of England. Those evil counselors invented what they call the King's Dispensing Power. Through this fictitious power the king can refuse to execute laws that have been enacted by king and Parliament for the security and happiness of the subjects. Therefore, they have, in fact, overturned those laws. In particular, they have tried to overturn those laws regarding the Church of England so that they can introduce the popish religion into the realm.

We have tried to warn the king how these actions disturb us, but those evil counselors have so twisted our good intentions that they have alienated the king more and more from us. The best remedy for all those evils is to call Parliament to protect the nation against the evil practices of those wicked counselors. But this cannot be done so long as the king and his counselors weaken the independence of Parliament by packing it with members who support their bad intentions and by disfranchising those who oppose their popish tendencies.

My wife, the Princess Mary, and I have a great interest in this matter. Since we have the right to succeed James to the throne . . . and since the English people have always expressed affection and esteem toward us, we feel we must protect their interests in a matter of such high

Parliaments and Councils of England Chronologically Arranged from the Reign of William I to the Revolution of 1688, Parry, ed., pp. 601-603. Language simplified.

Disenfranchise means to take away someone's right to vote.

131

consequence. We believe we must contribute as much aid as we can to maintain the Protestant religion, the laws and liberties of the kingdom, and to secure for the English people their continual enjoyment of their just rights. We have been asked by a great many lords and by many gentlemen, and other subjects of all ranks, to aid them in this cause.

▶On what grounds, if any, do you think someone has the right to invade another's territory?

Therefore, we have decided to go to England, and bring with us a large enough force to defend us from the violence of those evil counselors. We have prepared this declaration so that our intentions will be fully understood. Our expedition is intended only to make sure that a free and lawful Parliament will be assembled as soon as it is possible. Since the king's most recent summoning of Parliament was contrary to ancient custom, his charters will be considered as null and void. Those magistrates whom he has unjustly dismissed shall now resume their normal posts and duties. The ancient laws governing the election of members to Parliament from the boroughs of England shall be reinstated. The members of Parliament, being thus lawfully chosen, shall sit in full freedom so that the House of Lords and the House of Commons can make laws they consider necessary for the protection of the Protestant religion in England and to make sure that the realm will never again fall under tyrannical government. Finally, we invite and require all persons, all the peers of the realm, all lords lieutenants, deputy lieutenants, and all gentlemen, citizens, and other commons of all ranks, to assist us, so that we may prevent all those miseries which result from tyrannical government and slavery, and so that we may set aright all those violences and disorders that have overturned the Constitution.

The Bill of Rights

An act for declaring the rights and liberties of the subjects and for settling the succession of the crown. The House of Lords and the House of Commons, assembled at Westminster, lawfully, fully, and freely representing all the people of this realm, did upon the thirteenth day of February, 1689, present to their majesties, William and Mary, the following declaration.

Whereas the late King James II, with the assistance of several evil counselors, judges, and ministers, did attempt to undermine the Protestant religion and the laws and liberties of this kingdom.

And whereas King James II abdicated [renounced] the government and made the throne vacant, his highness the prince of Orange took over the government and called a Parliament to establish laws which will prevent another attempt to destroy our religion, laws, and liberties.

The Charters of England Complete; also Magna Carta and the Bill of Rights, Luffman, ed., pp. 412-417. Language simplified.

William and Mary gained the throne of England early in 1689, an event that became known as the Glorious Revolution.

132

Therefore, the Parliament declares:

1. That the king's supposed power of suspending laws without the consent of Parliament is illegal.

4. That levying taxes for the use of the king without the consent of Parliament is illegal.

5. That it is the right of the subjects to petition the king. Prosecuting anyone for petitioning the king is illegal.

6. That raising and keeping a standing army within the kingdom during times of peace without the consent of Parliament is illegal.

7. That those subjects who are Protestants may keep arms for their own defense as allowed by law.

8. That the king should not interfere with election of members of Parliament.

9. That the freedom of speech and debate in Parliament should not be taken away by any court outside of Parliament itself.

10. That excessive bail should not be required, excessive fines imposed, nor cruel and unusual punishments inflicted.

13. And that to correct grievances and amend, strengthen, and preserve the laws, Parliament ought to be held frequently.

▶Which of these clauses do you consider the most important? Why?

The New Coronation Oath, 1689

The archbishop or bishop shall say, "Will you solemnly promise and swear to govern the people of this kingdom of England, and the dominions thereto belonging according to the statutes agreed on in Parliament, and the laws and customs of the same?" The King and Queen shall say, "I solemnly promise so to do."

The New Coronation Oath. Language simplified.

The Triennial Act, 1694

Whereas, by ancient laws and statutes of this kingdom, frequent Parliaments ought to be held; and whereas frequent and new Parliaments bring about the happy union and good agreement of the king and people: It is hereby declared and enacted that a Parliament shall be held once every three years at the least. And be it further enacted that within three years at the most after the adjourning of this present Parliament, the king shall call for the assembling and holding of another Parliament. From hereafter the king shall call together a new Parliament within three years after the assembling of any Parliament. And be it further enacted that from henceforth no Parliament shall sit longer than three years.

The Triennial Act. Language simplified.

133

FOR THOUGHT:

How did the English continue their governmental traditions in the seventeenth century? What new changes did they make?

25 THE GROWTH OF PARLIAMENT

A HISTORICAL ESSAY

The Parliament of Great Britain developed out of medieval institutions that adapted to changing economic, political, and social forces. No precise date can be set for the founding of Parliament. In 1250 no such institution existed. By 1350 it was an accepted part of England's government. During those hundred years, the English people shaped traditional principles and practices to create the ancestor of today's Parliament.

The English monarchs never had absolute power. Medieval kings consulted with the great nobles of the realm to win their support for new undertakings. Even William the Conqueror and his descendants, who greatly increased the power of the crown, could never make royal power absolute. However, William required each noble to swear direct allegiance to the king to prevent the nobles from raising armies against him. William also made sure that the lands of his powerful vassals were scattered so that no rival could take the control of an entire area away from the king.

Henry II reigned from 1154 to 1189.

William's great-grandson, Henry II, continued to graft new ways to govern on the old ways. He gathered a staff of jurists to make laws for the kingdom. The laws were taken from the Anglo-Saxon common law, and they were enforced by two Anglo-Saxon institutions—the jury and the sheriff. To these, Henry added traveling justices who enforced the law all over the nation.

By the time John came to the throne in 1199, England was the most unified kingdom in Europe. But John in his greed for power alienated Philip Augustus of France, Pope Innocent III, and most important, his English nobles. In order to fight Philip, John raised feudal dues in England and levied taxes without consulting his barons. Then Pope Innocent III placed England under an interdict and excommunicated John when John appointed one of his followers head of the English Church without the pope's consent. At the mercy of the pope, defeated in France in

134

1214, and faced with insurrection among his nobles, John could only submit when the barons presented him with Magna Carta in 1215.

Magna Carta set forth the rights Englishmen had inherited from Anglo-Saxon rule and from feudal contracts. It required the king to observe these rights and to recognize new rights. Although Magna Carta was written by the nobles in their own interest, it provided some protection for the Church, the towns, and the common people. Thus later generations could use Magna Carta to justify shifts in political control from the monarch to Parliament. They cited the clause that required the king to consult the people's representatives before levying new taxes, and another that permitted the barons to revolt if the monarch violated the law. All of these changes, however, came within the framework of institutions which were centuries old.

Magna Carta was the last major accomplishment of the great nobles acting alone. Economic and social changes soon reduced their political power. With the growth of commerce, the country gentry and the burgesses began to accumulate great wealth. With this wealth they acquired political power, for they paid much of the taxes that supported the crown. In addition the kings began to hire soldiers so that they no longer depended on the armies of their vassals. New weapons, such as the longbow, were inexpensive enough that kings could buy them for all their soldiers.

Gentry refers to men who own large tracts of land but do not have titles of nobility.

Sometime during the thirteenth century, the kings began to consult wealthy commoners before beginning military expeditions. Their motive was to win consent for new taxes. When Edward I called the first parliaments, he included wealthy commoners as well as nobles. The nobles expected to share in the decision-making. But the gentry and burgesses understood that they had been called only to grant Edward money. However, during these meetings they were able to put their grievances before the king. Eventually they realized that they had many similar problems and that they would get better results if they acted as a group. Together they could withhold money from the king until he satisfied their demands. Again a basic change had evolved within an accepted institutional framework.

By the middle of the fourteenth century, Parliament had thus become a bargaining force in the English government. Yet its power was very limited. The gentry and burgesses met in the House of Commons; the nobility and Church leaders met separately in the House of Lords. The House of Commons was unable to act without the House of Lords, and Parliament met only when the king called it. Nor did Parliament have any authority to enact laws; it could only exert pressure on the king. In the centuries that followed, however, the kings did not make laws without Parliament's consent. Parliament also won the right to impeach the king's ministers.

Lords hold their seats by hereditary right or by royal appointment. The members of the Commons are elected.

Impeach means to make charges against someone in office. This person is later tried by an appropriate body.

▶The students in this picture are protesting a
budget cut in their school. For what other purposes,
if any, should groups of students use their power?

The Tudor monarchs, Henry VII, Henry VIII, and Elizabeth I, often
called on Parliament to approve their actions. However, James I and
his son, Charles I, tried to live within their income from royal lands
and taxes so that they would not have to call on Parliament. When
Charles needed funds in 1640 to continue a war with the Scots, the
members of Parliament were bitter and frustrated by eleven years of
inactivity. They executed the Earl of Strafford and the Archbishop of
Canterbury, advisers to the king, and they petitioned the king for meetings of Parliament every three years. These and other measures ignited
civil war between the supporters of the king and the supporters of
Parliament. Under the leadership of the Puritan, Oliver Cromwell, Parliament was victorious.

The Puritans had suffered for many years from the crown's intoler-
ance of their beliefs. They wanted to execute Charles, and in 1649, the

136

king was beheaded. The Puritans dissolved the monarchy and proclaimed England a Commonwealth, a word used at that time to indicate a republic. Cromwell headed the government, and in 1653 he was given the title of Lord Protector. But in 1660, shortly after Cromwell died, England had had enough of the republican experiment which broke so far from national traditions. Parliament called Charles II, son of Charles I, to the throne.

During the twenty-eight years of the Restoration period, Charles II and his brother, James II, scorned Parliament much as the early Stuarts had done. To add to the political friction, James II tried to return Catholicism to England. In 1688 seven barons sent a petition for help to William of Orange, who had married James's daughter Mary. William invaded England, and the English navy and much of the army deserted to his side. James fled to France hoping for aid from the Catholic monarch Louis XVI. But his plea failed.

After James fled, Parliament formally offered the throne to William and Mary. During their reign, Parliament's power began to increase. The new monarchs accepted the Bill of Rights which stated that the sovereign could not change or suspend the laws, keep a standing army, levy taxes, or set up special courts without the consent of Parliament. The Bill of Rights also provided for frequent meetings of Parliament and gave subjects the right to petition the king. The Toleration Act, passed in 1689, guaranteed religious freedom to all but Catholics and Unitarians. In 1694 the Triennial Act provided that Parliament could stay in session for only three years and that a new Parliament had to be called within three years after its last meeting. Parliament finally established itself as the supreme body of the English government by the Act of Settlement, passed in 1701. This law provided that if William and Mary died childless, the throne would pass to Protestant members of the royal family. Parliament had become so powerful that it could decide who would succeed to the throne.

However, Parliament needed a smaller group of leaders to formulate national policy. Leadership fell to those in Parliament who controlled the votes. It became customary for the monarchs to appoint their ministers from this group so that the monarchs would act in accord with the majority of Parliament. When ministers lost the confidence of Parliament, they resigned, and a group with parliamentary support continued in their place. Hence, Great Britain developed a cabinet system of government in which the executive officers are also the legislative leaders. The leader of the ministers is the Prime Minister, who now acts as the chief executive of Britain. Today, the Prime Minister and the other ministers are the leaders of the majority party in the House of Commons.

While the reforms of the late seventeenth century strengthened Parliament, they did not give the vote to more people. Moreover, as people

William and Mary ruled jointly until her death in 1694. He died in 1702.

In 1707, the Act of Union formally united Scotland and England in the kingdom of Great Britain.

left the farms to work in the industrial towns, boroughs that were once heavily populated became ghost towns. But representation in Parliament did not change. The situation became so ridiculous that the industrial city of Manchester sent no representatives to Parliament, while a borough that had actually been washed into the English Channel sent two. Powerful families bought these ghost towns, the so-called "rotten boroughs," and thus their seats in Parliament. Or they bribed the few remaining inhabitants to vote for their candidates for Parliament.

This question came to a head during England's war with the American colonies. King George III lost most of his supporters because he was losing the war. A reform bill written by Edmund Burke cut back the number of honorary household positions the king could appoint, thus eliminating one way George had controlled Parliament.

Burke's bill was followed by a wave of reform. The reformers fought to reapportion representation in Parliament and give the new industrial cities a voice in the government. They also wanted to extend the vote to more adult males; it was generally limited to wealthy property owners. Parliament divided sharply on reform. Some members, including Burke, were totally opposed to extreme and rapid reform. Others, including Burke's former ally, Charles James Fox, pushed for rapid change.

The split over reform hastened the formation of the two party system in Parliament. During the eighteenth century, Parliament had been divided into several groups who gathered around the great families. Only rarely did they join on national issues, and these alliances collapsed when the issues were resolved. But during the reform battle, which lasted more than forty years, the two-party system of today emerged.

In 1832 shrewd political manipulation gave the party for reform, the Whigs, a majority in the House of Commons. The Whigs immediately pushed through the Reform Bill of 1832 over the opposition of the Tories. The Tory House of Lords vetoed the bill because it reapportioned representation in the House of Commons. The reapportionment would reflect the population movement to the cities and give the Whigs more seats. The bill also gave suffrage to less wealthy property owners. After its defeat, the Whig leader, Earl Grey, schemed with the working-men's organizations to force the Lords to pass the bill by threatening riots and runs on the Bank of England. Then Grey forced the king to promise that he would create new peers from among the Whigs. Once in the House of Lords, these Whig peers would vote for reforms. Faced with these pressures, the Lords finally passed the bill. Once again Great Britain had blended change with the traditions of the past.

Other reform measures followed. During the last half of the nineteenth century, Benjamin Disraeli, the Conservative Prime Minister, and William Gladstone, the Liberal Prime Minister, both worked to expand

As a member of Commons, Edmund Burke supported the American Revolution, for he felt it reaffirmed traditional institutions. But he opposed the French Revolution for its destruction of the good as well as the bad. He favored conservative reform to promote gradual change.

Charles James Fox supported Burke's reform bill reducing royal appointments. But he split with Burke over the French Revolution and the method of reform for Britain.

The Whigs, composed mostly of gentry and businessmen, upheld Parliament over the crown. They became prominent during the Glorious Revolution. Whigs became the party of reform.

Earl Grey was prime minister from 1830 to 1834.

the vote. They pushed through reform measures in 1867, 1884, and 1885 that gave the vote to most adult males and reapportioned seats in Parliament more fairly. Legislation in 1872 required that voting be held by secret ballot. In 1918 another reform measure gave the vote to all adult men and to most women over the age of thirty. In 1928 women at last received the same voting rights as men. The fight to extend the vote had lasted almost one hundred years. Each new measure brought changes to old institutions.

Another major reform measure cut the power of the House of Lords. Early in the twentieth century, the House of Lords consisted of three groups: several hundred peers who had inherited their offices, about forty peers who represented the aristocracy of Scotland and Ireland, and a few officials of the Anglican Church. This aristocratic body held a veto power over new legislation passed by the House of Commons. Usually the Lords did not veto bills that had widespread popular support. However, in 1909 they refused to pass a bill connected to the budget.

In response, the House of Commons passed the Parliament Act of 1911. This act provided that all bills concerning money passed by the House of Commons became law within a month whether or not the House of Lords passed them. Other bills would become law without the approval of the House of Lords if three successive sessions of the House of Commons passed them within two years. The Lords agreed to this legislation because King George V threatened to appoint new peers in order to pass this law if the House of Lords did not submit. Once again Great Britain successfully changed one of its oldest institutions without abolishing it or using violence.

The long history of the development of Parliament shows one way in which people have won democratic rights. Over the years, the English built one small reform on another. Their political culture supported this sort of change because change early became an important part of the nation's traditions.

Gradually English subjects won the rights of citizens. First their representatives agreed to pay taxes to the king. Then they began to petition him for reforms. Later they withheld financial aid until their petitions were granted. They demanded regular meetings of Parliament and a system in which Parliament instead of the king controlled the executive branch of the government. Finally, when the vote was extended during the nineteenth and twentieth centuries, citizens through their chosen representatives in Parliament had won the greatest share of power. But they still kept their ancient institutions. Thus Great Britain still has a queen or king who opens Parliament each year by delivering a speech. But the speech is written by the Prime Minister, the chosen representative of all the citizens of Great Britain.

Benjamin Disraeli, twice prime minister, gave new life to the Conservative party through his social reform program. William Gladstone was the dominant personality of the Liberal party for nearly 30 years. He was prime minister four times.

▶Are there any political rights or privileges that should be different for men and women?

139

For full descriptions of these activities, turn to the **Student Book of Activities and Readings** included among the materials for individual and group activities.

Activity 5A: Comparison of the British House of Commons and the United States Congress (individual or group)
In recorded interviews, a member of the House of Commons and a member of the United States Congress discuss the ways in which these two government institutions operate. Listen to these two interviews and answer questions about them in the related Study Guide. Use your answers to develop a chart comparing the House of Commons and Congress.

Activity 5B: Essay or debate on the House of Lords (individual or group)
This activity contains a description of the House of Lords. After reading it, prepare a written essay or a debate on the following topic: Resolved: An aristocratic, hereditary House of Lords has no place in a modern democratic country.

The Anatomy of Absolutism

STATING THE ISSUE

Political scientists have identified three major types of political systems: primitive and traditional, authoritarian, and democratic. You have already studied a traditional system, that of feudal Europe. During the Middle Ages, most political decisions were made by the lord of a manor rather than by a central government. Customs guided most of these decisions.

Authoritarian political systems also existed in the ancient world. In an authoritarian system, one person or a small group of persons make most of the political decisions. Many ancient kingdoms and empires had a centralized authoritarian political system but traditional local governments.

Only a few democratic political systems existed in ancient times. Athens had democratic institutions, but only free, adult males took part in the political process. Neither women nor slaves had a voice in government. As Chapter 5 indicated, England began to develop democratic institutions during the Middle Ages. However, only the wealthy took part in government up to the nineteenth century.

Until recent years, most of Europe lived under some form of authoritarian government. Perhaps the most famous example was in seventeenth-century France, when Louis XIV reigned as Europe's most powerful monarch. Louis had much less authority than modern dictators who control more powerful armed forces and have modern methods of communication at their command. Yet for his time, Louis was so powerful that historians call his reign an age of absolutism, a term that means complete and unchallenged power.

Chapter 6 examines the government and the society of Louis XIV. The readings give evidence about seventeenth-century French decision-makers, the decision-making process, the political culture, the political institutions, and the role of the citizen. When you finish this chapter, you should be able to define absolutism using these five concepts to organize your definition.

1589	Henry IV becomes king of France.
1593	Henry converts to Catholicism.
1598	Edict of Nantes grants religious toleration to Protestants.
1643	Louis XIV becomes king at the age of five.
1643-1661	Cardinal Mazarin is chief minister and effective ruler of France.
1648-1653	The Fronde, an unsuccessful uprising of nobles and parlements, takes place.
1661	Louis declares himself his own first minister.
1661-1687	Louis builds the Palace of Versailles.
1662-1683	Jean Baptiste Colbert serves as Louis' finance minister.
1685	Louis revokes the Edict of Nantes.
1715	Louis XIV dies.

26 AN ABSOLUTE MONARCH IN ACTION

When a courtier once asked Louis XIV about the nature of the French state, the king is reported to have replied, "I am the state!" The king's retort indicated that he understood a basic characteristic of government: The nature of government depends on the characteristics of those who make the decisions. Therefore, to understand absolute monarchy in the France of Louis XIV, you must examine evidence describing the characteristics of the king.

Fortunately, diaries, journals, and eyewitness descriptions of Louis XIV and his court are plentiful. They tell how Louis worked, what he loved and hated, and why he acted as he did. But the historian must remember that these accounts also reflect the jealousy, loyalty, interests, and opinions of those who wrote them.

Reading 26 presents three selections that reveal some of Louis' characteristics. The first was written by the king himself. The second and third were written by the Duc de Saint-Simon, a noble in Louis' court. As you read, let the following questions guide you:

Louis XIV's Description of Kingship

In 1666 Louis wrote a memorandum to his son to tell him about the functions and conduct of a king.

Two things were absolutely necessary for ruling: very hard work on my part, and a wise choice of persons capable of carrying out my work.

As for work, my son, you will probably read these lines when you dread work far more than you love it. You will have finished your schooling and will be happy to be free of lengthy study. Yet it is work by which one reigns and for which one reigns.

I set a rule for myself to work regularly twice each day for two or three hours at a time. This regular work did not include the hours I spent privately working on matters of state, nor the time I was able to give when special problems arose. I permitted people to talk to me about urgent problems at any time.

I cannot tell you how important my resolution to work was. I felt myself uplifted in thought and courage. I joyfully scolded myself for not having been aware of work's importance earlier. My timidity, especially on occasions when I had to speak in public, disappeared in no time. I felt that I was king and born to be one. I experienced a delicious feeling which you will not know until you are king. You must not think, my son, that the affairs of state are like some thorny philosophical problem. A king must first of all be guided by his own good sense, which is natural and effortless. A king is the principal cause of good work being done. He cannot act without seeing his effect on the state. Success, even in small matters, gratifies us as well as success in great affairs. And there is no satisfaction equal to that of noting every day some progress you have made in the happiness of your people which comes from the work you have done.

My son, the work of a king is agreeable. One must try to learn the news concerning every province and every nation, the secrets of every court, the moods and weaknesses of every prince and every foreign minister. He must be well informed on all matters from commerce and science to art and philosophy. He must find out the secrets of his subjects, and discover the selfish interests of those who approach him with their real motives disguised. I know of no other pleasure I would take in place of the work of a king.

Memoires pour l'instruction du dauphin, in **Oeuvres de Louis XIV** (Paris: 1806), Vol. I, pp. 19-25. Translated by John M. Good.

▶Do you agree or disagree with Louis' opinion of hard work? Do you think success in one's work always brings the self-satisfaction and assurance that he experienced?

A Noble's Appraisal of Louis XIV

The Duc de Saint-Simon, a member of a prominent noble family, recorded in his memoirs the manners and customs of Louis' court at Versailles. The following excerpts first describe Louis' character and then his daily routine.

Duc de Saint-Simon, **Memoirs of Louis XIV and the Regency,** Bayle St. John, trans. (Washington: M. Walter Dunne, 1901), Vol. III, P. 359. Language simplified.

At twenty-three years of age, Louis became king in fact as well as in name, under the most favorable conditions. His ministers were the most skillful in all Europe; his generals the best; his court was filled with clever men.

Louis XIV was made for a brilliant court. His figure, his courage, his grace, his beauty, his grand bearing, even the tone of his voice and his majestic and natural charm set him apart from other men. Even if he had been born a simple private gentleman, he still would have excelled in all social festivities. However, intrigues against the king during his childhood made Louis suspicious of intelligent, educated, noble and highly principled men, and as he advanced in years, he began to hate them. He wished to reign by himself, and his jealousy on this point soon became a weakness. He concerned himself with little things; he never could reach great things. The superior ability of his early ministers and generals soon wearied him. He liked no one to be in any way superior to him. He chose his ministers, therefore, not for their knowledge, but for their ignorance; not for their capacity, but for their want of it. He concerned himself with the smallest details. He would even instruct his cooks, though he taught them things they had known for years.

▶Do you think vanity is necessarily harmful to good leadership?

His vanity, his unreasonable desire to be admired, ruined him. His ministers, his generals, his mistresses, his courtiers soon understood this fatal weakness. They praised him and spoiled him, for it was the one way they could approach him. This is why his ministers, drawn from the nonnoble class, had so much authority. They had better opportunity to flatter him.

A Day in the Life of the King

Duc de Saint-Simon, **Memoirs of Louis XIV and the Regency,** St. John, trans., Vol. III, pp. 30-37. Language simplified.

Grandes entrées means privileged permission to enter the king's chamber.

At eight o'clock the chief *valet*, who alone had slept in the royal chamber, awoke the king. The chief physician, the chief surgeon, and the nurse entered at the same time. At the quarter, the grand chamberlain was called and those who had what was called the *grandes entrées*. That was the time to speak to the king, if anyone had anything to ask of him. The chamberlain gave him his dressing gown; immediately

144

after, other privileged courtiers entered, and then everybody, in time to find the king putting on his shoes and stockings.

As soon as he was dressed, he prayed to God at the side of his bed, after which the king passed into his cabinet.

He found there a very numerous company. He gave orders to each for the day. It was then a good opportunity for talking with the king.

All the court meantime waited for the king in the gallery. Here the king gave audiences, spoke with whomever he might wish to speak secretly, and gave secret interviews to foreign ministers.

The king went to mass, where his musicians always sang an anthem. While he was going to and returning from mass, everybody spoke to him who wished. During the mass the ministers assembled in the king's chamber where distinguished people could go and speak with them. The king, returning from mass, asked almost immediately for the council.

On Sunday, and often on Monday, there was a council of state; on Tuesday a finance council; on Wednesday a council of state; on Saturday a finance council. Rarely were two held in one day or any on Thursday or Friday.

Thursday morning was almost always blank. It was the day for audiences that the king wished to give. On Friday after the mass, the king was with his confessor.

Upon returning home from walks or drives, anybody might speak to the king from the moment he left his coach till he reached the foot of his staircase. He changed his dress and rested in his cabinet an hour or more, then went to Madame de Maintenon's, and on the way anyone who wished might speak to him.

Madame de Maintenon was the most important of Louis' mistresses. In 1684, a year after the death of the queen, Louis married Madame de Maintenon, on condition that neither she nor their children could claim the throne. Madame de Maintenon had great influence over Louis.

At ten o'clock his supper was served. A quarter of an hour after the king came to supper, anyone spoke to him who wished. This supper was always on a grand scale, the royal household at table, and a large number of courtiers and ladies present.

After supper the king stood some moments encircled by all his court; then, with bows to the ladies, passed into his cabinet. He passed a little less than an hour there, seated in an armchair with the royal family.

The king, wishing to retire, went and fed his dogs; then said good night, passed into his chamber where he said his prayers, then undressed. He said good night with an inclination of the head, and while everybody was leaving the room gave the order to the colonel of the guards alone. Then began what was called the *petit coucher*, at which only the specially privileged remained. They did not leave until he got into bed. It was a moment to speak to him.

Petit coucher means a reception held in the king's private sleeping chamber just before he went to bed.

FOR THOUGHT:

How did the political institutions of Louis XIV and the decision-making process he used suit his personal characteristics?

The household furnishings shown on these two pages are in the Louis XIV style. What are the characteristics of these furnishings? Were they designed mainly for comfort or for some other reason? In what way, if any, do they suit Louis XIV's court? What does the furniture in your home reveal about your parents and you?

146

3

27 DECISION-MAKING IN AN ABSOLUTE MONARCHY

Whether it was a question of going to war, regulating industries, exiling outspoken nobles, raising taxes, or adding a wing to his palace at Versailles, Louis XIV alone held the decision-making power in France between 1661 and 1715. For more than half a century, he alone passed the laws of France and arranged to have them enforced.

At least three factors affected the decisions Louis made. First, Louis was directly influenced by those around him. Courtiers and ladies in favor at Versailles supplied him with information and offered possible solutions to problems. Therefore, they could often persuade him to carry out their pet projects. Second, Louis' beliefs about the role of government and the goals of society helped to shape his decisions. Finally, Louis made decisions on the basis of whether the advantages of a decision outweighed its disadvantages.

Reading 27 examines some of the information, the beliefs, and the expectations that led Louis to revoke the Edict of Nantes. This edict, issued by Henry IV in 1598, granted religious freedom to the Huguenots, or French Protestants, among the most able and prosperous of the bourgeoisie. The edict also gave the Huguenots control of about a hundred fortified towns in south-central France, providing them with great strength.

However, the Huguenots held their power for only a short time. To Cardinal Richelieu, the king's chief minister, they represented a threat to the Catholic monarchy. By 1629 Richelieu had captured the last of their towns and taken away their political power. All that remained from the Edict of Nantes was the promise of religious toleration.

Louis XIV also found the Huguenots a challenge to his absolutism. He wanted his authority to extend into all matters, including religion. On the advice of those around him, he first attempted to convert the Huguenots. Then in 1685, assured that there were few Protestants left in France, Louis revoked the Edict of Nantes on the grounds that it no longer served any purpose. But, in truth, many of the Huguenots had not converted. The revocation forced about 50,000 families to flee France. As a result, the country lost much of its commercial and industrial vitality. As you study Reading 27, form hypotheses to explain why Louis removed this last protection from his Protestant subjects. You can use the following questions to help you analyze the evidence given in the reading:

1. What role, if any, did most French people play in the decision to revoke the Edict of Nantes?
2. Did Louis XIV think of Frenchmen as subjects who should obey the government without taking part in it or as citizens with an active voice in decision-making?
3. How was the decision to revoke the Edict of Nantes made?

Louis XIV's Proclamation Revoking the Edict of Nantes

In this proclamation, Louis gave his reasons for reversing the edict. Remember that these were the reasons as he saw them.

James Harvey Robinson, Readings in European History (Boston: Ginn and Company, 1906), Vol. II, pp. 287-288. Language simplified.

Louis, by the grace of God, king of France, to all present and to come, greeting:

King Henry IV, our grandfather of glorious memory, hoped to keep the peace he had gained for his subjects after the great losses they had suffered in domestic and foreign wars. This peace had been troubled by the Protestant religion during the reigns of his predecessors. Accordingly, at Nantes in April 1598, he granted an edict to regulate the way in which the government and the Church should treat those who followed that religion. He also regulated the places in which the Protestants could worship and established special judges to administer justice to them. The purpose of the edict was to make possible a peaceful country in which the king could labor to return Protestants to the Roman Catholic Church.

God having at last brought perfect peace to our people, we are now able to devote our attention to accomplishing the goal to reunite the Protestants with the Catholic Church.

And now we see, with the aid of God, that we have attained our goal, since most of our Protestant subjects have returned to the Catholic faith. Therefore, since the Edict of Nantes and all other acts made in favor of the Protestants have become unnecessary, we have decided that we can do nothing better than entirely revoke the edict and all similar acts, in order to rid ourselves of the memory of the troubles, confusion, and evils which this false religion has brought about in our kingdom.

The Ideology of Absolutism: Divine Right of Kings

Bishop Jacques Bossuet was a well-known scholar and an excellent speaker. For eleven years, he was tutor to Louis' son. To help him understand the purpose of absolute monarchy, Bossuet wrote Politics Drawn from the Very Words of Holy Scripture. *The following excerpt explains Bossuet's theory of the divine right of kings. Louis XIV accepted the ideas expressed in these passages.*

The person of the king is sacred, and to attack him in any way is an attack on religion itself. Kings represent the divine majesty and have been appointed by Him to carry out His purposes. Serving God and respecting kings are bound together.

But kings should not believe that they are masters of their power to use at their own pleasure; they must use it with fear and self-restraint, as a thing coming from God, remembering that God will demand an account of how His power has been used.

Kings should tremble then as they use the power God has granted them; and let them beware if they use it for evil purposes. We have

Bishop Jacques Bossuet, **Politics Drawn from the Very Words of Holy Scripture,** as quoted in Robinson, **Readings in European History,** Vol. II, pp. 274-277. Language simplified.

*Top, Louis XIV and his court walking in the gardens of Versailles
Bottom, Louis XIV dressing*

Louis XIV receiving a visitor

The pictures on these two pages show typical scenes in Louis XIV's court. What do these pictures tell you about how people gained access to France's key political decision-maker, the king? What kinds of people were able to gain access to him?

151

known of unjust kings who use the power God has given them to act contrary to His laws and to perform deeds of violence and to slay God's children!

The royal power is absolute. Many writers who hate absolutism have tried to confuse it with arbitrary government, in which the king uses his power for his own pleasures. But arbitrary government and absolute government are completely different.

The king is not responsible to anyone on earth for his acts. Without this absolute authority, the king could neither do good nor prevent evil. His power must be such that no one can hope to escape him.

The king is not a private person. He belongs to the public. The will of the people is included in his will. As all perfection and all strength are united in God, so all the power of the individual subjects is united in the person of the king.

The power of God embraces the whole earth and holds it together; the power of the king spreads throughout his realm and holds it together. Should God withdraw His power, the earth would fall to pieces; should the king's authority end in the realm, all would be confusion.

O kings, use your power boldly, for it is divine and good for human kind. But use it with humility. You are given this power by God. You are still feeble, still mortal, still sinners. And you are still answerable to God, needing to give Him a greater account of yourself than ordinary men.

Saint-Simon on the Revocation

Just as he recorded the details of Louis' court, Saint-Simon described the major issues of governmental policy. As always, he injected his own views and interpretations.

Madame de Maintenon, the king's mistress who had become his wife, was exceedingly religious. She found that the king believed he was a religious reformer, because he had always persecuted non-believers, or those he was led to believe were non-believers. Madame de Maintenon saw that she could further her own aims for making all France Catholic through the king.

Moreover, the king had been poorly educated, and his ignorance made him easy prey for the Jesuits. He became even an easier prey when, with increasing age, he became very religious without adding to his knowledge. In this state of mind, it was easy to persuade Louis that a tremendous blow against the Protestants would bring him more grandeur than any of his ancestors had. Furthermore, he was persuaded that such an act would strengthen his power.

The monarchs distinguished absolute and arbitrary rule thus: An absolute ruler could in no way be limited by his subjects or the law. But he was bound by the will of God and by tradition. Despots, or arbitrary rulers, recognized no limits at all.

▶In your opinion, who, if anyone, has any "divine" right over other people? Why?

Duc de Saint-Simon, **Memoirs of Louis XIV and the Regency,** St. John, trans., Vol. III, pp. 12-14. Language simplified.

Jesuits were distinguished for missionary work and studies in science and humanities. Devoted to the papacy, they tried to reclaim Protestant Europe and promote Catholic reform. Because the Jesuits were both controversial and powerful, many Catholic monarchs attempted to destroy them.

The revocation of the Edict of Nantes was the result of a frightful plot, in which Madame de Maintenon was one of the chief conspirators. The act drove a quarter of the population of France from the realm, ruined the country's commerce, and weakened the state in every direction. It allowed the soldiers to loot the property of the Huguenots, authorized punishments that killed thousands of innocent people, ruined the merchant class, tore hundreds of families into pieces, armed relatives against relatives, and banished manufacturers to foreign lands. The revocation sent nobles, rich old men, as well as religious, learned, and virtuous people, to the galleys solely because of their religion. Those who wished to escape such torture pretended to accept a religion they hated!

Although many people informed the king of these persecutions, others filled his ears with news of Protestant conversions. They told him that ten thousand converted in one city, six thousand in another—and apparently these conversions took place all at once. The king congratulated himself on his power and on his religious devotion. He believed that he alone had the honor of converting God's lost children. The bishops wrote articles and the Jesuits gave sermons full of his praises. Louis had never before believed himself so great in the eyes of man, and so advanced in the eyes of God.

FOR THOUGHT:

How did the philosophy of Bishop Bossuet reflect the institutions, the decision-making process, and the political role of most French people during the seventeenth century?

28 COLBERT AND MERCANTILISM: A STUDY IN ADMINISTRATION

Louis XIV could not personally administer all his laws and orders everywhere at once. Instead he appointed a group of officials to carry out his commands throughout the kingdom. Louis did not often ask the nobles to fill these positions. But because of their feudal heritage, he knew they would still remain loyal to him as his vassals. They kept their titles and high social status while Louis took the last of their political power. Louis forced them to live at Versailles where he could watch their every move. He spied on them, set them against each other by favoring one, then another, and kept them entirely subject to his

Saint-Simon exaggerated the consequences of the revocation, but he described the types of things that occurred accurately.

Galleys were boats rowed by prisoners. Thousands of men were condemned to spend the rest of their lives, a short time at best, chained to galley oars. See the picture on page 161.

▶For what reasons, if any, should people accept laws that go against their own beliefs?

153

power. The courtiers spent each day in great luxury, waiting to be received by Louis.

Louis appointed members of the wealthy middle class as his trusted officials. He offered them money, land, and titles. Among them were Jean Baptiste Colbert, the king's finance minister. Colbert was the son of a draper and the nephew of a rich merchant. At the age of thirty-two, he entered the service of Mazarin, Louis XIV's chief minister then, and he quickly became a financial adviser. Just before Mazarin died, he recommended Colbert to the king. Eventually Colbert became the most influential of Louis' ministers because he developed industry and commerce and made economic reforms. But Colbert knew that his high position and great power would last only as long as he pleased the king.

Colbert redeveloped the still feudal French economy around the economic policies of mercantilism. Mercantilism was a theory of trade based on the idea that the real wealth of a nation consisted of money and precious metals in the treasuries of the government. To accumulate money, a nation had to sell more than it bought, thus producing what was called a favorable balance of trade. A mercantilist nation taxed imports heavily to discourage people from buying them. It also developed manufacturing because manufactured goods sold for more money than raw materials. And it established colonies to supply the raw materials to feed industries, thus making it unnecessary to depend on foreign countries for its needs.

Under Colbert, France became the leading mercantile power of Europe. The selections in Reading 28 will help you determine how Colbert reached his goal. At the same time, you will see how Louis administered his realm through men like Colbert. Think about the following questions as you read:

1. What role did the government take in making economic decisions in seventeenth-century France?
2. What were the major characteristics of the officials whom Louis XIV appointed? Why did he pick these men as his administrators?

An Edict Establishing the Royal Tapestry Works

In 1667 Louis XIV issued this edict in his own name, but the ideas were Colbert's.

P. Boissonade, **Colbert** (Paris: Marcel Rivière, 1932), pp. 305-307. Translated by John M. Good.

The manufacture of tapestries has always seemed useful. Prosperous countries have established tapestry industries and have offered special favors to attract the best workers . . . .

Our desire to make industry flourish in our kingdom has led us to reestablish tapestry production by purchasing the Gobelins mansion and several houses nearby. We have summoned painters with the highest reputation, tapestry workers, sculptors, goldsmiths and silversmiths, cabinet-makers, and other outstanding artists and craftsmen to come there. We have given each of them apartments and special privileges, and so should attract more workers. We hope that outstanding workers in all kinds of manufacturing will come at our invitation to give us their skills, so that the work done in Gobelins will be of higher quality than the best work in foreign countries. To insure our success, we have believed it is necessary to issue these regulations . . . .

1. The manufacture of tapestries and other works shall be done in the mansion of the Gobelins, the houses, land, and the other buildings belonging to us. On the main entrance of the mansion a marble tablet shall be set up, inscribed with our coat of arms and the words: ROYAL MANUFACTURE OF FURNISHINGS FOR THE CROWN.

2. The factories and buildings shall be administered by our beloved loyal minister, M. Colbert . . . .

4. M. Colbert, and M. Le Brun under him, will keep the factory supplied with good painters, masterworkers in tapestries, jewelers, foundry workers, engravers, stoneworkers, cabinetmakers, dyers, and other good workers in all the arts and crafts.

11. The workers employed in these manufacturing plants will live in the houses nearest the Gobelins mansion. The workers will not be required to quarter soldiers and officers . . . .

17. We forbid any merchant or other person from buying or importing any foreign tapestries. If anyone should sell foreign tapestries . . . in our realm, the tapestries will be confiscated and he shall pay a fine of half their value.

A Letter from Colbert to the Intendants

Rather than leave the administration of local areas to the nobles who had their manors there, Louis appointed intendants to report all matters directly to the crown. In 1670 all the intendants received the following letter from Colbert.

The king desires to stop the manufacturers of France from violating his wishes. Accordingly, his Majesty has resolved to send inspectors into all the provinces of the kingdom to inform the judges, the merchants, and the workers of his wishes. So that the intendants may help, we have prepared this directive.

Giles and Jehan Gobelin opened a dye works in Paris in the mid-fifteenth century. In 1601 two Flemish weavers added a tapestry works to the Gobelins establishment. The Gobelin family sold the factory to Louis XIV in 1662. Colbert united it with other factories in 1667 to organize the royal tapestry works.

Charles Le Brun, painter, decorator, and architect, founded the Royal Academy of Painting and Sculpture. He directed all Louis' artistic undertakings for 20 years, including the decorations at Versailles.

Most seventeenth-century European countries required their citizens to take soldiers into their homes, since there were no barracks. The families had to bear all expenses of feeding and housing the soldiers. Kings often sent soldiers to stay with citizens who opposed them. For example, Louis forced the Huguenots to quarter troops.

Lettres, Instructions, et Memoirs de Colbert, P. Clement, ed. (Paris: 1863), Vol. II, pp. 835-837. Translated by John M. Good.

These pictures show two tapestries made at the Gobelins tapestry works. How do these tapestries portray Louis XIV? What do they indicate about Louis' motives in setting up the Gobelins works?

1. The inspector shall report to the intendant.

2. The inspector, having received his orders from the intendant, will go immediately to the nearest manufacturing center and consult with the mayor and the aldermen. He shall find out if the regulation for manufactures has been registered and published.

3. A community room will be established in the city hall where the examiners can inspect and mark the merchandise of the clothmakers. The examiners can settle on the spot any disputes which might develop because of defects in the cloth, and they will instill fear of the laws in the minds of the clothworkers. Since the cloth merchants can readily

157

spot good quality or defects in the merchandise, and since it is in their interest that the cloth be perfect, the aldermen shall elect one of the prominent merchants to help inspect and mark the cloth.

11. The inspector shall read the regulation on manufacturing to the guild masters. He shall inform them that if they break the regulation, their goods will be confiscated and unraveled. The goods they manufacture must be uniform throughout the kingdom in length, width, and strength.

18. The inspector will find out about all the important fairs held in his department and will go there to inspect the merchandise sold, to see if it bears the seal of passing inspection and to see if it meets the quality called for in the regulation. If the cloth does not, he shall seize it and unravel it on the spot.

▶ Do you feel that certain industries should be regulated and protected by government? If so, which ones?

Colbert Instructs an Intendant on His Duties

Colbert wrote many letters to the intendants. The following two are examples of how the finance minister managed the affairs of the kingdom. The intendant in question had assumed some of the functions of the tax court.

Lettres, Instructions, et Memoirs de Colbert, Clement, ed., Vol. II, pp. 266, 270-271. Translated by John M. Good.

Rouen was the ancient capital of Normandy in northern France.

To M. de Creil, intendant of Rouen, January 27, 1673:

I have reported to the king the way you have conducted the affairs of Normandy. His Majesty has ordered me to write you that he has found you have actually set up an additional court there to settle tax disputes. You have administered things that should be administered by the magistrates and the financial court. He has, therefore, ordered me to tell you that if you do not remedy these errors, he will have to dismiss you from your position.

You ought to examine closely all the regulations dealing with taxes and tax-farms, and all other regulations dealing with the duties of intendants. You should conduct yourself according to these rules and never deviate from them.

You alone have the responsibility to see that the magistrates and the financial court interpret the tax regulations correctly. When they do not obey them, you should inform the king's finance council at Versailles, and request that the king give you special power to correct the situation.

In seventeenth-century France, the right to collect taxes in a particular area— i.e., tax-farm—was sold to individuals or companies. Tax-farmers collected money beyond the amount of the taxes. This extra money went into their own pockets.

To M. de Creil, intendant of Rouen, February 3, 1673:

I have read your memorandum explaining your dispute with the financial court. You should not hastily reject the advice the king has ordered me to give you on this matter.

158

I must again tell you that it is difficult, if not impossible, to mislead me on this subject. I believe I have already told you that you must deal only with those matters which are assigned you by the regulations. However, your own memorandum gave you away. It made it quite clear that you were administering the property taxes. The administration of these taxes belongs to the magistrates and the financial court.

I assure you that I did not know that there were from twenty to twenty-four tax collectors in each parish. The number to be chosen each year is stated in the regulations. Tell me all you have to say on this subject, so that I can inform the king.

Of all the abuses in taxation we have heard about, one stands out. Apparently some assistants to the collectors of the property tax have been cooperating with court magistrates to make special assessments on people who appear before the court. The money collected from these assessments supposedly is to pay court costs, but it has been going into the collectors' pockets instead. Please inform me if this is going on in Rouen. Either remedy the situation yourself or advise me about it.

▶Do you think corruption within the government is inevitable? How would you try to control it?

FOR THOUGHT:

In what ways, if any, did the policy called mercantilism fit Louis XIV's political beliefs and the needs of his government?

29 LOUIS XIV: THE ANATOMY OF ABSOLUTISM

A HISTORICAL ESSAY

In 1643, at the age of five, Louis XIV became king of France. In 1661, Cardinal Mazarin, Louis' chief minister, died, and the king took control of the affairs of the state. For the next fifty years, the so-called Grand Monarch dominated Europe's political, economic, and social scene. "I am the state," which Louis is supposed to have boasted, catches the spirit of the age in which the modern centralized state was born.

Before modern governments could develop, sovereign states had to replace feudal governments. To be sovereign, a state must control the administration of justice and the use of force. In a sovereign state, people who are not government officials cannot pass legal judgments or control their own armed forces. Therefore, medieval states were not sovereign because manorial courts administered justice and the nobility controlled their own armed forces.

159

▶Do you believe laws should be made by a country's national government or by local governments to fit local requirements?

England emerged as the first of Europe's truly sovereign states. William the Conqueror made all nobles swear direct loyalty to him, giving him the beginnings of control over the armed forces. Later kings added sheriffs and traveling justices to centralize law enforcement. In England the evolution of Parliament linked the interests of the nobility and the landed gentry with the crown. England had only one Parliament for the whole country instead of many local representative bodies such as France had. Parliament had both a House of Lords and a House of Commons, but landowners dominated them equally. In the House of Commons, landed gentry mixed with representatives from the towns, many of whom were also landowners. By the middle of the seventeenth century, three times as many nobles as representatives of the Church sat in the House of Lords. No king could govern England long if Parliament opposed him. Hence, a grudging partnership between king and Parliament grew up. England became a sovereign state in which the few governed everyone else.

France's government developed in a very different way. In the last half of the sixteenth century, France was torn by civil and religious wars. The civil wars were fought because of the lack of government. Bands of armed men wandered about the country plundering manors and towns. The religious wars were caused by the struggle for power between the Catholics and the French Protestants, called Huguenots. When rival bands of Protestants and Catholics met, battles usually flared up and many people were killed.

These civil and religious wars lasted for thirty years. But neither side could subdue the other. Gradually a group of people grew up among both Catholics and Protestants who came to believe that too much was being made of religion. They thought there should be enough room in France for both religions since the alternative seemed to be constant war. A leading philosopher of this group, Jean Bodin, began to argue that every society must have one power strong enough to make and enforce laws. This argument developed into the idea of royal absolutism and the sovereign state.

In 1589 both the French king and the leader of the Catholic party were assassinated. Henry of Navarre, leader of the Huguenots, became king as Henry IV. Henry converted to Catholicism in 1593 in order to end the bitter religious conflicts. In 1598 he issued the Edict of Nantes which granted religious toleration to Protestants. Although some Catholics opposed him, he gradually won acceptance for his new policies.

Next Henry turned his attention to strengthening the government. He began to collect taxes regularly, control local officials, and discipline the army. With all of Henry's changes, he never found it necessary to call together the Estates-General, the representative assembly. After a fanatic killed him in 1610, his widow did call the Estates-General. But so many quarrels broke out within it that no program could be adopted. She dismissed it in 1615. For many years to come, national government was to be conducted by the king, not by a representative body.

Cardinal Richelieu, the chief minister of the next king, Louis XIII, tried to strengthen the state through mercantilist policies. To raise money, he sold titles of nobility to rich merchants. To stop local wars, he destroyed most fortified castles and took away the fortified cities that the Huguenots had built. These reforms slowly made the king and his minister the head of a sovereign state, which Louis XIV inherited in 1643 when he became king at the age of five.

While Louis was still a child, his chief minister was Cardinal Mazarin. In 1648 a revolution called the Fronde broke out, led by the nobility

▶This picture shows a galley in Louis XIV's navy. Each galley was rowed by men who had been condemned for life because they were criminals or because they remained Huguenots after the Edict of Nantes was revoked. Do you think criminals should be condemned to hard labor? What should the purpose of sentences given to criminals be?

and the members of the law courts, called parlements. The revolution was really a struggle for power. The nobles wanted to reduce the king's power and increase their own. But because the nobility had no support from the bourgeoisie, also represented in the parlements, the uprising failed. In later years, both the bourgeoisie and the peasants welcomed strong kings to protect them from self-seeking nobles. This development helped the growth of royal absolutism in France.

When Mazarin died suddenly in 1661, everyone expected the twenty-three-year-old king to appoint another first minister to rule in his name. Louis had shown little interest in the affairs of state. But instead, he announced that henceforth he would manage all government affairs himself. "You will assist me with your advice, gentlemen, when I ask for it," he told his disappointed and skeptical ministers. "I order you to sign nothing, not even a passport, without my command."

What his ministers thought to be a passing whim began fifty-four years of rigid personal rule. Like other absolute rulers, Louis thought of the nation as his personal estate and its inhabitants as his obedient children. But at the same time, Louis had certain responsibilities to live up to. As God's representative on earth, according to the divine right theory, Louis had to be remote but all-seeing, dignified but gracious, glorious but just.

Louis' clothing—flowing cloaks, high-heeled shoes, and broad-brimmed hats with waving ostrich plumes—emphasized his regality. He wore wigs made of dark hair with rows of curls falling over the shoulders. The sun, source of light and life, became Louis' personal emblem. Flatterers called him the "Sun King," and they said he strongly resembled Apollo, the Greek god of the sun. Louis fed his vanity by surrounding himself with statues, paintings, and tapestries of Apollo.

Richelieu and Mazarin had destroyed the political power of the French nobility. Louis made the nobility totally dependent on his court. Nobles who wanted political appointments had to stay near the king, waiting for him to make his choices. Nobles who sought social prestige could find it only at Versailles. Nobles who needed special favors courted the king's good will. "Out of sight, out of mind" was the sorry fate of many a nobleman, for Louis' usual punishment for minor offenses was to exile a noble to his provincial estate.

Life at Louis' court was a constant round of ritual, pleasure, and intrigue. For himself, the Sun King set strict rules, devoting many hours to the details of government and the demands of court etiquette. The nobles had to follow the rigid court etiquette because Louis believed that formality and ceremony were essential to the royal court. Every moment of the royal day was scheduled. The privileged nobles who attended him from the moment he awoke handed him his washcloth, his clothing, and his wig. Others were allowed into his outer bedroom only, or into one of the reception rooms. Throughout the remainder of the day, the nobles waited for a word with their king.

The palace at Versailles expressed Louis' image of himself. It was difficult to preserve the image of a dignified Sun King amid the commotion of a large city. So Louis moved his court from Paris to Versailles, twelve miles away, where Louis XIII had had a hunting lodge. In the 1660's Louis began building there a vast complex of magnificent palaces surrounded by splendid gardens and woods. The main palace stretched for more than a quarter of a mile. The king's apartments occupied only a small portion of this building. Here and in the other palaces were the apartments of the courtiers who came with their families and attendants. The main palace also had the great ceremonial halls, the most famous of which is the Hall of Mirrors. Gilded furniture, rich tapestries, and grand paintings adorned all the rooms.

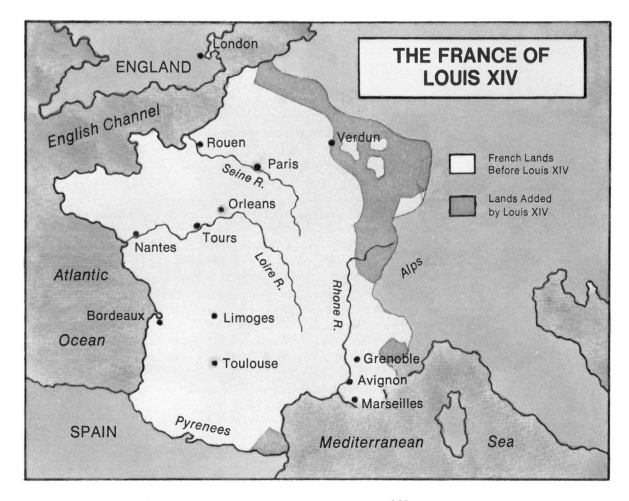

THE FRANCE OF LOUIS XIV

French Lands Before Louis XIV

Lands Added by Louis XIV

Socially Louis surrounded himself with the aristocracy. But the key to his political success lay in the bourgeoisie. To run his government, the king selected men from the wealthy middle class who depended on him for social and political advancement. To hold their loyalty, Louis passed laws that profited them and, at the same time, built the prosperity, power, and glory of France. But the bourgeoisie's power did not give them equal status with the nobles at court.

The king used a number of committees as an aid in running the government. These committees held frequent meetings which the king usually led. But though committee members discussed policy and gave advice, they never voted. Louis alone made the final decisions. Then his royal ministers sent these decisions to provincial administrators called intendants. Because the intendants represented the royal will and reported to the king, they had full power over local officials. Town councils and nobles, who claimed political rights given them by ancient charters and tradition, were helpless against them. This total control of the state by the king characterized seventeenth-century absolutism.

Jean Baptiste Colbert, Louis' most important minister, was a member of the bourgeoisie. Colbert adopted the economic policies of mercantilism and reorganized the economic life of France to serve the state. To achieve the main goal of mercantilism—filling the royal treasury— Colbert had to make France economically self-sufficient. He developed new industries, which were protected by tariffs and strictly regulated. Through Colbert, the king gave monopolies and subsidies to important industries, built roads and canals, widened rivers, and developed a navy to protect foreign trade. He built a large merchant marine and established colonies in Asia and North America to provide raw materials and markets. But after Colbert's death, France rapidly declined as a mercantile power.

Louis poured the income brought in by Colbert's policies into the glitter of Versailles and into the building of a modern army and navy. The French army numbered 100,000 in peacetime, the largest in the seventeenth century, and it reached four times that size during Louis' wars. Well equipped and trained, it was easily the most efficient military force in Europe. Louis used the army continuously in wars that filled more than half his fifty-four years of power. He hoped to reach the so-called "natural boundaries" of France—the Pyrenees to the south, the Alps to the east, and the Rhine River to the north. Since Italians, Spaniards, Germans, Belgians, and Dutch lived within these areas, their monarchs fought wars against Louis.

Alarmed at his expansion, England led the opposition to Louis. The fighting spread beyond Europe to the English and French colonies in Asia, the West Indies, and North America. Louis' extremism, his ambition, and his self-infatuation led him to wage war on such a grand

▶ Do you think war is ever justified?

164

scale that he eventually exhausted his mighty army as well as his overflowing treasury.

By 1715 when Louis XIV died, the French government was clearly sovereign. The king had won control of the administration of justice and the use of armed force in the nation over the opposition of the nobles. The nobles had lost their influence in the decision-making process by opposing both the king and the commoners.

English nobles increased their power by allying themselves with the gentry in Parliament. They could also influence their king by withholding taxes. On the other hand, French nobles paid almost no taxes and thus they lacked a powerful tool. In addition, their failure to use the Estates General constructively led to its decay. Louis XIV reigned unchecked. He treated his people as subjects with no rights rather than as citizens with civil, political, and social rights. As a result, seventy-four years after his death, a bloody revolution took place in France.

Individual and Group Activities for Chapter 6

For full descriptions of these activities, turn to the **Student Book of Activities and Readings** included among the materials for individual and group activities.

Activity 6A: Presentation of drama performed at the court of Louis XIV (group)

This activity contains part of a French play that was popular at the court of Louis XIV. Select a section to act out, rehearse it, and perform it before the class.

Activity 6B: Study of the music played at the court of Louis XIV (individual)

This activity contains a group of pictures showing musical instruments and the settings in which musicians performed at the court of Louis XIV. Examine these pictures while listening to a recording of seventeenth-century French music. Then decide why this music was suitable for Louis' court, and present your ideas in an oral report or a written essay.

The Birth of Modern Science

CHAPTER

7

While kings and parliaments revolutionized political systems in the western world, other people revolutionized ways of thinking. These people were scientists who did not accept the theories established by ancient thinkers and churchmen about the physical universe. To them nothing in nature was so sacred that it could not be questioned. Out of this questioning grew a scientific revolution which changed the entire world.

The birth of modern science took place during the sixteenth and seventeenth centuries. Many of the greatest people in the history of science lived during this period. The key concept that developed from this early scientific movement was rationalism. Rationalism is the belief that people can prove all things by using their reason, by questioning and experimenting. Rationalism led to a new method of looking for truth—scientific or controlled investigation.

The laws of nature that these early scientists discovered challenged many traditional beliefs about the individual's position in the universe. Like other things in nature, the scientists said, people and their society must also function according to natural laws. By the end of the eighteenth century, the traditional teachings of the churches, the schools, and the governments were being questioned. Some western thinkers, applying the method of scientific investigation, began to look for natural laws that governed people and their relationships to other people. They believed that once these laws were discovered, people would be able to create better societies.

Today the scientific method has become a part of every side of life. Sociologists, anthropologists, political scientists, economists, psychologists, and historians use it in their specialized studies of the individual and his society. The inquiry approach used in this textbook grew out of the scientific method. The scientific environment of today's world stems from the revolution in thought that took place in the sixteenth and seventeenth centuries. The readings that follow should help you to discover what this new thinking was like, why it developed when it did, and what was important about it.

1126-1198	Avorroës introduces Aristotelian science to Europe.
1266-1268	Roger Bacon writes **Opus Majus.**
1267-1273	St. Thomas Aquinas writes **Summa Theologica.**
1543	Nicholas Copernicus publishes **On the Revolutions of the Heavenly Bodies.**
1571-1601	Tycho Brahe carries on astronomical observations.
1609	Johannes Kepler discovers new laws about the movement of the planets.
1609-1613	Galileo Galilei begins his telescopic observations and supports the Copernican theory.
1620	Francis Bacon publishes **Novum Organum.**
1637	René Déscartes publishes works on mathematics and mechanics.
1662	King Charles II charters the Royal Society of England.
1687	Sir Isaac Newton publishes **Principia Mathematica** explaining gravitation.
1690	John Locke publishes **Two Treatises of Government.**
1704	Newton publishes **Opticks.**

30 MEDIEVAL SCIENCE

Like the Renaissance, the Reformation, parliamentary government, and absolutism, modern science has its roots in the Middle Ages. Medieval scholastics were among the first to look for answers to many scientific questions. These scholastics were mostly monks who tried to explain away the conflicts between faith and reason. Their movement was religious in nature, and they did not seek answers to scientific questions for the same reasons as modern people. They looked for answers that would justify their religious beliefs.

The medieval scholastics relied on the teachings of authorities, chiefly the ancient Greeks and the Church, to explain the physical world. Therefore, they added little to scientific knowledge. They made few discoveries, and their methods of coming to conclusions differed from the methods of modern science. But the scholastics did bring one important change to western thinking. They claimed that observation was as reliable as faith in discovering truth. And they patiently observed many natural phenomena, making careful notes. The conclusions they drew from these observations generally were not scientific, but their attention to detail was. By the thirteenth century, scholastic thinking had spread to the universities where many of the teachers were monks.

To understand fully the revolutionary nature of later scientific developments, you must first understand how the medieval scholastics looked at the physical world. Most important among the scholastics was St. Thomas Aquinas, whom you studied in Chapter 2. Reading 30 contains excerpts from his writings and from those of several other medieval thinkers. As you read, keep the following questions in mind:

1. What part did observation play in the explanations given by Adelard and Neckam? What part did reason play?
2. According to St. Thomas Aquinas, how could man find the truth? according to Roger Bacon?

A Medieval Scientist Explains Natural Phenomena

Adelard of Bath was a twelfth-century English scholastic. He is best known for his study of Arabian mathematics and science. The following selection is from Adelard's work, Natural Questions, *which appeared between 1107 and 1133. Through the use of dialogue, it shows how a medieval scientist explained the physical world.*

Adelard of Bath, **Quaestiones Naturales,** M. Muller, ed. (Ashendorff, Germany: Munster, 1934). Translated by John M. Good.

NEPHEW: Why is seawater bitter and salty?

ADELARD: I believe that the heat of the sun and the planets causes the saltiness. The ocean flows through the hot zone of the earth near the equator. The planets overhead also have their course through the same zone. The great heat of the stars heats the sea and it becomes salty. One fact which supports this theory is that seawater when it is dried by the sun on the rocks near the ocean turns into salt . . . .

NEPHEW: If, as the common people believe, all rivers flow into the sea, then why do they not increase the size of the ocean?

ADELARD: If you follow the common people you will tumble into a pit. They understand nature so poorly that they are like men in a dream, and when they talk about nature they positively snore. It is not true that all rivers run into the sea, though many do. But just as some run into it, some run out of it. The sea gives as well as receives, and, therefore, does not increase in size. In fact, since so many underground streams flow out of the ocean and the stars evaporate so much of its water, some people have asked why the ocean does not decrease in size.

NEPHEW: Lo! I am confused again. If rivers run from the sea, why are they not salty when they reach us?

ADELARD: They lose their salt on the route to us. Though they were salty when they started, the rivers were strained in their passage through the center of the earth and leave their saltiness there . . . .

An Encyclopedia of Scientific Knowledge

Alexander Neckam was an English clergyman who lived from 1157 to 1217. At the end of the twelfth century, Neckam tried to put all scientific knowledge into one encyclopedia called On the Nature of Things. *In it he tried to show the moral lessons that could be gained from scientific knowledge.*

Alexander Neckam, **On the Nature of Things,** as quoted in James Harvey Robinson, **Readings in European History** (Boston: Ginn and Co., 1904), Vol. I, pp. 439-440. Language simplified.

According to a fable, the wren gained royal power among the birds by a clever plan. The birds had agreed that the royal power would be given to the bird that could fly the highest. The wren hid itself under the wing of the eagle, the highest flying bird of all. Then, when the eagle flew as high as it could, the wren flew out and perched on the eagle's head, declaring itself the victor.

This fable teaches us about those who use the works of others to gain their position and then take the credit for themselves. As a philosopher says, "We are all like dwarfs standing on giants' shoulders." We must be careful to give credit to our ancestors for those things which we should not claim for our own glory. We should not follow the example of the wren, which, with little effort of its own, claimed to have outdone the eagle.

▶Do you agree with the moral lesson Neckam drew from the fable of the wren? How much credit should you give others who help you succeed.

Aristotle and Medieval Science

Averroës, a Spanish-Arabian philosopher of the twelfth century, spread many of the writings of Aristotle through western Europe. His views about Aristotle were typical of most educated men of the late Middle Ages.

Averroës, **Corpus Commentariorum Averrois in Aristotelem,** as quoted in Robinson, **Readings in European History,** Vol. I, p.456. Language simplified.

Metaphysics is the division of philosophy which explores the ultimate state of existence.

Aristotle was the wisest of the Greeks. He fully developed logic, physics, and metaphysics. All the works on these subjects written before his writings do not deserve to be mentioned. He overshadowed all of them. He put the finishing touches on these sciences as well, for none of those who have come after him have added anything at all to what he discovered. To find all of this in one man is strange and miraculous. Undoubtedly Aristotle deserves to be called divine rather than human.

St. Thomas Aquinas
on the Sources of Truth

Aristotle taught many ideas that contradicted the teachings of the Church, including the idea that man gains knowledge through reason alone. St. Thomas Aquinas was very much influenced by many of Aristotle's ideas. In the following excerpt from his Summa Theologica, *written between 1267 and 1273, he tries to resolve the conflict between reason and faith.*

St. Thomas Aquinas, **Summa Theologica**. Language simplified.

Some men believe that we do not need any more knowledge than that which we earn by using our power of reason. They believe that man should not seek answers to questions that cannot be solved by reason.

▶ Do you think that religious explanations for events should be included in science books?

December 20, 1972

CALIFORNIA TEXTS WILL HAVE EVOLUTION AS THEORY, NO GOD

In a final vote taken last week, the California State Board of Education decided not to include the Biblical account of man's creation in its science textbooks. But it will insist that evolution is treated as theory rather than fact.

The battle between creationists and evolutionists has grown hot in the state recently, and for awhile it looked as though Genesis might compete with Darwin in a basic science series for grades K through 8.

While the controversy was still going strong, the National Academy of Science passed a resolution urging the state board to reject religion in science books. Nineteen Nobel Laureate scientists joined in signing a letter of protest to the board which said they were "appalled" that it might be considering including religious as well as scientific explanations in science books.

I answer that in addition to what we can learn by reason, we must learn knowledge that is revealed by God. God's revealed truth is necessary for our salvation. Man cannot learn some truths by use of his reason alone; hence, it was necessary to give him those truths by Divine Revelation. Even those truths about God that we can learn by using our reason had to be revealed. All men must know these truths about God in order to be saved, but only a few intelligent men can discover them by use of reason. Those who believe only in reason should read in Ecclesiasticus, Chapter 3:25: "For God has shown man much that goes beyond what he learns from reason."

Roger Bacon
on the Sources
of Knowledge

The English monk, philosopher, and scientist, Roger Bacon, was dissatisfied with the traditional explanations about the nature of the physical world. The following selection is from his Opus Majus *which appeared between 1266 and 1268.*

I now wish to explain the principles of experimental science. Without experience nothing can be sufficiently known. There are two ways of acquiring knowledge—by reasoning and through experience. By reasoning we can draw a conclusion and grant that the conclusion fulfills the test of reason. But reasoning does not alone make the conclusion certain. Only experience can make us accept a conclusion with certainty. A man who has never seen fire is able to prove by adequate use of reason that fire burns and injures things and destroys them. Still, his mind would not be satisfied, and he would not avoid fire. He would place his hand or some other substance in the fire so that he could prove by experience the conclusion he had reached through reason. When a man has had the actual experience of fire, his mind is certain of its effects and rests knowing the truth. Reasoning does not suffice, but experience does.

Roger Bacon, **Opus Majus**, Robert Belle Burke, trans. (Philadelphia: University of Pennsylvania Press, 1928), Vol. II, p. 583. Language simplified.

▶Should you use experience as your main test of truth? Or should you rely on reason and on the opinions of other people?

FOR THOUGHT:

How accurate would a history textbook be if it were written using the principles described in Reading 30?

31 THE SIXTEENTH- AND SEVENTEENTH-CENTURY SCIENTISTS

The scholastics, like Adelard of Bath and Roger Bacon, did much to advance science. However, these men were few in number, and their work had little effect on medieval thought. Following the scholastics came the humanists of the Renaissance, who were taught by monks in the universities of Italy and France. The humanists read the works of Aristotle and the other ancients, and they found many ideas to stir their Renaissance curiosity. The humanists, like the scholastics before them, added little to scientific knowledge. But they passed on many ideas that later led people to reexamine accepted beliefs.

Beginning with the publication of Nicholas Copernicus' book *On the Revolutions of the Heavenly Bodies* in 1543, European scientists made discovery after discovery about the natural world. Copernicus, a Polish churchman and astronomer, lived from 1473 to 1543. He revived and advanced the theory of a heliocentric universe that had been mentioned in some ancient writings. The heliocentric theory states that the sun is the center of the universe, and the earth is one of several planets revolving around the sun. Copernicus' theory contradicted the theory put forth by Aristotle and systemetized by Ptolemy, a second-century Greek astronomer. The Ptolemaic theory claims that the earth is the center of the universe, and the sun, moon, stars, and planets revolve around it. This geocentric, or earth-centered, theory was accepted by the Church. The Church held that God had put people on the earth at the center of the universe, and, therefore, people were the focus of God's attention.

Copernicus worked out his theory some twenty to thirty years before he published it. As a clergyman he understood that it contradicted Church doctrine. Therefore he hesitated to publish it until shortly before his death, when he felt he could no longer hold back what he believed to be true. His book did not attract widespread attention, and most who did hear of it refused to believe it. But a few scientists picked up his theory, and the revolution that Copernicus started quietly took hold.

The scientists of the sixteenth and seventeenth centuries added more to man's knowledge of the physical world than all the scientists before them. The documents in Reading 31 will help you to decide if it was just coincidence that so many scientists lived at one time and that most of them came from the rising middle class. Use the following questions to guide your study:

1. What advantages did these scientists have over earlier scientists? For example, how were they helped by wealthy people, new institutions, and changing attitudes?
2. What obstacles did these scientists have to overcome? How did the conflict between science and religion influence their work?

Copernicus Describes His Frame of Reference

The following selection is from the preface to the book On the Revolutions of the Heavenly Bodies. *In it, Copernicus explained how the ideas of the past and present both helped and hindered him.*

For a long time I had thought about the uncertainty of the doctrine about the orbital paths of the heavenly bodies. Therefore, I took pains to read through the writings of all the philosophers I could find, in order to discover if one of them had stated that the paths of the planets might be different from those described by the traditional doctrine. And I did find, first in Cicero, that at least one of the ancient philosophers thought that the earth moves. Afterwards, I read in Plutarch that others shared the same belief. Plutarch says: "The common opinion is that the earth stands still; but Philolaus and Pythagoras believe that it moves about the sun in an oblique circle." Heraclides also taught that the earth moves, that it rotates upon its axis as a wheel rotates about its hub.

After learning of these theories that contradict the accepted doctrine, I myself began to think about the motion of the earth. And although my theory might contradict the accepted doctrine, I knew that others who had come before me had been allowed to change the paths of the planets to account for inaccuracies in the doctrine. They had been allowed to suggest that other circles should be added to the basic path of a planet, so that the course of a planet consisted of one basic path about the earth and a number of loops or secondary orbits. I believed, therefore, that I would be allowed to suggest a theory for the motion of the earth in order to give a more satisfactory explanation for the movements of the other planets.

Nicholas Copernicus, **On the Revolutions of the Heavenly Bodies,** as quoted in A.E.E. McKenzie, **Major Achievements of Science** (New York: Cambridge University Press, 1960), Vol. II, pp. 5-6. Language simplified.

Cicero (106-43 B.C.) was a Roman lawyer, philosopher, and essayist. Plutarch, who died c. 120 A.D., was a Greek essayist and biographer. Philolaus (second half of the fifth century B.C.), Pythagoras (582-507 B.C.), and Heraclides (fourth century B.C.), were all Greek philosophers.

▶Do you feel that everyone has the right to challenge accepted beliefs? How should people go about trying to change beliefs they do not accept?

Two Letters by Galileo

Galileo Galilei, an Italian scientist who lived from 1564 to 1642, attacked many of Aristotle's teachings, including Aristotle's theory that heavy weights fall faster than light ones. In 1609 Galileo built a telescope and discovered the moons of Jupiter. This and other observations upheld Copernicus' theory, and Galileo soon published his findings. However, in 1616 the Church denounced the heliocentric theory and told Galileo not to teach it. Nevertheless, in 1632 he published another work in which he advanced the theory. Galileo was then called before the Court of the Inquisition in Rome where he denied his belief publicly. He lived his last years outside Florence working quietly at his studies. The following excerpts from Galileo's letters describe the problems he faced and the advantages he enjoyed.

A LETTER TO MADAME CHRISTINA OF LORRAINE, GRAND DUCHESS OF TUSCANY

McKenzie, **Major Achievements of Science**, Vol. II, p. 8, copyright © 1960. Reprinted by permission of the publisher, Cambridge University Press. Language simplified.

Some years ago, I discovered in the heavens many things that had not been seen before our own age. Because they were new and because what I saw contradicted some of the commonly accepted ideas about the physical world, a large number of professors rose up against me—as if I had placed these new things in the sky with my own hands in order to upset nature and overturn the sciences.

These men are still resolved to destroy me and anything that is mine by any means they can. They know I believe that the sun stands motionless in the center of the universe and that the planets revolve around it. They know I believe the earth rotates on its axis and revolves in an orbit around the sun along with the other heavenly orbs. They know also that I support my position by not only refuting the arguments of Ptolemy and Aristotle, but by producing many arguments that explain my position. They realize that my ideas contradict commonly accepted beliefs, but since they cannot defend their position with science, they defend it by appealing to the authority of the Bible.

▶ How should people who hold to accepted beliefs go about trying to defend and preserve them?

First, they have tried to make people believe that my ideas are contrary to the Bible and therefore, heretical. I admit that it is both pious and prudent to say that the Bible is always true—when the true meaning of the words is understood. But I believe nobody will deny that the Bible is often vague and that the words of the Scriptures carry hidden meanings. Hence, to rely upon only the words of the Bible might lead us to error. For the sake of those who wish to understand these hidden meanings, wise men must explain the true sense of these passages.

A LETTER TO COSIMO II DE MEDICI, GRAND DUKE OF TUSCANY

Stillman Drake, **Discoveries and Opinions of Galileo** (New York: Doubleday & Co., 1957), pp. 24-25. Language simplified.

In ancient times, Caesar Augustus named a star after his uncle, Julius Caesar. This star appeared during Augustus' reign, but unfortunately it disappeared in a brief time. (The star was one of those heavenly bodies that the Greeks and Romans called comets.) But we are able to read the heavens far more accurately. No sooner had your immortal graces begun to shine on earth when we saw bright stars in the heavens that celebrated your virtues for all time. Behold, then, four stars that will bear your famous name. They do not belong to the millions of unnoticed fixed stars. Rather they belong to the bright ranks of the planets. They move about the most noble Jupiter, as if they were sons of the planet.

It pleased Almighty God to have me teach you mathematics four years ago. Since then it has been clear that it is divine will that I serve Your Highness. As a result I have received your generosity and help. Who could wonder, then, that my heart seeks day and night to find some way to let you know how grateful I am to you? And so, most serene Cosimo, since I discovered these stars while you were my patron, I have decided to name them with the august name of your family. I have called them the Medicean Stars.

The Charter of the Royal Society

During the 1640's, many English scientists began to meet to share their ideas. King Charles II granted them the following charter in 1662.

We have long resolved to extend not only the boundaries of our empire, but also those of the arts and sciences. Therefore, we look with favor upon all forms of learning, but we especially wish to encourage those philosophical studies which use experiments to shape a new philosophy or correct the old. In order that such studies, which have never been brilliant in any part of the world, may shine brightest among the English people:

Know ye that we have granted and declared that from henceforth and forever there shall be a society, consisting of a president, council, and fellows, which shall be called the Royal Society. The studies of this society are to promote the sciences of natural things and useful arts by means of experiments.

And further, for the improvement of the experiments, arts, and sciences, we have granted that the Royal Society shall be allowed to meet and share information and knowledge with anyone, strangers and foreigners included. And they may not be interrupted, disturbed, or molested by anyone. Provided, however, that the Royal Society shall confine such meetings to matters philosophical, mathematical, or mechanical.

The Record of the Royal Society of London, 3rd ed. (London: The Royal Society, 1912), pp. 59, 67-68. Language simplified.

32 THE SIGNIFICANCE OF THE SCIENTIFIC REVOLUTION

The discoveries of Copernicus and Galileo represented a revolt against traditional beliefs. Their theories and calculations destroyed the neat image of an earth-centered universe taught by ancient and medieval authorities. Other scientists confirmed and expanded their findings. But no satisfactory explanation existed of how this universe operated until the great English scientist, Sir Isaac Newton, provided one. Building on the work of those before him, Newton formulated the law of gravitation showing that objects or masses attract each other. The force of this attraction, gravity, holds the solar system together around the sun. Newton saw the world as a great machine operating according to unchanging laws. The effects of this view of the world were to be long and far-reaching.

Copernicus, Galileo, and Newton speculated about the nature of the universe. Other people considered different scientific questions and made further discoveries in astronomy, physics, and mathematics. In their search for answers about the natural world, all these scientists formulated hypotheses and tested them for accuracy. In so doing, they developed the scientific method of investigation.

Ancient and medieval philosophers had stressed deductive reasoning. In deductive reasoning, one begins with a general statement of an assumed truth and from it draws conclusions about specifics.

Francis Bacon gave one of the first formal statements of scientific reasoning in his *Novum Organum*. Bacon, a contemporary of Galileo, was an English philosopher, essayist, and statesman. By collecting data about natural phenomenon and comparing them, he hoped to discover general laws that govern nature. He used so-called inductive reasoning —going from specifics to general laws—and laid the basis for scientific investigations.

176

Reading 32 contains selections from the writings of Sir Isaac Newton and Francesco Redi, a little-known Italian scientist. Newton explains the principles of the scientific method, and Redi describes his studies of insects found in decayed meat. Think about the following questions as you read:

1. According to Newton, how can one discover the truth about nature? What method did Redi use? How do their methods compare with those of St. Thomas Aquinas and Roger Bacon?
2. Why did Newton and Redi pursue scientific research? How do their purposes compare with those of the medieval scientists?

Sir Isaac Newton on the Scientific Method

Besides the law of gravitation, Sir Isaac Newton (1642-1727) formulated laws about light and color. He also discovered the branch of mathematics called calculus at about the same time as a German mathematician. In the following selections from two of his works, Principia Mathematica *and* Opticks, *Newton explains his method of discovering natural laws.*

PRINCIPIA MATHEMATICA, 1687

In science, we develop our theories from the phenomena we observe, and afterwards we develop general theories for all similar phenomena by inductive reasoning. This was how the laws of motion and gravitation were discovered. And even though we cannot determine why bodies gravitate toward each other, it is enough to know that they are attracted to each other—to know that gravity really does exist and acts according to the laws we have explained. Gravity accounts for all the motions of the planets and of our sea.

Sir Isaac Newton, Principia Mathematica, Andrew Motte, trans. (New York: Daniel Adee, 1848), pp. 506-507. Language simplified.

OPTICKS, 1704

In natural philosophy, we must investigate difficult problems with the scientific method before we make our conclusions. This method consists of experimenting and observing and in building up conclusions by inductive reasoning. Inductive reasoning is the best way to form general conclusions about the nature of things. As long as the general theory explains all the phenomena that are similar to the specific one, the general conclusion can be accepted without qualifications. But if any exceptions to the theory should be observed, then the theory must be modified.

Newton, Opticks, as quoted in Great Books of the Western World (Chicago: Encylopaedia Britannica, 1952), Vol. XXXIV, p. 543. Language simplified.

►Do you think the scientific method should be the only method used to discover truth? Why?

Francesco Redi Describes His Experiments with Decayed Meat

Until the seventeenth century, most men believed that flies and other insects came from decayed meat. Both Aristotle and the Old Testament supported this theory. Francesco Redi, an Italian scientist, discussed this theory in Generation of Insects, *published in 1668. In the following selection, he explains the method of investigation he used to test and disprove the traditional view.*

Dissecting equipment

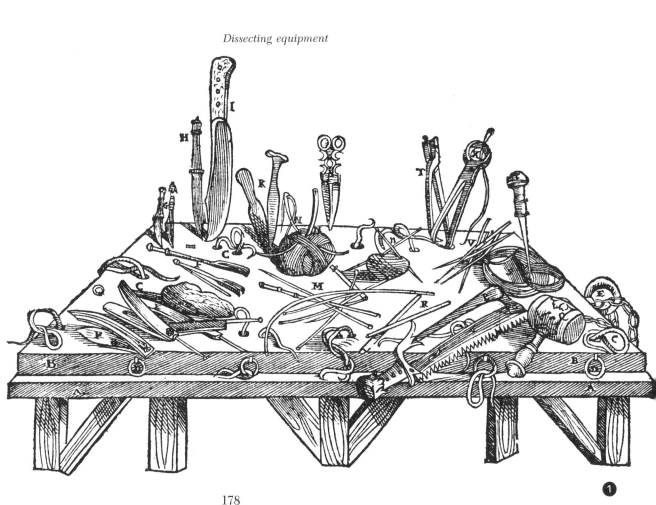

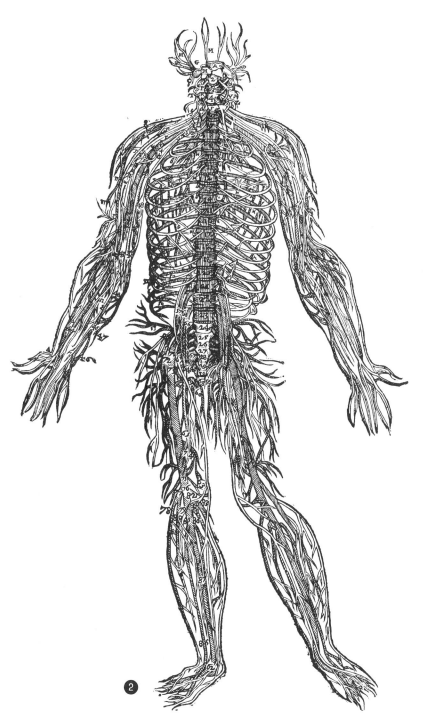

In 1543 a Flemish physician named Andreas Vesalius published a book from which the pictures on these two pages were taken. Like Redi, Vesalius believed in experimentation and careful observation. How might his work have contributed to the development of modern medicine?

Spinal nervous system

Francesco Redi, **Generation of Insects,** as quoted in Raymond Phineas Stearns, **Pageant of Europe,** rev. ed. (New York: Harcourt Brace Jovanovich, Inc., 1961), pp. 355-356, copyright © 1947, copyright © 1961 by Harcourt Brace Jovanovich, Inc. Reprinted by permission. Language simplified.

Through many observations, I am inclined to believe that all living things born in times past and born now come from the seeds of the parents. I do not believe that decaying meat and other putrid [rotten] matter produce insects, but I believe that they provide a place for insects to nest. And in order that you will see well the truth of what I say, I shall now talk of my observations of these insects.

At the beginning of June, I had three serpents killed. As soon as they were dead, I put them in an open box to decay. Not long after, I noticed they were all covered with worms . . . . Even the naked eye could see the worms grow larger as they devoured the meat. From one day to another, as I could observe, the number increased . . . . [After] eating all except the bones, all escaped through a little hole that I made, without my finding where they went. On June 11, I put in three others of the same snakes. After three days, I saw worms which increased in numbers and size, but they were not all the same color . . . . After they had consumed the flesh, they sought to escape, but I had closed all the [holes]. I observed on the nineteenth of the same month that some of the large and small ones had . . . [stopped moving] and had taken a form similar to an egg. On the twenty-first all had taken that form. All were white at the beginning, then they became rather red. Some remained red, others became dark . . . . I separated the red eggs and put them in glass vases well covered with paper, and on the eighth day from every red egg came a fly . . . of a vivid green and marvelously bright . . . . From the black eggs after fourteen days came large and black striped flies, with hairy stomachs and red skins, of the type we see daily buzzing about meat . . . .

I began to wonder if all the worms [did not come] from the flies only, and not from the putrid flesh; and I was confirmed . . . by the fact that I had always seen on the meats before they were infected flies of the same species that afterward were hatched. But my wondering would have been in vain if experimenting had not confirmed it. In the middle of July, I put in four flasks, a snake, some fish, four eels, ... and a cut of veal, and covered the mouths well with paper and string and sealed tightly; then in bottles I put the same meats and left the mouths open. Not much time passed until the fish and meat of these second bottles became infested [with worms], and in these could be seen flies entering and leaving at will; but in the closed bottles I have not seen a worm.

FOR THOUGHT:

How are the methods of Newton and Redi related to inquiry techniques in the social studies?

33 THE BIRTH OF
MODERN SCIENCE

A HISTORICAL ESSAY

The scientific revolution began when many forces came together during the sixteenth century. The Renaissance had helped to turn the attention of western people away from the spiritual world and toward the world about them. The Reformation had weakened the medieval religious order. Explorers had traveled all over the world and shattered traditional ideas about the earth. Powerful monarchs had begun to upset feudal society. Mercantilism and the expanding economy had shifted the center of economic life away from self-sufficient manors. And scholars had revived the ideas of the past, using the themes of Greek humanism to create a new social order.

This new age encouraged people to challenge ancient ideas about the physical world. As a result, the pace of scientific discovery quickened. Each decade saw important new scientific advances. Most of the new knowledge came in the fields of astronomy, physics, and mathematics. Comparable developments in biology and chemistry did not take place until the nineteenth century. Despite its limited range, however, the new science of the sixteenth and seventeenth centuries produced many more discoveries than any earlier age.

Only a few learned people understood the findings of the new science. Most Europeans distrusted science because it challenged the traditional view of man as the center of God's universe. Powerful leaders in the universities and churches tried to prevent the spread of the new findings. Religious wars and witch-burnings swept Europe during both the sixteenth and seventeenth centuries. Even most of the humanists, who did so much to shape Renaissance attitudes, were hostile to science and its new methods. But nothing could hold back the new ideas.

The scientific revolution began in Poland with a Roman Catholic churchman, Nicholas Copernicus. Copernicus attacked the geocentric, or earth-centered, system described by the Greek astronomer, Ptolemy, around 150 A.D. According to Ptolemy's system, the planets, the sun, and the moon revolve around the earth in a complicated system of circles within circles.

Copernicus found this ancient astronomy inadequate in two ways. First, he could not believe that God had put together such a clumsy piece of heavenly clockwork. Second, he knew that the observed position of some of the planets did not agree with their position as predicted

Religious persecution of supposed witches began early in the fourteenth century. Many who were interested in scientific experimentation were convicted of witchcraft and executed in the sixteenth and seventeenth centuries.

181

by the Ptolemaic system. Copernicus searched further into the records of the ancient astronomers. He found a few who thought that the universe was heliocentric, or sun-centered. Some even claimed that the earth had a double motion—a daily rotation around its axis and an annual revolution, or orbit, around the sun.

In 1543, after many years of study, Copernicus finally published *On the Revolutions of the Heavenly Bodies.* It caused little stir at first, although some of its readers denounced it. They could not believe that the earth moved at a great speed through the heavens. If so, why didn't they fall off? Some of this opposition to Copernicus' scheme was justified. He kept the ancient idea that the planets revolved around the sun in circles, all moving at the same speed. Thus his system was not much more reliable in predicting the location of the planets than Ptolemy's was.

Gradually, however, the basic principles of Copernicus' work won support from a growing number of people. Printing presses spread the idea of a heliocentric universe all over Europe. Other astronomers conducted investigations that supported Copernicus' work. In Denmark, Tycho Brahe made detailed observations of the planets. Brahe, however, never accepted the Copernican system in full. Brahe's assistant, Johannes Kepler, did accept the Copernican system, and he used Brahe's data to make new calculations. Kepler determined that the planets do not move in circular orbits or at a uniform speed, but in elliptical orbits and at different speeds depending on their distance from the sun. Galileo's observations of the moons of Jupiter further supported heliocentrism. Both Aristotle's beliefs and common-sense observation that "saw" the sun "move" around the earth had clearly been proved wrong.

Just as the Aristotelian-Ptolemaic view of the universe gave way to Copernicus' system, Aristotle's mechanics gave way to those of later scientists. Aristotle based his ideas about motion on deductions, not experiments. Later scientists conducted experiments and discovered mathematical laws that proved most of Aristotle's ideas about mechanics wrong. For example, Simon Stevin, a self-taught Dutch mathematician and military engineer, did an experiment that disproved Aristotle's belief that heavy bodies fall faster than light ones. Stevin wrote:

Mechanics is the branch of physics that deals with motion and the effects of forces on material bodies.

> The experiment against Aristotle is this. Let us take two leaden balls, one ten times heavier than the other. Allow them to fall together from a height of thirty feet upon a board from which a sound is clearly given out and it shall appear that the lighter does not take ten times longer to fall than the heavier, but that they fall so equally upon the board that both noises appear to be the same sound.

This picture shows the medieval view of the sky as a star-studded globe through which a lucky person might poke his or her head and see into heaven. If you held this point of view, how might you have reacted to the ideas of Copernicus and other astronomers?

183

Galileo showed conclusively that Aristotle's belief about falling objects was false. He developed a precise mathematical law that explains the rate of speed at which objects fall. But Galileo's major contribution to science was his careful working out of the relationship among hypotheses, experimentation, and mathematics. In his experiments, he did not use anything that could not be reduced to measurable quantities and expressed in numbers. In addition, he rejected explanations based on magic or religion.

Kepler tried to discover why each planet remains in orbit about the sun. Although he understood how the planets move, he never discovered the physical force behind this movement. He thought that the sun sent out some sort of magnetic force, driving the planets in their eternal orbits. But Kepler's work, together with Galileo's, enabled Sir Isaac Newton to develop the theory of gravitation which explains the motion of the planets and all physical objects.

At about the time of Galileo, René Déscartes, a French scientist, made important advances in mathematics and mechanics. Probably his greatest scientific contribution was analytical geometry, a combination of algebra and geometry. He also added much to the study of physics.

Déscartes went beyond the study of science to investigate philosophy as well. He came to believe that all physical life was based on unchanging mathematical laws and could be explained by using mathematics. In the philosophical system he built around his belief, Déscartes attempted to explain man. He said, people think and because they think, they exist. Déscartes' work, added to that of all the other scientists of the sixteenth and seventeenth centuries, served as the basis for Newton's accomplishments.

The work of Sir Isaac Newton brought to a climax the first phase of the scientific revolution. By using the work of Copernicus, Stevin, Kepler, Déscartes, Galileo, and other scientists, he developed the theory of gravitation. This theory states that every particle of matter in the universe attracts every other particle with a force equal to the product of their masses and inversely proportional to the square of the distance between them. For example, an object such as an apple is attracted to the earth and therefore "falls down" to the earth when released from its twig. But the earth is also attracted to the apple, and, indeed, the earth "falls up" to the apple by a tiny amount. In like manner, the moon, the earth, and the sun attract each other. This mutual attraction keeps the universe moving.

Newton's theory of gravitation combined a great mass of evidence into one theory that gave a precise explanation of a mechanical world. This mechanistic view of nature set the course for studies in the physical sciences well into the nineteenth century.

The scientists of the sixteenth and seventeeth centuries gave human-kind an even greater gift than new knowledge. They developed a modern scientific method. Most medieval thinkers reasoned deductively. They started with a general idea often taken from the Bible or from an ancient scholar. For example, they examined the idea, "God made man in His own image." Then they reasoned from it: "If God made man in His own image, man must be the center of the universe. Hence, the sun must circle around the earth."

In the place of this deductive logic, the scientists of the sixteenth and seventeenth centuries developed ways of reasoning using inquiry. First they identified a problem. Then as they examined the problem, they developed hypotheses or possible solutions. They gathered evidence to support or reject each hypothesis by observation and experimentation. Then they drew conclusions, which they often expressed in mathematical terms. As a final step, they developed theories—bodies of carefully organized knowledge that explain a wide variety of generalizations and facts and that can be used to predict. The theory of gravitation is an excellent example. This scientific method has probably done more to change the way in which people live and think than any other single development in human history.

Several organizations such as the British Royal Society and the French Academy of Science, were established in the seventeenth century to promote scientific activity. But on the whole, scientific developments affected only a well-educated minority. Most people continued to believe what their senses told them and to keep traditional ideas about God, nature, and their relationship to them. In time, however, the new scientific investigations had an important effect on western society. Newton's theory of gravitation stripped away the mystery of God's universe for many people. People saw the world as a machine created by God, the Great Engineer. Once He had set the machine in motion, it would operate forever according to unchanging laws. This idea altered forever what historians call the climate of opinion. People who accepted the ideas of the new science could not continue to believe in witchcraft and in miracles.

The new science also caused western people to reexamine themselves and their values. The philosophers of the eighteenth century, the so-called Age of Enlightenment or Reason, had absorbed the teachings of the Newtonians. They tried to find a philosophy that would explain society in terms of the natural laws that regulate it. They believed that if people could discover these laws and change their society to fit them, they would reach perfection and happiness.

One example, to be examined in a later chapter of this book, may make the point clear. In 1690 John Locke, a contemporary of Newton,

▶Do you believe that human society can ever reach perfection?

185

published *Two Treatises of Government.* Locke believed that God gave humankind certain natural rights, namely the rights to life, liberty, and property. People developed governments to protect these natural rights. If a government tried to take these rights away, its citizens had the right to revolt. This argument—an outgrowth of Newton's ideas about natural laws governing the universe—became the theoretical justification for both the Glorious Revolution in England and the American Revolution.

To the men of the Enlightenment, the way of scientific progress indicated the way of social progress. They adopted the scientific method and applied it to all issues—religious, political, economic, and social. They attacked existing institutions in a search for natural law, freedom, reason, and humanitarianism. Their efforts helped to create the modern world in which scientific reasoning plays such an important role.

Individual and Group Activities for Chapter 7

For full descriptions of these activities, turn to the **Student Book of Activities and Readings** included among the materials for individual and group activities.

Activity 7A: Interview and essay on a modern scientist's work (individual)
Interview a scientist to find out what he does. Then write an essay in which you describe his work and its place in contemporary life.

Activity 7B: Comparision of modern science and seventeenth-century science (individual)
Read through the Study Guide accompanying this activity which has been designed to help you compare modern science and seventeenth-century science. Then select and read several articles from recent issues of news magazines and answer the questions on the Study Guide. Finally try to present the differences between seventeenth-century science and modern science in an interesting way, perhaps with a painting, a collage, or a short story.

Economic Growth
in a Market Economy

STATING THE ISSUE

The values, folkways, and institutions that dominated Europe during the Middle Ages gave way to many pressures for change. In one of the most dramatic of all these changes, Europeans created new ways to answer the basic economic questions. Medieval Europeans relied on tradition to guide their economic decisions, but later Europeans turned to the marketplace.

In a market economy, the consumer decides what goods will be produced, how they will be produced, and who will receive them. If consumers flock to buy one style of shoes, manufacturers will produce more of that style and stop producing less popular ones. In order to compete successfully, they will combine human, natural, and capital resources as efficiently as they can. Manufacturers will divide the income among themselves, their workers, and the suppliers of natural and capital resources according to the contribution each one makes.

The change from a traditional to a market economy took place over many centuries. It involved both agriculture and industry. Both the social system and the political system contributed to the pace of economic change. Whole societies had to accept new ways before the market could dominate economic life.

The economy began to grow at a more rapid rate during the latter half of the eighteenth century, particularly in Great Britain. There a unique combination of economic, political, and social changes led to rapidly accelerating economic growth. Later, new cities were built around factories, mills, and mines. Modern industrialized, urbanized society had been born.

Chapter 8 investigates both the slow development of the market economy and the dramatic jump in economic growth during the eighteenth century. The readings provide evidence to help you see why these developments took place.

1095-1291	Crusades open trade between East and Europe.
c. 1300	Toulouse revises guild laws.
1662-1683	Jean Baptiste Colbert serves as Louis XIV's finance minister.
1700-1845	Six million acres of British farmland are enclosed.
1709	Abraham Darby reduces coal to coke.
1754	Royal Society for the Encouragement of Art, Manufactures, and Commerce begins.
1761	Bridgewater Canal opens.
1769	James Watt perfects steam engine. Richard Arkwright patents water frame.
1775	James Watt and Matthew Boulton open steam engine factory.
1776	Adam Smith publishes **The Wealth of Nations.**
1799	Unions are outlawed in Britain.
1830	Twenty thousand miles of roads are built in Britain.

34 THE EMERGENCE OF THE MARKET

    Europeans did not consciously invent the market economy as Thomas Edison invented the electric light bulb. Rather, many political, economic, and social changes gradually pushed western man toward making economic decisions in a different way. Many of the values and institutions of European life had to change before the market economy could develop.

    During the Middle Ages traditional ways dominated economic life and prevented the development of a market economy. A market economy must have free laborers who can move from place to place seeking the best jobs. Most medieval Europeans, however, were bound to the land as serfs. The development of a market economy depends upon centers of commerce where goods can be traded. During the Middle Ages, few Europeans lived in cities where trade could take place. If a market is to develop, the society must be able to move goods from place to place easily. In medieval times, pirates, wars, tolls, and taxes on commerce made transporting goods difficult. Finally, if it is to develop a market economy, the society must value material wealth and give high social status to those who produce wealth. Medieval Christians valued heavenly reward above earthly gain and put merchants in a low place on the social scale.

By the eleventh and twelfth centuries, Europe had already begun to remove those controls on the economy that had prevented the rise of a market system. As the centuries passed, changes in European culture picked up speed. By the eighteenth century, the European economy resembled the model of a market economy more than it resembled the traditional model. The documents in Reading 34 will help you develop a hypothesis about what caused the changes in the European economic system. As you study these documents, let the following questions guide you:

1. What changes in the political and social systems of Europe helped the market economy to develop?
2. How did changes in values in Europe influence the development of the market economy?

A Serf Makes
a New Contract

Inflation created a need for money in the late Middle Ages, and many lords worked out new contracts with their serfs. In return for cash, the lords released the serfs from their obligations. Following is an example of such a contract from 1278.

Let everyone know that we have freed from the yoke of serfdom, William, the son of Richard of Wythington. Previously William has been our serf, along with all of his children and all of his possessions. Now, neither we nor those who follow us as lord of this manor shall be able to require services upon our land from William and his children.

William will receive the house and land he now occupies by paying to us and our successors forty shillings each year, rather than pay the old manorial rents.

James Harvey Robinson, Readings in European History (Boston: Ginn and Co., 1906), Vol. I, pp. 405-406. Language simplified.

Toulouse Revises Its Guild Regulations

Medieval guild regulations turned men away from the trades, blocked new production techniques, banned the sale of goods from other towns, and even ruled on the morality of the guildsmen. (See Chapter 2, Reading 11.) In time, however, town governments lifted many of these restrictions. The following selection from the early fourteenth century gives an example of revised guild regulations.

Sister Mary Ambrose, Statutes on Cloth-making, as quoted in **Essays in Medieval Life and Thought,** John H. Mundy et al., eds. (New York: Biblo & Tannen, 1955), pp. 172-180. Translated by John M. Good.

A number of worthy men of Toulouse [France] have come to the councilmen of the city complaining of many conflicts between the drapers, weavers, carders, and finishers of woolen cloth.

Therefore, the councilmen of Toulouse, having conferred with many experts and members of these trades, issue the following ordinance.

All weavers may work at their profession, day and night, wherever it pleases them in the city or the suburb.

Moreover, these weavers may sell their cloth at any price that pleases them.

All apprentices who complete their residence with master weavers may work in their own workshops or wherever it pleases them, so long as they do their work honestly and well.

All men and women who make cloth in their homes may hire weavers to work for them.

Colbert and the Merchants of Marseilles

The files in the office of Colbert were filled with letters like this one to the merchants of Marseilles in 1664.

Robinson, **Readings in European History,** Vol. II, pp. 279-280. Language simplified.

A livre was a French coin, first issued in gold, then in silver, and finally in copper. It was discontinued in 1794.

Considering how helpful it would be to this land to reestablish foreign and domestic commerce, we have decided to establish a council devoted to questions of trade.

We also inform you that we are budgeting a million livres each year out of the royal treasury to encourage manufactures and increase navigation.

We are working constantly to abolish all tolls which are collected on the rivers.

We have already spent more than a million livres on the repair of roads, and we shall spend more.

We will take money from the royal treasury to help those who wish to reestablish old industries or begin new ones.

All merchants who trade on the sea will receive gifts of money for each ton of merchandise they export or import if they buy ships or build new ones.

▶Do you feel that all traditional practices and values necessarily prevent change? What examples can you give?

A Comment on English Society

Daniel Defoe (1660?-1731) is best known for his novel, Robinson Crusoe. *But Defoe was also a keen observer of English society and a fine example of the well-to-do middle-class man who had achieved social prominence. The following selection is taken from* The Complete English Tradesman, *written between 1725 and 1727.*

Since we engage in so much trade, it is no wonder that the tradesmen in England become noblemen and country gentlemen. Nor should we wonder that the gentlemen of the best families marry tradesmen's daughters, and apprentice their younger sons to tradesmen. How often these younger sons make enough money in trade to buy the estates of their elder brothers, who had inherited the lands of their fathers and then wasted their inheritance by high living.

Unlike other countries, gentlemen can be merchants in England. In fact, trade in England makes gentlemen. After a generation or two, the tradesmen's children or grandchildren become as good as gentlemen, members of Parliament, statesmen, judges, bishops, and noblemen.

Daniel Defoe, **The Complete English Tradesman,** as quoted in **The Works of Daniel Defoe,** John S. Nimmo, ed. (Edinburgh, Scotland: William P. Nimmo, 1869), pp. 548-590. Language simplified.

Richard Baxter on Labor and Riches

Richard Baxter (1615-1691) was the most famous Presbyterian clergyman of his time. Presbyterianism was founded by a Scottish clergyman, John Knox, in the mid-sixteenth century. It is essentially an outgrowth of Calvinism. Baxter developed Calvin's economic ideas (Chapter 4, Reading 19) in a book called A Christian Directory. *The importance of these ideas is apparent when they are compared with those of St. Thomas Aquinas (Chapter 2, Reading 11).*

God has commanded you to work for your daily bread, and not to live on the sweat of others. He that will not work must be forbidden to eat. Indeed, it is necessary for the health of our bodies, which will grow diseased if we are idle. And if our body becomes diseased, so does our soul.

Richard Baxter, **A Christian Directory** (London: 1673), pp. 108, 111, 378. Language simplified.

▶Do you think there are cases in which people who do not work should be given support?

191

Moneylenders

These pictures show several scenes from early modern Europe. Which of these scenes would have held back the development of a market economy? Which of them would have contributed to the development of a market economy?

Serfs working on a manor

A town market

An apprentice mason and an apprentice carpenter display their skills before the head of the guild. He will decide if they are qualified to join the guild as master craftsmen.

193

Merchant ships

Finally, it is lawful and right to save money and become wealthy. To seek riches solely for pleasures of the flesh is wrong. But you may do those things which will most likely give you success and lawful gain. You are supposed to improve all of the talents your Master has given you. You do not fulfill your calling if you choose the least profitable method of gaining riches.

The Wealth of Nations

Adam Smith wrote The Wealth of Nations *in 1776. This classic volume describes the way in which a market economy worked to produce goods and services without government interference.*

Adam Smith, **The Wealth of Nations** (New York: American Home Library Co., 1902), Vol. I, pp. 107-112. Language simplified.

The sole purpose of all production is to provide the best possible goods to the consumer at the lowest possible price. Society should assist producers of goods and services only to the extent that assisting them benefits the consumer.

The price charged to the consumer for any commodity goes to pay for three things: rent for land or the cost of producing raw materials, the wages of the workers who produce the commodity, and the profits of the person who owns the machinery used to make it and to carry it to the market. When the price of an article is neither more nor less than the total cost of these three elements, it is sold at what may be called its natural price. The commodity is then sold for precisely what it is worth, or for what it really cost the person who brought it to market.

If too much of a product is brought to market, the market price falls below the natural price. And the amount of money needed to pay for the use of land, raw materials, labor, and profit is not received in full. Therefore, those who rent land and sell raw materials will not allow all of their goods to be used to produce the article, fewer laborers will work, and the owners of machinery and carriers will not use all of their stock in the production and transportation of the article, since none of them obtained the cost of their contribution to its production. When this happens, less of the commodity will be produced. Eventually, there will only be enough of the article produced to satisfy the demand, and its market price will return to its natural price.

On the other hand, if not enough of a commodity is brought to market, the market price rises above the natural price. Those who are given money for their land and their raw materials, for their labor, and for their profits will be paid more than what they consider to be their costs. Therefore, those who supply land and raw materials will prepare more of their resources for making the article, more laborers will work to produce it, and the owners of machinery and carriers will use more of their stock to produce and transport it. When this happens, more of the commodity will be produced. Eventually, there will be enough to satisfy the demand, and its market price will return to its natural price.

FOR THOUGHT:

You have been reading about a variety of changes in Europe's political, economic, and social systems and in the values of Europe's people. Could the market economy have developed if any of these changes had not taken place?

35 POLITICAL AND SOCIAL CHANGES

During the last years of the eighteenth century, economic development in Great Britain jumped ahead. The dramatic growth of production on farms and in factories took place because of unusual political, social, and intellectual forces. An economy cannot grow rapidly if the government takes little interest in economic affairs. Britain's government encouraged economic growth. In similar fashion, the social and intellectual forces of a nation must also contribute to its economic development.

In most countries, economic growth depends on a small elite—the people with the most prestige and power in a society. Members of an elite can make changes in political, social, and intellectual conditions. Usually the elite make these changes through the government. In some countries, such as Japan, the traditional ruling class decided to throw out old ways. In other countries, such as the Soviet Union, a group of revolutionaries seized power and forced the society to industrialize rapidly. In a third group of countries, such as the United States, business people who wanted a larger share of the market provided most of the stimulus for economic growth. But even these men and women depended upon the government to pass favorable laws.

An elite cannot make changes in a relatively democratic society unless the rest of the population also wants the changes. Hence, the social structure of a nation and its intellectual life influence economic expansion. By the late eighteenth century, the elite in Great Britain lived in a society in which large groups of people were ready for change.

Reading 35 explores the political, social, and intellectual background of late eighteenth-century Britain. As you read, think about the following questions:

1. What kinds of things did the government do to encourage economic growth?
2. How did the system of social classes and the intellectual life of the nation contribute to economic growth?

A Nobleman Builds a Canal

In 1774 John Campbell, a Scottish author, published A Political Survey of Great Britain *in which he described the efforts of Parliament to encourage many projects throughout Britain.*

John Campbell, **A Political Survey of Great Britain** (London: 1774), pp. 263-264. Language simplified.

This canal, built by the Duke of Bridgewater, was the first in England. It cut in half his cost of transporting coal from his mines to Manchester.

A nobleman decided to build a canal to carry coals from Worsley Bridge to Manchester. Since the canal would be used by the public as well as by himself, an act of Parliament, passed in 1759, allowed him to do this work. With the building of this canal, the value of canals was more clearly understood.

As a result, it was decided to carry the canal over the Mersey and Bolland rivers and to extend it to where the river becomes naturally navigable. This extension would open a passage to Liverpool. The powers needed to carry out this design made a third act of Parliament necessary.

The act was passed after the inhabitants of the country through which the proposed canal was to pass, who would benefit from it, petitioned Parliament. The duke agreed to take upon himself the whole expense of building the canal, without asking for an increase in the rates charged to use it.

The canal, originally designed for the convenience of the duke, now became a great public utility. The extension of the canal excited an interest in building other canals in bordering counties.

Defoe on the Roads of the Midland Counties

The following selection is from the appendix to Daniel Defoe's A Tour Through the Whole Island of Great Britain, *which*

196

appeared between 1724 and 1727. This excerpt is typical of Defoe's efforts to inform the British of ways to strengthen the economy.

I have taken notice of bad road conditions in the Midland counties because these counties carry on a great deal of trade with London and with each other.

Because road conditions were so bad, the people of the counties brought them to the attention of Parliament. Parliament has created turnpike trusts to solve the problems. These trusts are allowed to charge tolls for use of the road by carriages, cattle, and travelers on horseback. The tolls are very small—a horse and rider is charged a penny, a coach three pence, a cart four pence, a wagon six pence, and so on. Cattle are charged by the head. Although the rates vary from place to place, none of the people who pay the tolls think the rates are too high. The benefits they obtain from good road conditions make up for the small charge.

Daniel Defoe, **A Tour Through the Whole Island of Great Britain** (London: G. Strahan, 1727), Vol. II, pp. 179-180. Language simplified.

Defoe overstates his point here since there was considerable opposition to the turnpikes up to about the middle of the eighteenth century.

An Enclosure Act

Medieval organization of British estates continued well into the eighteenth century. Practices such as farming narrow strips of land and grazing cattle on common pastures prevented landlords from introducing crop rotation and other farming techniques that required large fields. In order to bring more land under their control, the landlords attempted to enclose, or fence off, the fields for their own use. But many medieval contracts still upheld the rights of the tenant farmers.

Sometimes the landlords were able to make agreements with the tenants to buy their plots. Sometimes they simply expelled the tenants. But when tenants refused to give up their ancient rights, the landlords turned to Parliament for enclosure acts. Between 1700 and 1845, more than 4,000 acts enclosed 6 million acres of British farmland.

January 26, 1769

A petition was read to the House of Commons from the chief owners of land in Chipping Norton and Salford in the County of Oxford. Since there are several open and common fields which are of small advantage to the landowners in these two parishes, the petitioners asked Parliament to consider a bill to enclose these lands, with each landowner receiving a just share. The petitioners declared that enclosing and dividing the lands as explained in the petition will considerably improve their respective estates.

Journals of the House of Commons (Reprinted by order of the House of Commons, 1803), Vol. XXXII, pp. 150, 239, 253, 326-327, 350. Language simplified.

T. S. Ashton, **An Economic History of England: The Eighteenth Century** (New York: Barnes & Noble, Inc., 1954), pp. 20-22. Reprinted by permission of the publisher and Methuen & Co., Ltd.

March 20, 1769

Lord Charles Spencer reported that his committee has considered the petition of the smaller landowners of Chipping Norton and has heard their legal counsel. The committee also heard the counsel of the original owners who wish to enclose the lands. The committee found that the parties concerned by the enclosure (with the exception of a very small minority) had agreed to the bill.

▶In an issue such as enclosure, there are two sides to the question. In this case, which side would you have supported? Why?

April 4, 1769

A bill for enclosing and dividing certain open and common fields in Chipping Norton and Salford in the County of Oxford was read a third time.

Resolved: That the bill pass.

English Society in the Eighteenth Century

T. S. Ashton, one of England's most respected economic historians, has been one of the strongest critics of the idea that industrialization in England brought untold suffering to millions. In this excerpt from An Economic History of England: The Eighteenth Century, *Ashton analyzes English society.*

Squires were part of the landed gentry.

English society was a class structure. . . . [But] there was no sharp distinction between those who [made] their incomes from rents and those who lived on the gains of commerce or industry. Landed families . . . put their younger sons into trade; and great proprietors busied themselves with transport and manufacture. Successful traders, manufacturers, and bankers usually sought, before they ended their days, to become country squires. They might hope to set their sons among the great of the land, or at least to marry their daughters in such a way as to ensure that their grandchildren would be ennobled . . . . Class [differences] were rungs of a ladder on which many climbed and descended. Their existence, and the differences in incomes with which they were associated, may be [offensive] to modern [feelings], but they led to [the desire to become equal]; and the . . . rungs were many and closely spaced . . . . [Class differences] were the product of centuries of history—a fact that has not been sufficiently appreciated by those . . . looking at English progress in technology and wealth.

▶Do you find the idea of social classes arranged in order from higher to lower offensive? Why, or why not?

198

The Social and
Intellectual Climate

The following selection is taken from Herbert Heaton's Economic History of Europe. *Heaton describes the changes in ideas and attitudes that encouraged economic growth in Britain during the 1700's.*

Popular interest in industrial improvement resembled the wave of curiosity and [interest in experimentation] that [swept] agriculture. Societies were set up to [encourage] technical progress. In London the Society for the Encouragement of Arts, Manufactures, and Commerce offered money, medals, and other rewards . . . .

Herbert Heaton, **Economic History of Europe,** rev. ed. (New York: Harper & Row, Publishers, Inc., 1948), abridgment of pp. 407-408, 482-483, copyright 1936, 1948 by Harper & Row, Publishers, Inc. Reprinted by permission.

▶The Society for the Encouragement of Arts, Manufacturers, and Commerce made this prize offering in 1776. Should governments today offer similar prizes to encourage economic and cultural developments? Or should such encouragement be left to private citizens and private foundations?

PREMIUMS

OFFERED BY THE

SOCIETY,

Inſtituted at **LONDON,**

FOR THE

ENCOURAGEMENT

OF

ARTS, MANUFACTURES,

AND

COMMERCE.

LONDON:

Printed by Order of the SOCIETY,

By J. BROWNE, Bridge - Street, near the City Obeliſk.

M.DCC.LXXVI.

Meanwhile, as individuals or as members of learned societies, the scientists of all nations were in touch with each other . . . . The scientists were also getting into closer touch with industry and agriculture, for their knowledge of physics and chemistry was now reaching a point where it could answer some technical questions.

The decades after 1750 were thus marked by a quickening spirit of inquiry and search for new things. Magazines, encyclopedias, dictionaries, and yearbooks chronicled new machines and methods . . . . All things seemed possible . . . .

FOR THOUGHT:

How did the political, social, and intellectual forces in Great Britain during the eighteenth century affect its economic development?

36 ECONOMIC AND TECHNOLOGICAL CHANGES

The geography of Britain favored the growth of its economy. As an island-nation, Britain had escaped the destructive effects of the major European wars. By the early 1700's, Britain produced enough grain for its 5½ million inhabitants and still had some to export. Britain also had rich coal deposits that provided a ready source of fuel. Moreover, Britain's geography aided the transportation of goods, since ships could navigate the rivers thirty miles upstream. And few hills or mountains stood in the way of the building of roads.

However, it was British inventiveness and enterprise that made use of the nation's natural advantages. For example, once James Watt perfected the steam engine, the great coal reserves could be converted into fuel to turn the wheels of industry. Coal became one of Britain's most valuable resources. Similarly, improvements in canals and roads made it possible for people and goods to move more easily from the mines and farms to the factories, cities, and ports.

Reading 36 focuses on the economic and technological changes in eighteenth-century Britain. Using these selections, you should be able to develop several hypotheses about how economic and technological changes contributed to the rapid growth of the British economy. As you read, compare the changing economic scene with the changing political and social scene. Let the following questions guide you:

1. Why were the technological improvements described by Young, Tull, and Mrs. Darby developed during this period of history?
2. How did these technological developments influence the British economy?

Arthur Young on Agriculture

Arthur Young (1741-1820) devoted his life to spreading scientific methods of farming although he himself failed miserably at farming. As he traveled throughout England and the European continent, he kept journals of new farming methods. In the following excerpt from The Farmer's Tour Through the East of England, *Young describes some of the most important agricultural developments in England.*

Arthur Young, The Farmer's Tour Through the East of England (London: Strahan & Nicoll, 1771), p. 150. Language simplified.

As I shall presently leave Norfolk, it is proper to give a slight review of the farming methods which have made the name of this county so famous in the farming world.

Norfolk is a county in eastern England.

From forty to sixty years ago, all the northern and western and part of the eastern areas of the county were sheepwalks, worth as little as six pennies an acre. The great improvements have been made by means of the following methods.

First: By enclosing without the help of Parliament.
Second: By a generous use of marl and clay.
Third: By the introduction of an excellent four-year rotation of crops.
Fourth: By growing turnips.
Fifth: By growing clover and ray grass.
Sixth: By landlords granting long leases.
Seventh: By the country being divided chiefly into large farms.

A mixture of clay and marl was spread over the soil to make it fertile.

Ray grass is used for pasture and hay.

Jethro Tull on Sowing Seed

Jethro Tull, who lived in the early 1700's, studied agricultural methods in England, France, and Italy. He developed several inventions that made farming more efficient, including a horse-drawn drilling machine that planted each seed in the ground. His writings had great influence on British agriculture.

Jethro Tull, Horse-Hoeing Husbandry or An Essay on the Principles of Vegetation and Tillage (London: A. Millar, 1751), p. 60. Language simplified.

In Wiltshire they sow the greatest quantity of seed that I have ever heard of. I am informed by the owners themselves that on some land they sow eight bushels of barley to an acre. In good years they expect one grain to produce four more. I have heard that in dry summers an acre sown with eight bushels of seed will produce only four bushels of grain at harvest.

Wiltshire was primarily a pastoral and agricultural county in southern England.

But, in drilling, the seeds all lie at the same correct depth, none deeper and none shallower than the rest. There is no danger that the seeds will be buried or uncovered. The farmer need not concern himself with these problems.

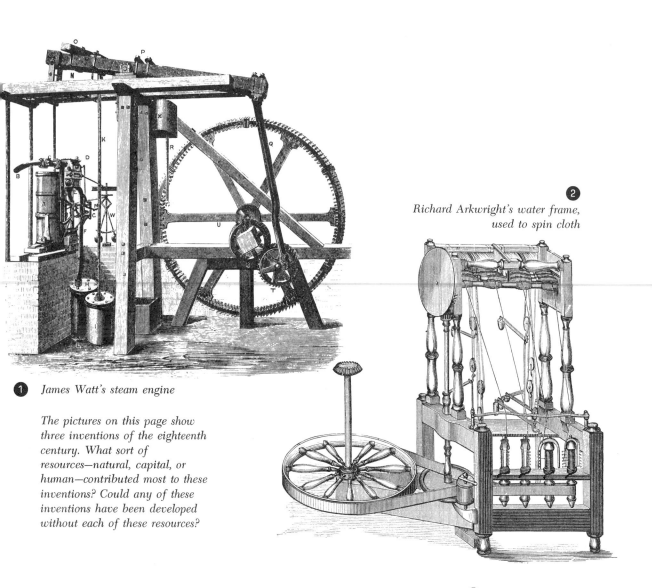

2 Richard Arkwright's water frame, used to spin cloth

1 James Watt's steam engine

The pictures on this page show three inventions of the eighteenth century. What sort of resources—natural, capital, or human—contributed most to these inventions? Could any of these inventions have been developed without each of these resources?

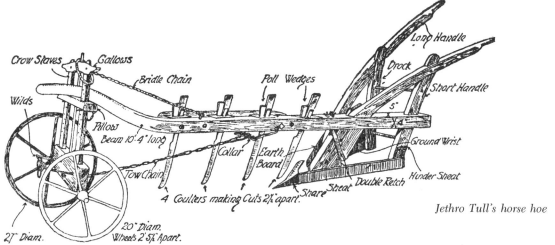

Crow Staves Gallows

Wilds

Bridle Chain

Pillow
Beam 10'4" long

Tow Chain

Poll Wedges

Collar Earth Board

4 Coulters making Cuts 2½ apart.

27" Diam.

20" Diam.
Wheels 2'5½" Apart.

Long Handle

Drock

Short Handle

S

Ground Wrist

Hinder Sheat

Sheat Double Retch

Share

Jethro Tull's horse hoe **3**

Improvements at the Darby Iron Works

In the following letter, Mrs. Abiah Darby explains how her husband's father improved his method of making iron. Abraham Darby (1677-1717) produced iron that had been smelted, or melted, together with coke. Coke is produced by removing the chemical impurities from coal that make iron brittle.

My husband's father attempted to mold and cast [shape] iron pots, etc. in sand instead of loam. Most manufacturers used loam even though it was a tedious and expensive process. Sometime later he suggested that it might be practicable to smelt iron with pit coal. He first tried with raw coal as it came out of the mines, but it did not work. Not discouraged, he had the coal coked into cinder, and then the process succeeded to his satisfaction.

Had not these discoveries and improvements been made, the iron trade would have dwindled away. Wood for charcoal became very scarce, and landed gentlemen raised the prices of cord wood [wood used for fuel] very high. Indeed, we would not have been able to get it. But after pit coal was introduced, the demand for charcoal was very much lessened and, in a few years, I believe we will not use it any more.

FOR THOUGHT:

How were the technological changes described in Reading 36 related to the political, social, and intellectual changes that were discussed in Reading 35?

English Historical Documents 1714-1783, D. B. Horn and Mary Ransome, eds. (New York: Oxford University Press, 1957), pp. 468-470. Language simplified. Reprinted by permission of Manchester University Press, publishers of T. S. Ashton, **Iron and Steel in the Industrial Revolution,** original source adapted.

Loam is a coarse molding sand used in melting and casting.

When coke came into use, many ironworks moved away from the forests and close to the coalfields.

37 THE DEVELOPMENT OF MODERN ECONOMICS

A HISTORICAL ESSAY

Three developments had to take place before a market economy could replace the traditional economic system of the Middle Ages. First, people had to use money to pay for goods and services instead of making payments in labor or in goods. Second, society had to respect making money as a legitimate goal in life instead of condemning it as people of the Middle Ages had done. Finally, the control of tradition and command over economic decision-making had to be broken.

Changes in traditional practices and values began slowly in a number of different ways. Traveling merchants weakened the self-sufficient local economies by creating a demand for all sorts of new products. These men traveled in caravans, their horses and mules loaded with goods brought from distant countries. As they moved over the countryside, the merchants stopped at towns where they took shelter near the walls surrounding the towns. In time they set up trading posts there, and new communities grew around the posts. These new trading communities were not affected by ancient manorial and guild restrictions. As a result, they developed separate laws and institutions, and they began to use money to conduct their business.

Money also began to play a part on the manors. The growing cities needed more and more food which they bought from the manors, thus bringing cash to the countryside. And the nobles living in the countryside wanted to buy some of the merchants' goods. To do so, they needed more money. As a result, they began to demand that feudal dues be paid with money rather than with bushels of wheat or dozens of eggs. They arranged to have their serfs and tenants pay them a certain sum of money—a so-called fixed cash payment—each year. But then prices rose. The grandson of a noble who had fixed his dues found that he could buy only one-third as much with the same income. As nobles grew poorer, their social status fell. At the same time, merchants and bankers became richer and their social status rose.

The Crusades encouraged the activities of the merchants and the development of new towns. Many future capitalists were able to collect enough money in the Crusades to set up businesses. The Crusades also helped to change the value system of the nobility by bringing them into contact with the dynamic cultures of the East.

The creation of larger, more stable political units also helped to produce economic change. Between the tenth and sixteenth centuries, new governments covering large areas grew up in Europe. These new governments did away with tolls, issued standard coinage, developed standard weights and measures, and encouraged manufacturing and finance. They sponsored voyages of exploration, which eventually turned the world into one vast market. Colonies flooded Europe with gold and silver that were used to make coins. These colonies gave Europeans new knowledge, new markets, and new sources of raw materials.

Changes in economic attitudes were less visible, but they were equally important. For example, Calvinists judged a person's worth by what he did on earth. They thought of the energetic merchant as a godly

Capitalism is an economic system that permits private ownership of the means of production. A capitalist is a person who invests funds in a business to produce profits.

204

person, not an evil one. The Calvinists also argued that surplus wealth should be used productively. Instead of spending their money for fighting, display, and luxuries, they spent it on capital goods—tools, factories, and mills.

An economic revolution was in the making. In the tenth century, Europeans had seldom used money. However, by the seventeenth century, money was widely used in many of the European economies. People who had money to buy goods and services made their demands known. Industry then produced *what* the market wanted. The market also determined *how* its resources should be used to produce the desired goods. The market economy based on supply and demand could shift resources into an industry and out again, as Adam Smith explained. The market economy determined where natural, capital, and human resources should be used and in what proportions. The market began to answer the basic economic questions—what goods and services to produce, how to produce them, and for whom to produce them.

The pure market economy exists only when four conditions are present: 1) a very large number of small producers, no one of which is large enough to have a significant influence on either the quantity produced or the market prices; 2) each producer making an identical or substitutable product so that consumers will form no preferences; 3) easy entrance into industries, and easy exit for those who fail in them; and 4) absence of collusion, or secret agreements, among producers on prices, quantities, or quality of goods sold.

By 1750 most economic decisions in Britain were being made in the market. And most industries met the four conditions necessary for a pure market system. The textile industry may serve as an example. England had thousands of small independent textile companies. These companies made identical or very similar products. One piece of woolen cloth could be easily substituted for another of the same length and width. Entry into the textile industry was easy. Legally, anyone could start a business. And since most textile companies were small, a manufacturer needed only a small amount of capital to start one. Finally, because many companies scattered all over England made the same kinds of cloth, collusion was almost impossible.

But the development of a market economic system does not necessarily lead to dramatic economic growth. Economic growth means an increase in the total amount of goods and services produced each year. Without economic growth, the standard of living cannot improve. Increased production must come from using natural, capital, and human resources more efficiently. Great Britain's natural resources were limited by nature, although the nation did get additional raw materials from the colonies. Hence, the chief reasons for dramatic economic growth in Britain were improved uses of capital and human resources.

▶ Do you feel an obligation to invest any extra money you may have at sometime in the future to help the economy? Or should you spend extra funds for vacations or luxury goods?

205

Britain's population grew dramatically in the eighteenth century. Earlier marriages had led to a rising birthrate, and better living conditions resulted in a lower death rate. More people were available to farm the land, populate the colonies, and work in the factories. A larger population also meant a larger market.

The growing enclosure movement changed the distribution of population and encouraged economic growth. In 1700 most estates were divided into three fields. Tenants held strips in each field and made decisions about crops and livestock together. Often tenants were afraid to use new machinery or new farming techniques. To change the traditional ways of dividing and using land, the landlords enclosed, or fenced off, their lands. Their newly enlarged farms prospered, and the landlords were able to experiment with crop rotation, fertilizers, new seeds, and machinery. By the middle of the eighteenth century, fewer farmers could produce enough food for Britain's growing population.

►Should society help people displaced by economic change?

But enclosure often ruined small landowners. They could not compete with wealthy farmers because machinery and new techniques were costly. Many sold their few acres to the large landowners and moved to cities to open stores, become craftsmen, or work in new industries. They were joined in the cities by the cottagers, those farm laborers who had owned no land. Changes in agriculture had provided the human resources for industry.

Industries such as coal mining, glass production, salt mining, and shipbuilding began to grow steadily during the middle of the sixteenth century. All these industries required new machines. These machines, known as capital goods, further quickened economic growth. The British built their first factories and large shipyards and steadily developed engineering skills. They borrowed some technology from the continent and invented much of their own.

Richard Arkwright (1732-1792) patented the water frame in 1769. He also helped to start the factory system by establishing large cotton mills.

New sources of power helped the economy to grow during the eighteenth century. Arkwright's water frame harnessed waterwheels to textile machines, and the river banks of Britain were soon clogged with mills. The effects of the steam engine were even more dramatic. In 1769 James Watt developed a steam engine that used far less coal than earlier models. Watt and Matthew Boulton opened a steam engine factory in 1775. Soon Watt's engines powered factories, canal locks, mines, and forges. In the early nineteenth century, steam engines were put into boats and railroad locomotives.

A nationwide transportation network, begun in the 1700's, linked all parts of the country, thus also encouraging the growth of the economy. After 1760 canals became important as thousands of barges, pulled by horses, carried tons of freight across industrial Britain. By 1830 twenty thousand miles of roads connected Britain's cities, cutting in half the transportation time of freight and passengers. Railroads later replaced both canals and roads as the major carriers of freight, but they came well after Britain was on its way to industrialization. These improvements in transportation made Britain into a single economy in which each area used the resources and markets of the whole country.

Most individuals did not have enough capital to build new canals, factories, roads, and machinery. Some borrowed from friends and relatives, while others borrowed from banks. But many set up joint stock companies in which the investors bought shares of stock in a company for the right to a share of the profits.

Changes in values and institutions also spurred economic growth. The leaders of the new agriculture came mainly from members of the nobility who wanted to improve their estates. Many younger sons of noblemen entered trade or manufacturing. At the same time, commoners had the opportunity to change roles and improve their status. The children of poor noblemen sometimes married the sons and daughters of wealthy merchants and manufacturers. Thus all classes of society took part in Britain's industrial growth. Mechanics, parsons, and mill workers were among the inventors of textile machinery.

Government also played an important economic role. Besides passing enclosure laws, Parliament set up a patent system to assure inventors profits from their work. It chartered the Royal Society for the Encouragement of Art, Manufactures, and Commerce. The Royal Navy protected the merchants transporting goods by sea, and local governments protected the roads from highwaymen.

What were the immediate results of industrialization? Fifty years ago, most historians gave gloomy answers to this question: low living standards, poor working conditions, slum housing. More recent research points to other conclusions. Small landowners who were forced to sell their land and take unskilled jobs in industry at low wages saw their living standard fall. But the cottagers who moved from farm to factory probably suffered no decline in living standard. And the standard of living among skilled workers rose steadily throughout the nineteenth century.

Similar generalizations can be made about working conditions. Farmers had always worked hard, but they had been their own bosses and set their own hours. They probably worked no harder or longer in the textile mills, but they took orders from foremen and were forced to follow rigid schedules and quotas. The wives and children of the farmers had usually worked with them on the farms. In many industries, their lives became much harder. But industrialism also created thousands of artisans and small shopkeepers whose lives were generally quite satisfactory.

▶This picture is a painting by William Hogarth. It shows the impoverished Earl of Squanderfield, pointing to his family tree, arranging for his son to marry the daughter of a rich commoner. Do you think people today should marry within their own social class? financial bracket? religion? age group? educational background? race? Why or why not?

Conditions in the industrial cities varied. They were often over-crowded, with inadequate water supplies and primitive sewage systems, particularly where the unskilled lived. But such conditions existed in London well before the city industrialized. Moreover, many of these conditions cannot be blamed on industrialism alone. Disease spread because of insufficient medical knowledge and facilities. City planners lacked good water and sewer pipes. Municipal governments were poorly organized and often prevented by out-of-date laws from meeting the challenges of industrialism.

These and other problems of industrialism led to new economic institutions and philosophies in Britain. Since individual workers had no bargaining power, they banded together in unions to make collective demands. Unions first developed in the crafts where it was difficult to replace people with scarce skills. Later the unskilled factory workers joined together to form unions. Workers also organized cooperatives that bought goods in large quantities and sold them to the members at a discount. They opened mechanics institutes to train the unskilled, and they published their own newspapers.

The workers also became involved in politics, first through the established parties and then through the Labor party. Some radical political groups also formed, favoring the overthrow of capitalism. But most workingmen's groups won change through the representative institutions of the British government. In this way they won a voice in the decision-making of their new industrial society.

Unions were outlawed in 1799 by an act prohibiting the combination of workers for the purpose of seeking improved working conditions and wages. However, the act was rarely invoked, and when it was, the penalties were not severe.

The Labor party was organized between 1900 and 1902. In 1924 the party was elected by enough seats in Parliament to govern Britain briefly. But it was not until 1945 that the party gained a large enough majority to put through its programs.

Individual and Group Activities for Chapter 8

For full descriptions of these activities, turn to the **Student Book of Activities and Readings** included among the materials for individual and group activities.

Activity 8A: Scrapbook or collage illustrating economic growth in the contemporary world (individual or group)

Collect material dealing with economic growth in the contemporary world from several issues of a weekly news magazine or a Sunday newspaper. Use the material to make a scrapbook or a collage.

Activity 8B: Interpretation of a graph dealing with the problem of unlimited economic growth (individual)

This activity contains a discussion of some of the long-term consequences of unlimited economic growth. Copy one of the graphs in the activity and explain what it tells about the problem of unlimited economic growth.

The French Revolution

CHAPTER

9

A revolution is a major reorganization of government and society that involves violence and results in replacing one governing group with another. Many of the events that newspapers call revolutions do not fall under this definition. For example, most of the changes of government in Africa and Latin America are not revolutions but rather so-called coups d'etat. That is, these countries have changed their rulers by violence or the threat of violence, but they have not changed the basic structure of their government or their society.

Modern historians have classified true revolutions into six types. This chapter focuses on one of these types, sometimes called the Great Revolution. Great revolutions create major changes in a society. They change its political and social structure, they influence who controls property, and they spark the development of new philosophies to explain people's proper relationships within the society. Great revolutions separate one age in a nation's history from those that follow.

Great revolutions have both underlying causes and immediate causes. The underlying causes create a potentially explosive situation. The immediate causes set off the spark that leads to the actual revolt.

Chapter 9 analyzes the causes of the revolution in eighteenth-century France and traces its developments. Although the revolt did not break out until 1789, the events that caused it took place over many years. Understanding the causes of this violent revolution in one society can help you learn how to analyze similar events in the modern world.

210

1690	John Locke publishes **Two Treatises of Government.**
1762	Jean Jacques Rousseau publishes **The Social Contract.**
1789	**What Is the Third Estate?** by Abbé Sieyès urges major reforms.
	Third Estate forms the National Assembly.
	Parisians storm the Bastille.
	National Assembly abolishes feudalism and adopts the Declaration of the Rights of Man and the Citizen.
1791	Louis XVI accepts the constitution establishing constitutional monarchy.
1792	National Convention declares France a republic.
1792-1799	France fights most of Europe in wars of revolution.
1793	National Convention executes Louis XVI.
1793-1794	Jacobins institute the Terror.
1794	National Convention removes the Jacobins from power.
1795	National Convention drafts constitution setting up Directory.
1799	Napoleon's coup d'etat succeeds.
1804	Napoleon becomes emperor of France.
1815	Napoleon is defeated at the battle of Waterloo.

38 THE OLD REGIME

By 1789 France was the most advanced country in Europe. Its 24 million people had been united in a single national state for centuries. In contrast, England and Scotland together numbered only 10 million people, and they had been united officially for less than a century. Paris was second only to London in size, and it was the center of the intellectual movement of the time. France was also Europe's richest nation. France's foreign trade had increased five times since the death of Louis XIV. It now exported more goods to the rest of Europe than England did. In addition, France had the strongest military force in Europe.

But none of these developments had affected France's government, which had changed little since Louis XIV's death. France remained an authoritarian state. The king continued to rule without the help of the French parliament, the Estates-General, which had not met since

1614. Instead of asking representatives of his subjects for advice, the king depended on appointed officials. Nobles dominated government service, the army, and the higher church offices. And their power and influence continued to rise.

France's social system also remained much as it had been since feudal times. Everyone belonged to one of three estates, or classes, of society. The First Estate was the clergy, which made up less than 1 percent of the population. The Second Estate was the nobility, forming less than 2 percent of the population. The Third Estate included everyone else.

The church had a far greater influence than its size would suggest. It was the largest individual landowner in France, with between 5 and 10 percent of the nation's land. But the profits from this land were divided unequally. Most of them went to the small percentage of higher clergy who came from the nobility.

The nobility owned about 20 percent of the land, but they did not raise crops or livestock themselves. Instead, they rented out their land to peasants, who made up most of the Third Estate. Each peasant farmed a small plot for which he had to pay a complex variety of dues. In addition, the nobles kept certain feudal privileges, such as the right to hunt on their land.

The peasants resented the dues they had to pay as well as the nobles' privileges, particularly since the landowners did little to improve conditions on their property. But on the whole, the peasants were better off in France than elsewhere in Europe. Many of them owned their own farms, about 40 percent of the nation's land.

Working people in the towns also belonged to the Third Estate. These people shared none of the privileges of the nobles and clergy. Although most of them were probably as well off as people of similar positions in other countries, their standard of living was low compared to the French upper classes. Then during the eighteenth century, they were hit hard by inflation. Prices rose by about 65 percent while wages rose by only about 22 percent. As a result, town workers began to resent their position in French society.

In addition to the town workers, the Third Estate also contained a rising middle class made up of merchants, legal and governmental workers, and other professional people. Throughout the eighteenth century, this group increased in power and wealth. Because so much prestige went along with land ownership, many wealthy members of this group bought land. By 1789 they owned almost 20 percent of French land. For this reason, the rising middle class had become rivals of the nobility.

Reading 38 contains four excerpts from eighteenth-century documents that dramatize some of the social, political, and economic conditions of eighteenth-century France discussed in this introduction. As you read, keep the following questions in mind:

1. What complaints did various groups within the French population have against the conditions under which they lived?
2. What caused these conditions? Who did these people blame?

Jean Jacques Rousseau Dines with a French Peasant

Jean Jacques Rousseau (1712-1778) was one of the most important intellectuals and writers of the eighteenth century. In 1732 he traveled through central France. The following account tells of his meeting with a French peasant during his travels.

Having turned off the road one day to take a closer look at an attractive spot, I lost my way. After several hours of wandering around, I went into a peasant's hut. In Switzerland, peasants have enough resources to help a stranger, and I expected the same hospitality in France. I offered to pay for my dinner. He gave me skimmed milk and some coarse bread made of barley, saying that it was all he had. I ate hungrily, but did not get enough to satisfy my appetite.

The peasant watched me closely and listened to my story. After a while, he said that he judged me to be a good and honorable young man, not a person who had come to betray him for money. So he opened a little trapdoor near the kitchen and went down some stairs. He soon reappeared with a nice brown loaf of bread made of wheat, a piece of ham, and a bottle of wine. To this he added an omelette, and I enjoyed an excellent dinner.

When I offered again to pay him, his anxiety returned. He refused to take my money. When I asked him why, he at last said with a shudder "revenue-officers and excisemen." He told me that he hid his wine and bread so that he would not have to pay the excise tax and that he was a lost man if anyone suspected that he had money. I never forgot what he said. It began in my heart the hatred against oppression from which these people suffer. This man did not dare to eat the bread which he had earned by the sweat of his brow and could only escape financial ruin by pretending to be poor. I left his house angry and touched because a beautiful country had fallen prey to barbarous farmers of taxes.

Jean Jacques Rousseau, **Confessions** (London: 1904), pp. 148-149. Language simplified.

Tax collectors gave rewards to people who told them of property owners with goods on which taxes had not been paid.

Revenue-officers and excisemen were tax collectors.

213

The cartoons on this page show how two artists pictured the relationships among the three estates in eighteenth-century France. What are those relationships?

An English Physician
Comments
on Life in Paris

John Moore, an English physician, traveled on the European continent for a year. He wrote the following account in 1779.

John Moore, **A View of Society and Manners in France, Switzerland, and Germany** (London: 1803), Vol. I, pp. 27-28. Language simplified.

Everything in France has been arranged for the benefit of the rich and powerful. Little or nothing is done, however, for the comfort of the average citizen. This conclusion strikes the visitor as soon as he enters Paris.

The city of London is lighted at night. In addition, the city has raised sidewalks along the streets for the comfort and convenience of pedestrians. Paris, however, is poorly lighted and has only one or two raised footpaths. People who cannot afford carriages must grope their way along. They must duck behind pillars or run into shops to avoid being run down by carriages. Coachmen drive carriages as near to the walls as they like, scattering people before them.

In France monarchy has been raised on high. The monarch has lost sight of the bulk of the nation. He pays attention only to the few members of the nobility who come within his sight at the court.

▶To what degree should society try to provide for the comfort of all citizens rather than only of a small group?

An English Agricultural
Reformer Describes a French
Peasant Woman

Arthur Young visited France in 1787, 1788, and 1789. He was particularly interested in agricultural conditions which the following incident concerns.

Arthur Young, **Travels in France,** Miss Betham-Edwards, ed. (London: George Bell & Sons, 1892), pp. 197-198. Language simplified.

I was walking up a long hill to ease my mare when a poor woman joined me. She complained about the times, and said it was a sad country. She said that her husband had but a small piece of land, one cow, and a poor little horse. Yet they had to pay forty-two pounds of wheat and three chickens as tax to one lord and eighty-eight pounds of oats, one chicken, and a shilling to another. In addition, they had to pay heavy land taxes as well as other taxes.

Nobles were exempt from paying land taxes.

People said, she reported, that some of the great folks were going to help the poor ones. She did not know who they were or how they might help. But she said that the taxes and special privileges were destroying the peasants. From a short distance, this woman appeared to be sixty or seventy years old. Her body was bent with labor and her face covered with lines. But she was only twenty-eight.

An Englishman who has not traveled cannot imagine the appearance of most French countrywomen. They probably work harder than the men. This work, combined with women's labor of bringing a new race of slaves into the world, destroys feminine appearance. This attitude toward women in France can be traced directly to the government.

▶Should women who have children work outside the home? Why or why not?

A French Noble Comments
on the Rising Middle Class

The Marquis de Bouillé (1739-1800) was an enlightened French nobleman. During the revolution, he took part in an unsuccessful attempt to help the royal family escape. His comments about the middle class that follow apply to France in the 1770's and 1780's.

Marquis de Bouillé, **Memoires,** ed. F. Barrière (Paris: 1859), p. 123. Translated by Edwin Fenton.

The riches which commerce brought to the kingdom went only to commoners because the prejudices of the nobles did not allow them to enter commerce or manufacturing. The increase in wealth contributed to inflation, and inflation cut back the wealth of landowners who received a fixed money income. Trade also caused the growth of cities, some of which became as large as the capitals of other countries. The nobles left their estates to ruin themselves in Paris. But the commoners stayed home and piled up wealth. All the little towns became centers of commerce and manufacturing. They were filled with the middle classes who were richer and more industrious than the nobles. Many of them administered the lands of the great landowners and made money at it.

The middle class received a better education than the nobles. They needed an education more since they had to earn a living while the nobility got government jobs although many of them had neither talent nor merit. The middle class, meanwhile, got only secondary positions. Both in Paris and in the provincial towns the middle class was superior to the nobility in wealth, talent, and personal merit. Although well aware of their superiority, they were constantly humiliated. Military regulations kept them from leading positions in the army. They were kept out of the upper clergy because bishops and other top officials were chosen from the nobility. Even the judges rejected them. Most courts admitted only nobles to membership.

FOR THOUGHT:

Under what circumstances might the various groups who suffered under the Old Regime have decided to unite to change their society?

39 THE REVOLUTION IN PEOPLE'S MINDS

Reading 38 showed that many people in eighteenth-century France had serious complaints about their lives. Peasants complained about having to pay taxes or dues to the government, the landowners, and the Church. The rising middle class complained because the nobility had so many more privileges than they did as well as greater prestige. Wage earners complained about inflation. And many members of the nobility and the clergy complained because the king ruled France without consulting them.

Two of these groups of people—the middle class and the nobility—had much in common despite the differences in their positions. Both groups were educated. Both owned property of some sort. Both wanted a larger voice in political decision-making. In the eighteenth century these two groups began to use different arguments to express their complaints. They based these complaints on a new philosophy that grew out of a period in European intellectual history that was called the Enlightenment.

The philosophers of the Enlightenment followed the lead of natural scientists such as Sir Isaac Newton. Newton had found laws which governed the movement of heavenly bodies. The philosophers of the Enlightenment tried to find similar laws that governed people's lives. These new ideas spread rapidly through Europe, particularly through the educated French classes. They provided intellectual reasons for revolt.

Reading 39 consists of excerpts from two of these philosophers, John Locke and Jean Jacques Rousseau. As you read, keep the following questions in mind:

1. What was the state of nature according to Locke and Rousseau? What did people gain and lose by leaving it?
2. How did these two philosophers justify revolt against an established government?

Two Treatises
of Government, 1690

John Locke, a contemporary of Sir Isaac Newton, published Two Treatises of Government *in 1690. Locke was trying to justify the Glorious Revolution and England's new government. His work later supplied the philosophical support for revolutions in both the American colonies and in France.*

John Locke, **Two Treatises of Government** (London, 1690). Language simplified.

► How can you support the statement that all men are equal when people differ so much in talents, abilities, and character?

To understand political power, we must consider the condition in which nature puts all men. It is a state of perfect freedom to do as they wish and dispose of themselves and their possessions as they think fit, within the bounds of the law of nature. They need not ask permission or the consent of any other man.

The state of nature is also a state of equality. No one has more power or authority than another. Since all human beings have the same advantages and the use of the same skills, they should be equal to each other. The state of nature has a law of nature to govern it. Reason is that law. It teaches that all men are equal and independent, and that no one ought to harm another in his life, health, liberty, or possessions. All men are made by one all-powerful and wise Maker. They are all servants of one Master who sent them into the world to do His business. He has put men naturally into a state of independence, and they remain in it until they choose to become members of a political society.

If man in the state of nature is free, if he is absolute lord of his own person and possessions, why will he give up his freedom? Why will he put himself under the control of any person or institution? The obvious answer is that rights in the state of nature are constantly exposed to the attacks of others. Since every man is equal and since most men do not concern themselves with equity and justice, the enjoyment of rights in the state of nature is unsafe and insecure. Hence each man joins in society with others to preserve his life, liberty, and property.

Since men hope to preserve their property by establishing a government, they will not want that government to destroy this objective. When legislators try to destroy or take away the property of the people, or try to reduce them to slavery, they put themselves into a state of war with the people who can then refuse to obey the laws. When legislators try to gain or give someone else absolute power over the lives, liberties, and property of the people, they abuse the power which the people had put into their hands. It is then the privilege of the people to establish a new legislature to provide for their safety and security. These principles also hold true for the executive who helps to make laws and carry them out.

Perhaps some will say that the people are ignorant and discontented and that a government based on their unsteady opinion and uncertain humor will be unstable. They might argue that no government can exist for long if the people may set up a new legislature whenever they do not like the old one. But people do not easily give up their old forms of government. In England, for example, the unwillingness of the people to throw out their old constitution has kept us to, or brought us back to, our old legislature of king, lords, and commons.

However, it will be said that this philosophy may lead to frequent rebellion. To which I answer, such revolutions are not caused by every little mismanagement in public affairs. But if a long train of abuses, lies, and tricks make a government's bad intentions visible to the people, they cannot help seeing where they are going. It is no wonder that they will then rouse themselves, and try to put the rule into hands which will secure to them the purpose for which government was originally organized.

The Social Contract, 1762

Jean Jacques Rousseau was one of the most influential of the eighteenth-century philosophers. Although he disagreed with some of Locke's ideas, his writings generally supported Locke.

I assume, for the sake of argument, that mankind at some time reached a point when the disadvantages of remaining in a state of nature outweighed the advantages. Under these conditions, the original state of nature could no longer endure. The human race would have perished if it had not changed its way.

Men, being human, cannot develop new powers. But they can unite and control the powers they already have. Men in the state of nature could get together, pooling their strength in a way that would permit them to meet any challenger. They had to learn to work together under central direction.

A real concentration of human powers could be brought about only by an agreement among individual men. But each individual man relies on his own strength and his own freedom of action to protect and preserve himself. How can he limit his strength and his freedom of action without injuring himself?

Some form of association must be found which can rally the whole community for the protection of the person and property of each of

This rustic villa was built by the French queen, Marie Antoinette. Here she and the ladies of the French court pretended to be peasants.

What do these two pictures suggest about the influence of Rousseau on French life?

The Goddess of Reason is carried through the streets of Paris in 1789.

its citizens in such a way that each man, because he is a voluntary member of the association, still obeys his own will and hence remains as free as he was before. That is the basic problem solved by the social contract.

The essence of the social contract can be stated simply: Each individual surrenders all his rights to the community. Since each man surrenders his rights without reservation, all are equal. And because all are equal, it is to everyone's interest to make life pleasant for his fellows.

Since all rights have been surrendered to the community without reservation, no one has any claim against the group. If any rights were left to individuals, then each man would try to extend those rights he had reserved for himself. This situation would mean that a state of nature still existed. All rights must be surrendered; none may be reserved.

The heart of the idea of the social contract may be stated simply: Each of us places his person and authority under the supreme direction of the general will; and the group receives each individual as an indivisible part of the whole.

In order that the social contract may not be a mere empty formula, everyone must understand that any individual who refuses to obey the general will must be forced by his fellows to do so. This is a way of saying that it may be necessary to force a man to be free; freedom in this case being obedience to the will of all.

▶Should an individual surrender all of his rights to a community, or should he keep some rights?

FOR THOUGHT:

On which groups in French society would the ideas of Locke and Rousseau have the most influence? Why?

40 THE AIMS OF THE REVOLUTION

Citizenship can be divided into three parts—civil rights, political rights, and social rights. Civil rights give citizens liberty of the person; freedom of speech, thought and faith; the right to own property; and the right to justice. Political rights give citizens the power to take part in political decision-making by voting and holding political offices. Social rights give citizens economic security through such measures as social security laws and the right to a free public education.

Citizenship has been restricted to a small select group throughout most of history. Even this group has lacked some of the rights of a full citizen, particularly political rights. In modern times, citizenship has gradually been extended to more and more people. In some modern societies, all citizens enjoy all three parts of citizenship. They have civil rights, political rights, and social rights.

The French Revolution marked the first step toward full citizenship for the great majority of the French people. The revolution was triggered by a governmental financial crisis. Louis XVI had spent vast fortunes on wars, among them the American Revolutionary War. Attempts to reform the tax system in order to raise more money failed because of the opposition of the nobility and clergy. Both of these groups did not have to pay most taxes. Therefore, Louis decided to call a meeting of the Estates-General, the parliamentary body which had last met in 1614. He hoped this body would establish new taxes.

The Estates-General immediately became deadlocked about how to vote. In the past, the three estates had met separately, and each estate had cast one vote. This system made it possible for the clergy and the nobility, who made up the First and Second Estates, to outvote everyone else. Yet these two estates made up less than 3 percent of the total population. The Third Estate wanted every delegate to vote as an individual because it had as many representatives in the Estates-General as the other two estates combined. Since some members of the nobility and the clergy sympathized with the objectives of the Third Estate, this reform would give power to the group who represented most of the people of France.

Six weeks after the Estates-General met for the first time, the members of the Third Estate declared themselves the National Assembly. They invited the First and Second Estates to join them as the new lawmaking body of France. Three days later, Louis XVI barred the Assembly from its meeting place. Its members, joined by a few people from the nobility and clergy, then gathered in an indoor tennis court. They swore to continue meeting until they had drafted a constitution for the nation. After a period of indecision, Louis finally gave in to their demands.

Early in July, rumors began to circulate that Louis' troops were approaching Paris to dissolve the Assembly. Angry mobs of unemployed and hungry workers began to roam the streets, demanding food and looking for weapons. On July 14, a mob attacked the Bastille, an old fortress used for a prison, and killed most of the guards. Riots then broke out all over the countryside. Peasants broke into manor houses, destroying records of manorial dues and tax payments. A revolution had begun that kept Europe in turmoil for twenty-five years and marked the first major step toward citizenship for most of France's people.

Reading 40 contains two documents written in 1789 that give evidence about this revolutionary period. As you read them, think about the following questions:

1. What complaints about the way in which French society is organized can you find in *What Is the Third Estate?*
2. What rights did the Declaration of the Rights of Man and the Citizen grant to the French people?

A Revolutionary Pamphlet

Following Louis XVI's announcement that the Estates-General would meet, many people wrote pamphlets urging major changes in the Old Regime. Abbé Sieyès was one of the most influential of these pamphlet writers. He had been a minor administrative official in the French church and a reader of Locke and Rousseau. He published What Is the Third Estate? *in January 1789.*

The plan of this pamphlet is very simple. We have three questions to ask:

What is the Third Estate? Everything.

What has it been in the political order? Nothing.

What does it demand? To become something.

What does a nation need to function and become prosperous? It needs private enterprise to make goods and services and public functions to govern.

Private enterprise involves four groups of people. The first group is made up of families who farm. The second group takes these farm products and develops them for use by consumers. Merchants and dealers make up the third group. They carry the goods to consumers and manage trade. The fourth group is made up of other productive people essential to a society. They range from domestic servants to scientists, lawyers, or doctors. These four groups of people do the work which supports society. Who does this work? The members of the Third Estate.

Public functions can also be classified under four well-known headings: the Sword, the Robe, the Church, and the Administration. Members of the Third Estate make up nineteen-twentieths of these groups. They do all the really hard work which the privileged orders refuse to do. The First and Second Estates hold only the well-paid and honorary positions. They have said to the Third Estate: "Whatever your services or talents, you shall go thus far and no farther. It is not appropriate that you should be honored."

If the privileged orders were abolished, the nation would be something more rather than something less. Thus, what is the Third Estate? Everything, but an everything that is shackled and oppressed. What would it be without the privileged orders? Everything, but an everything free and flourishing. Nothing can progress without it. Everything

Emmanuel Joseph Sieyès. **Qu'est-ce que le Tiers-Etat?** (Paris: 1789). Translated by Edwin Fenton.

The Sword refers to the military. The Robe refers to the law and the administration of justice.

▶On what basis should people receive honors in a society?

223

would go better, however, without the other estates. The nobility does not really belong to the social organization. Indeed, it may be a burden on the nation.

All parts of the government's executive power have fallen to the group which furnishes the leaders of the Church, the Robe, and the Sword. Nobles prefer each other out of a spirit of brotherhood. In truth, the nobles reign.

It is the court and not the monarch that rules France. The court makes, unmakes, appoints, and discharges ministers, and creates and appoints people to positions. The court is the head of the immense aristocracy which overruns all of France.

Declaration of the Rights of Man and the Citizen

On August 26, 1789, after ten days of deliberation, the National Assembly adopted the famous Declaration of the Rights of Man and the Citizen. The Declaration was intended as a pledge of what the members of the Assembly wanted to accomplish.

Thomas Paine, **Rights of Man: Being an Answer to Mr. Burke's Attack on the French Revolution,** ed. Moncure Daniel Conway (New York: G. P. Putnam's Sons, 1894), pp. 351-353. Language simplified.

The representatives of the French people have been organized as a National Assembly. They believe that ignorance, neglect, or contempt of the rights of man lead to corrupt governments. They have decided to set forth in a solemn declaration the natural, inalienable, and sacred rights of man. Hence, the National Assembly recognizes and proclaims in the presence of the Supreme Being, the following rights of man and the citizen:

CETTE FOIS-CI LA JUSTICE EST DU COTÉ DU PLUS FORT.

LE NOBLE PAS DE DEUX

A votre tour M.ᵉ l'Abbé!... la Danse n'est pas ce que j'aime, elle m'est deffendue par état.
allons sans grimace et de bonne volonté soiez d'accord avec nous et vive la Liberté
bien entendu que nous payerons les Violons.

These three cartoons were drawn early in the French Revolution. They show
how the cartoonists viewed the changes taking place in the relationships
among the estates. Do these cartoonists agree with the suggestions of Abbé
Sieyès?

REVEIL DU TIERS ETAT

Ma foute, il étoit tems que je me réveillasse, car l'oppression de mes fers me donnoit le cauchemar un peu trop fort.

1. Men are born and remain free and equal in rights.
2. All governments should try to protect man's natural rights. These rights are liberty, property, security, and resistance to oppression.

Sovereignty means the ultimate source of power.

3. Sovereignty rests in the people. No group or individual may exercise any authority that does not come directly from the people.
4. Liberty consists of being able to do anything that does not injure anyone else. A person may exercise his natural rights so long as he does not interfere with the natural rights of others. The limits to which natural rights may be exercised can be determined by law.
5. Law can only forbid activities that are harmful to society.
6. Law is the expression of the general will. Every citizen has a right to take part personally or through his representative in making laws. All citizens are equal in the eyes of the law. They are equally eligible for all honors and for all public positions according to their abilities.
7. No man shall be accused, arrested, or imprisoned without following the practices laid down in the laws.

This provision is commonly called an **ex post facto** law.

8. The law shall provide for such punishments as are strictly and obviously necessary. No one shall be punished for a law passed after an act was committed.
9. All persons shall be held innocent until proved guilty. Hence, if a person is arrested, he shall not be treated more severely than required to arrest him.
10. No one shall be disturbed because of his opinions, including his views about religion, provided he does not disturb the public order established by the law.
11. The free communication of ideas and opinions is one of the most precious rights of man. Every citizen may speak, write and print freely, being responsible for any abuses of this freedom as defined by the law.
13. Taxes must be assessed on all citizens equally in proportion to their ability to pay.
14. Citizens have the right to determine whether a tax is necessary, to consent to it freely, to supervise how tax money is used, and to decide how taxes should be assessed and paid and how long they should last.
17. Property is a sacred and inviolable right. No one may be deprived of property unless public necessity clearly requires it and unless he receives a just payment.

FOR THOUGHT:

Which part of citizenship—civil rights, political rights, or social rights—seems most important in these two documents?

41 THE FRENCH REVOLUTION AND THE WESTERN HERITAGE

A HISTORICAL ESSAY

The French Revolution brought sweeping changes to France's political, social, and economic systems. It was the beginning of the French people's long struggle to change their status from subjects to citizens. Like the American Revolution, the revolt in France had an influence far beyond its own borders. By establishing the belief that freedom and citizenship could be won by violent revolt, it encouraged other countries to follow in its path.

The French Revolution took place in what was in many ways the most advanced country of its age. France had been a unified nation for centuries with a common language, common traditions, and a common set of loyalties. It was the center of the Enlightenment, which was the eighteenth-century intellectual movement. Moreover, France was potentially the most powerful nation in Europe. It had the largest population united under a single government, and its agriculture and trade were prospering. The French Revolution was not an uprising of Europe's poorest people. Instead, it was an attempt by most of the French people to overthrow political, social, and economic institutions that had not changed with the times.

Agriculture dominated the economy of eighteenth-century France. More than 80 percent of the population was rural. But the French peasants were no longer serfs, as some peasants elsewhere in Europe still were. In fact, peasants owned about 40 percent of the land, and they rented or worked on most of the rest.

Nevertheless, the French peasants had two major complaints. First, they objected to the remaining feudal rights of the nobles. These rights included the right to collect various fees and dues, the right to control village mills, bake ovens, and wine presses, and the right to hunt on peasants' lands. Second, the peasants objected to unequal taxation. They had to pay many taxes from which the nobles, the clergy, and many wealthy members of the middle class were exempt.

Most wealthy people who were not nobles had made their fortunes in trade, as lawyers, or as government officials. But though their fortunes were rising, their prestige and power were not. Better educated than the nobility, they resented the privileges that society granted to nobles. Many of these people read the works of Locke, Rousseau, and other

Britain led France in at least two ways, its parliamentary government and its new industrialism.

▶Should people resent others who have privileges that they do not have?

227

philosophers of the Enlightenment and found intellectual reasons for their dissatisfaction.

Workers in the towns also had complaints. Like other non-nobles, they had no influence in the government and low status in the society. During the eighteenth century, prices rose three times as fast as wages, keeping down the workers' standard of living. In the late 1780's, unemployment and a sharp rise in the price of bread made their lives even worse.

The nobility had been regaining power in the society since the death of Louis XIV. By the 1780's, they once again held most of the top positions in the government, the army, and the Church. They paid little attention to their manors except to collect fees and taxes, and they lived in the king's court at Versailles or in one of the cities. But the nobles had no formal way to influence the king's decisions. Many nobles wanted to have a role in the political system, and they resented the absolutist nature of the king's rule.

In England, Parliament had played an increasingly important role in government for centuries. But the French kings had not called a meeting of the Estates-General, the French parliament, since 1614. They gave their subjects neither civil nor political nor social rights. Their constant wars stretched the financial resources of their governments. In the 1780's, war debts, the out-of-date tax system, and a slight depression brought on a governmental economic crisis. When the nobility refused to pay new taxes, Louis XVI decided to call a meeting of the Estates-General.

French society was divided into three estates—the clergy, the nobility, and everyone else. Each estate was represented in the Estates-General. Traditionally each estate met and voted separately. The votes of two estates were required to pass a bill. But the Third Estate had as many delegates as the first two combined. Its members demanded that all representatives should vote as individuals. When the king refused to agree, the members of the Third Estate, joined by a few nobles and clergy, proclaimed themselves the National Assembly.

Although Louis XVI tried unsuccessfully to prevent the Assembly from meeting, he finally backed down and allowed it to meet. But secretly he began to gather his troops together. Rumors spread that the nobles were also gathering their forces. As a result, first unrest, then panic, and finally riots broke out in the cities and the countryside.

To restore order and legalize the revolution, the National Assembly ended the privileged positions of the nobles on August 4, 1789. Within two weeks, the Assembly also passed the Declaration of the Rights of Man and the Citizen. These two acts gave civil rights to French citizens. They mark the first step in the development of full citizenship for the nation.

Among these wars was the American Revolution. Louis XVI sided against England, spending large sums for military expenses and in loans to America.

A FAUT ESPERER Q'EU'JEU LA FINIRA BEN TOT

Vive le Roi . Vive la Nation.

J' SAVOIS BEN QU'JAURIONS NOT TOUR.

During the following two years, the National Assembly worked on a new constitution. It created a limited monarchy somewhat like that of Great Britain. The king became subject to the laws passed by the National Assembly. But delegates to the Assembly were to be chosen by electors. Property qualifications and other restrictions limited the vote to about 50,000 men, only a small minority of the French people.

The new government, launched on October 1, 1791, collapsed about ten months later. Even before this government had taken over, many nobles, representing much of France's leadership, had fled France. These so-called emigrés, supported by Austria and Prussia, organized counter-revolutionary forces on the borders of France. Many of the clergy had joined the emigrés when the government took over land belonging to the Church and sold it to raise money. A short time later,

How did the cartoonist portray the change in the condition of the peasants brought about by the events of August 4, 1789?

The emigrés were nobles who left, or emigrated from, the country.

229

Louis and his family tried to join the emigrés. But they were captured, returned to Paris, and imprisoned.

Finally, war drained the new government of its resources. The Assembly had declared war on Austria and on the emigrés in April 1792. Prussia soon joined the forces against France. Because France had lost most of its officers who had been nobles, it suffered severe defeats. By the summer of 1792, the new government could no longer defend the revolution.

Deputies to a National Convention met in September 1792 to draft a new constitution setting up a republic. Radicals began to win control. Led by an extreme group called the Jacobins, the Convention accused Louis XVI of treason, tried and convicted him, and sent him to the guillotine in January, 1793.

Louis' execution marked the beginning of the Jacobin rise to power. Jacobins soon filled all twelve positions on the Committee of Public Safety, set up originally as a sort of war cabinet. Led by Maximilian Robespierre, the Committee began a reign of terror. They tried, convicted, and executed hundreds of people whom they accused of counter-revolutionary activities. In a great outburst of nationalism, the French enthusiastically supported their new government.

In early summer 1794, the Jacobins stepped up the executions. Nearly fifteen hundred people perished under the blade of the guillotine within six weeks. The terror had gone too far. Robespierre's enemies set out to remove him. Late in July, he too fell victim to the guillotine. The National Convention continued to meet until October 1795, but it removed the Jacobins from power and drafted a new constitution. During this long period, the civil rights proclaimed early in the revolution were ignored by the revolutionary government.

In 1795 a new government was set up. It was called the Directory because five Directors, chosen by a two-house legislature, made up the executive branch. Only the wealthy could vote for members of the legislature. The Directory faced heavy opposition. Many Frenchmen wanted to return to a limited monarchy, while poorer people demanded a voice in the government. The Directory held on chiefly because some of its successful generals won widespread public support for the government.

Napoleon Bonaparte was the most notable of these generals. After winning several sensational military victories, he schemed to take control of the government. In a coup d'etat in 1799, Napoleon forced the legislature to accept his leadership and to adopt a constitution that gave him supreme power. By 1803, he had brought the fighting to a temporary halt, stabilized the government, and begun to strengthen the gains of the revolution. In 1804, he became emperor, a title which the French people supported by a plebiscite. France had returned officially to absolutist rule.

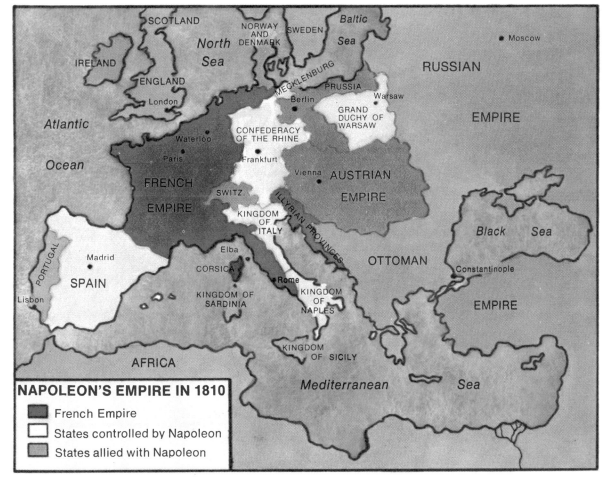

NAPOLEON'S EMPIRE IN 1810

- French Empire
- States controlled by Napoleon
- States allied with Napoleon

During the next eleven years, France fought one foreign war after another with virtually all of Europe. The French won victory after victory, spreading the ideals of the revolution across Europe. Finally, England, Austria, Russia, and Prussia combined forces to defeat and capture Napoleon. He gave up his throne and was exiled to the island of Elba. The French then restored the grandson of Louis XVI, Louis XVIII, to the throne and set up a limited monarchy. But Napoleon escaped from Elba in 1815. For a hundred days he seized control of the nation once more until he was defeated again at the battle of Waterloo. This time he was exiled to the distant island of St. Helena. Louis XVIII returned to the throne.

But Napoleon had succeeded in reorganizing the nation. A child of both the Enlightenment and the revolution, he had unusual capacities as a politician. His government put down outlaws, imposed and collected taxes from everyone, and invited all Frenchmen who would work

The son of Louis XVI, who would have been Louis XVII, had died.

231

with the government to return to the nation. Napoleon reformed government administration by opening public service to any citizen with talent. Public offices could no longer be inherited, bought or sold, or given out as favors. In addition, Napoleon assured the civil right of religious freedom for all religious groups.

Napoleon also combined the three hundred legal systems of the Old Regime, a number of parliamentary and royal laws, and the thousands of laws enacted by revolutionary assemblies. Five legal codes, the so-called Napoleonic Codes, emerged. These codes included a new property law that eliminated the old feudal rights.

But political rights were another matter. Napoleon wrote a new constitution that appeared to set up parliamentary institutions and granted universal male suffrage. Yet actually Napoleon ran the state. He shared the decision-making power with no one.

Nevertheless, the French Revolution had remade the society. It abolished legal classes and opened up a new social system in which men and women with talent could rise in social status. It changed the economic order by sweeping away feudal rights and transferring ownership of all Church lands and many of the lands of the nobility to others. And it changed the political system by opening public offices to everyone and establishing major civil rights throughout the society. A start had been made on the long process by which the subjects of Louis XVI became full citizens of the modern French republic. And in nations throughout the western world, the principles of the revolution—liberty, equality, and fraternity—inspired men and women to overthrow absolutist governments and set up new societies in which they too won full rights as citizens.

Individual and Group Activities for Chapter 9

For full descriptions of these activities, turn to the **Student Book of Activities and Readings** included among the materials for individual and group activities.

Activity 9A: Interpretation of the lifestyle of Napoleon (individual)
This activity shows a group of pictures that illustrate the lifestyle of Napoleon in the years following the French Revolution. In a brief essay based on these pictures, discuss whether Napoleon thought of himself as representative of the ideals of the revolution or the monarchy.

Activity 9B: Comparison of a contemporary national revolution with the French Revolution (individual)
Select a contemporary national revolution and investigate it. Then write a short paper comparing the revolution that you have selected with the French Revolution.

The Movement for Equality
and Full Citizenship

STATING THE ISSUE

Throughout the modern world, people want equality and full citizenship. Over the past several centuries the movement to win full citizenship has grown in western Europe and the United States. During the late 1700's and early 1800's, people in both the United States and France won full civil rights. These rights included freedom of speech, freedom of the press, and freedom of assembly. During the 1800's and early 1900's, men and women in both Europe and North America won political rights. These rights included the right to vote and to hold elected political offices. Beginning in the late 1800's, people began to win social rights. These rights included the right to free education and to a minimal standard of living that included security for old age, medical care, and adequate housing.

All of these civil, political, and social rights grew out of long and sometimes violent struggles. These struggles included the Glorious Revolution in England, the French Revolution, and the American Revolution, and a number of lesser known and largely unsuccessful revolutions in other parts of Europe. Since the end of World War II, the people of Asia and Africa have joined the struggle for equal rights. At times western powers have opposed the movement of former colonial peoples toward equal rights.

The movement to win equal rights for everyone began to develop about two hundred years ago. Yet the philosophical support behind this movement has existed since the time of the ancient Athenians. Chapter 10 begins with an account of some of these philosophical arguments for equality. It then explores some of the barriers to equality in the West during the 1800's and examines the movement for social rights that began at that time. The essay at the end of the chapter describes the movement for equality throughout the history of the West.

52 B.C.–46 B.C.	Marcus Tullius Cicero writes **The Republic** and **The Laws.**
c. 4 B.C.–c. 30 A.D.	Jesus lives in Palestine.
1776	Thirteen British colonies in North America issue Declaration of Independence.
1787	United States Constitution is written.
1789	French proclaim Declaration of the Rights of Man and the Citizen.
1791	United States adopts Bill of Rights.
1810–1825	Most Latin American nations win independence from Spain.
1830	France establishes a constitutional monarchy.
1848	Liberal revolutions erupt in France, Austria, Italy, and Prussia.
	Karl Marx and Friedrich Engels publish **Communist Manifesto.**
1865	United States abolishes slavery.
1867	Britain begins a half century of massive reform legislation.
1920	Most western European countries have universal suffrage.
	Women in United States gain right to vote.
1947	European colonies in Asia and Africa begin to win independence.

42 WESTERN JUSTIFICATIONS FOR EQUALITY

Many societies have rejected the idea that all people are equal. The Chinese teacher and philosopher, Confucius, argued that people were divided into two kinds—the superior, well-educated rulers, and the inferior, uneducated ruled. The ancient Greeks thought they were superior to foreigners. Medieval people accepted the social distinctions that divided people into nobility, clergy, and commoners. In India the Hindu religion supports the division of the Indian people into unequal castes. Primitive tribes often think that older people are superior to younger ones and that all men are superior to women. And many modern writers have defended the inequalities that come from unequal distribution of wealth.

234

While one group of writers pointed to inequalities among people, other men and women wrote about what people have in common. They argued that what people share is much greater than what separates one person or group from another. They based this argument on widely differing sets of assumptions. Reading 42 contains five justifications of equality. As you read, keep the following questions in mind:

1. On what grounds did each writer justify his belief in equality?
2. Do these writers stress civil rights, political rights, social rights, or all three?

A Roman View

During the first century B.C., the Roman republic had to adjust to new demands created by the development of an empire. At this time Cicero argued for the extension of Rome's republican institutions, justifying equality as he did so.

God has created man and has given him foresight, intelligence, memory, prudence, and reason. Of all the creatures God created, only man has the ability to reason and think. What is more divine in all of heaven and earth than reason? When it is fully developed and perfected, reason becomes wisdom. Both man and God possess reason in common. Those who have reason also have right reason, and right reason is law. Hence, we must believe that men and God have law in common. Those who share law must share justice, and those who share justice must be members of the same commonwealth.

Cicero, The Republic and the Laws, as quoted in Francis William Coker, Readings in Political Philosophy (New York: The Macmillan Company, 1938), pp. 146-147.

A Christian View

The New Testament passage below is one of many that express the Christian belief in equality.

When the Son of man shall come in his glory, and all the holy angels with him, then shall he sit upon the throne of his glory: And before him shall be gathered all nations: and he shall separate them one from another, as a shepherd divideth his sheep from the goats: And he shall set the sheep on his right hand, but the goats on the left.

Then shall the King say unto them on his right hand,

The Gospel according to St. Matthew, Chapter 25: 31-40, from The Dartmouth Bible, Roy B. Chamberlin and Herman Feldman, trans. (Boston: Houghton Mifflin Co., 1961), pp. 941-942.

Come, ye blessed of my Father,
inherit the kingdom prepared for you
    from the foundation of the world:
For I was ahungered, and ye gave me meat:
    I was thirsty, and ye gave me drink:
I was a stranger, and ye took me in:
    Naked, and ye clothed me:
I was sick, and ye visited me:
I was in prison, and ye came unto me.
Then shall the righteous answer him, saying,
        Lord, when saw we thee ahungered, and fed thee?
            or thirsty, and gave thee drink?
        When saw we thee a stranger, and took thee in?
            or naked, and clothed thee?
        Or when saw we thee sick, or in prison,
            and came unto thee?
And the King shall answer, Inasmuch as ye have done it unto one
of the least of these my brethren, ye have done it unto me.

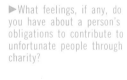

▶Under what conditions, if any, should modern people treat strangers in this way?

▶What feelings, if any, do you have about a person's obligations to contribute to unfortunate people through charity?

An American View

Among the most eloquent American statements on equality is the Declaration of Independence. In his autobiography, Thomas Jefferson, chief author of the document, credited Locke and other philosophers of the Enlightenment for many of his ideas.

When, in the Course of human events, it becomes necessary for one people to dissolve the political bands which have connected them with another, and to assume among the Powers of the earth, the separate and equal station to which the Laws of Nature and of Nature's God entitle them, a decent respect to the opinions of mankind requires that they should declare the causes which impel them to the separation.

We hold these truths to be self-evident, that all men are created equal, that they are endowed by their Creator with certain unalienable Rights, that among these are Life, Liberty, and the pursuit of Happiness. That to secure these rights, Governments are instituted among Men, deriving their just powers from the consent of the governed. That whenever any Form of Government becomes destructive of these ends, it is the Right of the People to alter or abolish it, and to institute new Government, laying its foundation on such principles and organizing its power in such form, as to them shall seem most likely to effect their Safety and Happiness.

▶ Do you agree that people should overthrow a government, using violence if necessary, when that government violates basic rights? Why or why not?

A Communist View

The Communist Manifesto *was written in 1848 by Karl Marx and Friedrich Engels. The following passages present some of the basic ideas of Communism.*

All history is the history of class struggles.

Freeman and slave, patrician and plebian, lord and serf, guildmaster and journeyman, oppressor and oppressed have constantly opposed one another. They carried on uninterrupted battles which ended each time either in a revolutionary remaking of society or in the common ruin of the opposing classes.

The present period of history, the period of the bourgeoisie, has simplified class antagonisms. Society is splitting into two hostile camps or two classes facing each other: the Bourgeoisie and the Proletariat.

When it has won control, the bourgeoisie has ended all feudal ideal relationships among people of different classes. It has abolished all feudal ties that bound people to their "natural superiors." It has left no other connections between people than naked self-interest.

Communist Manifesto, and Other Writings by Karl Marx, Max Eastman, ed. (New York: Modern Library, Random House, 1932), pp. 321-337. Language modernized.

A patrician was a member of a noble family in Republican Rome. A plebian was a Roman commoner.

The proletariat is the lowest social or economic class of a community.

Here Marx refers to the personal obligations involved in the feudal system and discussed in Chapter 2.

Communism, like other proletarian movements, hopes to form the proletariat into a class, overthrow the bourgeoisie, and conquer political power for the proletariat.

Communism does not wish to abolish all property, but only to abolish bourgeois property. Bourgeois property stands as a symbol for the exploitation of the many for the benefit of the few. In this sense, Communist theory may be summed up in one phrase: the abolition of private ownership of the means of production.

Labor receives only a minimum wage, that is, the amount absolutely necessary to keep the laborer alive. What the laborer receives merely prolongs his existence. We want to stop the practice of paying the laborer this minimum amount so that the owners of property can make large profits with which they increase their supply of capital. Communism will take away the power of some men to require others to work for the profits of a few.

By bourgeois property, Marx meant ownership of the means of production such as factories, farms, and tools.

An Anthropological View

Ashley Montagu, a well-known American anthropologist, is the author of the pamphlet from which the following excerpts are taken. The pamphlet was published by the Anti-Defamation League of B'nai B'rith, a Jewish organization dedicated to the elimination of racial and religious discrimination.

Ashley Montagu, **What We Know About "Race"** (New York: The One Nation Library, Anti-Defamation League of B'nai B'rith, September 1958), pp. 15-16, 39.

No one claims that some differences in intelligence may not exist between different ethnic groups. Such differences may very well exist. It is probable that they do. For no two groups when compared with one another are ever exactly alike in any of the respects in which they are compared; just as no two individuals are ever exactly alike. But this is a very different thing from saying that ethnic groups differ considerably from one another with respect to intelligence. There is no evidence whatever for such a statement, in spite of many attempts to find that evidence. On the contrary, the evidence that most scientists agree upon indicates that between one ethnic group and another the biological endowment for intelligence is much the same. And by intelligence is meant *the ability to make a successful response to a situation.*

Finally, let this be said: the facts about "race," intelligence, and environment are helpful and important in enabling us to understand the human condition a little more clearly. But what is really important to understand is that the idea of equality in no way depends upon these facts. The idea of equality, equality of opportunity and equality of rights, does not depend upon the idea that human beings are of equal biological endowment. Rather, that idea depends upon the ethical principle that every man by virtue of the fact that he is human is therefore entitled to all the rights and privileges that go with being human, and the greatest of these rights is the right to development.

FOR THOUGHT:

What institutional arrangements—political, economic, and social—do you think each writer would propose to bring about equality?

43 CHALLENGES TO THE IDEA OF EQUALITY AND FULL CITIZENSHIP

The American and French revolutions began what one famous historian has called the Age of Democratic Revolutions. Revolutionary movements spread across western Europe as far as Russia. Inspired by examples in the United States and western Europe, people in Latin America also began to demand civil and political rights.

During the nineteenth century, people who believed in equality had much to complain about. Although civil rights had been won in part in Great Britain, the United States, and France, they were not yet universal. Many societies gave their citizens no political rights at all. Even in advanced countries, at the beginning of the nineteenth century the vote was restricted to males who owned property. Nor did any government try to assure social rights by guaranteeing a minimum standard of living.

Both the writers of the period and the actual conditions in society challenged the idea of equality and full citizenship. Reading 43 contains excerpts from five documents written during the nineteenth century. Each of them poses a challenge to the idea of equality. As you read them, keep the following questions in mind:

1. What sort of rights—civil, political, or social—were violated by the ideas or practices described in each document?
2. What arguments were used to defend inequality in each of these documents?

239

François Guizot
Defends Inequality

Louis Philippe came to the throne of France by revolution. The July Revolution of 1830 in Paris overthrew the tyrannical King Charles X, and France established a constitutional monarchy. But even though the king's power was checked by the Chamber of Deputies, the deputies were elected only by those citizens who could afford a tax of two hundred francs. That meant that less than 1 percent of the nation voted. And no one could be a deputy unless he paid a tax of five hundred francs. François Guizot, the chief power in the Chamber of Deputies, defended these discriminatory laws and argued for continued bourgeoisie control of the government. His arguments and the other deputies' response to them appear in the following selection.

François Guizot, **Histoire Parlementaire de France,** as quoted in Thomas C. Mendenhall et al., **The Quest for a Principle of Authority in Europe, 1715–Present** (New York: Holt, Rinehart and Winston, Inc., 1948), p. 150, copyright 1948 by Holt, Rinehart and Winston, Inc. Reprinted by permission.

Gentlemen, nothing can eliminate inequality in this world. There are some rights which are the same for all; but there are some others which are not the same for all. *(Exclamations from the left)* Come now, are political rights the same for all? ... You label this one of the difficulties of our political system; as for me, I don't consider this a difficulty. I am not a believer in universal suffrage. I am convinced that universal suffrage is the death of liberty as well as of order. *(Approval from many quarters)*

I consider inequality and the distribution of political rights as a condition inevitable in a great society, and as the consequence of actual, material, and intellectual inequalities which necessarily exist within this society. *(Approval from the center)* ... I hope that those French people who because of their lot are not yet sufficiently independent or able to enter into political life will progressively improve themselves. In this fashion political rights will spread at the same rate as the individuals called upon to enjoy them become capable of doing so.

America's Peculiar Institution

During the early nineteenth century, the United States was still partly an extension of European civilization. Most Americans had either been born in Europe or were descended from Europeans. And in their new land, they changed old institutions to fit their needs. Among these was the one described by Frederick Law Olmsted after he had traveled through the South.

Frederick Law Olmsted,
The Cotton Kingdom
(London: S. Low, 1861), Vol.
II, pp. 193, 201-204, 207.

▶The marchers pictured here walked the fifty miles from Selma, Alabama, to the state capital of Montgomery in 1965 to encourage people to vote. For what reasons, if any, do you think citizens should try to get other citizens to register and vote?

I am now about to describe what I judged to be the most profitable estate that I visited. The slaves upon it formed about one twentieth of the whole population of the county, in which the blacks considerably outnumber the whites.

Each overseer regulated the hours of work on [one of the four estates of the] plantation. I saw the negroes at work before sunrise and after sunset. At about eight o'clock they were allowed to stop for breakfast, and again about noon, to dine. The length of these rests was at the discretion of the overseer or drivers, usually, I should say, from half an hour to an hour. There was no rule.

The number of hands directed by each overseer was considerably over one hundred. The best overseers, ordinarily, are young men, the sons of small planters, who take up the business temporarily, as a means of acquiring a little capital with which to purchase some negroes for themselves.

▶ Is there any reason why women should not do as hard physical work as men do?

The ploughs at work, both with single and double mule teams, were generally held by women, and very well held, too. I watched with some interest for any indication that their sex unfitted them for the occupation. Twenty of them were ploughing together, with double teams and heavy ploughs. They were superintended by a negro man who carried a whip, which he frequently cracked at them, permitting no dawdling or delay at the turning; and they twitched their ploughs around, jerking their reins, and yelling to their mules, with apparent ease, energy, and rapidity.

The whip was evidently in constant use. There were no rules on the subject that I learned; the overseers and drivers punished the negroes whenever they deemed it necessary and in such manner, and with such severity, as they thought fit. "If you don't work better," or "if you don't recollect what I tell you, I will have you flogged," I often heard. I said to one of the overseers, "It must be disagreeable to have to punish them as much as you do?" "Yes, it would be to those who are not used to it—but it's my business, and I think nothing of it. Why, sir, I wouldn't mind killing a nigger more than I would a dog." I asked if he had ever killed a negro? "Not quite that," he said, "but overseers were often obliged to. Some negroes are determined never to let a white man whip them and will resist you, when you attempt it; of course you must kill them in that case."

▶ Should people use corporal punishment to maintain discipline? For example, should school officials be permitted to paddle students in order to discipline them? Why or why not?

I happened to see the severest corporeal [bodily] punishment of a negro that I witnessed at the South while visiting this estate. I suppose, however, that punishment equally severe is common; in fact, it must be necessary to the maintenance of adequate discipline on every large plantation.

"Was it necessary to punish her so severely?" [I asked the overseer who had brutally beaten a girl who had run off from work.] "Oh yes, sir" (laughing again). "If I hadn't, she would have done the same thing again to-morrow, and half the people on the plantation would have followed her example. Oh, you've no idea how lazy these niggers are; you Northern people don't know anything about it. They'd never do any work at all if they were not afraid of being whipped."

242

The Working Class
in Britain

The industrialization of Britain helped to create such conditions as those described in the following selection. This excerpt comes from testimony given before a parliamentary committee in the 1830's.

Have you ever been employed in a factory?—Yes.

At what age did you first go to work in one?—Eight.

How long did you continue in that occupation?—Four years.

Will you state the hours of labour at the period when you first went to the factory, in ordinary times?—From 6 in the morning to 8 at night.

Fourteen hours?—Yes.

With what intervals for refreshments and for rest?—An hour at noontime.

When trade was brisk what were your hours?—From 5 in the morning to 9 in the evening.

Sixteen hours?—Yes.

How far did you live from the mill?—About two miles.

Was there any time allowed for you to get your breakfast in the mill?—No.

Did you take it before you left your home?—Generally.

During those long hours of labour could you be punctual; how did you awake?—I seldom did awake spontaneously; I was most generally awoke or lifted out of bed, sometimes asleep, by my parents.

Were you always in time?—No.

What was the consequence if you had been too late?—I was most commonly beaten.

Severely?—Very severely, I thought.

In those mills is chastisement toward the latter part of the day going on perpetually?—Perpetually.

So that you can hardly be in a mill without hearing constant crying?—Never an hour, I believe.

Do you think that if the overlooker were naturally a humane person, it would be still found necessary for him to beat the children, in order to keep up their attention and vigilance at the termination of those extraordinary days of labour?—Yes; the machine turns off a regular amount of cardings, and of course they must keep as regularly to their work the whole of the day; they must keep with the machine, and therefore however humane the slubber may be, as he must keep up with the machine or be found fault with, he spurs the children to keep

"Report of Committee on Factory Children's Labour," as quoted in **Parliamentary Papers**, 1831-1832, Vol. XV. pp. 95-97.

A slubber twisted the carded wool or cotton to prepare it for spinning.

up also by various means, but that which he commonly resorts to is to strap them when they become drowsy.

At the time when you were beaten for not keeping up with your work, were you anxious to have done it if you possibly could?—Yes; the dread of being beaten if we could not keep up with our work was a sufficient impulse to keep us to it if we possibly could at all.

Social Classes in Nineteenth-Century Russia

Russia, the largest of all European countries, was the least developed power of nineteenth-century Europe. The changes that had swept Europe for three hundred years had barely reached it, and those that did occur affected only the aristocracy. A British traveler, Sir Donald Mackenzie Wallace, made the following observations after a visit to Russia in the late nineteenth century.

Sir Donald Mackenzie Wallace, **Russia: On the Eve of War and Revolution,** Cyril E. Black, ed. (New York: Vintage Books, Random House, 1961), pp. 92-93.

To [the traveler] it seems that class distinctions form one of the most prominent characteristics of Russian society. In a few days he learns to distinguish the various classes by their outward appearance. He notices perhaps nothing peculiar in the nobles, because they dress in the ordinary European fashion, but he easily recognizes the burly, bearded merchant in black cloth cap and long, shiny, double-breasted coat; the priest with his uncut hair and flowing robes; the peasant with his full, fair beard and unsavory, greasy sheepskin.

Meeting everywhere those well-marked types, he naturally assumes that Russian society is composed of exclusive castes; and this first impression will be fully confirmed by a glance at the Code. On examining that monumental work, he finds that an entire volume—and by no means the smallest—is devoted to the rights and obligations of the various classes. From this he concludes that the classes have a legal as well as an actual existence.

The Code is the **Code of Laws of the Russian Empire,** completed in 1833 and modeled on the **Corpus Juris Civilis** of Justinian. It consisted of 15 volumes.

European Imperialist Ideas

In the late 1800's Europeans scrambled for colonies in the nonwestern world. The following stanzas from a poem by Rudyard Kipling, a British writer, indicate a common European attitude toward the native populations of the colonies.

Take up the White Man's burden—
  Send forth the best ye breed—
Go bind your sons to exile
To serve your captives' need;
To wait in heavy harness,
  On fluttered folk and wild—
Your new-caught, sullen peoples,
  Half-devil and half-child.

Take up the White Man's burden—
  The savage wars of peace—
Fill full the mouth of Famine
  And bid the sickness cease;
  And when your goal is nearest
  The end for others sought,
Watch Sloth and heathen Folly
  Bring all your hope to nought.

Rudyard Kipling, "The White Man's Burden," as quoted in **Rudyard Kipling's Verse: Definitive Edition** (Garden City, New York: Doubleday & Company, Inc., 1938), p. 373. Reprinted by permission of Mrs. George Bambridge, Doubleday & Company, Inc., and A. P. Watt & Son.

FOR THOUGHT:

Do you think that people would be justified to use force in order to win the civil, political, and social rights denied them by the practices described in these documents? Why or why not?

44 THE DEVELOPMENT OF SOCIAL RIGHTS

The movement for equal rights and full citizenship has taken place at different times in various countries. Each set of rights—civil, political, and social—has many separate aspects. Rights in each of these three areas have been won one at a time rather than by a single sweeping reform. Moreover, rights which citizens won in one country were often denied for many years to the citizens of another nation.

People's demands for social rights have been growing for many years. The modern movement for these rights began to develop during the nineteenth century in western Europe and the United States. One of the earliest demands was for free, public education. Demands for various kinds of social insurance, such as old age pensions, workmen's compensation, and unemployment insurance, followed close behind. Today the movement to expand social rights continues steadily.

The movement for social rights was opposed by supporters of the philosophy of laissez–faire. Literally, laissez–faire means "allow to do." Applied to politics, it implies that government should interfere as little as possible in economic affairs. Extreme supporters of laissez-faire were opposed to most government regulations. They argued that government should not tax citizens except for absolute essentials, such as national defense. And they opposed policies by which the government redistributed wealth, such as through public welfare or free education for all.

Reading 44 examines several arguments for social rights which suggest additional government regulation, extraction, or distribution. As you read, keep the following questions in mind:

1. On what grounds did each of these writers defend giving social rights to citizens?
2. How did each writer propose to use regulation, extraction, or distribution by government to achieve his goals?

The Movement for Free Public Schools

During the 1800's, reformers on both sides of the Atlantic began to support the idea of free education for all. The American reformer Horace Mann led the movement for public schools in the United States. The following excerpt from his writing presents some of the arguments he used.

Life and Works of Horace Mann (Boston: Lee and Shepard, 1891), Vol. IV, pp. 114-116. Language simplified.

▶Should people who send their own children to private schools pay taxes to send other people's children to public schools? Why or why not?

Except in New England and a few other local areas, no state or community supports free public schools. The failure to provide free schooling comes mainly from false ideas about the nature of property. Everyone knows that increased privileges such as free education will involve increased taxation to pay for them. Hence, rich men oppose free education because they will be taxed to pay for schools for children of the poor. People who have already paid to educate their own children do not want to be taxed to pay for the education of other people's children. Because of this situation, we should examine the meaning of the right to property. We should also try to determine whether property rights or the right to education are more important.

I believe in a principle of natural law which has divine origins: every human being who comes into the world has an absolute right to an education. This principle implies that government must provide education for everyone. In a democratic society, government must provide enough education to qualify everyone for the civil and social duties of citizenship. This education should teach people how to take care of their health, how to be good parents, how to be a witness or a member of a jury, how to vote, and in general how to be a good citizen.

For whose benefit did God create property in the first place? Surely not for any one man or one generation, but for the benefit of all people from the beginning to the end of time. No man who owns property has a natural right to use it without respecting the rights and claims of future generations. Much of our property has been inherited from past generations rather than earned during our own lifetime. Adult society should act as a trustee managing all property for the benefit of future generations. All children have a claim to some part of the world's property inherited by the present generation. This property should be used to support the schools.

Social Legislation in Germany

During the 1870's, various types of socialism began to appeal strongly to European working people. Among other things, socialists demanded that the government insure workers against sickness, accidents, and old age. Non-socialists began to worry about this development. Otto von Bismarck, a member of the Prussian aristocracy, was then Chancellor of Germany. He decided to push through a series of measures for social insurance in order to head off the demands of the socialists. This excerpt from an interview with Bismarck makes his motives clear.

I went to the Chancellor's palace at the appointed time, and I remained with him for an hour and a half. The Prince sat at his writing table with his face towards the door, and looked particularly well and hearty. He said: "A beginning must be made with the task of reconciling the laboring classes with the State. Whoever has a pension assured to him for his old age is much more contented and easier to manage than the man who has no such prospect. Compare a servant in a private house and one attached to a Government office or to the Court; the latter, because he looks forward to a pension, will put up with a great deal more and show much more zeal than the former. People call this State Socialism, and having done so think they have disposed of the question. It may be State Socialism, but it is necessary."

He paused for a moment, and then continued: "Large sums of money would be required for carrying such schemes into execution, at least a hundred million marks, or more probably two hundred. But I should

Moritz Busch, **Bismarck** (New York: The Macmillan Company, 1898), Vol. 2.

The term Prince here refers to Bismarck.

not be frightened by even three hundred millions. Means must be provided to enable the State to act generously towards the poor. The contentment of the disinherited, of all those who have no possessions, is not too dearly purchased even at a very high figure. They must learn that the State benefits them also, that it not only demands, but also bestows."

Social Reform in Great Britain

More and more workers won the right to vote during the 1800's in Great Britain. At first many of them joined the liberal party which pressed for social reforms. David Lloyd George became one of the most important leaders of the Liberal Party. In this excerpt from one of his speeches, he explains why he supported social legislation.

David Lloyd George, **Better Times: Speeches by the Right Hon. D. Lloyd George** (London: Hodder & Stoughton Limited), 1910.

▶Should society support a wife and children when a husband dies?

What happens today in the working of the great economic machine? A workman breaks down in his prime, and permanently loses his power of earning a livelihood. He has done his best to contribute to the common stock, and he can do no more. Why should he be allowed to starve and his children to die of hunger in this land of superabundant plenty? A workman dies, having done his duty as faithfully to his country as the soldier who falls on the stricken field. He has contributed the whole of his strength and skill towards building up its might and riches. Has the country no obligation to see that those left behind receive their daily bread? Here is the richest country in the world. What a shabby country it must be that it does not see that the widows and orphans of those who have served it faithfully are not suffering from want.

Take another case. A good workman is thrown out of employment. Whose fault is it? Perhaps some greedy financiers who, in their eagerness to get very rich, overstep the bounds of prudent speculation. There is a crash. A panic follows. The trade routes are blocked with the debris, and hundreds of thousands, nay, millions of workmen in many lands are forced to remain idle until the roads are cleared and traffic is resumed. The workmen are not to blame.

Is it just, is it fair, is it humane to let them suffer privation? I do not think the better-off classes, whose comfort is assured, realize the sufferings of the unemployed workmen. What is poverty? Have you felt it yourselves? If not, you ought to thank God for having been spared its sufferings and its temptations. Have you ever seen others enduring it? Then pray God to forgive you if you have not done your

▶The pictures on this page show American government agencies that provide the type of services that Lloyd George described. To what degree, if any, are these services a right rather than a privilege?

best to lighten it. By poverty I mean real poverty, not the limitation of your luxuries. I mean the poverty of the man who does not know how long he can keep a roof over his head, and where he will turn to find a meal for the pinched and hungry little children who look to him for food and protection.

The day will come, and it is not far distant, that this country will shudder at its toleration of that state of things when it was rolling in wealth. I say again, that apart from its inhumanity and its essential injustice, it is robbery, it is confiscation of what is the workman's share of the riches of this land. During years of prosperity the workman has helped to create these enormous resources of wealth which have accumulated in the country since the last period of depression. Hundreds of millions are added to the national wealth during the cycle of plenty. Surely, a few of these millions might be spared to preserve from hunger and from torturing anxiety the workmen who have helped to make that great wealth.

FOR THOUGHT:

Why do you think the movement for social rights began to develop later than the movement for civil and political rights?

45 THE IDEA OF EQUALITY IN THE WESTERN TRADITION

A HISTORICAL ESSAY

During most of human history, equality was only a philosophical idea held by a few advanced thinkers. But in day-to-day affairs, inequality remained the rule. This inequality touched every part of life. People with political power held others powerless. The wealthy refused to share their economic prosperity with slaves, serfs, or workers. And social inequality based on a rigid class structure ruled everywhere.

During most of human history, people have been denied basic civil rights such as freedom of press, speech, and assembly. Their governments treated them as subjects rather than as citizens, denying them the right to vote and to hold political office. And until the 1500's, social rights, such as the right to a free public education or a minimal standard of living, were unknown.

250

The idea of equality and the demand for full citizenship which it implies have never died, however. Supporters of equality have always believed in one fundamental idea: what people have in common is far more important than what separates them. Despite differences in birth, wealth, or power, all people have the same human experiences—birth, death, hunger, thirst, affection, sorrow, delight. Humans alone understand the humor of life. They alone face the brevity of existence and know the inevitability of death.

Western thinkers were the first to justify equality philosophically. One source of this concept lies in the Greek belief in the dignity of the individual. Belief in human equality also grew from the arguments of the Roman thinker, Cicero. He believed that humans shared with God the ability to reason. This talent entitled everyone to political rights. Jesus also championed equality by preaching that entrance into God's kingdom depends in part on how a person treats the poor and unfortunate during earthly life.

Centuries later, Karl Marx argued for equality from an entirely different basis. He denounced private ownership of the means of production as the basis of all inequality and demanded the abolition of both social classes and government to assure full and equal treatment for all. Politicians in democratic countries, such as Lloyd George in Great Britain and every twentieth-century president of the United States, have worked to bring more equal treatment and status without changing the basic structure of the society's institutions. Anthropologists and other social scientists have helped to extend all these reforms by demonstrating that no inherited differences in ability or talent exist among people of different races or between men and women.

In the western world, the movement for equality and full citizenship has gained strength in different countries at different times. On the whole, the United States, Great Britain, and France led the way, while other western European nations followed in their paths. During the 1800's and 1900's, people in Russia, Latin America, Asia, and Africa adapted western ideas of equality to their own social settings and joined the movement toward full citizenship.

In the United States, Great Britain, and France people first tried to win civil rights. Next they demanded political rights. Once people had won the vote, they began to struggle for social rights. In other nations the movements for civil, political, and social rights often took place at once. Nations in Asia and Africa gradually won independence after World War II, which ended in 1945. Many of these nations tried to grant simultaneously rights of all three types that westerners had won over centuries of struggle. Some of them failed in this first attempt.

In the three nations that led the struggle for equality and full citizenship, the movement first pressed for the rights of free white men. Later, movements rose to grant women's rights, the rights of native minority

▶To what extent do you believe that the things people have in common are more important than the things that sometimes separate them, such as color, faith, income, or national origin?

251

peoples, and the rights of people who lived in colonies. In Asia and Africa after World War II, however, some nations tried to grant equal rights to all groups of people at once. This development shows the power of the concepts of equality and full citizenship once people have seen them demonstrated anywhere in the world.

England led the way in the long movement to establish civil rights. The Norman conquerors of England kept several of the Anglo-Saxon institutions they found there. These institutions included the king's council, the sheriff, common law, and the jury system. Later, traveling justices who served the king helped to establish one set of laws throughout the kingdom. Although these laws treated nobles differently from commoners, they were the basis of civil rights in the lands which England ruled or colonized. Eventually many of these rights were written into national law in such measures as the Bill of Rights and the Toleration Act, both passed in 1689. Over the years, the laws and the courts began to treat people of all social classes in the same ways.

Political rights also grew slowly in England. At first, only the nobility, the clergy, and certain knights and burgesses who held property could vote to send representatives to Parliament. Over several centuries, the House of Lords and the House of Commons weakened the power of the king, primarily by winning control of the purse strings. By the 1800's, Great Britain had a well-established parliamentary system. However, few people could vote, and many people such as Catholics, Jews, and the poor, were barred from holding many political offices.

British colonists to America expanded these civil and political rights when they emigrated. Most American colonies granted the vote to many more people than had been done in England and made many more people eligible to hold public office. The colonists insisted on the right to freedom of the press. They firmly established the most advanced system of civil and political rights in the world when they wrote the Constitution in 1787. This famous document, and the Bill of Rights that accompanied it, established full civil rights for most citizens. These documents also laid the institutional basis for the movement toward full political rights for white males that followed a few years later.

While these changes were taking place in the United States, a revolution had broken out in France. This revolt had far greater immediate effect on civil rights than on political rights. By abolishing the estate system and removing the church from its privileged position, the French Revolution took a huge step toward establishing equal treatment before the law. Napoleon and his successors cut back voting rights. But the ideas of the Revolution—universal male suffrage, the right of everyone to hold public office, and the right of people to govern themselves through a legislature—took powerful hold of the minds of Frenchmen and of many other Europeans.

See the analysis of this movement in Chapter 5.

In 1734 the courts declared that a New York publisher, John Peter Zenger, could print criticisms of the government as long as they were factually accurate without committing libel. This decision helped to establish freedom of the press in the colonies.

252

During the hundred years before the outbreak of World War I in 1914, most northeastern European countries granted universal manhood suffrage, removed economic and religious qualifications for office-holding, and set up parliamentary political institutions. Again Great Britain led the way. In 1828 Parliament repealed the Test Act which had required public officials to swear that they believed in the Anglican faith. The Catholic Emancipation Act of 1829 gave Catholics the right to vote and to hold public office. In 1858 Parliament removed political restrictions on Jews. A series of reform bills gradually extended the vote to all males, established equal electoral districts, required the use of the secret ballot, and reduced the power of the House of Lords. Two bills passed in 1918 and 1928 extended the vote to women several decades after other nations had granted this basic right.

By this time most northeastern European nations had established universal suffrage and parliamentary institutions. France established the Third Republic after Germany defeated her in a war which ended in 1871. The Netherlands, Belgium, and the three Scandinavian countries all became constitutional monarchies granting full civil and political rights, while Switzerland emerged as a democratic republic. Universal manhood suffrage became the rule in Italy, Hungary, Austria, Spain, Greece, Bulgaria, Serbia, and Turkey. Most of these nations also established parliamentary institutions with limited powers. Even Russia called a meeting of its parliament, the Duma, in 1905. After World War I, almost all of these nations, as well as new countries such as Czechoslovakia and Poland that emerged from the war, established parliamentary governments. They granted a wide variety of civil and political rights to both men and women.

The movement for social rights began alongside the movement for civil and political rights. Free public education led the way. By 1900, most young people in western Europe had learned to read and write in the new public schools. Several countries, particularly Great Britain and Germany, set up social insurance systems. Governments began to regulate or build housing for the poor, provide public medical treatment, extend free education through college, and expand other social rights. Gradually voters passed a set of laws that established a minimal standard of living for everyone in the society. This standard represents the social rights that citizens in democratic countries now expect as a part of full citizenship.

None of these reforms came automatically. Behind each one lay a long history of agitation and struggle by millions of men and women. The famous reformers have their names in books and on laws, but none of them could have succeeded without the support and often the initiative of typical citizens who demanded full rights and sacrificed to win them.

►The pictures and chart on pages 254-256 illustrate several ways in which Americans win, keep, or use their rights. To what degree do you feel responsible for winning or protecting your civil, political, or social rights?

254

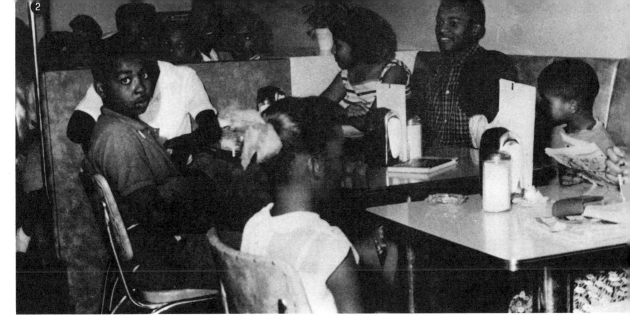

*These black people staged a sit-down in an Oklahoma luncheonette in the
late 1950's. They were seeking the right to be served.*

VOTING PARTICIPATION IN PRESIDENTIAL ELECTIONS

Number and Percentage of Potential Voters Who Voted in the Presidential Election of 1968

States	Voting Age Population (Thousands)	Votes Cast (Thousands)	Percent Voting Age Voting	States	Voting Age Population (Thousands)	Votes Cast (Thousands)	Percent Voting Age Voting
Ala.	2,034	1,050	51.6	Nev.	276	154	55.9
Alaska	123	83	67.5	N. H.	421	297	70.6
Ariz.	932	487	52.2	N. J.	4,376	2,875	65.7
Ark.	1,169	620	53.0	N. M.	519	327	63.1
Calif.	11,645	7,252	62.3	N. Y.	11,702	6,790	58.0
Colo.	1,153	810	70.3	N. C.	2,873	1,587	55.3
Conn.	1,817	1,255	69.1	N. Dak.	357	248	69.4
Del.	300	214	71.5	Ohio	6,225	3,960	63.6
Fla.	3,772	2,188	58.0	Okla.	1,504	943	62.7
Ga.	2,776	1,250	45.0	Ore.	1,237	819	66.2
Hawaii	376	236	62.8	Penn.	7,252	4,748	65.5
Idaho	398	291	73.2	R. I.	545	385	70.6
Ill.	6,565	4,619	70.4	S. C.	1,400	667	47.6
Ind.	2,952	2,124	71.9	S. Dak.	382	281	73.6
Iowa	1,650	1,168	70.8	Tenn.	2,345	1,249	53.2
Kans.	1,350	873	64.7	Texas	6,205	3,079	49.6
Ky.	2,021	1,056	52.2	Utah	552	423	76.6
La.	2,012	1,097	54.3	Vt.	246	161	65.6
Maine	570	393	68.9	Va.	2,579	1,359	52.7
Md.	2,137	1,235	57.8	Wash.	1,794	1,304	72.7
Mass.	3,344	2,332	69.9	W. Va.	1,079	754	69.9
Mich.	4,953	3,306	66.8	Wisc.	2,468	1,689	68.4
Minn.	2,089	1,589	76.0	Wyo.	183	127	69.5
Miss.	1,274	655	51.4	Dist. of			
Mo.	2,792	1,810	64.8	Col.	497	171	34.3
Mont.	398	274	68.9				
Neb.	854	537	62.9	**TOTALS**	**118,465**	**73,203**	**61.8**

These Indians occupied the town of Wounded Knee, South Dakota, demanding an investigation of government treatment of Indians.

In this context, elite means a powerful minority group.

Different countries have won different degrees of civil, political, and social rights. For example, in the Soviet Union, citizens have never had most of the civil and political rights common in the West. Soviet citizens do not have freedom of speech, press, and assembly. Although they have the right to vote and to hold office, effective political power lies in the hands of a small elite which dominates the Communist Party. But Soviet citizens have perhaps the most complete system of social rights in the world, considering the resources of Soviet society. These social rights have been granted by the regime rather than won by the demands of citizens.

In western democracies, citizens continue to win new rights through political action. Since World War II, both black Americans and Native

Americans have begun to demand equal civil, political, and social rights. Women in the United States have also awakened to the awareness that they have been denied many rights. The Women's Liberation Movement grew out of this awareness. Political and civil rights give all these minorities an opportunity to make their cases heard and to demand full equality. Soviet citizens do not have this opportunity because they lack civil and political rights.

The movement for equality and full citizenship now embraces the entire world. Once peculiarly western, it now has an international flavor. Newspapers and magazines often praise the technological contributions of the West to humankind. But they sometimes fail to stress the impact of the ideas of equality and full citizenship that the West has also exported. Perhaps these concepts have as much to contribute to human happiness as the triumphs of modern technology.

Many American Indians now prefer to be called Native Americans.

▶Do you ever think of women as a minority group that lacks some of the rights men have? Why or why not?

▶What do you think gives life more meaning and contributes more to human happiness—the ability to put people on the moon or the assurance of full civil, political, and social rights in a modern democratic society?

Individual and Group Activities for Chapter 10

For full descriptions of these activities, turn to the **Student Book of Activities and Readings** included among the materials for individual and group activities.

Activity 10A: Picture collection to illustrate the idea of equality in contemporary society (individual or group)

Collect a group of pictures that suggest the idea of equality in some form. Use the pictures to make a filmstrip, a scrapbook, or a collage to demonstrate different modern interpretations of the concept of equality.

Activity 10B: Interview and investigation of the women's liberation movement as a contemporary interpretation of the idea of equality (individual or group)

Investigate the background of the women's liberation movement so that you have a basic understanding of it. Then interview a member of the movement to learn how she interprets the idea of equality. Present your findings in a skit or an oral report in class.

Nationalism

Most modern people give their primary loyalty to their nation. People identify themselves as French, Chinese, Peruvian, or American even when they live in foreign lands. Their nation is the most important institution around which they organize their social, economic, and political lives. The citizens of each nation share an interdependent economy and usually the same language. They choose officials to run their nation's political system and to deal with other nations. No other institution attracts so much devotion in so many areas of life.

The nation-state has not always played such a central role in human affairs. During most of western history, people gave their allegiance to other institutions or to individuals. In ancient Greece, people gave their greatest loyalty to their city-state. The people who lived in the vast Roman Empire included Goths, Egyptians, Greeks, and many others who gave their primary loyalties to their own group rather than to Rome. During the Middle Ages, people divided their loyalties among their lords, their families, and the Church. The city-state once again claimed first allegiance during the Renaissance in Italy. Nationalism became a vital force only during modern times.

What is a nation? What is nationalism? Like democracy, socialism, and imperialism, definitions of nation-state and nationalism have varied according to time and place. These two words had different meanings to sixteenth-century English people, nineteenth-century Italians, and twentieth-century Germans. This chapter will examine some of the different meanings of nationalism. As you study, you will discover some of the problems of developing a historical definition of a term, that is, a definition that changes with time and place. You will also examine the enormous influence that nationalism has had in the modern world.

1485-1603	Nationalism grows in Tudor England.
1789	National consciousness spurs revolution in France.
1790	Civil Constitution of the Clergy is passed.
1795-1814	Napoleon's conquests kindle nationalism in many countries.
1831	Joseph Mazzini forms nationalist society called Young Italy.
1848	France, Austria, Italy, and Prussia experience unsuccessful liberal revolutions.
1852	Camillo di Cavour becomes prime minister of Piedmont.
1862	Otto von Bismarck becomes prime minister of Prussia.
1866	Prussia defeats Austria in Austro-Prussian War.
1867	Prussia organizes North German Confederation.
1870-1871	Prussia wins Franco-Prussian War.
1871	German Empire proclaimed at Versailles.
	Bismarck becomes imperial chancellor.

46 TUDOR NATIONALISM

Although historians generally date the rise of modern nationalism with the French Revolution, most of them agree that elements of nationalist feeling appeared in England during the reign of the Tudor monarchs, who ruled from 1485-1603. By the sixteenth century, English monarchs had laid the foundations for a nation-state. Armies loyal to the monarchs and paid by them had replaced the feudal armies of the nobles. The monarchs had also forged strong links between themselves and the rich merchants and landed gentry. By inviting these groups to sit in Parliament, the monarchs had given them a voice in political decision-making and a sense of national purpose.

However, civil war broke out in 1455 and lasted thirty years. Two families, the Yorks and the Lancasters, competed for the right to rule, until Henry VII, head of the house of Lancaster, ended the civil war, united England again, and began the Tudor dynasty. He and most of the Tudors reduced the role of the nobles while increasing their own power.

As the Tudors unified the country, they also stimulated national loyalty. Henry VIII and Elizabeth I often appealed to national pride to win support for their policies. The strong government they created, able to resist foreign interference and keep peace and prosperity at home, won the loyalty of their subjects.

The following selections, taken from the literature and public records of sixteenth-century England, deal with the growth of nationalism under the Tudors. From these readings, you should be able to construct hypotheses about the nature of English nationalism and the way in which it was fostered under the Tudors. As you read, keep the following questions in mind:

1. What arguments does each of these selections make?
2. What do these arguments reveal about the nature of nationalism in Tudor England?

England Challenges the Pope

In Chapter 4 you read about England's break with the Roman Catholic Church. To legalize this break, Parliament passed a number of acts. The following excerpt has been taken from one of them— An Act for the Exoneration [release] from Exactions [taxes] Paid to the See [Church territory] of Rome.

The Statutes of the Realm (London: Printed by Command of His Majesty George the Third, 1817), Vol. III, pp. 464-471. Language simplified.

We, your obedient and faithful subjects, members of the House of Commons, most humbly beseech your most royal majesty.

The pope has imposed intolerable taxes on this realm. He also has tricked your subjects into believing that he had full power to dispense all human laws and customs of this your realm in all causes which are called spiritual.

In this, your grace's realm, we recognize no superior under God except your grace. We recognize no laws except those that have been made within this realm for its continued prosperity. The people of this realm have bound themselves by long use and custom to the laws made by our own consent and the consent of your grace and your predecessors. We refuse to obey the laws of a foreign prince or leader of the Church.

Be it provided: For the honor of Almighty God and for the tender love, zeal, and affection that you bear and have always borne for the wealth of this realm and its subjects, no person or persons of this your realm shall from henceforth pay any taxes to the pope.

Shakespeare's "Sceptred Isle"

The plays of William Shakespeare (1564-1616) were performed for English audiences of all classes. Some of Shakespeare's most popular works recaptured the history of England. Two excerpts from such works follow.

William Shakespeare, The Life of King Henry V as quoted in The Complete Dramatic and Poetic Works of William Shakespeare (New York: Holt, Rinehart and Winston, Inc., 1952), pp. 552, 563-564.

HENRY V, ACT 3, SCENE 1

Once more unto the breach, dear friends, once more;
Or close the wall up with our English dead.
In peace there's nothing so becomes a man
As modest stillness and humility:
But when the blast of war blows in our ears,
Then imitate the action of the tiger;
Stiffen the sinews, summon up the blood,
Disguise fair nature with hard-favour'd rage; . . .
Now set the teeth and stretch the nostril wide,
Hold hard the breath, and bend up every spirit
To his full height! On, on, you noblest English! . . .
Be copy now to men of grosser blood,
And teach them how to war. And you, good yeomen,
Whose limbs were made in England, show us here
The mettle of your pasture; let us swear
That you are worth your breeding; which I doubt not;
For there is none of you so mean and base
That hath not noble lustre in your eyes.
I see you stand like greyhounds in the slips,
Straining upon the start. The game's afoot:
Follow your spirit; and upon this charge
Cry "God for Harry! England, and Saint George!"

Henry V makes this speech to his troops as he prepares to battle the French at Agincourt. Henry ruled England from 1413 to 1422. He attacked France in 1415 to regain lands in France held by his ancestors and to press his claim to the French throne.

"The mettle of your pasture" means the fine quality of your upbringing.

Slips are leashes.

Harry is Henry V.

HENRY V, ACT 4, SCENE 3

No, my fair cousin:
If we are mark'd to die, we are enow
To do our country loss; and if to live,
The fewer men, the greater share of honour.
God's will! I pray thee, wish not one man more.
By Jove, I am not covetous for gold,
Nor care I who doth feed upon my cost;
It yearns me not if men my garments wear;
Such outward things dwell not in my desires:
But if it be a sin to covet honour,
I am the most offending soul alive. . . .

At this point, Henry is about to lead his men into the battle of Agincourt. He speaks here to bolster the Earl of Westmoreland's courage. Westmoreland (1364-1425), Henry's cousin and a member of one of the most powerful families in England, did not accompany Henry to France as Shakespeare has him do.

This day is called the feast of Crispian:
He that outlives this day, and comes safe home,
Will stand a tip-toe when this day is nam'd,
And rouse him at the name of Crispian.
He that shall live this day, and see old age,
Will yearly on the vigil feast his neighbours,
And say "To-morrow is Saint Crispian":
Then will he strip his sleeve and show his scars,
And say, "These wounds I had on Crispin's day.". . .
We few, we happy few, we band of brothers;
For he today that sheds his blood with me
Shall be my brother; be he ne'er so vile
This day shall gentle his condition:
And gentlemen in England now abed
Shall think themselves accurs'd they were not here,
And hold their manhoods cheap whiles any speaks
That fought with us upon Saint Crispin's day. . . .

►Henry puts honor above wealth and heroism above comfort. Where in your own value system would you place these characteristics?

RICHARD II, ACT 2, SCENE 1

William Shakespeare, **The Tragedy of King Richard II,** as quoted in **The Complete Dramatic and Poetic Works of William Shakespeare,** pp. 446-447.

John of Gaunt (1340-1399), Duke of Lancaster, makes this speech as he is dying. Gaunt was the wealthiest noble in England at his time and extremely powerful. His son became Henry IV, the first of the Lancaster kings. The Tudors were also his descendants.

This royal throne of kings, this sceptred isle,
This earth of majesty, this seat of Mars,
This other Eden, demi-paradise,
This fortress built by Nature for herself
Against infection and the hand of war,
This happy breed of men, this little world,
This precious stone set in the silver sea,
Which serves it in the office of a wall,
Or as a moat defensive to a house,
Against the envy of less happier lands,
This blessed plot, this earth, this realm, this England, . . .

The Last Fight of the *Revenge*

Sir Walter Raleigh, "A Report of the Truth of the Fight About the Isles of Azores," as quoted in C. W. Colby, **Selections from the Sources of English History** (London: Longmans, Green & Co., 1911). Language simplified.

Sir Richard Grenville (1542?-1591), commander of the British man-of-war, Revenge, *lost his ship in 1591 while attempting to capture Spanish treasure ships. His cousin, Sir Walter Raleigh (1552?-1618), came to Grenville's defense when rumors circulated that the commander had acted in a cowardly fashion. Raleigh, a poet and businessman who organized colonizing expeditions to America, held important court positions under Elizabeth I. The following selection is from Raleigh's defense of Grenville.*

262

All the powder of the *Revenge* was now spent, all its pikes broken, forty of its best men killed, and most of the remainder of the ship's company wounded. In the beginning of the fight the *Revenge* had only one hundred able-bodied men, and these men bravely sustained the volleys, boardings, and enterings of fifteen ships of war. For us there remained no comfort at all, no hope, no supply either of ships, men, or weapons; the masts all beaten overboard, the tackle [rigging] split, the upper works totally destroyed, with nothing left for defense except the very foundation of the ship.

Sir Richard Grenville finding himself in this situation, having endured fifteen hours of continuous assault by the enemy and now being totally surrounded by the enemy, commanded the master gunner, whom he knew to be a most brave and resolute man, to split and sink the ship. This action would take away from the Spanish the honor and glory of capturing the *Revenge*, a task to which they had devoted fifteen

263

hours, fifty-three ships, and over ten thousand men. After this order, Grenville persuaded the ship's company, or as many as he could, to surrender themselves to God and to no one else, so that these valiant men, after having bravely held off so large an enemy force, would not by their surrender to the enemy lessen the honor of their nation by prolonging their own lives for a few hours or a few days.

►Does it make sense to you to destroy ships or other property so they will not fall into the hands of the enemy?

The Scorn of Stephen Gosson

In 1579 Stephen Gosson (1554-1624), a contemporary of William Shakespeare, challenged the worth of plays, poetry, and other arts in a work called The School of Abuse. *In the following selection from Gosson's book, he criticizes fashions and the theater.*

Stephen Gosson, **The School of Abuse,** Edward Arber, ed. (London: Alexander Murray and Son, 1869), p. 39. Language simplified.

Elizabeth's reign from 1558 to 1603 is considered one of England's greatest periods. During this time, the English gained control of the seas, explored new lands and established colonies, and produced a culture in many ways as rich as that of the Italian Renaissance.

God has blessed England with a Queen, in virtue excellent, in power mighty, in glory renowned, in government politic, and in possessions rich. She breaks her foes with a mere nod of the head. She rules her subjects by a mere flick of the hand. She makes debate unnecessary because she has great foresight for the realm. She has filled the royal treasury because she has kept the peace, she has administered justice by order of law, and she has taken great pains to reform abuses. But we unworthy servants of so kind a mistress, bad children of so good a mother, ungrateful subjects of so loving a prince, wound her royal heart by taking advantage of her leniency. How often has her Majesty advised us about the standards of tasteful dress and how often have we violated those standards. How often has she warned us to avoid theaters which destroy our morals and how boldly have we gone into them.

FOR THOUGHT:

How did the people of sixteenth-century England define nation? How did they express their feelings of nationalism?

. 47 NINETEENTH-CENTURY NATIONALISM IN ITALY

The citizens of France developed intense loyalties to their nation through the French Revolution. When other European nations threatened their independence, the French united to fight for their revolutionary political and social ideals. Their strong feelings of patriotism drove them through Europe on conquests led by Napoleon Bonaparte.

The example of the French people unified under a common cause and a common set of ideals inspired nationalism in other European countries. And French occupation of conquered lands encouraged nationalism in another way. Many of the conquered peoples resented French domination and joined together to resist it. Long after the spirit of revolution had faded away, nationalistic feelings still remained.

In Italy, French rule encouraged nationalism by breaking down loyalty to the various republics, duchies, papal states, and foreign countries in power there. By driving out the existing governments and installing himself or members of his family as rulers, Napoleon demonstrated that a unified Italy was a reasonable possibility. But when he was exiled in 1814, the old rulers returned. Chief among the foreign countries controlling Italy was Austria which dominated the northern states of Lombardy and Venetia. In addition, relatives of the emperor of Austria controlled Parma, Modena, and Tuscany. (See map, page 266.)

But the foreign rulers could not hold back the patriots who struggled to develop nationalist feeling among the Italians. Among these patriots were intellectuals and journalists who had been inspired by the ideals of the French Revolution. They believed that liberty, equality, and fraternity could never triumph as long as foreigners ruled large sections of their country. Northern Italian business people also opposed Austrian rule. They thought that Austrian economic policies interfered with their business. The goal of the Italian patriots became to drive Austria out of Italy and to unify the separate Italian states into one nation.

The selections in this reading contain three examples of ways in which Italian patriots tried to unify Italy. As you read, think about these questions:

1. How did each of these writers believe that national feeling could best be developed in Italy?
2. What benefits did each of these writers think would result from a united nation?

Joseph Mazzini: Unity Under a Republic

One of the most enthusiastic Italian patriots, Joseph Mazzini (1805-1872), founded a society called Young Italy to urge Italian unity. His efforts did much to plant nationalist ideas firmly in Italian minds.

Joseph Mazzini, Joseph Mazzini, His Life, Writings, and Political Principles (New York: Hurd & Houghton, 1872), pp. 62-67. Language simplified.

Young Italy is a brotherhood of Italians who believe in progress and duty. We are convinced that Italy is destined to become one nation. We are convinced that Italians can unify the nation without outside help. Former efforts to bring unity failed not because of the weakness of the Italian spirit but because revolutionary efforts were misguided. Those who join this organization devote both their thought and action to achieve the great aim of making Italy one independent, sovereign nation of free and equal men.

The aim of this association is to bring about a revolution; but its work will be essentially educational. The association therefore declares the principles which will be taught to our countrymen.

Young Italy aims to create a country that is *republican* and *unified*.

UNIFICATION OF ITALY   1859-1870

Kingdom of Sardinia before 1859

From Austria to Sardinia in 1859

Added to Sardinia in 1860 to form the Kingdom of Italy

Added to Italy in 1866

Added to Italy in 1870

We aim to make Italy republican because under the law of God and humanity every nation is destined to form a free and equal community of brothers. A republican government is the only political system that insures this future.

Young Italy wants a republic because there are no strong, native monarchs in Italy. We have no powerful respected aristocracy to step in between the throne and the people. We have no dynasty of Italian princes that has a tradition of glory or service devoted to the nation. No king commands the affection of all the people.

We are republican because our traditions are essentially republican. Our memories of Rome and the Renaissance city-states are memories of republics. We have progressed most under these republics. Whenever monarchs ruled our land, Italy decayed. They brought on our ruin by subjecting themselves to foreigners.

Young Italy wants the country unified because without unity there is no true nation. Without unity there can be no real strength. Italy is surrounded by powerful, united, and jealous nations. Because she is, she needs strength before all things.

Vincenzo Gioberti:
Unity Under the Pope

Vincenzo Gioberti (1801-1852) was a Roman Catholic priest who became deeply involved in the movement for Italian unity and independence. He served as prime minister of Piedmont from 1848 to 1849. His plan for unification follows.

That the pope should be the civil leader of Italy is a fact proved by the nature of things, confirmed by many centuries of history, recognized on many occasions by both the people and the princes, and doubted only by those who hope to serve some foreign interest. In order to establish a unified confederation of Italian states it is not necessary for the pope to receive or assume new powers. All he must do is put back into operation his ancient right to govern Italy.

There are three essential aspects of the perfect political organization: unity, liberty, and independence of the fatherland from foreign interference. No public life is perfect if the people are not united, if they are not free of any foreign yoke and not strong enough so that they fear no foreign power, and if they do not enjoy full civil liberty. Civil liberty is the single essential element desired by all. Those who have civil liberty, that is, freedom from government oppression, do not need political liberty, or the right to participate in the government. Only

Vincenzo Gioberti, **Del Primato Morale et Civile degli Italiani,** as quoted in Thomas C. Mendenhall et al., **The Quest for a Principle of Authority in Europe, 1715-Present** (New York: Holt, Rinehart and Winston, Inc., 1948), p. 180, copyright 1948 by Holt, Rinehart and Winston, Inc. Reprinted by permission. Language simplified.

those who do not have civil liberty desire political liberty to free them-selves from ancient shackles. Now, from what I have shown, it is clear that Italy can win these benefits without war, without revolution, and without offense to any other authorities. That is to say, unity and liberty can be won by a confederacy of the various Italian states under the presidency of the pope, and they can maintain their independence by carrying out internal reforms within their own states.

Count Camillo di Cavour:
Unity Under
Native Princes

Count Cavour (1810-1861) was prime minister of Piedmont from 1852 to 1859 and from 1860 to 1861. At that time, Piedmont was a constitutional monarchy under Victor Emmanuel II. In the follow-ing selection, Cavour offers his reasons for wanting to unite Italy.

Gli Scritti del Conte di Cavour, D. Zanichelli, ed., as quoted in Mendenhall, et al., The Quest for a Principle of Authority in Europe, 1715-Present, p. 183. Language simplified.

▶Do you believe that your national identity as an American makes you capable of more intelligence and morality than if you belonged to no nation?

Cavour is referring to the revolutions in 1820, 1830, and 1848. These revolutions brought almost no changes to Italy.

The history of every age proves that no people can reach a high degree of intelligence and morality unless its feeling of nationality is strongly developed. The masses can understand only a few limited ideas. After religious ideas, the highest and the noblest are the concepts of fatherland and nationality. The political circumstances of our country now prevent the people from forming the concepts of fatherland and nationality. Consequently, the masses remain plunged in a state of de-plorable inferiority. Moreover, the mass of people cannot have a feeling of personal dignity if they cannot be proud of their nationality. They must be conscious of their dignity to be moral.

We ardently wish to free Italy from foreign rule. We agree that we must put aside all petty differences in order to gain this most impor-tant goal. We wish to drive out the foreigners not only because we want to see our country powerful and glorious, but because we want to elevate the Italian people in intelligence and moral development.

Unless Europe explodes in war or revolution, a possibility that seems less likely every day, the precious conquest of our nationality can be reached only through the combined action of the strongest forces in the country: the national princes supported by all different nationalist parties. The history of the last thirty years shows what little effect military or democratic revolutions have had. If the friends of our country put aside these useless methods, they will realize that they can help achieve the true good of our country by rallying behind those thrones which have their roots deep in the national soil. Such conduct will restore the unity so badly needed in the Italian community. These

KEEP HIM FREE

BUY
WAR SAVINGS STAMPS
ISSUED BY THE UNITED STATES TREASURY DEPT.

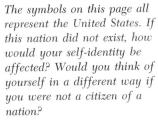

The symbols on this page all represent the United States. If this nation did not exist, how would your self-identity be affected? Would you think of yourself in a different way if you were not a citizen of a nation?

sincere, but misguided revolutionary patriots will then allow national princes to take advantage of the favorable political circumstances of our time to rid our land of all foreign rule.

FOR THOUGHT:

How did each of these writers define nationalism? How did the nature of nationalism in nineteenth-century Italy differ from nationalism under the Tudors?

48 NINETEENTH-CENTURY NATIONALISM IN GERMANY

Like Italy, Germany was divided into many small separate states in the nineteenth century. (See map, page 271.) Like the Italian patriots, many German intellectuals, business people, and politicians dreamed of and worked for a united Germany. Some believed a unified Germany would reduce barriers to trade. Others thought unification was the first step toward realizing the ideals of the French Revolution. Still others believed that a united Germany could better oppose French, Austrian, and Russian threats to take over or dominate individual German states.

The first serious attempt to unify Germany took place in 1848. In that year, a group of scholars, professional people, business people, and writers from most of the German states met in Frankfurt to draw up a constitution for a united Germany. The reformers were supported by landless peasants, artisans whose handicrafts were being replaced by machine-made products, and a small, but growing, working class. However, the Frankfurt Assembly did not deal with their problems. It created a bourgeois-controlled constitutional monarchy to be headed by the king of Prussia. Since it did not promise land reform for the peasants, economic security for the artisans, or social welfare measures for the workers, these groups withdrew their support. The king of Prussia also rejected the constitutional monarchy. Although he was in favor of uniting Germany under his throne, he did not want his power limited by a constitution. As a result, once the spirit of revolution died away, the king set out to unify Germany on his own terms.

Unification was finally achieved by the brilliant diplomacy and intrigue of Otto von Bismarck, prime minister of Prussia from 1862 to 1867. To end Austrian control of the German states, Bismarck provoked the Austro-Prussian War in 1866. Following the defeat of Austria, the

German states north of the Main River formed the North German Confederation under Prussian leadership, with Bismarck as chancellor. (See map, this page.) Austria and the German states south of the Main River were excluded from the new organization and were not united among themselves. Bismarck joined the southern German states to the North German Confederation by provoking war with France in 1870. Fearing France, the southern German states sided with Prussia. France was easily defeated and forced to give up Alsace and most of Lorraine to Germany. (See map, this page.) The German Empire, consisting of the southern German states and the states of the North German Confederation, was proclaimed in 1871 with the king of Prussia as emperor and Bismarck as chancellor.

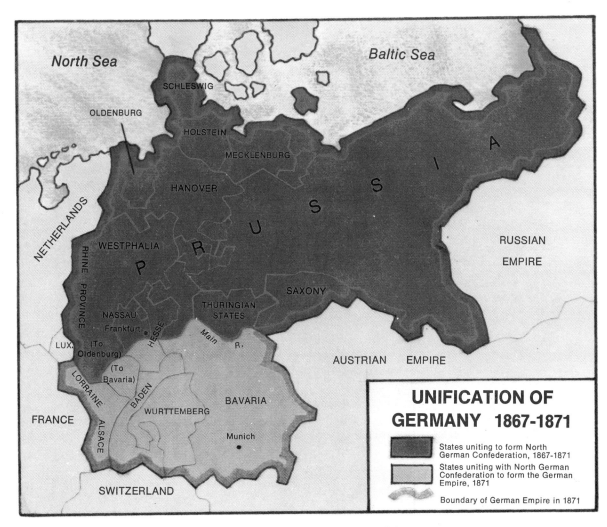

UNIFICATION OF GERMANY 1867-1871

States uniting to form North German Confederation, 1867-1871

States uniting with North German Confederation to form the German Empire, 1871

Boundary of German Empire in 1871

As nationalist feeling developed, Germany passed through three distinct stages. Before 1848, intellectuals and members of the bourgeoisie attempted to unify Germany under a liberal constitution. After 1848, the Prussian monarchy took on the task of nation building. Following 1871, there was an outpouring of nationalist feeling in literature, art, and music. For example, Richard Wagner (1813-1883) composed operas glorifying German heroes. The selections in Reading 48 illustrate some of the ways nationalism was expressed during each of three periods. As you read, keep the following questions in mind:

1. How are the major ideas of these three writers similar? How are they different?
2. Judging from these selections, how do you think German nationalism changed during the nineteenth century?

Wilhelm von Humboldt: Nationalism Before 1848

Wilhelm von Humboldt (1767-1835) was minister of education in Prussia from 1809 to 1810. In 1813, concerned about the fate of Germany once Napoleon was defeated, he drafted the following memorandum to plead for German unity.

Wilhelm von Humboldt, **Gesammelte Schriften,** as quoted in Mendenhall, et al., **The Quest for a Principle of Authority in Europe, 1715-Present,** p. 207. Language simplified.

Only a nation strong enough to meet aggression can preserve its inner blessings. It must be strong and free to build up self-reliance in the people, to pursue its national development peacefully, and to keep an advantageous position in the midst of the other European nations.

The feeling that Germany is a unit does not depend only on common customs, language, and literature. It also depends on the memory of rights and liberties enjoyed—and dangers suffered—in common. It depends on the memory of another age when our ancestors were more unified. If the individual German states continue their self-seeking, isolated status, they will learn it is impossible, or at least very difficult, to remain self-reliant. This situation would be very dangerous to the European balance of power. It would endanger the larger German states, even Austria and Prussia, and gradually weaken the German nationality.

Balance of power refers to the diplomatic principle that guided the Congress of Vienna in its decisions. It attempted to equalize the power of the major European nations to discourage aggression by any one of them.

There are only two methods by which a people can be held together: a real constitution or a mere confederation. A constitution is undeniably better than a confederation. It is more impressive, more binding, and more lasting.

272

Otto von Bismarck: Nationalism After 1848

The conditions under which Bismarck believed Germany could be unified are described in the following excerpt from one of his messages to the Prussian legislature.

In order for German patriotism to be active and effective, it needs to depend on a dynasty. Patriotism rarely rises to the surface if it is not linked with loyalty to a dynasty. In theory, it does emerge in parliament, in the press, in public meetings. In practice, however, the German needs either the attachment to a dynasty or the goad of anger to hurry him into action. Anger is not permanent. It is as a Prussian, a Hanoverian, a Württemberger, or a Bavarian rather than as a German that he is ready to give complete proof of his patriotism.

We cannot say that the Hanoverian, Hessian, and other dynasties have taken any special pains to win the affections of their subjects. Nonetheless, the people's patriotism to Germany as a whole is conditioned by their attachment to a particular dynasty. In order for a German to love his fatherland, he must have a prince upon whom he can concentrate his loyalty. Suppose that all the German dynasties were suddenly deposed. There is little likelihood that the German people would have enough national sentiment to hold themselves together.

Germans differ from other European peoples in that they attach themselves to dynasties. The dynasty is the indispensable cement which holds together a definite portion of the nation. The dynasties have shaped the identity of the German people. Neither family ties nor a similar historical development hold them together. They have only the dynasty.

Otto von Bismarck, **Otto von Bismarck: The Man and the Statesman,** A. J. Butler, trans. (New York: Harper & Row, Publishers, Inc., 1898), Vol. I, pp. 315-322. Language simplified.

Hanover, Württemberg, and Bavaria were all German kingdoms.

▶Do you feel that different peoples need different kinds of governments? That is, might one form of government be good for some people and another form good for others?

Heinrich von Treitschke: Nationalism After Unification

Heinrich von Treitschke (1834-1896) was a well-known German historian and an ardent nationalist. In his writings, he glorified the heroes of Germany's unification. The following selection is taken from lectures he gave as a professor at the University of Berlin between 1874 and 1896.

The state is the people united by laws as an independent power. By "people" we mean a number of families which permanently live together. The state is power, so that it may continue to exist alongside

Heinrich von Treitschke, **Selections from Treitschke's Lectures on Politics,** Adam L. Gowans, trans. (New York: Frederick A. Stokes Co., 1914), pp. 9-16, 21-24. Language simplified.

other equally independent powers. War and the administration of justice are the most important tasks of the state.

The idea of a world-state, including all of mankind, is disgusting. All different peoples (or nations), like individual men, have their own particular characteristics. From the great variety of these characteristics, the richness of the human race is seen.

The state is power first, so that it can maintain itself. The state protects the life of the people, regulating it in all ways. It never considers the feeling of the people; it demands obedience. Its laws must be kept, whether the people do it willingly or unwillingly. When the state can no longer see to it that the people obey, it perishes in anarchy.

The peoples that form real states are not those who have genius. Rather, real states are made by those peoples who have character. The history of the world proves this. The state is no academy of arts. If it neglects the establishment of its power in order to promote the ideal strivings of mankind, it renounces its nature and goes to ruin. This truth remains: The state can allow nothing to have more power than it has. In other words, it must be sovereign.

►Some people object to organizations such as the United Nations, pictured here, because they interfere with national sovereignty. Do you think a nation loses something vital to its identity if it permits an international body to make some of its decisions? Why or why not?

Of course, every state will limit its sovereignty in some respects when it makes treaties. But the rule of no power being higher than the state still holds, for every treaty is a voluntary limitation of power. However, establishing an international court of arbitration is not consistent with the nature of the state. No questions of importance could be submitted to such a court. In questions of vital importance, it is a matter of honor for the state to determine what it will do by itself.

The second essential function of the state is to make war. That we have failed to appreciate this is proof of how sentimental we have become. Without war there would be no state at all. All the states of history have arisen through wars. The protection of its citizens by arms remains the first and essential task of the state.

The great advances of mankind can be realized entirely only by the sword. How often did we use words to persuade the small German states of the value of uniting under Prussian leadership? They needed the convincing proof which Prussia furnished in the battles with Austria and France.

Political idealism demands wars. Materialism condemns them. We will destroy morality if we wish to eliminate heroism from humanity! It is the heroes of the nation who inspire youth.

▶ Treitschke limits heroism to deeds of war. Do you think that is a fair definition?

FOR THOUGHT:

How did von Treitschke define nationalism? How do his ideas of nationalism differ from those of the writers that you studied in Readings 46 and 47?

49 THE RISE OF NATIONALISM

A HISTORICAL ESSAY

Nationalism helps to explain much of the power of modern governments. A nation gives its people a historical tradition with which they can identify. It touches them daily as government agencies record and regulate their lives through birth registration, draft cards, tax collections, and welfare records. Through their vote citizens help to make the nation's laws. The citizens of a nation-state develop a sense of belonging to a group which creates a feeling of loyalty to that group.

Modern people give loyalty to their nation for some of the same reasons that people have always given loyalty to groups. Groups provide their members with a sense of identity and purpose. Just as people can identify with family groups, they can identify with a nation. Like community, social, and labor organizations, nations give people a sense of belonging and make them feel that they are serving a more important cause than their personal interests. Giving allegiance to the nation helps people to identify with a larger purpose.

Nationalism does not depend on family ties to define the group. Unlike community, social, or labor organizations, each of which promotes its own special interests, the nation serves the purposes of all its citizens. Unlike religions, which often include peoples of different countries, languages, customs, and histories, nationalism thrives best where people share a common territory, tongue, and tradition.

Nationalism developed in the West in comparatively modern times. In the ancient world people gave their loyalty to local political units. Athenians and Spartans, for example, were loyal to their city states, not to Greece. Roman soldiers marched to glorify the city of Rome rather than the empire. And the people of various backgrounds, languages, and customs who made up the Roman Empire thought of themselves as Egyptians or Greeks or some other group, not as Romans. Of all the ancient peoples, only the Hebrews came close to the idea of a nation. But for most of their history, they have lacked one of the basic requirements of nationhood—a homeland.

In medieval times, most men and women gave their loyalty to other persons. In theory, all people gave their spiritual loyalty to the Church, but loyalty to the Church as an institution was seldom as strong as loyalty to the local bishop or priest. The peasant and the knight gave their primary political loyalty to the local lord of the manor rather than to the king. The king had to depend on the personal loyalty of the barons and dukes who served him. Such personal relationships between lord and vassal were the cement of the medieval political system.

As the monarchs of the late Middle Ages strengthened their rule and won the loyalty of their subjects, national feeling began to develop. In England, for example, the feudal ancestors of the Tudors had slowly joined together their territories, extending their political power over them. The English state had existed for centuries, but the Tudors made the state into a nation. In the process, they won the allegiance of the English people.

In dynastic nationalism, the nationalist feelings of the people are attached to the monarch, who symbolizes the nation, rather than to an abstract idea of the nation-state.

Several factors helped the development of dynastic nationalism in Tudor England. The growth of commerce and a market economy created a new class of merchants who were not tied to the old feudal loyalties. Along with the growth of trade, the growth of cities led to the need for large-scale agriculture. Large landowners began to enclose their fields, forcing many small farmers to leave their land. As these small farmers lost their place in the old feudal system, they began to develop new loyalties to their nation.

276

The new class of merchants and commercial farmers found it in their interest to support monarchs who increased national power at the expense of the feudal lords, the Church, and foreign nations. To these merchants and farmers, feudalism had meant irregular taxes and almost constant warfare, both of which interfered with trade. They were willing to back Henry VIII in his break with the Church because Catholic doctrines opposed many of their economic practices. In 1588, when Spain threatened England's overseas trade, the merchants loaned their own ships to Queen Elizabeth's navy in order to defeat the Spanish Armada.

The Tudors began to recognize the value of a prosperous state and developed a partnership between the state and its economic interests. Mercantilism, as this partnership was called, benefited both sides. The state supported industry and commerce, increasing the profits of business people and commercial farmers. Increased profits meant greater wealth for the state in tax money. As a result of this economic partnership, industrial and commercial interests became identified with the nation itself.

Dynastic nationalism had two elements of modern nationalism: a strong centralized state and a powerful group that supported the nation above all other loyalties. But the nation did not have the support of all the people. In the manors and villages of agricultural Europe, many people remained loyal to their local lord, their church, and their village.

The French Revolution swept away many of these local loyalties. It destroyed many of the medieval institutions of French society and completed the nationalization of the French church. The revolutionary government extended the right to vote and passed laws making military service a duty. It added the idea of participation to the two elements of dynastic nationalism—the centralized state and loyalty to the nation.

Under the revolutionary nation-state, the French people developed a sense of national consciousness based on the principle that all people were citizens and that all citizens were equal before the law. The example of this revolutionary French government with its new ideals soon kindled nationalist feelings in the people of other nations. Although Napoleon's troops marched under the banner of liberty, equality, and fraternity, they did not follow the ideals of the Revolution. As a result, the people who lived under French rule soon longed for their own national governments.

The diplomats who tried to bring order to Europe following the collapse of the Napoleonic Empire blamed liberalism and nationalism for the French Revolution and the Napoleonic wars. They were determined to prevent these forces from returning. But the industrialization of Europe produced conditions that encouraged liberalism and nationalism. Large numbers of people were forced to move, usually from the

In 1790 the National Assembly passed the Civil Constitution of the Clergy making all bishops and priests civil officials. They were paid by the state and elected by the people of the diocese or parish. Because of opposition to this act, Napoleon negotiated the Concordat of 1801 with the pope. It provided that the state would still pay the salaries of the clergy, but the bishops would be nominated by the state and confirmed by the pope. The bishops would appoint the priests. The Concordat was in force until 1905.

The pictures on these two pages show a number of factors that have helped to encourage nationalist feelings. In what ways would each of these factors help to develop nationalist sentiments?

An astronaut on the moon

The Eiffel Tower in Paris, France

278

A World War I poster

The Centennial celebration of the Fourth of July in Philadelphia, 1876

An American history book

countryside into the cities. Social classes began to break down. In this rapidly changing society, the nation emerged as the main focus of people's loyalties.

At first, nationalism was linked with the principles of liberalism—the belief in the ability and goodness of people, in the importance of the rights of the individual, and in steady progress. Liberal nationalist beliefs inspired the revolutions of 1848. But the almost universal failure of these revolutions to build nations based on the principles of men like Mazzini dealt a serious blow to liberalism. One nation after another founded repressive governments. But despite the decline of liberalism, nationalism continued to grow.

Denied unity under liberal constitutions, Germans and Italians turned to powerful native monarchs to fulfill their nationalist ambitions. In Italy, the shrewd prime minister of Piedmont, Count Camillo di Cavour, brought about unification under the king of Piedmont. Otto von Bismarck, prime minister of Prussia, unified Germany under the Prussian king. In both cases, national unity depended on reducing the influence of foreign powers on the tiny duchies, principalities, and city-states in Italy and Germany. Therefore, diplomacy and war were essential for unification.

Nationalism proved to have a dividing as well as a unifying effect. Huge empires, such as Austria-Hungary, ruled many ethnic groups, each of which wanted its own independent state. These minorities rebelled many times during the last half of the nineteenth century. But most did not achieve their nationalist goals until the end of World War I.

Nationalism has had many functions at different times and places. As its functions changed, the very meaning of the term also changed. Dynastic nationalism in Tudor England means something different from participatory nationalism in revolutionary France. Nationalism in nineteenth-century Germany differed from both of these earlier nationalisms and from the kind of nationalism that helped to tear apart the Austro-Hungarian Empire. Hence people must be able to define terms like nationalism in two ways. They must know the dictionary definition of the concept, which is "devotion to the interests of a particular nation." And they must also know the special characteristics of nationalism at a particular time and place, such as in Tudor England or late nineteenth-century Germany.

In addition to nationalism, many other words must be given historical definitions. This means that a word must be defined as it is used in different times and places. Here are some of these words: socialism, communism, feudalism, democracy, authoritarianism, and Americanism. Unless people know both a dictionary definition and a historical definition of such terms, they cannot use them to convey precise meanings to someone else.

In many countries today, a number of forces have acted together to produce a new sort of modern nationalism. The pictures on pages 278–279 illustrate some of these forces. Modern nationalism may have replaced religion as the major faith to which most people give their first allegiance. Citizens of a nation-state join together in common loyalty to a set of ideals, just as medieval Christians used to do. They use symbols such as flags, much as Jews use the Star of David or Christians use the cross. *God Save the Queen* or *The Star Spangled Banner* become the hymns of this new faith. Citizens visit national shrines such as Lenin's tomb or Kennedy's grave just as Moslems go on pilgrimages to Mecca. The nation's heroes—Mao, Garibaldi, or Lincoln—become the saints and martyrs of the new faith. And like religion used to do, modern nations call on people to sacrifice their property or lives. The late President John F. Kennedy made this point clearly when he said: "Ask not what your country can do for you; ask what you can do for your country."

Individual and Group Activities for Chapter 11

For full descriptions of these activities, turn to the **Student Book of Activities and Readings** included among the materials for individual and group activities.

Activity 11A: Scrapbook or collage illustrating how nationalism operates in the world today (individual or group)

Collect a number of newspaper and magazine articles and pictures showing how nationalism operates today. Arrange your materials in a scrapbook or as a collage.

Activity 11B: Analysis of children's patriotic songs to show how music encourages nationalistic feelings (individual)

This activity contains several patriotic songs used in elementary school music classes. Read the words carefully and also listen to a recording of these songs. In a brief essay, explain how these songs might encourage the development of nationalistic feelings in young children.

War and Peace

CHAPTER
12

The modern world teeters dangerously on the edge of war that could destroy humankind. Therefore, international relations focus around two issues: preventing a war between the major powers from breaking out and preventing wars between smaller countries from spreading to the super powers. During the past 150 years, western leaders have tried two systems of international relations to protect national interests and avoid war. Both have failed.

Beginning with the Congress of Vienna in 1815, European leaders tried to create a balance of power among the major European nations—Great Britain, Austria, Prussia, Russia, and France. Such a balance required that no one nation or group of nations become strong enough to dominate the others. Under the system established at the Congress of Vienna, the peace of Europe lasted a hundred years except for minor wars. But the unification of Italy and Germany and the weakening of Austria-Hungary undermined the balance of power.

In 1914, for the first time since Napoleon had been defeated at Waterloo, all the major European powers plunged into war. In 1917, the United States joined the war on the side of France, Britain, and Russia and so began its involvement in the power struggles of the European nations. Following World War I, several American and European statesmen tried to develop a new system for keeping the peace. Rather than rely on a balance of power, they hoped to prevent war through a system of collective security. They established an international organization, the League of Nations, to settle international disagreements. However, the League did not have the power to enforce its rulings, and it collapsed with the outbreak of World War II in 1939.

Chapter 12 examines the causes and also the nature of World War I. It also discusses the attempts of the European nations to keep the peace after the fall of Napoleon in 1815.

1879	Germany and Austria-Hungary form a secret defensive alliance.
1882	Germany, Austria-Hungary, and Italy form Triple Alliance.
1894	France and Russia agree to mutual defensive aid against Triple Alliance nations.
1904	Britain and France form Entente Cordiale.
1905	In first Moroccan crisis, Germany tries to block French control of Morocco.
1907	Triple Entente unites Britain, France, and Russia.
1908	Austria's annexation of Bosnia-Herzegovina causes first Balkan crisis.
1911	Second Moroccan crisis arises between Germany and France.
1912-1913	Balkan countries defeat Ottoman Turks, and second Balkan crisis follows.
1914	Austrian archduke assassinated, and war breaks out in Europe.
1917	Revolution ends Russian monarchy, and Russia signs armistice with Germany.
	United States declares war on Germany.
1918	Russia signs peace treaty with Germany.
	Germany signs armistice.
1919	Germany signs Versailles Treaty, containing League of Nations charter.
1920	United States refuses to ratify peace treaty with League charter.
1939	League of Nations collapses with outbreak of World War II.

50 DECISIONS LEADING TO WAR

On June 28, 1914, Archduke Franz Ferdinand, heir to the throne of Austria-Hungary, and his wife Sophie were assassinated. This event was the spark setting off a war that soon involved every major power in Europe.

Franz Ferdinand was out of favor with most of the Austrian royal family. His wife, Sophie, was a Czech, and they did not approve of her. The archduke had also expressed liberal views about the Slavic minorities in the empire. He had suggested that the dual monarchy of Austria-Hungary should become a triple monarchy to give representation to the Slavic peoples. This policy also alarmed the leaders of Serbia, an independent Slavic nation. (See map, page 291.) For several years, Serbia had led a movement, known as Panslavism, aimed at uniting all Slavs into one nation. The archduke's plan would have destroyed this Serbian dream.

These tensions between Austria and Serbia had developed with the decline of the Turkish, or Ottoman Empire in eastern Europe. The Ottoman Empire stretched from the Middle East and North Africa through southern Europe. From the end of the fifteenth century until late in the seventeenth century, the Turks had controlled most of Europe south and east of the Danube River. This territory included most of the Balkan peninsula. (See map, page 291.) But the Ottoman Empire proved to be much too large. By 1900 many Slavic subjects in the Balkan region had won their independence and formed small states. But these states were not powerful enough to keep their independence without the help of one or another of the great European powers. As a result, Russia, Austria, Germany, and Italy competed for influence and possessions in the Balkan region.

In June 1914, Franz Ferdinand and his wife traveled to Bosnia-Herzegovina, part of the Austro-Hungarian Empire, to observe military operations. Many Serbs lived in Bosnia-Herzegovina. It had been the focus of much rivalry between Serbia and its ally, Russia, on the one hand, and Austria, on the other. In 1908 Austria-Hungary had annexed Bosnia-Herzegovina over the objections of Russia and Serbia. Franz Ferdinand and his wife reached the capital of Bosnia-Herzegovina, Sarajevo, on June 28. There, a young Serbian nationalist shot and killed them. This incident led to the outbreak of World War I.

Reading 50 is designed to help you understand how the decisions of European leaders brought on war in 1914. In your next class meeting, you will begin to recreate the decisions that followed the archduke's murder. Your class will be divided into five groups, representing the cabinets of Austria-Hungary, Germany, France, Great Britain, and Russia. Before coming to class, you should read the memorandum describing the aims of the country you will represent. You should also familiarize yourself with the positions of the other nations and examine the map on page 291. In class, each group will discuss the interests of the nation it represents and the alternatives open to it. Let the following questions guide you:

1. What are your country's interests? On which interests would you be willing to compromise if necessary?
2. What European nation do you believe is the greatest threat to your interests?
3. What countries might you count on to support you if you go to war? Under what circumstances, if any, would you go to war without their support?
4. To what countries do you owe support if they go to war? Under what conditions will you support them? Under what conditions will you refuse to support them?

Memoranda of Commitments and Interests

These five memoranda have been prepared specifically for this lesson. Although they are fictitious, the memoranda are based on actual evidence of the situation in Europe in 1914. And wherever possible, the memoranda use the language of the original correspondence.

MEMORANDUM TO THE AUSTRO-HUNGARIAN CABINET—JUNE 28, 1914

I. ALLIANCES

Since 1879 we have been allied with Germany, and since 1882 with Italy. Under the terms of our alliance with Germany, we have agreed to come to her aid if she is attacked by Russia or another nation supported by Russia. Germany has made the same promise to us. Under the terms of our alliance with Italy, we have agreed to aid her, along with Germany, if she is attacked by France. Finally, if any one of the members of the alliance is attacked by two or more powers, the other two members have promised aid. Since these alliances were concluded, Germany has proved to be a faithful ally; Italy has not.

In the two most serious crises we have faced in this century, Germany has remained loyal to the Austro-Hungarian Empire. Germany stayed by our side in 1908 when Russia went back on her promise to allow us to annex the provinces of Bosnia-Herzegovina. In return we had promised our neutrality if Russia wished to gain control of the Bosporus and Dardanelles. Russia probably went back on her promise because Serbia protested our annexation of provinces that included many Serbs. But Russia could not get support from her allies, France and Great Britain. As a result, Germany's friendship allowed us to annex Bosnia-Herzegovina.

In 1912 and 1913, Germany backed our efforts to stop the Serbians from taking territory in the Balkans at our expense and the expense of the Ottoman Empire. Once again Germany kept Russia from interfering with our plans. We have generally been able to count on the support of the German emperor, Kaiser Wilhelm, and his government, and it has been in our best interest to support his projects. We have done so on two occasions when Kaiser Wilhelm wished to block France's take-over of Morocco. In 1905 we were the only European power who backed the kaiser when he promised the sultan that he would not allow another European nation to control that country. In 1911 the kaiser gave in to France, who took over Morocco supported by her allies, Great Britain and Russia.

In 1879 Germany formed the Dual Alliance with Austria-Hungary. This was a secret defensive alliance aimed at Russia, whose support of Panslavism threatened the Austrian Empire. In 1882 Italy, angry at France for occupying North African territory it wanted, joined Austria-Hungary and Germany in the Triple Alliance.

The Bosporus and Dardanelles, narrow straits between the Aegean and Black seas, had been closed to all foreign warships in times of peace by the Straits Agreement of 1841. Russia had asked for special terms to allow its warships to go through the straits.

In 1912, Serbia, Bulgaria, Greece, and Montenegro drove the Ottoman Turks out of Europe, except from the city of Constantinople. Serbia, supported by Russia, demanded part of Albania as an outlet to the Adriatic. The Albanians proclaimed independence, and Russia withdrew its support of Serbia. Serbia then demanded part of Macedonia from Bulgaria, and in June 1913, Bulgaria attacked Serbia. Rumania, Greece, and Turkey helped Serbia defeat Bulgaria.

285

These boys in Nazi Germany are burning books condemned by the government.

►Which, if any, of the scenes shown in these pictures would make you decide to fight? Or do you feel that nothing is worth fighting for?

II. VITAL INTERESTS

Since the Congress of Vienna, we have tried to protect our holdings in Europe and maintain our influence in the Balkan states. As the Ottoman Empire has been forced to withdraw from the Balkan peninsula, we have stepped in to maintain peace in the area. This has been extremely difficult to do with the Serbs constantly agitating for an outlet on the Adriatic Sea and for the annexation of areas of our nation that contain large numbers of Serbs. Their frequent attacks on Austria, the assassination being the most recent and most severe example, has made it difficult for us to keep peace in the Balkans and prevent revolution by the subject peoples in our empire. With Germany's good will, however, we have been successful most of the time. Yet the activities of the Serbs have tried even the patience of the German emperor. Most important, however, has been Russia's attempt to extend her influence into the Balkans. Again, Germany's aid has helped us keep the Russians from making significant gains. But we must constantly be on our guard to see that Russia does not extend her influence at our expense.

MEMORANDUM TO THE GERMAN CABINET—JUNE 28, 1914

I. ALLIANCES

Austria-Hungary and Italy have been our allies since 1882, when we signed the Triple Alliance. This alliance was drafted by Chancellor Otto von Bismarck in an effort to protect our country from France, who has desired revenge since its defeat in the Franco-Prussian War in 1871. Under this alliance, we will support Italy if she is attacked by France. If we are attacked by France, Italy agrees to help us. If Austria is attacked by Russia or another country backed by Russia, we shall come to Austria's aid. And if we are attacked by Russia or another country backed by Russia, Austria will aid us. Finally, if two or more countries should attack one of the three parties to the alliance, the other two will come to that nation's aid.

When our emperor, Kaiser Wilhelm, tried to block the French takeover of Morocco in 1905, Austria stood by our side. Italy sided with the other great powers, and as a result France was able to make its move without interference. In return for Austria's loyalty, we have supported her Balkan interests. In 1908, when she moved to take over the provinces of Bosnia-Herzegovina, we sided with her against Russia. Since Russia could not get help from her western allies, Great Britain and France, we were able to assure Austria-Hungary's victory in that crisis. We again stood by Austria-Hungary last year when she moved to take away from the Serbs the gains they had made in the war against the Ottoman Empire. Again, Serbia's ally, Russia, was forced to back down. The events of the past nine years have cemented our friendship with the Austro-Hungarian Empire. Italy, however, has not proved to be a loyal ally.

In 1905 France, already having some power in Morocco, asked the sultan to make his country a full French protectorate. The German emperor, testing British support of France, landed in Morocco and declared it independent. He demanded an international conference, which met in 1906. Britain reaffirmed its support of France. Morocco remained independent, but French rights were reassured. In 1908 the sultan's brother took power, and in 1911 France helped him end a revolt. When a German warship appeared off Morocco, France took this as a threat of war. France and Germany finally made Morocco a French protectorate. In return Germany won territory in Africa.

II. VITAL INTERESTS

Since the kaiser dismissed Chancellor Bismarck in 1890, Germany has expanded her interests to include the entire world. Of course, we still wish to prevent France from seeking revenge against us. This interest, which was the only concern of Chancellor Bismarck, has been replaced in recent years by Germany's interest in extending her influence to other parts of the world.

We have stepped up our efforts to acquire overseas colonies. We have obtained some in Africa and Asia. At present they do not seem threatened by the immediate situation. However, any war that involves Germany includes the risk of losing these colonies. As part of our policy, Germany has also increased her efforts to build a navy to rival that of Great Britain. There is evidence that Great Britain is greatly concerned about our new naval power. In recent years we have also acquired influence in the Middle East. A treaty with the Ottoman Empire and a railway from Berlin to Baghdad should further increase our influence in that area of the world. In this cause we are supported by Austria-Hungary. Certainly, one of our most vital interests is Austria's continued domination of the Balkan countries, since it is much better to have an ally there than a potential enemy, such as Russia.

MEMORANDUM TO THE FRENCH CABINET—JUNE 28, 1914

I. ALLIANCES

We have an alliance with Russia, concluded in 1894. This alliance became possible when the Germans, our enemies in 1870 and 1871, refused to renew the Reinsurance Treaty of 1887. Under this treaty, Russia and Germany had each agreed to remain neutral if the other went to war. From Germany's refusal to renew the treaty, the Russians became aware of the German menace to peace, and tried to form an alliance with us. The terms of our alliance with Russia are as follows: We agree to aid Russia if she is attacked by Germany or Austria supported by Germany; Russia agrees to aid us if we are attacked by Germany or Italy supported by Germany.

On two occasions Russia's interests in the Balkans were threatened, and we have been asked to come to her aid. First in 1908, when Austria annexed Bosnia-Herzegovina, Russia called on us to stop Austria's take-over of two provinces that included a large number of Serbs. Then in 1913, Russia called on us to support her efforts to help the Serbs keep the territory they had won in a war against the Ottoman Turks. Again, Austria's interference deprived the Serbs and the Russians of their interests in the area. Our alliance with Russia is purely defensive, however, and we could not agree to support her in these actions. Even though Russia has been disappointed by our decisions in these cases, she remains a faithful ally.

When Wilhelm II became kaiser in 1888, a struggle for supremacy began between him and Bismarck. The kaiser took a lenient attitude toward the Socialists, whom Bismarck had attempted to suppress. Bismarck also held back Wilhelm's colonial ambitions.

German colonies in Africa included South-West Africa, part of present-day Tanzania in east Africa, and present-day Togo, Cameroon, Rwanda, and Burundi in West Africa. Germany also held islands in the Pacific: western Samoa, the northeast section of New Guinea, and two of the Solomon Islands.

By 1896 a railroad, financed chiefly by Germans, ran from Constantinople through Asia Minor. In 1898 Germany got a concession from Turkey to continue the railroad to Baghdad, capital of Iraq. France, Russia, and Britain felt that this development threatened their interests in the East. Protests and negotiations held up work until 1911. It was not completed until 1940.

Russia's fear of German aggression and France's fear of the Triple Alliance drove the two nations into a Dual Alliance, in 1894. Meanwhile an unofficial understanding—the Entente Cordiale—existed between France and Britain. Russia, Britain, and France formed the Triple Entente in 1907 when differences between Britain and Russia, long-time rivals in colonialism, were ironed out. This alliance did not involve formal military commitments.

288

In recent years our relations with Great Britain have grown warmer. In the two crises of 1905 and 1911, when the German emperor, Kaiser Wilhelm, tried to block our moves to make Morocco a protectorate, Great Britain stood firmly by our side. These two crises, plus the friendly way in which we have settled our differences regarding overseas colonies, particularly in Africa, have led to certain British commitments. Although we have no formal military alliance with Great Britain, we have worked out secret arrangements in which she has agreed to commit some of her troops to our defense if we are ever attacked by Germany.

II. VITAL INTERESTS

It has become an article of faith with the French nation that we shall win back the two provinces lost in the Franco-Prussian War—Alsace and Lorraine. Indeed, the spirit of revenge has run very high in our country since our defeat in that war. Not only the confiscation of two of our provinces, but the huge indemnity that Germany forced us to pay and the German military occupation of France until the indemnity was paid have caused ill feelings toward our neighbor on the east. We will never provoke war with Germany, but we shall not stand idly by while she is aggressive.

Indemnity is a sum of money paid to the victors in a war by the losers.

As for our overseas possessions, we have worked out agreements with the British, so that they will not threaten us. But if Germany sees an opportunity to gain imperial possessions at our expense, you can be sure that she will take it.

MEMORANDUM TO THE BRITISH CABINET—JUNE 28, 1914

I. ALLIANCES

At present we have no formal defensive or offensive alliances with any European power. We have tried to keep from becoming entangled in continental European diplomacy and intrigue.

Our relations with our neighbor, France, have been steadily improving in recent years. however. We have come to realize that our interests and the interests of France are parallel. We have settled most differences regarding possessions overseas, and we supported France in 1905 when the German emperor, Kaiser Wilhelm, tried to upset French plans for strengthening their control of Morocco. Our firm support of our friend probably averted war, since Germany was unable to obtain the support of her ally, Italy. In 1911, when the kaiser sent a gunboat to Tangier to stop France from getting a full protectorate in Morocco, we showed that we would not allow moves that violate our interests in the Mediterranean.

Tangier, an international zone and part of the domain of Morocco, lies at the northwestern tip of Africa on the Strait of Gibraltar. Tangier played a part in several of the Moroccan crises.

In the Mediterranean region, France has proved to be a better friend to our interests than other nations. Accordingly, we have conducted secret negotiations with the French to work out some arrangements for military aid if France suffers another attack from Germany. These arrangements are not known to the British public, nor even to most members of Parliament. We should be reluctant to reveal them at all, but we do have a commitment to honor.

Our relations with Russia have also been improving in recent years, especially since the friendly settlement of the Persian problem in 1907. Russia has agreed not to press her interests in that nation, and hence, we need not fear her threat to our Indian possession. We cannot support Russia's interests in the Balkan area, however, for her interests there do not coincide with ours. Russia's desire to obtain control of the straits leading from the Black Sea to the Mediterranean must be prevented. We cannot stand for such action, since Russian penetration in that area could endanger our control of the Mediterranean, so vital to our trade with our Asiatic colonies.

II. VITAL INTERESTS

Our most vital interest in continental Europe—Belgium—has been the one unchanging interest in British policy since the beginning of the eighteenth century. We have not tolerated control of Belgium by any great power. When France threatened Belgium in 1793, we took steps to defend our interests there. We shall do so again, since Belgium lies less than twenty-five miles from our coast. At present, Germany seems to be the greatest threat to Belgian neutrality.

Germany also threatens our vital interests in another area. Her plans to build a railway from Berlin to Baghdad make her a much more immediate threat to our Indian possession and to the Suez Canal than Russia. In recent years, Germany's naval building program has been alarming. We tried to stop this threat in 1912 with the Haldane mission, but Germany refused to give up the naval building program unless we agreed to remain neutral if she went to war. This, of course, we could not promise. Elsewhere we must protect our vital interests in our overseas colonies. We must not permit any power to challenge our control of India or our interests in the Suez Canal, Gibraltar, and the Mediterranean Sea.

MEMORANDUM TO THE RUSSIAN CABINET—JUNE 28, 1914

I. ALLIANCES

We are an ally of Serbia, one of the parties in the present conflict. We have supported her on several occasions, most recently when Austria moved in 1913 to take away territories from our fellow Slavs that they had acquired from the Ottoman Empire. Since we could not get the support of our western European friends, France and Great Britain, we were unable to block the Austrian action.

The British-Russian agreement of 1907 divided contested Persia into three areas. Russia was given the north and Britain the southeast, while the central area remained neutral. Russia agreed to stay out of Afghanistan, which would remain independent under British influence. Later in the same year, Britain supported a change in the Straits Agreement in Russia's favor, and Russia recognized British supremacy over the Persian Gulf. With this understanding, Britain, France, and Russia formed the Triple Entente.

The Suez Canal in Egypt connects the Mediterranean and Red seas. Until 1956 it was run by an investment company dominated by the British. Gilbraltar, a British crown colony, is located on the northwestern end of the Rock of Gibraltar, owned by Britain since 1704. The Strait of Gibraltar joins the Atlantic Ocean and Mediterranean Sea.

290

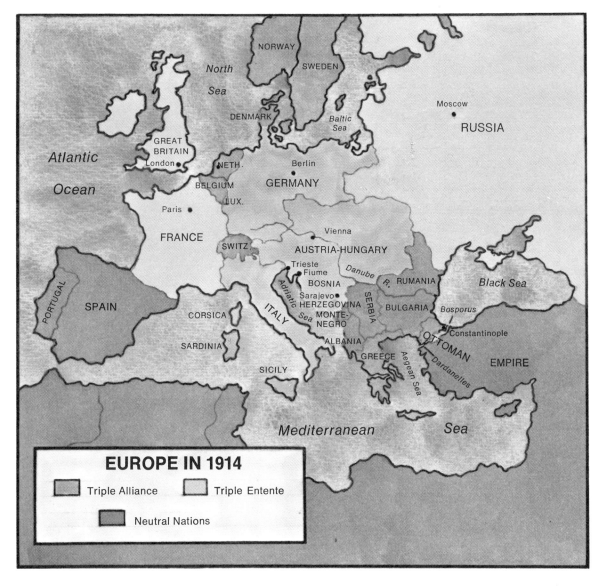

EUROPE IN 1914

| Triple Alliance | Triple Entente |
| Neutral Nations |

We also supported Serbia in 1908 when Austria-Hungary annexed Bosnia-Herzegovina. Originally we had agreed to allow this annexation to take place in return for an Austrian concession. They would allow us a free hand in gaining control of the straits leading from the Black Sea to the Mediterranean. But the Serbs protested the Austrian annexation, because millions of Serbs lived in the provinces of Bosnia-Herzegovina. Therefore, when Austria moved to annex these territories, we reversed our position.

In this crisis, as well as the one in 1913, we were unable to obtain support from either Great Britain or France. Great Britain, in particular, did not wish to support our further movement into the Balkans, since they are anxious to keep the straits in the hands of the Turks, who are less of a threat than we are to their shipping in the Mediterranean.

We have an alliance with France. This alliance was concluded in 1894, after the German emperor, Kaiser Wilhelm, refused to renew the Reinsurance Treaty, under which each of us promised to remain neutral if the other party went to war. The terms of our alliance with France are as follows: We agree to come to France's aid if she is attacked by Germany or by Italy supported by Germany; France agrees to aid us if we are attacked by Germany or by Austria supported by Germany. In most cases, France has honored her commitments to us, but she has not come to our aid in the two Balkan crises when we lost so much.

We do not have a military alliance with Britain, but we probably can count on her support if war should ever come. At the very least, she will not aid another power who is at war with us. Relations between our two countries have been getting better since 1907, when we reached a friendly settlement on the Persian situation. We have divided the country between us. We cannot count on Great Britain's support, however, if we endanger her vital interests. Great Britain jealously protects the free movement of her ships in the Mediterranean between the Suez Canal and Gibraltar, both of which she controls, and her interest in India, which one of her ministers once called "the jewel in the imperial crown."

II. VITAL INTERESTS

Our most vital interests, and those which concern us most in the present crisis, are in the Balkan states. These states, particularly Serbia, have always been friendly toward us, probably because they are our Slavic sisters and brothers. We have already lost much in this area at the hands of the Austrians, and the Germans also have threatened our interests there. The German plan to build a railway from Berlin to Baghdad also threatens our interests in the Middle East. Of course, we still have strong interests in the straits connecting the Black Sea and the Mediterranean. Since the Ottoman Empire is a German ally, a victory over Germany would perhaps give us this passage.

FOR THOUGHT:

What would you say was the attitude of the major European nations toward war at the time of these memoranda?

51 MODERN WAR: ITS EFFECTS ON EUROPEAN ATTITUDES

Technology has increased people's abilities to produce; it has equally increased their powers to destroy. In the Middle Ages, people at war fought face to face with swords and lances. In World War II, an American airplane dropped one bomb that killed or wounded 150,000 people the airmen had never seen.

Political developments have also contributed to the changing ways of war. In an effort to free themselves from their dependence on the feudal aristocracy, European monarchs of the fourteenth and fifteenth centuries raised armies of hired soldiers. The French Revolution replaced these hired soldiers with citizen armies drafted into the service of the nation. The democratic belief that all people should take part in the political process also assumes that all people will give their lives to the nation in time of war.

The technological, political, and ideological movements of the nineteenth century all made their mark on World War I. The industrialization of Europe created a new military technology. The spread of representative government changed military decision-making. The rise of nationalism changed the purposes for which people fought. The spread of equality changed the organization of the armed forces. On the battlefields of France, Russia, Turkey, and Italy, a new kind of war was fought. And the people of Europe—both soldiers and civilians—reacted to this new kind of war.

Reading 51 contains excerpts that show the reactions of young men who fought in the war. The first two excerpts are taken from letters written by German soldiers early in the war. The next two selections are taken from the literature written in reaction to the war. As you read the passages, try to answer these questions:

1. What feelings about the war do the letters from the young German soldiers reveal? For what were these young men fighting?
2. What does the excerpt from Erich Maria Remarque's novel indicate about the author's feelings about war? What point did Owen's poem make about war?

Two German Soldiers
React to War

The following excerpts are taken from letters two German soldiers wrote to their parents in the early months of World War I. Both of these young men had been law students before the war interrupted their lives. Both died before the end of 1914.

WALTER LIMMER, AGE 24

Philipp Witkop, **German Students' War Letters**, A. F. Wedd, ed. and trans. (London: Methuen & Company, Ltd., 1929), pp. 1-4, 17-20. Reprinted by permission of Methuen & Company, Ltd. and E. P. Dutton & Co., Inc.

Leipzig (still, I'm sorry to say), *August 3rd, 1914.*
    HURRAH! At last I have got my orders: to report at a place here at eleven o'clock tomorrow. I have been hanging about here, waiting, from hour to hour. This morning I met a young lady I know, and I was almost ashamed to let her see me in civilian clothes. You too, my good parents, you will agree that I am right in saying that I don't belong in this peaceful Leipzig any more. . . . We must have a broad outlook and think of our nation, our Fatherland, of God—then we shall be brave and strong.

England

Germany

English shops
owned by Germans
are looted.

The pictures on these two
pages show scenes in
several nations at the
outbreak of World War I.
What attitudes toward the
war do these pictures
imply? Why do you think
so many people felt this
way?

The United States

295

Leipzig, August 7th, 1914.

Every soldier must, to start with, be as I was a week ago, oppressed by the first mental picture of horrors which are no longer mere possibilities, but actually approaching realities; and on the day of the first battle the feeling of dread is bound to try and get possession of one's heart again, but now it won't find us shaky or unprepared. I personally have entirely regained my self-possession. I have thought out my position as if I had already done with this world—as if I were certain of not coming home again; and that gives me peace and security. Dear father, good mother, beloved brothers and sisters, please, please don't think me cruel for saying this, but it would be a good thing if already you too would, with brave hearts and firm self-control, get accustomed to the idea that you will not see me or any of my brothers again. Then if bad news does come, you will be able to receive it much more calmly. But if we all do come back, then we can accept that joy as an unexpected and all the more gracious and glorious gift of God. . . .

FRANZ BLUMENFELD, AGE 23

September 23, 1914 (in the train, going north).

. . . I want to write to you about something, which, judging from bits in your letters, you haven't quite understood: why I should have volunteered for the war? Of course it was not from any enthusiasm for war in general, nor because I thought it would be a fine thing to kill a great many people or otherwise distinguish myself. On the contrary, I think that war is a very, very evil thing, and I believe that even in this case it might have been averted [prevented] by a more skilful diplomacy. But, now that it has been declared, I think it is a matter of course that one should feel oneself so much a member of the nation that one must unite one's fate as closely as possible with that of the whole. . . . What counts is always the readiness to make a sacrifice, not the object for which the sacrifice is made.

This war seems to me, from all that I have heard, to be something so horrible, inhuman, mad, obsolete, and in every way depraving, that I have firmly resolved, if I do come back, to do everything in my power to prevent such a thing from ever happening again. . . .

▶Do you think a person should fight for his country even if he thinks it is wrong? Why or why not?

The War in Literature

World War I inspired many literary works dramatizing the reactions of the young men who fought in it. The first excerpt that follows is taken from the novel All Quiet on the Western Front, *written in 1929 by Erich Maria Remarque (1897-1970), a German. Remarque fled Germany when Hitler came to power. He lived first in Switzerland, and in 1939 he came to the United States.*

The second selection is one of many war poems written by Wilfred Owen (1893-1918). Owen, a German company commander on the western front, died seven days before the armistice.

Our trench is almost gone. At many places it is only eighteen inches high, it is broken by holes, and craters, and mountains of earth. A shell lands square in front of our post. At once it is dark. We are buried and must dig ourselves out. After an hour the entrance is clear again, and we are calmer because we have had something to do. . . .

Towards morning, while it is still dark, there is some excitement. Through the entrance rushes in a swarm of fleeing rats that try to storm the walls. Torches light up the confusion. Everyone yells and curses and slaughters. The madness and despair of many hours unloads itself in this outburst. Faces are distorted, arms strike out, the beasts scream; we just stop in time to avoid attacking one another. . . .

By midday what I expected happens. One of the recruits has a fit. I have been watching him for a long time, grinding his teeth and opening and shutting his fists. These hunted protruding eyes, we know them too well. During the last few hours he has had merely the appearance of calm. He had collapsed like a rotten tree. . . .

He won't listen to anything and hits out, his mouth is wet and pours out words, half choked, meaningless words. It is a case of claustrophobia, he feels as though he is suffocating here and wants to get out at any price. If we let him go he would run about everywhere regardless of cover. He is not the first.

Though he raves and his eyes roll, it can't be helped, and we have to give him a hiding to bring him to his senses. We do it quickly and mercilessly, and at last he sits down quietly. The others have turned pale; let's hope it deters [stops] them. . . .

Suddenly it howls and flashes terrifically, the dug-out cracks in all its joints under a direct hit, fortunately only a light one that the concrete blocks are able to withstand. . . .

The recruit starts to rave again and two others follow suit. One jumps up and rushes out, we have trouble with the other two. I start after the one who escapes and wonder whether to shoot him in the leg—then it shrieks again, I fling myself down and when I stand up the wall of the trench is plastered with smoking splinters, lumps of flesh, and bits of uniform. I scramble back.

The first recruit seems actually to have gone insane. He butts his head against the wall like a goat. . . .

Suddenly the nearer explosions cease. The shelling continues but it has lifted and falls behind us, our trench is free. We seize the hand-grenades, pitch them out in front of the dug-out and jump after them. The bombardment has stopped and a heavy barrage now falls behind us. The attack has come.

Erich Maria Remarque, **All Quiet on the Western Front**, A. W. Whein, trans. (Boston: Little, Brown, and Company, 1929), pp.104-115.

Claustrophobia is an abnormal fear of being closed in.

Drawn in 1918 by George Grosz, a German artist, Fit for Active Service *shows a doctor passing a potential draftee as fit for service. What does this drawing tell you about the changing attitudes toward the war?*

No one would believe that in this howling waste there could still be men; but steel helmets now appear on all sides out of the trench, and fifty yards from us a machine-gun is already in position. . . .

We recognize the distorted faces, the smooth helmets: they are French. They have already suffered heavily when they reach the remnants of the barbed-wire entanglements. A whole line has gone down before our machine-guns. . . .

I see one of them, his face upturned, fall into a wire cradle. His body collapses, his hands remain suspended as though he were praying. Then his body drops clean away and only his hands with the stumps of his arms, shot off, now hang in the wire.

The moment we are about to retreat three faces rise up from the ground in front of us. Under one of the helmets a dark pointed beard and two eyes that are fastened on me. I raise my hand, but I cannot throw into those strange eyes; for one mad moment the whole slaughter whirls like a circus round me, and these two eyes that are alone motionless; then the head rises up, a hand, a movement, and my hand-grenade flies through the air and into him. . . .

298

We have become wild beasts. We do not fight, we defend ourselves against annihilation [total destruction]. It is not against men that we fling our bombs, what do we know of men in this moment when Death with hands and helmets is hunting us down—now, for the first time in three days we can see his face, now, for the first time in three days we can oppose him; we feel a mad anger. No longer do we lie helpless, waiting on the scaffold, we can destroy and kill, to save ourselves, to save ourselves and be revenged. . . .

A scaffold is a platform on which a criminal is executed.

We stagger forward, and into our pierced and shattered souls bores the torturing image of the brown earth with the greasy sun and the convulsed and dead soldiers, who lie there—it can't be helped—who cry and clutch at our legs as we spring over them.

We have lost all feeling for one another. We can hardly control ourselves when our hunted glance lights on the form of some other man. We are insensible, dead men, who through some trick, some dreadful magic, are still able to run and to kill.

GAS ATTACK

Dulce et Decorum Est

The Poems of Wilfred Owen, Edmund Blunden, ed. (London: Chatto & Windus, 1946), p. 66, copyright 1946, copyright 1963. Reprinted by permission of Harold Owen and Chatto & Windus.

The title of the poem is Latin meaning, "It is sweet and dignified."

Bent double, like old beggars under sacks,
Knock-kneed, coughing like hags, we cursed through sludge,
Till on the haunting flares we turned our backs,
And towards our distant rest began to trudge.
Men marched asleep. Many had lost their boots,
But limped on, blood-shod. All went lame, all blind;
Drunk with fatigue; deaf even to the hoots
Of gas-shells dropping softly behind.

Gas! Gas! Quick, boys! An ecstasy of fumbling,
Fitting the clumsy helmets just in time,
But someone still was yelling out and stumbling
And floundering like a man in fire or lime.—
Dim through the misty panes and thick green light,
As under a green sea, I saw him drowning.

In all my dreams before my helpless sight
He plunges at me, guttering, choking, drowning.

If in some smothering dreams, you too could pace
Behind the wagon that we flung him in,
And watch the white eyes writhing in his face,
His hanging face, like a devil's sick of sin;

If you could hear, at every jolt, the blood
Come gargling from the froth-corrupted lungs,
Bitter as the cud
Of vile, incurable sores on innocent tongues,—
My friend, you would not tell with such high zest
To children ardent for some desperate glory,
The old Lie: *Dulce et decorum est*
Pro patria mori.

The Latin phrase means, "It is sweet and dignified to die for the fatherland."

FOR THOUGHT:

What hypothesis would you make on the basis of the evidence in this reading about the effect of the war on European attitudes toward war?

52 TO MAINTAIN THE PEACE

World War I, which ended in 1918, proved to be the most costly and terrible conflict in history. Western diplomats were determined that the destruction of this "Great War" would never be repeated. The goal was clear, but the methods were not.

The Germans had surrendered in 1918, hoping that peace would be built around the Fourteen Points, a declaration of war aims developed by President Woodrow Wilson of the United States. But translating Wilson's lofty ideals into a realistic peace treaty proved impossible. Several of the countries that had opposed Germany wished revenge on their hated enemy. In France especially, where the horrors of World War I were aggravated by the memory of the Franco-Prussian War, the desire for revenge had reached enormous proportions. Further complications arose from the promises the victorious Allies had made to each other during the war. Each nation expected those promises to be honored in the peace settlement. For example, Great Britain and France had promised Italy possession of Trieste and Fiume, two cities in Austria-Hungary, if Italy joined the allied cause. This promise and others violated the Fourteen Points.

General conditions in Europe also frustrated peacemaking efforts. Several nations faced serious food shortages. Former subjects of the Austro-Hungarian Empire had organized armies to seize territories they hoped to incorporate into their newly created, independent nations. The Communist Revolution in Russia threatened to spread to other lands in eastern Europe.

Faced with such complications, the peacemakers worked from January to June of 1919 in Paris drawing up a peace treaty to end the war and prevent future wars. On June 28 the representatives of the German government, who had not participated in the treaty negotiations, accepted the peace conditions imposed by the Great Powers: France, Great Britain, and the United States. Reading 52 presents Wilson's Fourteen Points as well as excerpts from the Treaty of Versailles and the German response to the treaty. Using these selections, you can begin to decide if the treaty was an instrument for keeping peace. As you read, keep these questions in mind:

1. What position did the documents in this reading take on each of the following issues: Alsace-Loraine? disarmament? colonies? Poland? the principle of nationalities being ruled by native governments? war guilt? reparations?
2. To what extent did the Treaty of Versailles follow the principles set down in the Fourteen Points?

The Fourteen Points

On April 6, 1917, at the request of President Wilson, the Congress of the United States declared war on Germany. Therefore, as a member of the Allied forces opposing Germany for about a year and a half, the United States earned the right to take part in the peace negotiations held in Paris. Unlike the European powers, the United States was not bound by promises made to other Allied governments. As a result, Wilson found it possible to announce his Fourteen Points on January 8, 1918.

We entered this war because violations of right had occurred which touched us to the quick and made the life of our own people impossible. What we demand in this war, therefore, is that the world be made fit and safe to live in; and particularly that it be made safe for every peace-loving nation which, like our own, wishes to live its own life, determine its own institutions, be assured of justice and fair dealing by the other peoples of the world as against force and selfish aggression. Our program is:

I. Open covenants [agreements] of peace, openly arrived at, after which there shall be no private international understandings of any kind.

II. Absolute freedom of navigation upon the seas.

III. The removal, so far as possible, of all economic barriers and the establishment of an equality of trade conditions.

IV. Adequate guarantees that national armaments will be reduced to the lowest point consistent with domestic safety.

Congressional Record, 65th Congress, 2nd Session, pp. 680-681.

V. A free, open-minded, and absolutely impartial adjustment of all colonial claims, based upon the principle that in questions of sovereignty the interests of the populations concerned must have equal weight with the government whose title is to be determined.

VI. The evacuation of all Russian territory and such a settlement of all questions affecting Russia as will assure her of a sincere welcome into the society of free nations under [her own] institutions.

VII. Belgium . . . must be evacuated and restored, without any attempt to limit the sovereignty which she enjoys.

VIII. All French territory should be freed and the invaded portions restored, and the wrong done to France by Prussia in 1871 in the matter of Alsace-Lorraine should be righted.

IX. A readjustment of the frontiers of Italy should be effected along clearly recognizable lines of nationality.

X. The peoples of Austria-Hungary should be accorded the freest opportunity of autonomous [independent] development.

XI. Rumania, Serbia, and Montenegro should be evacuated; occupied territories restored; Serbia accorded free and secure access to the sea; and international guarantees of the political and economic independence and territorial integrity of the several Balkan states should be entered into.

XII. The Turkish portions of the present Ottoman Empire should be assured a secure sovereignty, but the other nationalities which are now under Turkish rule should be assured an absolutely unmolested opportunity of autonomous development, and the Dardanelles should be permanently opened to all nations.

XIII. An independent Polish state should be set up which should include the territories inhabited by Polish populations, which should be assured a free and secure access to the sea.

XIV. A general association of nations must be formed for the purpose of affording mutual guarantees of political independence and territorial integrity to great and small states alike.

An evident principle runs through the whole program I have outlined. It is the principle of justice to all peoples and nationalities, and their right to live on equal terms of liberty and safety with one another, whether they be strong or weak.

Late in 1918, the Kingdom of the Serbs, Croats, and Slovenes was proclaimed. In 1929 it was renamed Yugoslavia. The kingdom was made up of the former provinces and states of Serbia, Montenegro, Croatia, Bosnia-Herzegovina, Macedonia, and Slovenia.

▶Should a nation work for absolute justice or accept the principle that more powerful nations will control weaker ones?

The Treaty of Versailles

After nearly six months of negotiations, the Treaty of Versailles was signed in the grand palace built by Louis XIV. The treaty included more than seven hundred articles. (See the map on page 303 for territorial changes.)

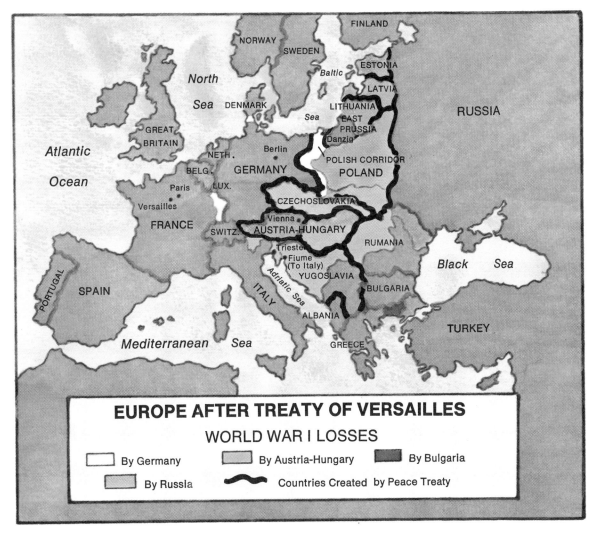

EUROPE AFTER TREATY OF VERSAILLES

WORLD WAR I LOSSES

- By Germany
- By Austria-Hungary
- By Bulgaria
- By Russia
- Countries Created by Peace Treaty

Article 42. Germany is forbidden to maintain or construct any fortifications either on the left bank of the Rhine or on the right bank to the west of a line drawn 50 kilometers to the east.

Article 45. As compensation for the destruction of the coal mines in the north of France and as part payment towards the total reparation due, Germany cedes [gives up] to France the coal mines in the Saar Basin.

Article 49. Germany renounces the government of the Saar in favor of the League of Nations as trustee.

At the end of fifteen years the inhabitants of said territory shall indicate the sovereignty under which they desire to be placed.

The Treaty of Versailles and After (Washington: United States Government Printing Office, 1947).

▶ Should the winning nation in a war try to make the loser pay? Why or why not?

[*Article 51, preface.*] The High Contracting Parties, recognizing the moral obligation to redress [correct] the wrong done by Germany in 1871 both to the rights of France and to the wishes of the population of Alsace and Lorraine, agree upon the following Articles:

Article 51. The territories which were ceded to Germany are restored to France.

Article 80. Germany acknowledges and will respect strictly the independence of Austria.

Article 81. Germany recognizes the complete independence of the Czecho-Slovak State.

Article 87. Germany recognizes the complete independence of the state of Poland.

Article 102. The Principal Allied Powers undertake to establish the town of Danzig as a Free City. It will be placed under the protection of the League of Nations.

Article 119. Germany renounces all her rights and titles over her overseas possessions.

Article 159. The German military forces shall be demobilized [disbanded] and reduced as prescribed hereinafter.

Article 160. By a date which must not be later than March 31, 1920, the German Army must not contain more than seven divisions of infantry and three divisions of cavalry.

After that date the Army of Germany must not exceed one hundred thousand men, including officers.

The total of officers must not exceed four thousand.

Article 231. The Allied and Associate Governments affirm and Germany accepts the responsibility of Germany and her allies for causing all the loss and damage to which the Allied and Associated Governments and their nationals have been subjected as a consequence of the war.

Article 232. The Allied and Associated Governments recognize that the resources of Germany are not adequate to make complete reparation for all such loss and damage.

The Allied and Associated Governments, however, require, and Germany undertakes, that she will make compensation for all damage done to the civilian population of the Allied and Associated Powers and to their property during the belligerency [war].

Article 428. As a guarantee for the execution of the present Treaty by Germany, the German territory situated to the west of the Rhine will be occupied by Allied and Associated troops for a period of fifteen years.

Article 431. If before the expiration of the period of fifteen years Germany complies with all the undertakings resulting from the present Treaty, the occupying forces will be withdrawn.

Poland became independent with the signing of the armistice in November 1918. The Versailles Treaty gave Poland a strip of German territory in order to provide Polish access to the Baltic Sea. This strip was called the Polish Corridor and divided East Prussia from the rest of Germany. However, Germans were free to cross the Corridor. The port city, Danzig, within East Prussia, was made a free city. In 1945 Danzig was transferred to Poland.

More objective evaluations of World War 1 have rejected the idea that all of the blame was Germany's. It is recognized that to some extent Germany tried to ease Austro-Serbian tensions in a last hope of avoiding war.

The German Response
to the Treaty

The final draft of the treaty was given to the representatives of the German government on June 28, 1919. Before signing the treaty, Count Brockdorff-Rantzau, the leader of the German delegation, made the following comment. Witnesses reported that he trembled with rage.

The peace to be concluded with Germany was to be a peace of right, not a peace of might. . . .

The peace document shows that none of [the] repeated solemn assurances has been kept.

To begin with the territorial questions:

In the West, a purely German territory on the Saar with a population of at least 650,000 inhabitants is to be separated from the German Empire for at least fifteen years merely for the reason that claims are asserted to the coal abounding there. . . .

The settlement of the colonial question is equally contradictory to a peace of justice. For the essence of activity in colonial work does not consist in capitalistic exploitation of a less developed human race, but in raising backward peoples to a higher civilization. . . . [Yet, the] treaty . . . deprives Germany of her colonies. . . .

President Wilson, in his speech of October 20th, 1916, has acknowledged that "no single fact caused the war, but that in the last analysis the whole European system is in a deeper sense responsible for the war, with its combination of alliances and understandings, a complicated texture of intrigues and espionage that unfailingly caught the whole family of nations in its meshes," "that the present war is not so simply to be explained and that its roots reach deep into the dark soil of history." [Yet] Germany is to acknowledge that Germany and her allies are responsible for all damages. . . . Apart from the consideration that there is no . . . legal foundation for the obligation for reparation imposed upon Germany, the amount of such compensation is to be determined by a commission nominated solely by Germany's enemies. . . .

The same is also true with regard to Alsace-Lorraine. If Germany has pledged herself "to right the wrong of 1871," this does not mean any renunciation of the right of self-determination of the inhabitants of Alsace-Lorraine. A cession of the country without consulting the population would be a new wrong, if for no other reason, because it would be inconsistent with a recognized principle of peace.

On the other hand, it is incompatible with the idea of national self-determination for 2½ million Germans to be torn away from their native

Harry J. Carrol, Jr. et al., The Development of Civilization (Chicago: Scott, Foresman and Company, 1961), Vol. II, pp. 396-398.

► Do you think the citizens of Germany's colonies wanted their civilization "raised"? Why or why not?

land against their own will. By the proposed . . . boundary, unmistakably German territories are disposed of in favor of their Polish neighbors. . . . This disrespect of the right of self-determination is shown most grossly in the fact that Danzig is to be separated from the German Empire and made a free state. . . . The same may be said with reference to the fact that millions of Germans in German-Austria are to be denied the union with Germany which they desire and that, further, millions of Germans dwelling along our frontiers are to be forced to remain part of the newly created Czecho-Slovakian State. . . .

FOR THOUGHT:

How could the Treaty of Versailles have been made more successful in keeping the peace?

53 WAR AND PEACE: INTERNATIONAL RELATIONS SINCE 1815

A HISTORICAL ESSAY

Three major wars have affected the course of international relations in the past two hundred years. The first of these wars lasted for a generation and was essentially a series of alliances against France following the outbreak of the Revolution in 1789 and the dictatorship of Napoleon Bonaparte. The second war lasted four years (1914-1918) and has become known as World War I because so much of the world eventually became involved. The third, World War II (1939-1945), was truly a global struggle.

Each war was widespread, requiring the formation of powerful alliances to defeat powerful opponents. Each was, in part, an ideological struggle between authoritarianism and democracy. At the same time, each war was an attempt to maintain the balance of power. And in each case the aggressor—Napoleon, Kaiser Wilhelm II, Hitler—was defeated. But the policies adopted to preserve the hard-won peace each time were different. Napoleon's defeat in 1814 launched a century of balance-of-power politics. The defeat of imperial Germany in 1918

306

introduced the concept of collective security. After World War II, both collective security and balance-of-power politics were used in new ways.

Napoleon had defeated most of Europe by following an old and simple rule: Divide and conquer. Not until 1813, after Napoleon's disastrous campaign in Russia, did the great nations of Europe effectively unite against him. Until then, each had pursued its own interests, often at the expense of other nations. And in 1814, having finally defeated the French, these nations squabbled about the spoils of war, again placing their own interests above international ones. Napoleon immediately seized the opportunity to escape from his exile on the island of Elba, and return to France. The allies hastily patched up their differences in the face of this threat and defeated Napoleon conclusively at Waterloo, Belgium, in June 1815.

This experience dramatically emphasized the need for a united front against aggression if peace were to be preserved. Yet the diplomats who met at the peace conference in Vienna were caught in the age-old dilemma: How does a nation protect its own interests without endangering those of other nations?

This dilemma created greater dilemmas at Vienna. Tsar Alexander I, whose armies had played the key role in defeating Napoleon, posed as the liberator of Europe. In return, he demanded handsome payment— the right to annex Poland. Great Britain, in the midst of rapid economic growth, was alarmed at the Russian plans for expansion. Russian power in central Europe and along the Mediterranean directly challenged British commercial interests and the lines of communication with India. Russia was supported at the Congress by Prussia who wished to become the dominant German power. Prussia was willing to cede to Russia certain Prussian territories inhabited by Poles in return for the Kingdom of Saxony.

The interests of the fourth Great Power, Austria, were opposed to both Russian and Prussian objectives. Austria was located in the center of Europe and had always been directly threatened by any other continental nation that became powerful. Accordingly, balance of power was the most sensible policy for Austria to pursue; and Prince Metternich, Austria's long-time foreign minister, used all his powers of persuasion to achieve it. He opposed the ambitions of Tsar Alexander and set himself against the forces of nationalism in Germany and Italy. He united with the British to insist that France be reinstated among the Great Powers.

In the end the decisions at Vienna agreed largely with the interests of Austria and Great Britain. Russia received only part of Poland, and France regained its equal status with the other Great Powers. The map of Europe was redrawn without regard for nationality: Austria added

Prince Metternich (1773-1859) was Austrian minister of foreign affairs from 1809-1848. The years 1815-1848 are often referred to as the Age of Metternich, because his policies were the core of international European policies.

Italians and more Slavs to its already diverse population, for example. Prussia did not get all of Saxony, but was given the Rhineland as compensation. This move served a dual purpose. It prevented Prussia from strengthening its central territory, and, at the same time, it created a barrier against future French expansion. Playing on the fear of revolution, Metternich had diverted Russian and Prussian ambition away from open hostility and counteracted the influence of Britain.

The Vienna settlement followed three basic principles: legitimacy, or a return to past conditions wherever possible; compensation, by which each nation received some rewards for its efforts in the common cause; and conservatism, or opposition to liberalism, nationalism, and change in general. In order to preserve the *status quo*, or the situation as it was, a revolutionary agreement required the Powers to meet periodically to review the state of affairs in Europe. Thus was born the Concert of Europe, which was the first attempt to form a collective security organization.

▶Under what conditions, if any, should people try to return to conditions that existed in the past?

Europe did not get involved in another general war for ninety-nine years after the Congress of Vienna. The few wars waged were on a limited scale. And the credit for the peace belonged primarily to the balance of power. No one nation was strong enough, or believed itself strong enough, to upset that balance. Collective security contributed little; the conferences called almost every year to examine controversial political questions soon broke up over the liberal-conservative issue.

Even the emergence of Germany as one of the most powerful European states did not destroy the balance of power for several decades. Otto von Bismarck was as strong a supporter of the Concert of Europe as were the diplomats at Vienna. Bismarck could have added German-speaking Austria to his empire in 1866, but he preferred an independent Austria acting as a buffer against Russia. His conservative policies pleased Russia while also promoting the best relations with Britain by not interfering in matters vital to that nation. Meanwhile, Bismarck encouraged French colonial expansion into areas where the British and Italians had gone. And he made several defensive alliances, notably with Austria and Italy, to prevent a French-dominated alliance against Germany from recovering French areas lost in 1871.

Such planning decisively shifted the balance of power to Germany. But France had been able to build up an alliance system of its own, with Russia and Great Britain. By 1914 it seemed as if Europe waited only for that one event, such as the murder of Franz Ferdinand, that would justify war. After the war broke out, the Great Powers of Europe proved unable to end it either by military victory or negotiation until the United States stepped in and brought it to a conclusion. Thus, when World War I was over, Europe had lost the leadership of the world to the United States.

In the final test—in the war that balance of power was to have prevented—the politics of a century were found wanting. At least this appeared so to President Woodrow Wilson who felt that a new system of keeping peace had to be found. And so he created the League of Nations, an organization of peace-loving nations that would take united action against aggression. This idea of collective security centers on the belief that aggressive war is a crime against humankind, and it is the duty of all states to unite against such aggression. Thus, collective security goes beyond the interests of individual states; it relies on the weight of world opinion.

The Covenant (charter) of the League of Nations, which was included in the Versailles Treaty, contained certain key provisions. Each member promised to respect the independence of all other member nations and to aid one another against aggression. All agreed to submit serious disputes to the League and in no case to turn to war until the League had had time to work out settlements. The members also promised to take united action against any nation that started war in violation of these provisions. This united action would first be economic and then military.

In theory, collective security would avoid war; in practice, it did not. The nations of the world were not ready to give up their individual interests for a world community. The United States can serve as an example of this generalization. The Senate refused to approve the Treaty of Versailles because the League Covenant would restrict national sovereignty.

Nor did the other major powers support collective security. France had accepted the League mainly because Wilson insisted, and France did not want to defy the power of the United States. French statesmen still believed more in balance of power than in collective security, and they soon established a new system of alliances aimed at isolating Germany. Great Britain, for its part, was no more eager to give up its power of independent action than was the United States.

The League, therefore, was not a closely knit organization with a common goal, but nations that worked together only when it served their purposes. And even if the nations agreed on a common objective, the League did not represent all the major powers of the world—an idea basic to collective security. The United States never joined, and the Soviet Union and Germany, potentially the most powerful European states, were members for only a short time. Finally, the Covenant of the League suffered because it was part of the Treaty of Versailles.

The League worked fairly well in its first ten years for a reason more negative than positive—a power vacuum existed in the world. The United States refused to accept the responsibility of its new world leadership, and it remained stubbornly removed from world affairs.

▶Should a nation be willing to give up control of its own sovereignty to an international organization? Why or why not?

Germany joined the League in 1926, but Hitler withdrew the nation in 1933. The Soviet Union joined only in 1934, allying itself with the West in the face of growing Nazi power.

A World War I savings stamps
poster

French women working in a factory

*In what ways do these pictures
show how various aspects of
modern history have changed the
nature of war?*

A battlefield in France, 1917

The United States Secretary of War drawing numbers from a bowl to begin the draft, June 1918

An airplane taking off from a battle cruiser

The Soviet Union wrestled with internal problems of Communism. Germany, France, and Britain were rocked by the economic and political results of the war. What disputes arose were minor, and the League rapidly settled them.

Yet when the League finally challenged the actions of a major power, its inability to stop aggression became apparent. In 1931 Japan invaded and occupied the large Chinese province of Manchuria despite League opposition. In 1933 Japan withdrew from the League. The message of Manchuria's conquest was not lost on other world leaders. In 1935 the Italian dictator Mussolini conquered the African kingdom of Ethiopia without effective opposition from the League. And two years later, having formed the Axis alliance with Germany, Italy also left the League of Nations. When Hitler annexed Austria and portions of Czechoslovakia in 1938, the League refused to understand his real goals.

Collective security is not necessarily unworkable; it simply was unrealistic at that time. During the two decades after World War I, great economic depression struck both Europe and the United States. The average citizen was more interested in lower taxes and increased social welfare than in international power plays. Moreover, public opinion in the western nations assumed the League could stop aggression without understanding that, having no armed forces of its own, it had to rely on the armies and navies of Britain and France. And the French and British people made it clear time after time that they did not want their countries to go to war. And so the concept of collective security mistakenly came to mean peace without fighting.

Hitler's aggressions eventually drove the western democracies to war in 1939, not because collective security was threatened but because Hitler challenged special interests. The alliance forged against the Nazis was composed of several states whose chief bond was their need to defeat Hitler. Once this objective was accomplished, their differences quickly reappeared. The Soviet Union wanted security from attack, which could be assured by adding territory to the homeland and occupying large areas of eastern Europe. The Soviet Union also wanted to spread Communist ideas. The United States hoped to establish democracy all over the world. Britain, shattered by two wars in thirty years, wanted to keep what remained of its past glory.

The Soviet Union and the United States both demanded a dominant voice in world affairs. Britain wanted some sort of balance to offset these two giant powers. Each has found partial satisfaction in the United Nations. The planners of the United Nations were more realistic than their predecessors, and they recognized that some nations are more powerful than others. Consequently, the United States, the Soviet Union, Britain, France, and China can veto decisions endangering their national interests. The planners also recognized that a "United Nations"

Meeting in San Francisco from April 25 to June 26, 1945, delegates from 50 nations drafted the United Nations Charter. The first meetings of the General Assembly and Security Council were held in London in January 1946.

must include all nations, and gradually almost every country in the world has been given membership. And the United Nations can call upon armed forces to back up the interests of collective security.

Yet the interests of democratic and Communist nations are so opposed that it has been very difficult to agree on common objectives through collective security. Accordingly, foreign policy has alternated between doses of collective security and balance-of-power. The United Nations has been used effectively in cases where the powers have wished to avoid personal involvement, and settlement by a third party is in their mutual interest. But in most cases the rival nations prefer to keep the power of decision-making in their own hands. While using the potentials of collective security through the United Nations, they have also made alliances to support their special interests. They have again created what is in effect a balance of power.

Individual and Group Activities for Chapter 12

For full descriptions of these activities, turn to the **Student Book of Activities and Readings** included among the materials for individual and group activities.

Activity 12A: Study of World War I propaganda through war posters of that period (individual)
This activity contains several posters from World War I. Carefully analyze them to see how they were useful propaganda tools. Then write a short explanation for each poster.

Activity 12B: Interview with a veteran of World War I and a creative interpretation of the experience (individual or group)
Arrange an interview with a World War I veteran in your community. Find out what the war was like from the point of view of an actual participant. Then think of a dramatic, literary, or artistic way to express your impressions from the interview.

Authoritarianism in Russia

Most of the forces that transformed western Europe had little effect on Russia. Some of these forces appeared there later than in the rest of Europe. Others never reached Russia at all. By 1900 Russia had fallen far behind her western neighbors. Serfdom had been abolished for only forty years. Serious efforts to industrialize were only ten years old. And the Russians had only begun to develop representative political institutions.

Russia faced many problems in the early 1900's. The abolition of serfdom left serious social and economic problems unsolved. Peasants resented the heavy taxes they had to pay and demanded more land. The living standards of workers and peasants had not improved because industrialization had not kept up with the growth of population. Russian intellectuals questioned the absolutist government run by the tsar. The inefficient government ran the nation badly. Finally, Russia was the weakest militarily of all the major powers.

When the Russian armies lost battle after battle early in World War I, the Russian people realized that their government could not even defend the nation. A year of revolution in 1917 crushed the old government. The tsar abdicated, and moderate reformers formed a provisional government. Then the Bolsheviks. a more radical group, organized a second revolution in October 1917. After overthrowing the provisional government, the Bolsheviks quickly made peace with Germany and Austria-Hungary. They also began to set up a new government under the leadership of V. I. Lenin, an early leader of the Bolsheviks.

Tsarist Russia had always been an authoritarian state. Lenin and his followers mixed traditional authoritarian values with the ideas of Karl Marx. Out of this development grew a new sort of authoritarian government more powerful and oppressive in some ways than Russians had ever known before. Chapter 13 analyzes the nature of this government and traces its historical roots.

314

1848	Karl Marx and Friedrich Engels issue <u>Communist Manifesto</u>.
1917	Nicholas II abdicates in February Revolution.
	Bolshevik Revolution in October gives V.I. Lenin control of government.
1924	Lenin dies.
1928	Josef Stalin seizes power.
	Stalin introduces first Five-Year Plan, forcing rapid industrialization.
1934-1938	Communist purges kill or imprison thousands.
1941-1945	Soviet Union fights Germany in World War II.
1946-1948	Communists take over eastern European countries.
1953	Stalin dies.
1953-1958	Nikita Khrushchev comes to power.
1956	Twentieth Congress of the Communist Party meets in Moscow.
1964	Communist Party forces Khrushchev to retire.
	Leonid Brezhnev and Aleksei Kosygin begin collective leadership.

54 ROOTS OF AUTHORITARIANISM: IMPERIAL RUSSIA

According to a nineteenth-century Russian official, Russian society at that time was supported by three pillars—autocracy, orthodoxy, and Russian nationalism. Autocracy referred to the absolute rule of the tsar as well as to the autocratic rule of each household by the head of the family. Orthodoxy referred specifically to the teachings of the Russian Orthodox Church, but more generally to the idea that no differences of opinion were allowed, because everyone had to believe in the revealed truth of the Orthodox Church. Russian nationalism stressed a program of Russification under which non-Russian nationalities were to be forcibly absorbed into the Russian culture.

Although this analysis of Russian society was oversimplified, it described the general character of Russia as it appeared to Donald Mackenzie Wallace, an Englishman who visited Russia in the last decades of the nineteenth century. The following selection is taken from Wallace's account of Russian society at that time. His detailed observations provided a picture of Russian traditions, habits, and values that have influenced the nature of the Communist dictatorship. The society he described was the society the Bolsheviks wished to destroy when they seized power in 1917, but it was also the society upon which they built their government. As you read Wallace's account, think about the following questions:

1. In what ways were the values and traditions of the Russian government and family system similar?
2. What communal or collective institutions existed in tsarist Russia?

An Englishman's View of Nineteenth-Century Russia

Sir Donald Mackenzie Wallace, **Russia: On the Eve of War and Revolution,** Cyril E. Black, ed. (New York: Vintage Books, Random House, Inc., 1961), pp. 7-9, 258-261, 270-271, 286-287.

Peter the Great was tsar from 1682 to 1725.

THE ADMINISTRATION

At the top of the pyramid stands the Emperor, "the autocratic monarch," as Peter the Great described him, "who has to give an account of his acts to no one on earth, but has power and authority to rule his States and lands as a Christian sovereign according to his own will and judgment." Immediately below his Majesty we see the Council of State, the Committee of Ministers, and the Senate, which represent respectively the legislative, the administrative, and the judicial power. . . . Though the Council is entrusted with many important functions—such as discussing bills, criticizing the annual budget, declaring war and concluding peace—it has merely a consultative character, and the Emperor is not bound by its decisions. . . .

For the purpose of territorial administration Russia proper . . . is divided into forty-nine provinces or "governments," and each government is subdivided into districts. . . .

Over each province is placed a Governor, who is assisted in his duties by a Vice-Governor and a small council. . . . Down to the time of the Crimean War [1854-1856], the Governors . . . ruled in a most arbitrary, high-handed style, often exercising an important influence on the civil and criminal tribunals. . . .

To keep this vast and complex bureaucratic machine in motion it is necessary to have a large and well-drilled army of officials. These are drawn chiefly from the ranks of the Noblesse [nobility] and the Clergy, and form a peculiar social class. . . .

316

THE PEASANTS

Ivan's household was a good specimen of the Russian peasant family of the old type. Previous to the Emancipation [of the serfs] in 1861 there were many households of this kind, containing the representatives of three generations. All the members, young and old, lived together in patriarchal fashion under the direction and authority of the Head of the House, called usually the *Khozain*—that is to say, the Administrator; or, in some districts, the *Bolshak*, which means literally "the Big One." Generally speaking, this important position was occupied by the grandfather, or, if he was dead, by the eldest brother, . . .

The relations between the Head of the Household and the other members depended on custom and personal character, and they varied greatly consequently in different families. If the Big One was an intelligent man, of decided, energetic character, . . . there was probably perfect discipline in the household, except perhaps in the matter of female tongues, which do not readily submit to the authority even of their owners; but very often it happened that the Big One was not thoroughly well fitted for his post, and in that case endless quarrels and bickerings inevitably took place. . . .

The house, with . . . the cattle, the agricultural implements, the grain and other products, the money gained from the sale of these products—in a word, the house and nearly everything it contained—were the joint property of the family. Hence, nothing was bought or sold by any member—not even by the Big One himself . . . —without the . . . consent of the other grown-up males, and all the money that was earned was put into the common purse. When one of the sons left home to work elsewhere he was expected to bring or send home all his earnings, except what he required for food, lodgings, and other *necessary* expenses; and if he understood the word "necessary" in too lax a sense, he had to listen to very plain-spoken reproaches when he returned. During his absence, which might last for a whole year or several years, his wife and children remained in the house as before, and the money which he earned could be devoted to the payment of the family taxes.

The peasant household of the old type was thus a primitive labor association, of which the members had all things in common. . . .

[The] predominance of practical economic considerations was exemplified also by the way in which marriages were arranged in these large families. In the primitive system of agriculture usually practiced in Russia, the natural labor unit . . . comprised a man, a woman, and a horse. As soon, therefore, as a boy became an able-bodied laborer he had to be provided with the two accessories necessary for the completion of the labor unit. To procure a horse . . . was the duty of the Head of the House; to procure a wife for the youth was the duty of "the female Big One." . . . And the chief consideration in determining

A patriarchal family is one that is ruled by the father.

▶ Should authors include remarks based on their own observations, opinions, or prejudices in accounts such as this one? Why or why not?

▶ Under what conditions, if any, should children be expected to contribute their earnings to their families?

317

► These pictures show scenes from Russian village life in the 1800's. For what purposes, if any, would a group have the right to upset this way of life in order to bring about economic and social changes?

the choice was in both cases the same. Prudent domestic administrators were not to be tempted by showy horses or beautiful brides; what they sought was . . . capacity for work. . . .

THE VILLAGES

[A] Russian village is something very different from a village in our sense of the term. . . . Among the families composing a Russian village . . . a state of isolation is impossible. The Heads of Households must often meet together and consult in the Village Assembly, and their daily occupations must be influenced by the Communal decrees. They cannot begin to mow the hay or plow the fallow field until the Village Assembly has passed a resolution on the subject. Under the old system, if a peasant became a drunkard, or took some equally efficient means to become insolvent, every family in the village had a right to complain, not merely in the interests of public morality, but from selfish motives, because all the families were collectively responsible for his taxes. . . .

Insolvent means unable to pay one's debts.

For the reason given above no peasant could permanently leave the village without the consent of the Commune, and this consent would not be granted until the applicant gave satisfactory security . . . If a peasant wished to go away for a short time, in order to work elsewhere, he had to obtain a written permission, which served him as a passport during his absence; and he might be recalled at any moment by a Communal decree. In reality he was rarely recalled so long as he sent home regularly the full amount of his taxes—including the dues which he had to pay for the temporary passport—but sometimes the Commune used the power of recall for purposes of extortion. If it became known, for instance, that an absent member was receiving a good salary or otherwise making money, he might one day receive a formal order to return at once to his native village, but he was probably informed at the same time, unofficially, that his presence would be dispensed with if he would send to the Commune a certain specified sum. . . .

Communal land in Russia is of three kinds: the land on which the village is built, the arable [farm] land, and the meadow or hay field, if the village is fortunate enough to possess one. On the first of these each family possesses a house and garden, which are the hereditary property of the family, and are never affected by periodical redistributions. The other kinds are both subject to redistribution. . . .

The whole of the Communal arable land is first of all divided into three fields, to suit the triennial [three-year] rotation of crops, and each field is then divided into a number of long, narrow strips—corresponding to the number of male members in the Commune—as nearly as possible equal to each other in area and quality. Sometimes it is necessary to divide the field into several portions, according to the quality of the soil, and then to subdivide each of these portions into the requisite

319

number of strips. Thus in all cases every household possesses at least one strip in each field; and in those cases where subdivision is necessary, every household possesses a strip in each of the portions into which the field is subdivided. It often happens, therefore, that the strips are very narrow, and the portions belonging to each family very numerous. Strips six feet wide are by no means rare. . . . Of these narrow strips a household may possess as many as thirty in a single field! The complicated process of division and subdivision is accomplished by the peasants themselves . . . .

As the whole of the Communal land thus resembles to some extent a big farm, it is necessary to make certain rules concerning cultivation. A family may sow what it likes in the land allotted to it, but all families must at least conform to the accepted system of rotation. In like manner, a family cannot begin the autumn plowing before the appointed time, because it would thereby interfere with the rights of the other families, who use the fallow field as pasturage. . . .

FOR THOUGHT:

In what ways might Russian society under the tsars have contributed to the growth of an authoritarian government under the Bolsheviks?

55 ROOTS OF AUTHORITARIANISM: COMMUNIST IDEOLOGY

In April 1917, a sealed train left Switzerland for Petrograd, today called Leningrad, carrying the exiled prophet of the Bolshevik Revolution, V. I. Lenin. The Germans knew that Lenin wished to push the Russian Revolution to a Bolshevik victory. They agreed to help him reach his homeland, hoping that he would create greater disorder among the Russian people and thus weaken the Russian war effort.

The provisional government was struggling with the immense problems of Russia's continued participation in World War I and the severe economic and social crises aggravated by the war. When Lenin arrived in Petrograd, he proclaimed that he had come to complete the revolution. He attacked the provisional government, accusing it of being the servant of big business. He called for peace at once, on almost any terms. He promised that the Bolsheviks would give the factories to the workers and the land to the peasants. When they seized power seven months later, they began to carry out this program.

Bolshevik ideology was based on the ideas of Karl Marx and Friedrich Engels. In the *Communist Manifesto*, written by both men, and in *Das Capital*, written by Marx alone, Marx and Engels had accused the capitalists of Europe of taking advantage of the proletariat. By running the government in the name of the proletariat, the Bolsheviks aimed to use political power to take control of the factories, machines, and other means of production away from the bourgeoisie. They would then place control in the hands of the people.

Reading 55 is concerned with the ways in which government was to be used to create a Communist society. The following selections are taken from the writings of Marx and Engels, Lenin, Josef Stalin, and Nikita Khrushchev, all influential men who helped to shape Communist thought. As you read, keep these questions in mind:

1. How does Marx describe the classless society? In what ways have the Soviet Communists enlarged or changed his views?
2. What methods do the Communist writers support to achieve their goals? How can you explain their different methods?

The *Communist Manifesto*

This excerpt from the Communist Manifesto *discusses the role of the proletariat in the period immediately following a successful Communist revolution.*

The first step in the revolution by the working class is to raise the proletariat to the position of the ruling class, in order to win the battle of democracy.

The proletariat will use its political power to seize all capital from the bourgeoisie. It will centralize control of all means of production in the hands of the state, that is, in the hands of the proletariat organized as the ruling class. The proletariat will also increase the total amount of productive forces, such as factories, as rapidly as possible.

In the beginning, these changes cannot be made except by interfering with the rights of property and by changing bourgeois production methods. These measures will require changes in the old social order. They are unavoidable if the goal is to revolutionize entirely the mode of production.

Eventually class distinctions will disappear and all production will be concentrated in a vast association made up of the whole nation. At this time the public power, or state, will lose its present political character. Today political power is merely the organized power which one class uses to oppress another. During its contest with the bourgeoisie, the proletariat will be forced to organize itself into a class. By

Karl Marx and Friedrich Engels, **Communist Manifesto,** as quoted in **Essential Works of Marxism,** Arthur P. Mendel, ed. (New York: Bantam Books, 1961), pp. 32-33. Language simplified.

▶Under what conditions, if any, can you justify making basic social, political, and economic changes by the use of force?

▶Every Easter Tsar Nicholas II gave an expensive and elaborate Easter egg, such as this one, to his wife. Do you think a political leader should have so much wealth that he can give expensive presents when many of the people in his country go hungry?

revolution, it will make itself into the ruling class and will sweep away by force the old conditions of production. Along with these conditions, it will sweep away the reasons for class antagonisms and for classes in general. Thereby, it will abolish its own supremacy as a class.

In place of the old bourgeois society, with its classes and class antagonisms, we shall have an association in which the free development of each is the condition for the free development of all.

Lenin on the Nature of the State

Lenin contributed much to Communist theory, particularly the emphasis on the use of a disciplined and aggressive revolutionary party to seize power. His ideas have become so basic to Communist ideology that it is often called Marxism-Leninism.

V. I. Lenin, The State and Revolution, as quoted in Essential Works of Marxism, Mendel, ed., p. 171. Language simplified.

The dictatorship of the proletariat means the organization of the most advanced members of the oppressed classes into the ruling class in order to suppress the oppressors. This dictatorship cannot result only in an expansion of traditional democracy, but into a democracy of the poor. To do this, the dictatorship of the proletariat will put restrictions

322

on the freedom of the oppressors, the exploiters, the capitalists. We must suppress them in order to free humanity from wage slavery. Their resistance must be crushed by force for where there is suppression and violence by the oppressors, there is no freedom and no democracy.

Only in communist society does it become possible to speak of freedom. In communist society, the resistance of the capitalists will have been completely crushed. When they have disappeared, there will be no social classes, that is, no differences between the members of society in their relationship to the means of production. The state can then cease to exist, resulting in a state of freedom. Only then can people have a truly complete democracy without any restrictions whatever.

Stalin on the Role of the Party

After Lenin's death in 1924, a four-year power struggle developed among other party leaders. Josef Stalin (1879-1953) triumphed in 1928 after ruthlessly maneuvering his rivals out of positions of power. He kept tight control of the Communist Party until his death.

The Communist Party is the highest form of organization of the proletariat. The Party is the main guiding force within the proletarian class and among the organizations of that class. The Party is an instrument in the hands of the proletariat for achieving the dictatorship of the proletariat.

The proletariat needs the Party to achieve the dictatorship of the proletariat. It needs the Party still more to maintain, strengthen, and expand the dictatorship and win the complete victory of socialism.

Now, what does to "maintain" and "expand" the dictatorship mean? It means filling the millions of proletarians with the spirit of discipline and organization. It means making the proletarians into a barrier against the destructive influences of petty bourgeois habits. It means strengthening the organizational work of the proletarians to reeducate the petty bourgeois. It means helping the masses of the proletariat to reeducate themselves as a force that can abolish classes and prepare the way for the organization of a socialist system of production. It is impossible to reach all of these goals without a solid and disciplined Party.

The Twentieth Party Congress

The Twentieth Congress of the Communist Party met in Moscow in 1956. At that time, Nikita Khrushchev, then leader of the Party and premier of the Soviet Union, delivered a "secret speech" in which he denounced Stalin and his practices. He also called for a restatement of Communist aims and methods. This is part of the program adopted.

323

COMMUNIST EUROPE

Union Republics of U.S.S.R.

U.S.S.R. Satellite Nations

RUSSIAN SOCIALIST FEDERAL SOVIET REPUBLIC

★ Moscow

ESTONIA
LATVIA
LITHUANIA
EAST GERMANY
CZECHOSLOVAKIA
POLAND
BYELORUSSIA
HUNGARY
UKRAINE
RUMANIA
MOLDAVIA
BULGARIA
Black Sea
GEORGIA
ARMENIA
AZERBAIDZHAN
Caspian Sea
KAZAKH
UZBEK
KIRGHIZ
TADZHIK
TURKMEN
Mediterranean Sea

The New Communist Manifesto, Dan L. Jacobs, ed. (Evanston, Illinois: Row, Peterson and Co., 1962). pp. 235-236.

The dictatorship of the proletariat, born of the socialist revolution, played an epoch-making role by ensuring the victory of socialism in the U.S.S.R. In the course of socialist construction, however, it underwent changes. After the exploiting classes had been abolished, the function of suppressing their resistance ceased to exist. The chief functions of the socialist state—organization of the economy, culture and education—developed in full measure. The socialist state entered a new period of development. The state began to grow over into a nation-wide organization of the working people of socialist society. Proletarian democracy was growing more and more into a socialist democracy of the people as a whole.

324

The working class is the only class in history that does not aim to perpetuate its power.... Since the working class is the foremost and best organized force of Soviet society, it plays a leading role also in the period of the full-scale construction of communism. The working class will have completed its role of leader of society after communism is built and classes disappear....

As socialist democracy develops, the organs of state power slowly will be transformed into organs of public self-government. The Leninist principle of democratic centralism, which ensures the proper combination of centralized leadership with the maximum encouragement of local initiative, the extension of the rights of the Union republics and greater creative activity of the masses, will be promoted. It is essential to strengthen discipline, constantly control the activities of all the sections of the administrative apparatus, check the execution of the decisions and laws of the Soviet state and heighten the responsibility of every official for the strict and timely implementation of these laws....

FOR THOUGHT:

How did the ideology you have been reading about influence the development of an authoritarian political system in the Soviet Union?

56 THE INDIVIDUAL IN SOVIET SOCIETY

After the October 1917 revolution, the Bolsheviks made peace with Germany. They gave up land on their western borders and made other concessions. Then civil war broke out. The Bolsheviks eventually won, but Lenin and his followers inherited a land in chaos. The war had taken millions of lives, and it had destroyed both farms and factories. In addition, peasants, workers, and intellectuals had turned against the nobles, merchants, and manufacturers. When the production of both farm products and manufactured goods fell, the revolution seemed to be in danger.

For a time, Lenin and his followers compromised with the past. Beginning in 1921 they permitted some private ownership of industry and farms and some private trade under a plan called the New Economic Policy. The economy recovered. But beginning in 1928, Lenin's successor, Josef Stalin, began a series of Five-Year Plans to bring industry under state ownership and force peasants onto collective farms.

Communist Party officials slowly eliminated all organized opposition to their rule. They used the secret police to search out individuals and organizations hostile to the revolution. The secret police arrested former members of the tsarist government, former capitalists, and even many Communists who did not agree with the regime. After 1928, Stalin used the police to eliminate opponents and potential opponents of his Five-Year Plans. Of the Soviet Union's 25 million peasant families, about one million owned their own farms. Stalin tried to force them to unite their lands to form collective or state farms. If they refused, the secret police drove them from their land, took their property, and either deported them to labor camps or shot them.

Stalin also used the secret police to attack potential opponents within the ranks of the Party, including many of his oldest friends and colleagues. A number of purges took place. Estimates of how many people were killed or sent to forced labor camps range from 6 to 14 million. Late in the 1930's, Stalin purged the secret police itself, getting rid of other potential opponents. The purges effectively wiped out opposition to the Communist Party. The present Soviet government does not execute people wholesale or run forced labor camps. But the purges still serve as a warning to anyone who may be thinking of starting an opposition movement to the Party.

Reading 56 contains two excerpts about the nature of life in the Soviet Union today. Each focuses upon the role of dissenters in Soviet society. Each implies something about the nature of authoritarian rule there. As you read, think about the following questions:

1. What do the dissenters described in this article want? Does their dissent imply dissatisfaction with all aspects of Soviet life?
2. How has the government treated these dissenters?

A Novelist Criticizes the Regime

Alexander Solzhenitsyn, who won the Nobel Prize in 1970 for his novel, One Day in the Life of Ivan Denisovich, *has been a leader in several movements to win civil rights for Soviet citizens. The following articles describe this struggle.*

DISSENT IN RUSSIA: THE THIN WEDGE

"Dissent in Russia: The Thin Wedge," **Newsweek** (February 1, 1971), pp. 29-33. Copyright © February 1, 1971 by Newsweek, Inc., 1971. Used by permission.

In his dual role as a man of letters and a man of science, Solzhenitsyn personifies a turning point for the Soviet Union. In recent months, a growing number of prominent scientists have joined artistic dissenters in open protest against the Soviet repression of individuality. And this union of the artistic and scientific intelligentsia [intellectuals] is the most important milestone in the course of Soviet dissent since the death of Joseph Stalin. . . .

Outspoken Actress
Melina Mercouri

United Press International

From one of the best known political families in Greece
(**Miss Mercouri during news conference yesterday**)

WHETHER the subject is politics, love, life, husband-stealing, the stage or a director she doesn't like, Melina Mercouri is one Greek who has a word for it—or, rather, many words, some corrosive.

"My biggest amusement is to talk," she said recently. "That is why I hate the junta." Yesterday the junta that now rules Greece decided Miss Mercouri had talked too much and too corrosively. It an-

Woman in the News

nounced that it was depriving her of her citizenship and confiscating her property.

In taking these extreme steps, the junta is ostracizing a woman celebrated in her homeland for more than her acting career. Miss Mercouri comes from one of the best-known political families in the country.

Her grandfather, whom she once described as "like d'Artagnan," was Mayor of Athens for more than 30 years. Her father, who died in London last week, served several terms in the Greek Government as Minister of the Interior.

► Melina Mercouri left Greece because of the lack of intellectual and artistic freedom there. Do you think she should have stayed and tried to change Greece's government or was she right to leave?

Few of the dissenters are western-style democrats; what they seek is an enlightened *Soviet* system. But even that relatively modest demand confronts the cautious bureaucrats in the Kremlin with the gravest challenge of the post-Stalin era. . . . The government's painful dilemma—whether to bend with the winds of change or to crack down savagely on dissent—may ultimately hold the key to the success or failure of the Marxist experiment in Russia.

In a sense, the father of current Soviet dissent was Nikita Khrushchev. By inaugurating the de-Stalinization campaign in 1956, Khrushchev raised many hopes and, quite unintentionally, sparked the birth of a literary counterculture. Under Khrushchev, Solzhenitsyn was permitted to publish his novel, *One Day in the Life of Ivan Denisovich*—a searing indictment of Stalin's prison camps. Even this much dissent, however,

A kremlin is the walled center of many old Russian cities. The most famous is the Kremlin in Moscow, the seat of the present-day Soviet government.

Khrushchev began a campaign against what he called "the cult of personality," an attempt by the regime to praise Stalin for everything good in Soviet life.

327

alarmed the gray bureaucrats who succeeded Khrushchev, and soon the government began to crack down again. . . .

Dissent did not approach its present stage, however, until men like Solzhenitsyn edged off the sidelines. Solzhenitsyn's first timid step into political involvement—a series of wartime letters to a friend in which he criticized Stalin—had earned him eight years in a labor camp. After his release, he carefully avoided politics, settling down to a quiet job teaching mathematics in a provincial city. But . . . it was his evolution into a novelist of conscience that eventually brought him back to criticism of the regime. Thus, in 1967, he wrote to the Writer's Union demanding an end to the censorship that had "smothered, gagged, and slandered" his novels, *The First Circle* and *Cancer Ward.* The next year, Andrei Sakharov, an illustrious physicist who is known as one of the "fathers" of the Soviet hydrogen bomb, published a liberal manifesto in which he declared: "Intellectual freedom is essential to human society." And last year, biologist Zhores Medvedev . . . lashed out furiously at censorship of the mails.

►Why should people risk their career—even their lives—to end censorship?

At first, the new dissenters were unorganized. . . . Soviet law forbids the formation of anything that resembles a political opposition group. But events were soon to convince some scientists that they would be better off hanging together. Last May . . . Medvedev was arrested and hustled off to a mental institution. Solzhenitsyn joined the vast public outcry that quickly won the biologist his freedom and eventually even a new job. . . .

Even though they were kept from the attention of the average Russian, these actions made waves that are still rippling across the world of Soviet art and science. Still other eminent figures have been drawn into the fray. As the official press heaped fresh abuse on Solzhenitsyn, the cellist Mstislav Rostropovich—who had taken the novelist into his country *dacha* [house] outside Moscow—leapt to his friend's defense in an open letter to four Russian newspapers. When the authorities retaliated by barring Rostropovich from a scheduled concert, two other distinguished musicians—violinist David Oistrakh and pianist Sviatoslav Richter—refused to participate in the concert until Rostropovich had been reinstated. . . .

►Should people risk their careers and positions to defend friends who are attacked?

Yet for all their fame, men like Rostropovich, Oistrakh, and Richter are not vitally important to the bureaucrats who rule the nation. "The Soviet regime can get along perfectly well without its poets or musicians," says one western Kremlinologist. "But it can't get along so well without its technical elite." It is thus a cause of considerable concern to the men in the Kremlin that many Russian scientists feel increasingly alienated from their society. . . . Scientific dissent is also fostered by a growing awareness that censorship and political orthodoxy are severe handicaps to Soviet research [and] technological capabilities. . . .

A Kremlinologist is a specialist in Soviet affairs.

328

Despite their prominence, the dissident scientists and their allies in the arts have no monopoly on protest in Russia. [Still, their impact] . . . is considerable. Some foreign observers, however, discern a potentially damaging split in the "respectable" opposition among the intelligentsia. According to this theory, one group—composed of influential men like Solzhenitsyn and Sakharov—hopes to change Soviet society from within and hews more or less strictly to legal forms of protest. The other faction, made up of younger dissenters—most of them artists—is frustrated by a lack of influence and, as a result, has moved into activities that lie outside Soviet law.

"They fight the authorities," one Russian says. . . . "They confront them directly. They do not have the fear of the labor camp in their bones." Thus, in addition to filing formal protests, lending moral support when their friends stand trial, and signing petitions . . . these rebels stage illegal demonstrations, write articles, stories, and poems in *samizdat* form, and pass around smudged carbon copies of *A Chronicle of Current Events*, the Soviet Union's principal underground newspaper. . . . Obviously, the government could crush the protest movement overnight if it wanted to . . . . Instead, it has given many dissenters a little leash, and it has allowed "subversive" publications like the *Chronicle* to circulate fairly widely.

Samizdat means self-published. Samizdat are handwritten or typewritten manuscripts that circulate secretly.

THE HUMAN RIGHTS COMMITTEE

The Human Rights Committee joined by Aleksandr Solzhenitsyn differs from similar groups of Soviet dissenters in one important respect: Its founders are scientists, men who hold a privileged position in Soviet society and who traditionally have more leeway in criticizing the government. This fact, however, makes the committee a particular embarrassment to Moscow. Consequently, of its three founders, probably only renowned physicist Andrei Sakharov is relatively invulnerable to attack. His colleagues, physicists Valery Chalidze and Andrei Tverdokhlebov, could face active official harassment and even prosecution.

In spite of this, Chalidze recently discussed his committee's plans and goals . . . in a rare interview. . . . "Our organization is legal because Paragraph 126 of the Soviet Constitution guarantees the right of association. . . . The committee's task is not to unmask and demand but study and recommend—taking into account the real conditions here and the difficulties of the state in this sphere. It demands patience.

"Do you want us to make a revolution? Don't be silly. We will merely study human rights as guaranteed in Soviet law. . . . "One of the things the committee will seek to study is the violation of human rights in this country. . . .

"What influence will our committee have? . . . If the public has matured enough to be able to absorb the ideas proclaimed by the French

"The Human Rights Committee," **Newsweek** (December 21, 1970), p. 57. Copyright© December 21, 1970 by Newsweek, Inc. Used by permission.

Revolution, then we could say that we have some influence. And if the government ignores us? We will just go on making recommendations and more recommendations."

FOR THOUGHT:

In what ways does the treatment of dissenters in the Soviet Union today reflect the traditions of tsarist society and the ideology of the founders of the Bolshevik Party?

57 THE NATURE OF AUTHORITARIANISM IN THE SOVIET UNION

A HISTORICAL ESSAY

When the Bolsheviks seized power in 1917, Russia had only begun to develop the kind of modern society already well established in Great Britain and the United States. In 1917 three-fourths of Russia's 160 million people were illiterate peasants. They used the same agricultural techniques that had been used for centuries. Russian industry had begun to modernize during the 1890's, but it still trailed well behind the rest of Europe. And Russia's political system remained the most autocratic in Europe. To aggravate all these internal difficulties, Russia was surrounded with hostile neighbors who wanted the Bolshevik experiment to fail.

After 1917 the leaders of the Communist Party set out to accomplish in several decades what western European nations had achieved in centuries. To a large extent they were successful. The Soviet Union emerged from World War II as a major military power. Today it ranks as one of the world's strongest industrial nations. It has almost wiped out illiteracy and has given positions of power and prestige to people with talent. It has helped to spread Communist ideology far beyond Soviet borders. Its scientists have exploded hydrogen bombs and developed the technological know-how that enabled them to launch the first space vehicle. All of these impressive achievements have been packed into just over fifty years.

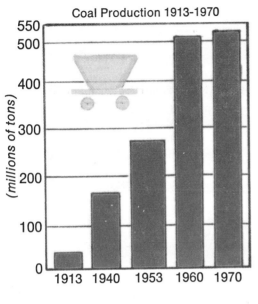

Coal Production 1913-1970

(millions of tons)

550, 500, 400, 300, 200, 100, 0

1913 1940 1953 1960 1970

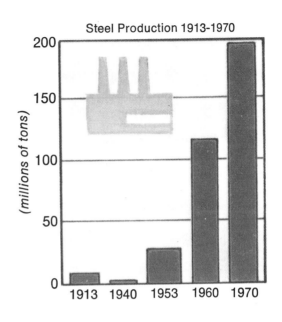

Steel Production 1913-1970

(millions of tons)

200, 150, 100, 50, 0

1913 1940 1953 1960 1970

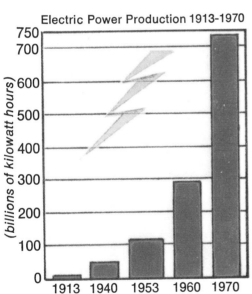

Electric Power Production 1913-1970

(billions of kilowatt hours)

750, 700, 600, 500, 400, 300, 200, 100, 0

1913 1940 1953 1960 1970

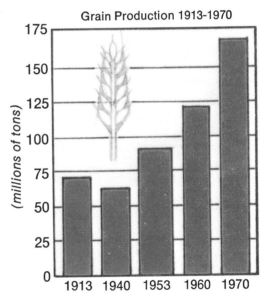

Grain Production 1913-1970

(millions of tons)

175, 150, 125, 100, 75, 50, 25, 0

1913 1940 1953 1960 1970

ECONOMIC ACHIEVEMENTS OF THE SOVIET UNION

These charts illustrate four economic achievements of the Soviet government. How much progress has been made? How do you account for the uneven rate of progress?

331

The powerful elite that controls the Communist Party has guided the Soviet Union to these impressive achievements. The members of this elite make the laws and appoint people to administer them. They distribute human, capital, and natural resources to produce the goods and services they believe necessary and desirable. Although control of the arts has been relaxed since Stalin's death, the Communist Party still keeps a close watch over the production of literature, music, plays, and paintings. The news media are also carefully controlled.

The influence of the past helped to shape the Soviet Union's present society. Autocratic political traditions accustomed the Russian people to authoritarianism. The Tatar people who conquered the Russians in the thirteenth century used an authoritarian system of government. When the Tatars were finally expelled, the tsars kept the authoritarian political system. In succeeding centuries the Russians learned to obey their rulers without question. The Russian Orthodox Church, closely tied to the tsarist government, reinforced the idea of submission to authority. So did the Russian family structure which was centered around obedience to the father. Even the organization of the *mir*, the Russian village, stressed the authority of the group rather than the rights of the individual. All these conditions helped to prepare the people of tsarist Russia for the authoritarianism of the Bolshevik Party.

Western political thought also contributed to the development of an authoritarian state in the Soviet Union. In order to create a classless society, Karl Marx supported a dictatorship of the proletariat that would destroy bourgeois society. Marx believed that the bourgeoisie used parliamentary governments to suppress workers. He argued that the proletariat should seize control of the political system and establish a classless society. A dictatorship of the proletariat would follow. During this period workers would exterminate their bourgeois oppressors and convince everyone of the truth of Marxist doctrines. In this way the state would soon disappear.

Lenin interpreted Marx's conception of the dictatorship of the proletariat to mean control by the Communist Party. About 23,000 people belonged to the Bolshevik faction of the Russian Social Democratic Party early in 1917. Lenin argued that this hard core of revolutionary leaders should seize the government in the name of the proletariat. Only this small elite, Lenin argued, knew what was best for the Russian masses. Left to their own desires, the peasants would simply seize the land, place it under private ownership, and solidly establish capitalist society in Russia. But the Communist elite would work toward the abolition of privately owned factories and farms. If necessary, they could force former bourgeois owners to work for the state, or they could liquidate them. They could also force the peasants to give up their private holdings and join farm collectives. Lenin argued that the

Elite means the best or more skilled members of a group.

The Tatars were an Asiatic people who established an empire in Russia around 1240. The Tatar domination was broken in 1480.

elite could remake Russian society only by using force and working through the Communist Party.

The Communist Party expanded slowly during the first years after the revolution. It admitted its millionth member in 1926. After Stalin began the Five-Year Plans in 1928, the Party expanded more rapidly. In addition to politicians, it needed economists, engineers, urban experts, and diplomats to manage the many tasks of a changing society. When Stalin died in 1953, the Party numbered almost 7 million. During the next two decades, Party membership doubled, although even then it was only about 6 percent of the total population.

The Communist Party has a hierarchical structure. (See chart, this page.) Each member belongs to a cell which meets in a local factory, farm or village. But the real power of the Party is centered in the fifteen-member Politbureau. This group dominates the All-Union Central Committee, which meets twice a year, and the All-Union Party Congress, which meets every four years. These organizations have become mere rubber stamps for the decisions made by the Party elite.

Although the Constitution of the Soviet Union guarantees civil rights to citizens, the Soviet government has violated or abolished every one of these rights. For many years, citizens took the jobs to which economic

▶Should a society admit everyone to membership in its key political institutions? Why or why not?

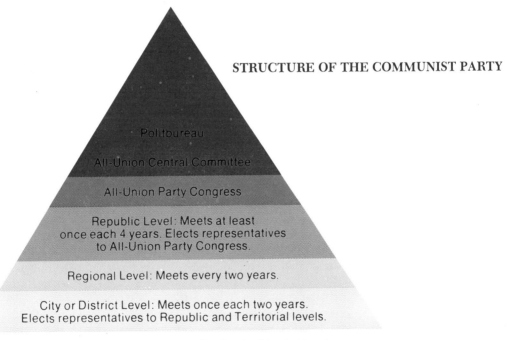

STRUCTURE OF THE COMMUNIST PARTY

Politbureau

All-Union Central Committee

All-Union Party Congress

Republic Level: Meets at least once each 4 years. Elects representatives to All-Union Party Congress.

Regional Level: Meets every two years.

City or District Level: Meets once each two years. Elects representatives to Republic and Territorial levels.

Cells in factories, farms, army, schools, etc. Meet at least once a month. Elect representatives to City or District Level.

planners assigned them rather than seek the work of their choice. Today Soviet citizens cannot emigrate freely, and many cannot get permission to travel abroad. During the 1930's people who spoke or wrote in opposition to the government were usually sent to labor camps. Even today, Soviet citizens cannot speak or write in opposition to the Party without being punished. Although Soviet citizens may worship in churches and synagogues, no member of the Communist Party may do so. Ownership of property is also restricted. Soviet citizens may own dwellings, automobiles, and other personal property, but they may not own capital goods. Finally, Soviet courts so consistently support the Party position that many outside observers do not believe they bring justice to Soviet citizens.

Nor do Soviet citizens have political rights as they are known in the West. They do not participate in any real decision-making. Almost all Soviet citizens do vote in elections. But the people they choose to attend the Soviet of the Union and the Soviet of Nationalities meet for only a few days at a time. They pass unanimously and without meaningful debate every bill submitted to them by their leaders, who are controlled by the Communist Party. And although theoretically any Soviet citizen may run for office, nomination is controlled by organizations approved by the Communist Party, the only party in the Soviet Union.

However, the Soviet Union has a much better record in social rights. Compulsory, free education has almost wiped out illiteracy. Through the use of competitive examinations, poor and rich alike have an equal chance for higher education and, through it, for greater success in society. The Constitution requires everyone to work, and few people are unemployed. Moreover, the standard of living has risen steadily, although it still falls far below western standards. The Party has tried to provide adequate housing and medical care as well as provisions for old age and disability. The Party has also tried to provide some cultural life through plays, operas, athletic organizations, and similar activities.

For many years, westerners referred to the Soviet Union as a totalitarian state. This term implies that the government has complete and total control over the life of Soviet citizens. Admittedly, the government's huge army and its control of all other armed forces, such as the police, make open resistance unthinkable. Government control of the media, such as newspapers, radio, and television, has helped to convince most citizens that the regime's decisions are correct. And the government also has enormous power because it controls the economy. In addition, the ruthless use of forced labor camps and purges in which millions of people died during the 1930's wiped out most sources of opposition.

Yet pockets of opposition still remain. A few intellectuals oppose the regime, some of them publicly. Others circulate privately printed newspapers. And several groups compete within the Party for control. No one group can rule if it offends too many other people, as Khrushchev found out when the Communist Party deposed him in 1964. And whenever farm and factory production dropped, government planners were forced to change some of their policies.

All these developments indicate that the Soviet Union is not a completely totalitarian state. Yet it lies as close to the totalitarian end of the political spectrum as any contemporary government, which its denial of both civil and political rights makes clear. Most Soviet citizens strongly support the principles of centralized economic planning that have catapulted their economy from one of the world's most backward to one of its most advanced. They have no desire to revolt, and they are proud of their nation's achievements. But as they reach a higher standard of living and come more in contact with the West, they have begun to demand some of the liberties they see elsewhere. They want to have all the civil and political rights that lie at the heart of the western heritage and have always been denied to them by both the tsars and the Communist Party.

▶ Are social rights more important than civil and political rights? Why or why not?

Individual and Group Activities for Chapter 13

For full descriptions of these activities, turn to the **Student Book of Activities and Readings** included among the materials for individual and group activities.

Activity 13A: Essay on how it feels to live under an authoritarian regime, based on evidence from contemporary newspapers (individual)
Collect as many newspaper articles as you can find that give evidence about how authoritarianism operates in the Soviet Union today. On the basis of this evidence, write an essay describing how you think a Soviet citizen today feels about his government and country.

Activity 13B: Essay on the treatment of Jews in the Soviet Union (individual)
Read a group of articles about the treatment of Jews in the Soviet Union. In a short essay, explain how the official Soviet policies toward Jews reflect the ideology of the Soviet Union.

Nazism in Germany

STATING THE ISSUE

In January 1933 Adolf Hitler became chancellor of Germany. For the next twelve years, he and his Nazi regime heaped indignity, terror, death, and destruction on the German people and their European neighbors. The ovens and gas chambers of the concentration camps and some of the ruins of bombed-out cities still stand as testimony to his scourge.

The twelve years during which Hitler ruled Germany and threatened the very survival of western civilization emerge as one of the most barbarous episodes in the history of humankind. Never before had any one man used the power of the state so ruthlessly. The Nazi era seems to most westerners to have been a monstrous mistake, as if for a time all humanist ideals were blotted out by the rantings of a demented man.

Yet Hitler's Nazism was the ugly and deformed child of western civilization. The ideology of his regime was taken from the writings of some of the West's most famous thinkers. Western technology gave him the means to carry out his vicious program; industrialization gave him the military strength to overpower all of Germany's neighbors except the Soviet Union and Great Britain. Nationalism brought millions to his cause. Even the institutions of democracy, particularly universal suffrage, added to his power. Hitler became dictator by using his great gifts as a public speaker to play on the fears of the German citizens to win their votes.

Chapter 14 analyzes Hitler's rise to power and describes some of the major events of the Nazi era. The essay at the end of the chapter relates Nazism to major trends in the western tradition.

1919	Weimar Constitution establishes a republic in Germany.	
1923	French troops occupy Ruhr Valley.	
	Inflation sweeps Germany.	
	Adolf Hitler fails to seize power in Munich. He writes **Mein Kampf** in jail.	
1929	Great Depression strikes Germany and all of Europe.	
1932	Nazis gain largest number of seats in Reichstag.	
1933	President Hindenburg makes Hitler chancellor.	
	Enabling Act gives Nazi government dictatorial powers.	
1935	Nuremberg Laws deprive Jews of rights.	
1936	German troops reoccupy Rhineland.	
1938	Germany annexes Austria.	
	Munich Pact concedes western Czechoslovakia to Hitler.	
1939	Germany invades Poland; Britain and France declare war on Germany.	
1940	Nazis occupy Denmark, Norway, Holland, Belgium, Luxembourg, and France.	
1940-1941	Germans launch air attacks on Great Britain.	
1941-1943	Germans are defeated in Soviet Union.	
1942	British check German advance in Africa at El Alamein.	
1944	Allies invade Italy and France to begin liberation of Europe.	
1945	Hitler commits suicide. Germany surrenders.	

58 THE GERMAN PEOPLE AND THE NAZIS

In 1929 a worldwide depression struck the industrialized countries of the western world. Unemployment soared to staggering heights, and production fell to new lows. In the United States and Great Britain, the government took on unusual powers to deal with economic problems. In France, the voters turned from one proposed cure to another. In Germany, the people gave power to Adolf Hitler.

Why did the German people turn to Hitler? Certainly part of the answer lies in Hitler's intrigues in the government and the use of his private army to terrorize his opposition. But part also lies in the will of the German people themselves. Although Hitler never received a majority of the popular vote in a free election, more than 17 million Germans voted for him in 1933.

337

Who supported Hitler and why? Reading 58 provides evidence with which you can begin to answer these questions. It contains a brief history of Germany from 1919 to 1933 and seven case studies representing various groups of Germans in the 1930's. These case studies are fictitious, but they are based on facts. Your teacher will ask each of you to read one of these case studies. As you study this reading, keep the following questions in mind:

1. What problems did the person in your case study face? What sort of a regime would seem most likely to solve his or her immediate problem?
2. What problems did the Weimar Republic face? How might these problems have aided the rise of Hitler?

The Weimar Republic and Hitler

Weimar, the city from which the republic took its name, is a noted cultural center located in the central part of Germany. The provisional national assembly met in Weimar in 1919 to form the German republic and draft its constitution.

Putsch means a secret, sudden plot to overthrow a government. On November 8, 1923, Hitler raided a Munich beer hall where Bavarian leaders were speaking. The leaders pretended to support Hitler and were soon freed. The next day 3,000 of Hitler's troops challenged the Bavarian militia and were defeated. Hitler fled, but was soon captured and sentenced to five years in prison. A growing sympathy with national socialism led to his release in 13 months. While in prison, Hitler wrote Mein Kampf.

In 1919, after centuries of autocratic rule, the German nation established a republic. A constitution written at Weimar skillfully combined elements of the parliamentary systems of western Europe and the independent executive system of the United States. Yet the new republic seemed doomed to fail from its beginning.

In the first place, the republican government signed the Treaty of Versailles. Most Germans believed that the treaty unfairly placed the total guilt for the war on Germany. The treaty also demanded that Germany be harshly punished. Therefore, the German people immediately opposed the new government. At the same time, those who had been responsible for World War I—the kaiser, members of his government, and the military leaders—escaped blame. As a result, the kaiser and the leaders of the military became identified with the glories of the fatherland. And the decline of Germany became identified with the republic.

In addition, the Weimar government was plagued by several groups that wanted to overthrow it. German Communists wanted the same kind of regime that had been established in the Soviet Union. Right-wing groups wanted a monarchy or a dictatorship. These groups caused several minor rebellions against the government, among them Adolf Hitler's Munich beer hall *putsch* in November 1923.

Third, even supporters of the republic contributed to its downfall. Instead of grouping themselves into a few major parties with wide appeal, they separated into many small parties. As a result, no single party was ever able to win a majority of seats in the Reichstag, the

German parliament. Only temporary coalitions of parties were able to carry on the process of governing. And whenever a minor disagreement arose among the parties of a coalition, the government fell.

Then in 1923 runaway inflation almost toppled the German economy. At one point, a bushel of potatoes cost a bushel of money, and the weekly salary of many Germans was worth only the price of one streetcar ride. Germany recovered from this inflation, but it was continually pressured to pay reparations as ordered by the Versailles Treaty.

However, after 1925 Germany seemed on the way to stable government and economic recovery. Such men as Gustav Stresemann temporarily weathered the political and economic storms. The war hero, Paul von Hindenburg, lent respect to the republican government when he became its president. During the middle and late 1920's, the German economy continued to recover, government crises diminished, and life returned to a more normal routine.

Hitler used the period after his unsuccessful rebellion and short prison term to organize his climb to power. He raised a private army for the Nazis—the Storm Troopers—by recruiting war veterans, the discontented, and hoodlums. He organized local party groups all over Germany to spread Nazi propaganda and recruit members. He even created a cabinet so that he would be prepared to administer the government whenever his opportunity came.

Then in 1929 a depression shook all of Europe and the United States. The German government was unable to deal with the growing economic distress. Hitler's National Socialist German Workers' party, or Nazi party, suddenly became a strong political force.

In the election of 1932 the Nazis won more seats in the Reichstag than any other party. The other leaders attempted to work around the Nazis by forming a coalition of all their parties. When this tactic failed, President Hindenburg called another election. Still the Nazi party remained the most numerous in the Reichstag. Hindenburg was then persuaded to appoint Hitler as chancellor, assuming that the other political leaders could then control him. But Hitler himself called a new election for March 1933. Until the election, he used his power in the government to terrorize his opposition. He wrecked newspaper offices and radio stations. As a final stroke, he burned the Reichstag building and blamed the fire on the Communists.

In the election, the Nazis won 288 of the 638 Reichstag seats. Together with their allies, the Nationalists, who had won 52 seats, Hitler had a majority of the legislature. On the first day that the new Reichstag met, the Nazis and Nationalists pushed through an Enabling Act which gave the Nazi-controlled government dictatorial powers for four years. Hitler had arrived. The Reichstag adjourned, never again to have an effective voice in the affairs of Germany during Hitler's rule.

Gustav Stresemann (1878-1929) entered the Reichstag in 1907. In 1918 he founded the conservative German People's party. He was chancellor in 1923 and foreign minister from 1923 until his death. Paul von Hindenburg (1847-1934), a hero of those wars, was appointed supreme commander of the Central Power forces in 1916. In 1925 he became president of Germany. Although he served until his death, during his last years he was not in full possession of his faculties. He was probably unable to understand fully the threat Hitler posed.

In German the Storm Troopers were called the Sturmabteilungen, or the SA. The SA guarded Nazi meetings and terrorized Hitler's opponents.

"Nazi" was a derisive term taken from the German way of pronouncing the first two syllables of national. However, it became the general name for the movement.

Seven Case Studies

CASE 1

Hermann Struts, a lieutenant in the German army, has been a lieutenant since World War I when he fought bravely on the western front. Coming from a long line of military officers and having graduated from the German military academy, Hermann is proud of Germany's military tradition. His pride is personal, because his family had been part of that tradition, and it is general, because Germany had always boasted a fine army that had secured the nation's well-being and leadership.

Yet Hermann has not been promoted for more than ten years. Because the German army had been so drastically reduced by the Treaty of Versailles, there have been relatively few promotions. In the old army, Hermann would have been at least a captain by now, because he is a resourceful officer. He probably would have been a major. Hermann resents the Versailles Treaty, which forced Germany to give up its military tradition. He believes this has forever injured Germany's honor, and his honor as a soldier. He feels that if the present government had vetoed the treaty and allowed the German army to resist it, neither Germany nor he would be in their present position.

CASE 2

Karin Hauptmann works in a textile factory in Berlin. Although her trade union has actively worked for better conditions and higher wages, it has not made many gains, primarily because the 1923 inflation and the present depression have weakened the entire economy. However, Karin believes that the union would succeed if the economy were stable. As it is, the union has kept her employed. When many of her friends were laid off, Karin's union persuaded the company managers to keep the senior employees. Factories where unions are weak kept only the younger employees, because the company managers say they are more productive.

Karin has been worried by the ideas many of her fellow workers have expressed recently. They have said that the greediness of the factory owners causes business cycles and that when the owners are forced to cut back production, they take it out on the workers. These fellow workers think the only way to end the depression is to let the workers control the factories and the government. Karin still believes that the workers get fair treatment as long as there are strong unions. Moreover, she thinks that managing the factories and the government should be left to people who understand these complicated jobs.

340

CASE 3

Eric von Ronheim, chief executive of an electric motor factory in Frankfurt, is extremely concerned about the present economic depression. Reduced production means lower profits for his company. If Germany had not been treated so harshly at Versailles, the nation would have enough resources to produce goods for consumption, and conditions would be far better. But the government had had to impose heavy taxes in order to pay the reparations the Allies had demanded. Indeed, much of his own profits are going into these taxes. Moreover, the over-taxed Germans have little money to spend on German goods, and so demand is dangerously low. Since other countries are also suffering from depressions, there is almost no foreign market for German goods. Even if Germany were to come out of the depression, Eric knows taxes would be increased to finish paying the reparations.

Eric is also worried about the menacing number of Communists in Germany who wish to organize the same kind of government as the Soviet Union has. If the Communists succeed, the capitalists would receive no mercy from the workers. And Germany would be controlled by its old enemy, the Soviet Union.

CASE 4

Karl Schmidt is a steelworker in the rich steel-producing Ruhr Valley. But like so many people in the Ruhr, he is out of work. The depression has forced many steel mills to shut down until there is a market for their goods. On the day Karl's mill closed, the owners announced that shrinking profits made it impossible to keep the workers on their jobs. Yet, Karl reasons, the owners still live in big houses and drive expensive automobiles. Why are the owners protected from this economic slump while the workers suffer? The government is helping the workers somewhat with unemployment compensation, but the payments are hardly enough to support Karl, his wife Anna, and their two children. Moreover, the government has declared that it has little money left, and it cannot continue the payments much longer.

As far as Karl understands, if the government would stop paying the reparations, perhaps it could help Germany recover. But Karl also knows that if the government stops its payments, the French might again occupy the Ruhr Valley, as they had in 1923. What is needed, Karl believes, is a government that listens to the workers—perhaps even one that is run by the workers, as some of his friends argue. And he feels Germany needs a government that can deny France and the other nations the reparation payments.

The Ruhr Valley is a great mining and industrial region in western Germany. Early in 1923 French troops occupied the Ruhr Valley because Germany had failed to meet its reparation payments. The German government then stopped all reparation payments and ordered the Ruhr inhabitants to stop all work until the troops left. To support the idle workers, the government issued worthless money. This contributed heavily to the 1923 inflation.

CASE 5

Lotte von Kohler, a prominent attorney who attended the University of Bonn, has a strong sense of the German cultural, literary, and historical traditions. She believes that the great gifts her people have contributed to western civilization have been ignored. Lotte dreams of a newly created republic uniting all the German democratic traditions and leading the way to a totally democratic Europe. She is upset by the unfortunate methods the Weimar Republic often uses to repress the parties of the extreme left more cruelly than those of the extreme right.

However, Lotte's sense of justice is more outraged by the demeaning attitude with which the Allies, particularly the French, view the German republic. She, and others like her who believe in Germany and human dignity, would like to prove to these countries that the Germans are a great race.

CASE 6

Wilhelm Schultz is a peasant who works with his parents on their farm in East Prussia. (See map, page 358.) His aunt and uncle live just a few miles away, in the area of East Prussia that the Versailles Treaty had sectioned off as the Polish Corridor. They send reports describing how the Poles mistreat the Germans. Wilhelm's grandparents live nearby in Danzig, but their relatives never visit them. Going to Danzig means crossing into Poland which has many travel restrictions. Wilhelm's schooling had taught him great love for the German heroes like Siegfried, and he was dismayed that his government had signed a treaty that put many Germans, like his aunt and uncle, under Polish rule. Then again, he watches people who violate basic Prussian values rise to respected positions in the government. He sees that these people are often drunk and rowdy. This is not the way Prussians should behave, Wilhelm thinks.

Wilhelm and his parents are finding times hard. The thriving port of Danzig had once been the market for his parents' goods. Now it is difficult to ship goods there because they have to cross the Polish Corridor. Besides, the Poles have opened a rival port to take business away from Danzig. Moreover, the depression does not make things easier. Finally, the Communists nearby in the Soviet Union are a constant threat to Wilhelm and his parents because they support the end of private property. Wilhelm and his parents are proud to call their land their own, for this gives them an added dignity. Communists want to take this land and this dignity from them—the last rewards the world seems to offer.

CASE 7

Gerda Munchen is the owner of a small Munich grocery store started by her parents. For years her parents had saved to send her to the university. But Gerda chose not to go to the university, and the money stayed in the bank. In 1923 Gerda had had a good use for it. Her two daughters were both brilliant; one wanted to be a doctor, and the other hoped to be a lawyer. The money in the bank would have paid for their education. But that same year inflation had hit Germany because the government had printed so much money to pay the reparations. Since the money was not backed by anything economically solid, it had become nearly worthless. Two weeks before her older daughter was to leave for the university, the bank had called to say that her savings were worth only enough to buy three postage stamps. This was certainly a blow to Gerda, but it was more of a blow to her daughters whose futures hung in the balance. They asked her what kind of faith they could put in a system that ruined hard-working people.

Now in 1930, there seems little to be done to regain the losses. People are not making any money and, therefore, cannot buy as many groceries as they had before. And the competition from the big department and chain stores makes it difficult for Gerda to compete. Again Gerda's economic difficulties are not her fault. Her daughters once more question the system that has brought these hardships to their mother and to them.

FOR THOUGHT:

What western values did the person in the case study you read have?

59 NAZISM IN THEORY

The Communist regime in the Soviet Union draws its ideology from the West. Karl Marx and Friedrich Engels were both Germans, schooled in the philosophical thought of nineteenth-century Europe. Their basic assumptions had come from the scientific thought and the romanticism of the two earlier centuries. The impact of industrialism on the workers had influenced them. So did the belief, fostered by the French Revolution, that change could best be brought about through armed revolt.

Yet what of Nazism? Hitler's ideology seems an outright denial of the major western values and ideals. Hitler was certainly not the heir of Greek humanism. He violated the fundamental legal principles of the Roman Empire. The moral teachings of Judaism and Christianity and the universal urge toward world peace were western ideals and values foreign to his thought. However, the West has presented many faces to the world. And some of the roots of Nazism grew in the same soil as the roots of democracy. Others have quite different origins within western tradition.

The selections in Reading 59 concentrate on the origins of Nazi ideology by presenting some of the major ideas that guided Hitler's government, which he called the Third Reich. He claimed that it would follow in the tradition of the First Reich, or Holy Roman Empire, and the Second Reich, the empire under Bismarck. As you read these selections, try to answer the following questions:

1. What were Hitler's concepts of the nation and nationalism? How were these concepts similar to or different from the concepts expressed by earlier German nationalists (Chapter 11)?
2. What were the basic elements of Nazi political theory as explained by Hitler and Huber?

Hitler on Race and Nationality

Adolph Hitler did not invent racism. The racist concepts expressed in the following passages of his writings were based on the works of two nineteenth-century philosophers, Count Joseph Arthur de Gobineau and Houston Stewart Chamberlain. Gobineau (1816-1882), a French writer and diplomat, was a supporter of anti-Semitism, antidemocracy, and the supremacy of the Nordic people of northern Europe. Chamberlain (1855-1927) was born in England, but after marrying the daughter of the German composer, Richard Wagner, he became a German citizen. He believed in the racial superiority of the Germans and justified violent anti-Semitism.

Adolf Hitler, **Mein Kampf,** Ralph Manheim, trans. (Boston: Houghton Mifflin Co., 1943), pp. 383, 393-394, 642-643.

▶ Should one individual be considered more valuable than another for any reason, such as his or her religion, color, intelligence, or moral character?

... [The] folkish philosophy finds the importance of mankind in its basic racial elements. In the state it sees ... only a means to an end ... the preservation of the racial existence of man. Thus, it by no means believes in an equality of the races, but ... recognizes their higher or lesser value and feels itself obligated ... to promote the victory of the better and stronger, and demand the subordination of the inferior and weaker.... It sees not only the different value of the races, but also the different value of individuals.... [It] cannot grant the right to existence [of] an ... idea if this idea represents a danger for the racial life of the bearers of a higher ethics; for in a bastardized and niggerized

344

world all the concepts of the humanly beautiful and sublime, as well as an idealized future [for] our humanity, would be lost forever.

Human culture and civilization on this continent are inseparably bound up with the presence of the Aryan. If he dies out or declines, dark veils of an age without culture will again descend. . . .

The state is a means to an end. Its end lies in the preservation and advancement of a community of physically and psychically homogeneous creatures. . . .

We must distinguish in the sharpest way between the state as a vessel and the race as its content. This vessel has meaning only if it can preserve and protect the content; otherwise it is useless.

Thus, the highest purpose of a folkish state is concern for the preservation of those original racial elements which bestow culture and create the beauty and dignity of a higher mankind. We, as Aryans, can conceive of the state only as the living organism of a nationality which not only assures the preservation of this nationality, but by the development of its spiritual and ideal abilities leads it to the highest freedom. . . .

As National Socialists we . . . establish the following principle concerning the nature of the foreign policy of a folkish state:

The foreign policy of the folkish state must safeguard the existence on this planet of the race embodied in the state, by creating a healthy, viable natural relation between the nation's population and growth on the one hand and the quantity and quality of its soil on the other hand. . . .

Only an adequately large space on this earth assures a nation of freedom of existence.

Aryans are not a race. They are descendants of an early language group with no distinctive racial characteristics. Yet the racism that began with Gobineau and ended with Hitler changed the term Aryan to mean non-Jewish, based on the fact that Hebrew is a language unrelated to Aryan tongues.

Hitler on the Role of the Nazis

When the National Socialist party [at first] appealed to the German people it resolutely refused to pledge itself to champion the cause of any separate group which was committed to the support either of religious or economic interests within the nation: its appeal was from the first directed to the heroic instincts of the people. It did not set its hopes upon those who always consider only the advantage of their own business or keep in view the members of the group associated with them; the National Socialist party looked to those idealists . . . who . . . are ready . . . to sacrifice their own existence to the eternal life of people and of Reich. . . .

Thus a new Party was formed . . . ; its membership was limited, but its leaders and fighters were not to be measured by economic standards: they possessed the essential quality of leadership. . . .

Adolf Hitler, **My New Order**, Raoul de Roussy de Sales, ed. (New York: Reynal & Hitchcock, 1941), pp. 290-291, 293.

►In a democratic society, should a political party admit to membership everyone who wants to join? Or should membership be restricted?

As a Party we were compelled to remain in a minority since we were mobilizing the most valuable elements in the nation—the fighters, those who were ready for sacrifice—and these have always formed not the majority, but the minority. . . .

And because we were racially the most valuable section of the German nation, because we proudly valued ourselves as such, because we courageously, boldly demanded that to us should be entrusted the leadership of the Reich and of the people, the people in ever growing numbers . . . acknowledged our leadership. . . .

The aim must be that all decent Germans shall be National Socialists: only the best National Socialists shall be members of the Party. . . .

Alfred Rosenberg: Race and Nationality

The most productive writer in support of the Nazi cause was Alfred Rosenberg. In 1941, Rosenberg became minister of the eastern territories occupied by the Nazis, and as such he was responsible for millions of deaths. In 1946, he was executed as a war criminal.

Raymond E. Murphy, Francis B. Stevens, Howard Trivers, Joseph M. Roland, "National Socialism: Basic Principles, Their Application by the Nazi Party's Foreign Organization, and the Use of Germans Abroad for Nazi Aims," prepared in the Special Unit of the Division of European Affairs (Washington: United States Government Printing Office, 1943), pp. 32-33.

The right of nationality should not represent something which is received in the cradle as a gift, but should be regarded as a good which must be earned. Although every German is a subject of the state, the rights of nationality should only be received when at the age of twenty or twenty-two he has completed his education or his military service or has finished the labor service which he owes to the state. . . . The right to nationality . . . must become an opportunity for every German to strive for complete humanity and achievement in the service of the Volk [people]. . . .

The prevailing concept of state nationality completely ignores the idea of race. According to it whoever has a German passport is a German, whoever has Czech documents is a Czech, although he may not have a single drop of Czech blood in his veins. . . .

National Socialism recognizes that, although the individual racial strains in German-speaking territory differ, they nevertheless belong to closely related races, and that many mixtures among the members of these different branches have produced new and vital strains, among them the complex but still *German* man, but that a mixture with the Jewish enemy race, which in its whole spiritual and physical structure is basically completely different and antagonistic . . . can only result in bastardization.

346

A Jewish-owned department store

A Ghetto streetcar

A Jewish couple

The pictures on this page show several ways in which the Nazis forced Jews to identify themselves and their businesses. What effect might this public indentification have had on the ways in which other people treated Jews? Do you think it might have encouraged people who were not Nazis to support the regime?

Ernst Huber:
The Führer Concept

The leading political scientist of Nazism, Ernst Huber, explains the basic leadership principles of the Nazi ideology.

Murphy et al., "National Socialism," pp. 34-35.

Führer means leader.

A plebiscite is a vote by which a group of people express an opinion for or against a proposal.

The Führer-state of the [German] people is founded on the recognition that the true will of the people cannot be disclosed through parliamentary votes and plebiscites but that the will of the people in its pure and uncorrupted form can only be expressed through the Führer. Thus a distinction must be drawn between the supposed will of the people in a parliamentary democracy, which merely reflects the conflict of the various social interests, and the true will of the people in the Führer-state, in which the collective will of the real political unit is manifested [shown]....

The Führer is the bearer of the people's will; he is independent of all groups, associations, and interests, but he is bound by laws which are inherent in the nature of his people.... The Führer is no "representative" of a particular group whose wishes he must carry out.... He is... himself the bearer of the collective will of the people. In his will the will of the people is realized. He transforms the mere feelings of the people into a conscious will... Thus it is possible for him, in the name of the true will of the people which he serves, to go against the subjective opinions and convictions of single individuals within the people if these are not in accord with the objective destiny of the people... He shapes the collective will of the people within himself....

Through his planning and directing he gives the national life its true purpose and value. This directing and planning activity is especially manifested in [his] lawgiving power....

FOR THOUGHT:

What elements of western traditions do you find in the writings of Hitler, Rosenberg, and Huber?

60 NAZISM IN PRACTICE

In late January 1933, when Hindenburg appointed Hitler chancellor, the Nazis had their opportunity to put their theories into practice. By a combination of intrigue, terror, and popular support,

Hitler gained control of the government and the electorate. After Hindenburg died in 1934, the chancellor saw his opportunity to consolidate his power. Nearly 90 percent of the Germans voted to let Hitler unite the offices of president and chancellor into the person of Der Führer. Hitler and his Nazi party thereafter completed the formation of the Nazi state.

The early efforts of the Nazis did much to create order out of the chaos in Germany. When Hitler became chancellor, about 6 million Germans were unemployed. Within a year nearly all the jobless were back at work. Hitler also replaced the unstable republican government with a highly organized political machine capable of quick, seemingly efficient decisions. In return for this new stability, prosperity, and pride, however, the German people had to accept the Nazi ideology.

In international affairs Hitler put Germany back into a position of importance and power. In September 1938 Hitler demanded that the Sudetenland, the eastern section of Czechoslovakia inhabited by Germans, be allowed to join Germany. To keep peace Great Britain's prime minister, Neville Chamberlain, and France's premier, Edouard Daladier, agreed. Hitler soon increased his demands, and this time Chamberlain refused. When war seemed imminent, a conference was called on September 29 in Munich. Once again to avoid war, Great Britain and France gave in to Hitler. Hitler then occupied the Sudetenland, and within six months, all of Czechoslovakia was dissolved.

Reading 60 contains documents that provide a partial chronicle of what Nazi rule meant in Germany and in Europe. As you read, think about the following questions:

1. How did Hitler establish the Nazi state? What was the relationship between Nazi political theory and the political organization of the Third Reich?
2. What did Hitler do about non-Germans, particularly Jews? How did Hitler treat the other nations of Europe? Did these practices follow logically from the Nazi ideology?

Establishment
of the Nazi Reich

These three acts demonstrate the way Hitler "legally" established his Nazi dictatorship. The first act was decreed immediately after the Reichstag fire, only five days before the election that gave the Nazis control of the legislature. The second and third acts were passed after the Enabling Act had given Hitler dictatorial power.

DECREE OF THE REICH'S PRESIDENT FOR
THE PROTECTION OF THE PEOPLE AND STATE

Murphy et al., "National Socialism," pp. 215, 220-221.

February 28, 1933

   The following is decreed as a defensive measure against Communist acts of violence endangering the state:

   Sections 114, 115, 117, 118, and 153 of the Constitution of the German Reich are suspended until further notice. Thus, restrictions on personal liberty, on the right of free expression of opinion, including freedom of the press, on the right of assembly and the right of association, and violations of the privacy of postal, telegraphic, and telephonic communications, and warrants for house searches, orders for confiscations as well as restrictions on property, are also permissible beyond the legal limits. . . .

► Under what conditions, if any, should a society suspend basic civil liberties?

LAW AGAINST THE NEW ESTABLISHMENT OF PARTIES

July 14, 1933

   The German Cabinet has resolved the following law. . . : The National Socialist German Workers' Party constitutes the only political party in Germany. Whoever undertakes to maintain the organizational structure of another political party or to form a new political party will be punished with penal servitude up to three years or with imprisonment of from six months to three years. . . .

LAW TO SAFEGUARD THE UNITY OF PARTY AND STATE

December 1, 1933

   The German Cabinet has resolved the following law. . . : After the victory of the National Socialist revolution, the National Socialist German Workers' Party is the bearer of the German state-idea and indissolubly joined to the state. . . . The Führer determines its statutes.

   In order to guarantee the closest cooperation of the party and the SA with the public officials, the Führer's Deputy and the Chief of Staff of the SA are made members of the Cabinet.

Racism in Practice

The following selections are taken from the Nuremberg Laws of 1935, which translated Hitler's racist theories into public policy.

Raymond Phineas Stearns, Pageant of Europe (New York: Harcourt Brace Jovanovich, Inc., 1947), pp. 815-816.

THE LAW FOR PROTECTION OF GERMAN BLOOD
AND GERMAN HONOR, SEPTEMBER 15, 1935

   Clearly realizing that the purity of the German blood is the prerequisite for perpetuating the German people, and inspired by an inflexible determination to secure the existence of the German nation for all time to come, the Reichstag has unanimously passed the following law. . . .

1. Marriages between Jews and citizens of German or kindred stock are prohibited. . . .

3. Jews shall not employ in their household female citizens of German or kindred stock under 45 years of age.

4. Jews shall not hoist the Reich or national flag nor display the Reich colors.

REICH CITIZENSHIP LAW AND DECREE

1. A citizen is one who belongs to the protective union of the German Reich and who is under special obligations to it.

2. Only such persons as are of German or kindred stock and who have proved by their conduct that they are willing and fit loyally to serve the German people and Reich are citizens. . . .

Reich citizens shall be the sole possessors of complete political rights.

▶ Should religion play a role in the choice of a marriage partner? Why or why not?

The "Final Solution"

This account is taken from the testimony of one of the Nazi executioners responsible for putting into effect Hitler's "final solution" to Germany's race problem. The site of the extermination camp he describes was Belzec, a village in southern Poland. Before this man could be brought to trial, he committed suicide.

Globocnik said: . . . "Your . . . duty will be to improve the workings of our gas chambers, which operate on the exhaust from a Diesel engine. We need a more toxic and faster working gas. . . . The Führer has ordered more speed. Dr. Herbert Lindner, who was here yesterday, asked me, 'Wouldn't it be more prudent to burn the bodies instead of burying them? Another generation might take a different view of these things.' I answered: 'Gentlemen, if there is ever a generation after us so cowardly, so soft, that it would not understand our work as good and necessary, then, gentlemen, National Socialism will have been for nothing. On the contrary, we should bury bronze tablets saying that it was we, we who had the courage to carry out this gigantic task!' ". . .

The next day we left for Belzec. . . .

The following morning, a little before seven there was an announcement: "The first train will arrive in ten minutes!" A few minutes later a train arrived from Lemberg: forty-five cars with more than six thousand people. Two hundred Ukrainians assigned to this work flung open the doors and drove the Jews out of the cars with leather whips. A

Leon Poliakov, Harvest of Hate: The Nazi Program for the Destruction of the Jews of Europe (Syracuse, N. Y.: Syracuse University Press, 1954), pp. 194-196. Reprinted by permission of the American Jewish Committee.

Mrs. Hermine Ryan

▶In 1973 West Germany and Poland asked the United States to extradite, or surrender to them, Mrs. Hermine Ryan to stand trial for war crimes. She was the former Hermine Braunsteiner, who had worked in a Nazi prison camp at Majdanek where she had helped to exterminate Jews. Do you think the United States should have extradited her? Why or why not?

The crematorium tower at the Majdanek prison camp

loud speaker gave instructions: "Strip, even artificial limbs and glasses. Hand all money and valuables in at the 'valuables window.'"

Then the march began. Barbed wire on both sides, in the rear two dozen Ukrainians with rifles. They drew near. Wirth and I found ourselves in front of the death chambers. Stark naked men, women, children, and cripples passed by. A tall SS man in the corner called to the unfortunates in a loud minister's voice: "Nothing is going to hurt you! Just breathe deep and it will strengthen your lungs. It's a way to prevent contagious diseases. It's a good disinfectant!" They asked him what was going to happen and he answered: "The men will have to work, build houses and streets. The women won't have to do that, they will be busy with the housework and the kitchen."

This was the last hope for some of these poor people, enough to make them march toward the death chambers without resistance. The majority knew everything; the smell betrayed it! They climbed a little wooden stairs and entered the death chambers, most of them silently, pushed by those behind them. . . . SS men pushed the men into the chambers. "Fill it up," Wirth ordered; 700-800 people in ninety-three square meters. The doors closed. . . . SS Unterscharführer Heckenholt tried to start the motor. It wouldn't start! . . . My stopwatch clocked it all: fifty minutes, seventy minutes, and the Diesel still would not start! . . . The men were waiting in the gas chambers. You could hear them weeping "as though in a synagogue," . . . The Diesel started up after two hours and forty-nine minutes, by my stopwatch. Twenty-five minutes passed. You could see through the window that many were already dead, for an electric light illuminated the interior of the room. All were dead after thirty-two minutes! Jewish workers on the other side opened the wooden doors. They had been promised their lives in return for doing this horrible work, plus a small percentage of the money and valuables collected. The men were still standing, like columns of stone, with no room to fall or lean. Even in death you could tell the families, all holding hands. It was difficult to separate them while emptying the rooms for the next batch. The bodies were tossed out. . . . Two dozen workers were busy checking mouths which they opened with iron hooks. "Gold to the left, no gold to the right." . . . Dentists knocked out gold teeth, bridges, and crowns, with hammers. Captain Wirth stood in the middle of them. He was in his element. . . .

The SS, or **Schutzstaffel**, was selected from the SA to serve as Hitler's personal guard.

The Nazis and the War

This indictment was made by the Nuremberg International Military Tribunal, composed of four judges, one each from the United States, Britain, France, and the Soviet Union. The tribunal met from

November 1945 until October 1946. Of the twenty-two Nazis it tried, twelve were sentenced to death and three to life imprisonment.

United States Department of State, Trial of War Criminals (Washington: 1945).

PLUNDER OF PUBLIC AND PRIVATE PROPERTY

The Defendants ruthlessly exploited the people and the material resources of the countries they occupied, in order to strengthen the Nazi war machine, to depopulate and impoverish the rest of Europe, to enrich themselves and their adherents, and to promote German economic supremacy over Europe.

1. They degraded the standard of life of the people of occupied countries and caused starvation, by stripping occupied countries of foodstuffs for removal to Germany.

2. They seized raw materials and industrial machinery in all of the occupied countries, removed them to Germany and used them in the interest of the German war effort and the German economy....

8. In further development of their plan of criminal exploitation, they destroyed industrial cities, cultural monuments, scientific institutions, and property of all types in the occupied territories....

GERMANIZATION OF OCCUPIED TERRITORIES

In certain occupied territories purportedly annexed to Germany the Defendants methodically endeavored to assimilate those territories politically, culturally, socially and economically into the German Reich.... The Defendants forcibly deported inhabitants who were mostly non-German and introduced thousands of German colonists....

1. From the month of August, 1940, officials who refused to take the oath of allegiance to the Reich were expelled.

2. From January 2, 1942, all the young people of the Departments of the Upper Rhine and the Lower Rhine, aged from 10 to 18 years, were incorporated in the Hitler Youth. From 1940 all the French schools were closed, their staffs expelled, and the German school system was introduced....

3. On September 28, 1940, ... the Germanization of all [French] ... names [was ordered]....

4. Two orders imposed by force German nationality on all French citizens. ...

FOR THOUGHT:

How was Hitler's program related to the developments in the West that you have studied in this course?

A HISTORICAL ESSAY

The alarming attraction of Europeans to totalitarianism nearly destroyed the value system of liberal democracy. During the 1920's and 1930's, every western country contained groups that wanted to establish Communist or Fascist regimes. Several of these groups were successful. In Italy, Benito Mussolini and his followers marched on Rome in 1922, captured control of the government, and began a Fascist regime that ruled Italy for the next twenty years. In Spain, General Francisco Franco destroyed the republic created by the revolution of 1931. He then established himself as a Fascist dictator. And Hitler seized control of Germany, plunging the world into war within a decade.

Fascism seems alien to western traditions that try to give all people freedom and equality. Both Communists and Fascists rejected democratic institutions for autocratic dictatorships. They denied people freedom by forcing them to meet the demands of the state. They rejected the principle of equality by putting party members above other citizens and the "master race" over so-called inferior peoples. They seized the economy so that it would produce the goods and services that the government demanded. Most horrible of all, they victimized and degraded millions of human beings by putting them into concentration camps, exiling them to work camps, or murdering them.

Fascism emerged in the West, and it was rooted in western traditions. In fact, the Führer concept on which the Nazi regime was built had its basis in Rousseau's concept of the general will. (See page 219.) Hitler stressed that he alone could give the Germans the leadership they needed to reach their destiny. As Ernst Huber explained, the Führer claimed to be the bearer of the will of the German people. And he convinced the German people that their ultimate mission was to rule the world.

Nazism drew many of its principles from nineteenth-century thinkers. The Romantics of the early part of the century claimed that the heart rather than the head was the best guide to action. Later nineteenth-century thinkers argued that people's will or life force, a sort of irrational drive, would guide them along the right path. Because reason was intellectual, without human feeling, and not always right, it could not show people the good and the true. Hitler drew heavily

▶ In what degree should we
let feelings rather than
reason guide our actions?

on this theme, calling on Germans to think with their blood rather than with their brains. Their will, as embodied in Hitler, would guide them to world supremacy.

The emotional concept of nationalism that supported Hitler's claim to leadership also came out of the nineteenth century. The Germans were a proud people who felt degraded by their loss in World War I. Hitler made them feel proud again when he challenged their former conquerors. He appealed to these feelings of nationalism and pride by asking them to give him their lives that he might fulfill Germany's historic mission.

Hitler's racist beliefs also originated in western thought. Some western societies have supported the idea that a natural aristocracy based on birth and breeding exists. The Nazis believed that the so-called Aryan race was superior to all other races. They said that the great corrupters of civilization were the Jews. This idea of German superiority and Jewish inferiority had a long history in Germany. The Roman historian Tacitus had described the Germans as a blond, blue-eyed people of exceptional strength and skill. Medieval literature often showed Jews as enemies of Christian civilization.

Hitler took his racist ideas directly from Count Joseph Arthur de Gobineau and Houston Stewart Chamberlain. Both men claimed that they had demonstrated their racist theories scientifically. Although Gobineau and Chamberlain were not Germans, their Aryan myth was adopted and popularized in Germany, in part through the operas of Richard Wagner. For this reason, many Germans found it easy to accept Hitler's racist doctrines.

Nazism also had its roots in the autocratic political systems of the West. In Germany, a strong autocratic tradition honored those Prussian kings who had expanded Prussian territory. The autocratic Bismarck had unified Germany. On the other hand, liberal democracy had always failed the nation. At the Frankfurt Assembly of 1848, the liberals had failed to unify Germany under a constitutional monarchy. Similarly, the democratic Weimar Republic had signed the humiliating Versailles Treaty.

The Weimar government was thus discredited from the start. Many groups formed to overthrow it, among them Hitler's Nazi party. The Weimar Constitution provided enough stability for the government to survive the early attacks against it. But more than twenty-five parties competed for control of the Reichstag. No one party ever obtained a majority. Loose coalitions, attempting to carry on the task of governing, fell apart over the slightest disagreement.

As ministries formed and fell, the German economy was disrupted. Then in 1923 inflation left the nation almost in ruin. Slowly, the Germans rebuilt their economy. But in 1929 Germany plunged with the rest of the West into a general economic collapse. By 1932 about 6 million workers were unemployed, and the budget deficit mounted to $400 million.

Onto this stage stepped Hitler. After the unsuccessful Munich *putsch,* Hitler resolved not to take over the government by force, but to infiltrate it by constitutional means. As chaos increased in Germany, more and more of the nation turned to the Nazis for answers to their problems. Gradually, Nazi representation in the Reichstag increased, until in 1932 no other party could get a majority without cooperating with the Nazis. Hitler was finally asked to become chancellor in 1933.

Hitler then set out to destroy the republic. Article 48 of the Constitution stated that the president could pass laws by decree if the Reichstag granted him this power. He could then suspend civil liberties and use the military to carry out his program. Hitler had this power extended to him by the Enabling Act of March 24, 1933. Then he used it to eliminate his opposition.

At last supreme, Hitler governed with unrestrained brutality and terror. He systematically murdered people who questioned him within and without his party. In the so-called "night of the long knives," he eliminated the leaders of the Storm Troopers who might challenge his position. Next, newspapers and radio stations that might oppose him were destroyed. Then religious leaders were shipped to concentration camps. Politicians who would not cooperate with the Nazi government were sent away. Teachers mysteriously disappeared.

Few in Germany escaped the control of the Nazi party. Painters could not paint, writers could not write, architects could not design without the consent of the government. Sports events were nationalized and supervised by the Nazis. Movies and plays became a way of spreading the propaganda of the state. Even courtship, marriage, and raising children were controlled by the government. It became a citizen's duty to produce offspring for the state.

Technological advances made this kind of control possible. Hitler could reach every German citizen instantly by talking into a radio microphone. And Hitler was one of the most spellbinding speakers in western history. Modern communications also made it possible for Hitler to collect and send information quickly.

Once Hitler gained control over Germany, he set out to win control over Europe. He violated the Versailles Treaty by building up his military force beyond the treaty limits and by remilitarizing the Rhineland. Then in March 1938 he annexed Austria, again in violation of treaty terms. None of the western democracies was either willing or able to stop him.

In September 1938, he outmaneuvered Great Britain and France to take possession of the western part of Czechoslovakia. Hungary and

▶What, if anything, should an individual do to prevent or protest policies established by the government?

357

GERMAN EXPANSION 1938-1941

Occupied by Germany

Annexed by Germany

Axis Powers

NORWAY
SWEDEN
FINLAND
Baltic Sea
U.S.S.R.
North Sea
DEN
GREAT BRITAIN
London
NETH
Berlin
GERMANY
E. PRUSSIA
POLAND
BELGIUM
LUX.
CZECHOSLOVAKIA
Atlantic Ocean
FRANCE
Munich
SWITZ.
AUSTRIA
HUNGARY
RUMANIA
Black Sea
YUGOSLAVIA
BULGARIA
PORTUGAL
SPAIN
CORSICA
ITALY
ALBANIA
TURKEY
SARDINIA
GREECE
Mediterranean Sea
SICILY
CRETE

Poland grabbed the rest of Czechoslovakia. In August 1939 Hitler signed a non-aggression pact with Stalin to gain time. Finally, in September 1939, he unleashed his *blitzkrieg*, or lightning war, on Poland, touching off World War II. Within the year, Hitler had conquered Denmark, Norway, the Netherlands, and Luxembourg. Then he invaded France.

Within six months, France fell under the might of Hitler's *wehrmacht*, or war machine. Hitler then turned against his former ally and invaded the Soviet Union. He also began to bomb Britain steadily, planning to invade it later. He sent troops to North Africa under the command of the brilliant General Erwin Rommel to destroy Britain's supply route through the Suez Canal. Mussolini aided him at every step until Italy's surrender in 1943.

Hitler and the Nazis subjected the people of Germany and of the conquered nations to cruelty and degradation unknown in western history. Millions of French, Danes, Belgians, Poles, and Norwegians were uprooted from their homes, transported to Germany, and forced to work in labor camps and factories. Millions of Europe's Jews died in the gas chambers of such concentration camps as Buchenwald, Auschwitz, and Dachau. And all of Europe suffered the horrors of modern war that involve entire populations, soldiers and civilians alike.

The Allies finally turned back Hitler's armies in 1942 at the battle of Stalingrad in the Soviet Union and at El Alamein in Egypt. In 1943, led by troops from the United States, the Allies invaded Italy. The invasion of France followed. On April 30, 1945, Hitler committed suicide in Berlin. On May 7, Germany surrendered. But millions of soldiers and civilians had died during the six long years of World War II.

Individual and Group Activities for Chapter 14

For full descriptions of these activities, turn to the **Student Book of Activities and Readings** included among the materials for individual and group activities.

Activity 14A: Interview with a rabbi or a refugee from Europe on what life was like under Nazism (individual or group)
Interview someone in your community who lived in Europe under Nazi rule or a rabbi who can discuss conditions under Nazism with you. If you can, record your interview for use in class, or write a report about it. Then prepare a short list of study questions for use by students who may listen to the recording or read the report in the future.

Activity 14B: Study of the influence of Hitler youth groups on young people in Germany (individual)
This activity shows a group of photographs that illustrate some of the activities of Hitler youth groups. In a brief essay based on these pictures, try to explain why many German young people participated enthusiastically in Hitler's youth programs.

The West
Since World War II

CHAPTER

15

Between 1870 and 1914, western Europe reached the peak of its civilization during modern times. Constitutional government spread rapidly. The standard of living rose with the development of industry and new farming techniques. A rich intellectual and cultural life flowered in Europe's growing cities. People all over the world read Europe's books, listened to Europe's music, and admired Europe's painting, sculpture, and architecture.

Europe dominated most of the rest of the world in other ways as well. Australia, New Zealand, and Canada had been British colonies for centuries. Europeans governed India and most of Southeast Asia, and they had carved out spheres of influence in China. After 1870, Europeans divided most of Africa and the Middle East into colonies. In 1870 the United States, just emerging from a tragic civil war and with a population of only 38 million, seemed no threat to European domination. And Russia was the most backward state in Europe, making little use of its huge population and vast natural resources because of its obsolete political, economic, and social systems.

Then came a series of blows that destroyed Europe's position. These included World War I, the Russian Revolution, the rise of the dictators, the great depression of the 1930's, World War II, the development of Communist states in eastern Europe, the collapse of the European empires, and the rise of the super powers—the United States, the Soviet Union, and China. Midway through this series of events, at the end of World War II, Europe reached the low point of its influence in the world during modern times. Then it began to make its presence felt again. Chapter 15 describes how Europe responded to its new position in the world after World War II. The last two readings in the chapter discuss how elements of western civilization have been spread to the rest of the world.

360

1945	The United States and the Soviet Union emerge from World War II as super powers.
	The Cold War begins.
1947	Truman Doctrine is set up.
	Marshall Plan gives economic aid to western Europe.
1948	Communists seize power in Czechoslovakia.
1948–1949	Berlin blockade and airlift take place.
1949	Western powers form NATO.
	Soviet Union explodes its first atomic bomb.
	Communists win mainland China.
1950–1953	Korean War takes place.
1952	European Coal and Steel Community is formed.
1954	Vietnam is divided into a Communist state in the North and
	a non-Communist state in the South.
1956–1973	Vietnam War is fought.
1957	Common Market is established.
1972	President Nixon visits Peking and Moscow.
1973	Premier Brezhnev visits United States.

62 EUROPE AFTER WORLD WAR II

During the period between 1870 and 1914, Europe could be divided into an inner and an outer zone. The inner zone included Great Britain, Belgium, the Netherlands, Denmark, the southern parts of Norway and Sweden, Germany, France, the western parts of the Austrian empire, Switzerland, and northern Italy. This zone contained most of Europe's industry and railway lines. Its citizens had the highest standard of living, the lowest death rates, and the best conditions of health and sanitation in Europe. The countries in this zone led the world in liberal reform movements, and their citizens were responsible for most of the great literature, art, music, and scientific thought of the era. Most of these nations had parliamentary governments. Yet although these countries had so much in common, they fought each other bitterly in two world wars.

In a way, the northeastern section of the United States might be added to this zone, as it had similar economic and social characteristics.

The southern and western sections of the United States were an "outer zone" to the northeast at this time.

The outer zone included most of Ireland, Spain, and Portugal, the southern part of Italy, and all of Europe east of what was then Germany, Bohemia, and Austria. This zone grew food and supplied raw materials for the inner zone. It sent young people to universities in inner Europe and hired technicians and engineers from there. Most of its governments were autocratic rather than democratic. Citizens in these nations made relatively few contributions to the arts or to scientific thought. And like the nations in the inner zone, these countries also became involved in two world wars within twenty-five years.

Many of the nations in both the inner and the outer zones had colonies or spheres of influence outside Europe. The maps on pages 363 and 364 illustrate the way in which Europe dominated the world in 1914. During the first wave of colonial expansion starting in the 1400's, European nations took over the continents of North America and South America, Australia, India, and other parts of Asia. During a second expansionist period beginning in the late 1800's, Europe and the United States seized Africa, most of the Middle East, and what was left of Asia and the Pacific Islands. Although these nations faced similar problems in governing their colonies, they were unable to work together to solve them. Instead they fought each other, partly because of imperialist rivalries. In the process, they lost control of the world.

The United States acquired Hawaii and the Philippine Islands during the 1890's.

World War I weakened the power of the nations in Europe's inner zone. Germany, Austria-Hungary, France, and Great Britain lost millions of young men. Most of the war was fought in the inner zone where factories, farms, and houses were destroyed. At the end of the war, the United States emerged as a new world power whose participation in the war had saved the allied cause. But both the United States and the Soviet Union, born in revolution in Russia in 1917, withdrew into sullen isolation during the twenty years between the end of World War I and the beginning of World War II. Then Hitler, allied with Italy's Mussolini, provoked World War II and destroyed western Europe's dominance of the world.

Neither the United States nor the Soviet Union joined the League of Nations.

By the end of this war, Europe was a shambles. The war had taken about 18 million military lives and at least as many more civilians. Much of Europe's industry had been destroyed or worn out, and millions of homes were gone. Europe's people were exhausted and anxious to lead normal lives again. Yet much decision-making power had fallen from their hands. The defeated nations, particularly Germany and Italy, were at the mercy of the victors. And the victors in Europe were caught between the two great super powers, the United States and the Soviet Union. Soon these two countries became locked in a bitter struggle known as the Cold War.

The nature of international relations changed in 1945 because now there were only two great powers. Moreover, each of the two was

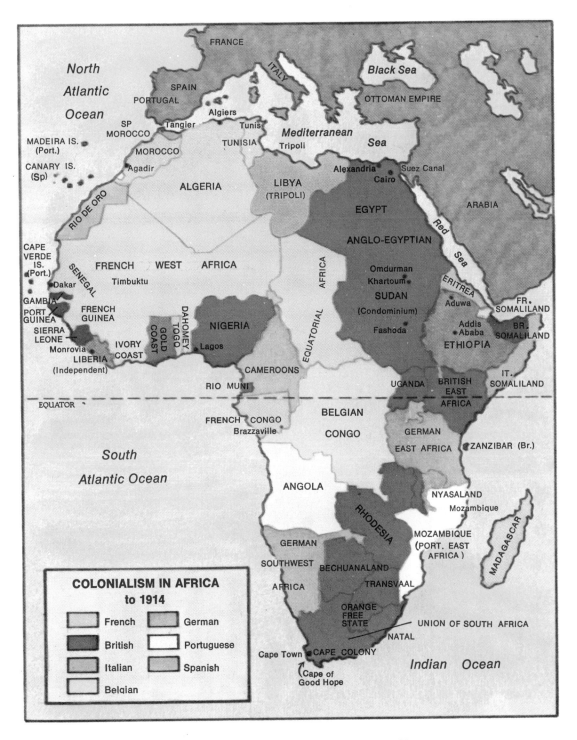

**COLONIALISM IN AFRICA
to 1914**

French
British
Italian
Belgian
German
Portuguese
Spanish

363

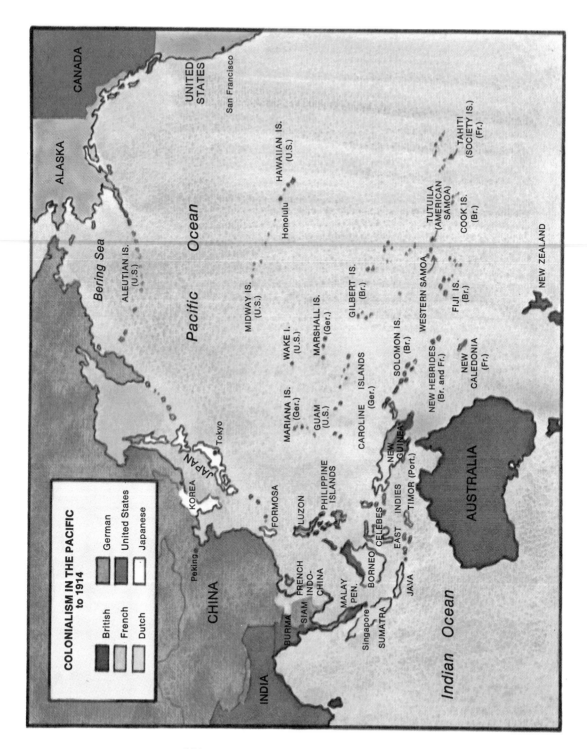

COLONIALISM IN THE PACIFIC
to 1914

British
French
Dutch
German
United States
Japanese

a new phenomenon in the world—a super power that spanned a continent and had immense resources, a huge population, and powerful armed forces. In addition, the United States had atomic weapons, which had the capacity to wipe out whole cities. And these two nations distrusted each other.

In an international system with a number of great powers, each nation must always watch what all the others are doing. But in a system with only two powers, each one always knows who the enemy will be. Military preparation of any kind seems a threat. After 1945 a series of actions by both the United States and the Soviet Union caused so much distrust and antagonism that people coined the term "Cold War" to describe international affairs during the period.

Between 1945 and 1947 the Soviet Union tried to solidify the gains it had made during the war. The Soviet government helped Communists who were fighting against the royalist government of Greece. It set up a Communist government in East Germany. It rejected proposals to put atomic weapons under international control. It supported the revolt of the Chinese Communist Party against the Chinese nationalists. And it vetoed many proposed activities of the United Nations.

▶ Do you think that the United States should put its nuclear arsenal under international control? Why or why not?

At about the same time, the United States began to develop policies to stop the spread of Communism. In 1947 under the Truman Doctrine, the United States supplied military equipment and advice to the Greek and Turkish governments to help these nations resist pressure from Communists. In the same year, the United States began the Marshall Plan which gave broad economic aid to western Europe. The Soviet Union refused to let satellite Communist governments receive aid under the Marshall Plan.

▶ How, if at all, can you justify spending money from American taxpayers to help Europe recover? Is it all right to help former allies? former enemies?

Early in 1948 Communists seized power in Czechoslovakia and turned that nation into a Soviet satellite. In the summer of 1948, the Soviet Union blockaded all land routes leading to Berlin, the former German capital occupied jointly by troops from the United States, the Soviet Union, Great Britain, and France. The United States responded with an airlift that kept the city alive for more than a year until the Soviet Union lifted the blockade. During this period, the United States and fifteen other nations developed a mutual defense system called the North Atlantic Treaty Organization. These NATO powers agreed to let West Germany rearm. Partly in response to these actions, the Soviet Union began to link the economies of eastern Europe together and signed military alliances with its satellites—Poland, Hungary, Rumania, Bulgaria, Czechoslovakia, and East Germany. And in 1949, Soviet scientists exploded their first atomic bomb.

While these events took place in Europe, Chinese Communists led by Mao Tse-Tung defeated the nationalist forces and proclaimed the Chinese People's Republic in September, 1949. Then Mao set up a

Korea had been divided along the 38th parallel after World War II, and all foreign troops had left. In 1950 communist North Korea attacked South Korea. Supported by a U.N. resolution, President Truman sent American troops to South Korea. Despite help from China and the Soviet Union, the North Koreans were eventually defeated and signed an armistice in 1953.

France tried to keep control of French Indochina, later called Vietnam, after World War II, but Communist guerrillas under Ho Chi Minh drove the French forces out. In 1954 Vietnam was divided into a Communist state in the North with a capital at Hanoi and a non-Communist South Vietnam with a capital at Saigon. Starting about 1956 the United States began to send advisers, military aid, and troops to Vietnam when it seemed that the Communists would take over the whole country. Thus the Vietnam war started.

Communist state modeled after the Soviet Union. For a time, particularly during the Korean War, China accepted aid from the Soviet Union. But relations between the two powers soon cooled. China asserted its right to lead Asian people toward Communism. Mao became the spokesman for a new kind of mass communism centered on the peasant. The Soviet Union now had a new rival. By the early 1970's, this condition helped to push the Soviet Union toward an improved relationship with the United States.

The rivalries of the three super powers and of the reawakened areas of western Europe reached every corner of the globe. The colonial revolt in Africa, Asia, and the Middle East reached its peak after World War II. In some cases, European powers withdrew peacefully as the British did from India. In other cases, only years of bitter warfare drove the Europeans out, such as the Dutch in Indonesia and the French in Indochina and Algeria. But inevitably the former colonies won their freedom. By the early 1960's, the old-style empires were gone.

In the meantime, western Europe had made a remarkable economic and political recovery from the tragedy of World War II. Spurred on at first by Marshall Plan aid, Western Europe experienced an economic boom focused around a new European Economic Community, also called the Common Market. At the same time, western European countries reestablished parliamentary democracy as the common form of government. But despite economic recovery, parliamentary governments, and new advances in education, the arts, and science, it was clear that Europe had lost its former position in the world. The United States, the Soviet Union, and China had become the new world leaders.

The international situation began to change early in the 1970's. The United States slowly withdrew from the long and bitter war in Vietnam. The Soviet Union and China continued to drift apart. Then President Nixon seized the initiative. He visited Peking and Moscow in 1972 and began to develop trade agreements and establish more cordial relationships with each of these powers. Once the ice was broken, the United States and the Soviet Union began to discuss ways to control nuclear energy and halt the arms race. When Soviet Premier Brezhnev visited Washington in June, 1973, he and Nixon announced a new round of agreements.

The Cold War seemed to be dying out. What effect would this development have on western Europe? The Common Market countries together had great economic power. Their ancient rivalries, which had plunged the world into two tragic wars, had been dulled. Perhaps western Europe could become a fourth super power alongside the United States, the Soviet Union, and China. At least it might become a force for moderation in the world, a force to carry on the humanistic principles which may yet be the West's greatest legacy to humankind.

FOR THOUGHT:

Why do you think power and influence shift among the nations of the world?

63 ATTEMPTS TO UNIFY EUROPE

Europeans have talked about unifying Europe for centuries. Usually this talk centered on international relations. European leaders developed the idea of the Concert of Europe—a form of international government by concert, or agreement—after the Napoleonic Wars. They also developed alliance systems during the late 1800's and early 1900's. Later they joined with non-European nations in the League of Nations and the United Nations. However, none of these developments led to the growth of real European unity either in feelings or in fact.

Since the end of World War II, western Europeans have discussed unity in three different ways. First, they have discussed and worked together for mutual defense. They joined organizations such as the North Atlantic Treaty Organization to counter the threat from the Soviet Union during the Cold War. As the United States began to withdraw from its defense commitments in Europe and to settle its quarrels with the Soviet Union, European nations began to talk about new mutual defense arrangements. In western Europe, only Great Britain and France have atomic weapons. Eventually, the cost of atomic weapons, the presence of powerful Soviet armies in eastern Europe, and the belief that the United States will become more isolationist may lead to the creation of a true western European army.

Second, Europeans have discussed political unity—the creation of a sort of United States of Europe. Several meetings have been held in which representatives of many nations discussed common problems. But it seems unlikely that a true Parliament of Europe with a single executive and judicial system will develop in the near future.

Third, Europeans have made genuine progress toward economic unity. The European Economic Community now ties together the economic systems of most of the nations which were part of the European "inner zone" between 1870 and 1914. The economic cooperation developed by the ECC, like possible defense efforts, may eventually encourage closer political ties.

The excerpts in Reading 63 trace the development of economic cooperation in Europe since the end of World War II. As you read, keep the following questions in mind:

1. What role did the United States play in the development of economic cooperation in Europe?
2. How strong is the European Economic Community compared to the United States and the Soviet Union?

The Marshall Plan

The New York Times, June 6, 1972, p. 14, ©1972 by the New York Times Company. Reprinted by permission.

George C. Marshall had been commander-in-chief of the American forces in Europe during World War II. At the time of the Marshall Plan, he was Secretary of State.

►Should workers be allowed to refuse to work for any reason if their country needs what they produce?

Arthur H. Vandenberg was a Republican senator from Michigan.

With Europe fat, prosperous and not a little smug, it is somewhat difficult to recall the conditions of a ruptured continent after its second major war of the century, with its institutions discredited, its cities ravaged, its survivors disillusioned and displaced. Twenty-five years ago today the United States initiated the Marshall Plan to attempt to remedy the situation.

The Europeans' troubles, said Will Clayton, Under Secretary of State for Economic Affairs, in a memorandum to his boss, George C. Marshall, lay with "the peasant who would not produce more than he and his family and his cattle could eat because with the money he might get from selling his surplus produce in the market he could not buy buttons and thread or farm tools."

The troubles, continued Mr. Clayton, . . . lay also with the "manufacturer of buttons and thread and cloth who could not produce for want of materials and fuel and because workers, being unable to satisfy their wants with money, were refusing to work." . . .

In March, 1947 President Harry S. Truman went to Congress to request a $400-million aid package for Greece and Turkey, which were under increasing pressure from Communist guerrillas in the wake of the British decision to end financial support in Greece. The chairman of the Senate Foreign Relations Committee, Arthur H. Vandenberg, told Mr. Truman that if he wanted to get the money he would have to "scare the hell" out of the country. Dean Acheson, later Secretary of State, proceeded to do just that. Mr. Acheson spoke of "an unbridgeable chasm" between the Soviet Union and the United States and declared that no two powers had been so far apart on fundamental issues since Rome and Carthage. In less than three months President Truman had the aid bill on his desk for signature.

The threat of Communist take-overs was, as Mr. Truman later put it, "only half the walnut." The other half was the staggering accumulation of wealth by the United States and in addition the problem of distributing it.

Self-interest was involved. Once Western Europe was on its feet, American planners thought, it would be a stronger ally in the cold war. Western Europe would also represent an important market for American goods and an ideal base for American companies eager to expand. . . .

What had started as special assistance for . . . Greece and Turkey was extended in the Marshall Plan to a formal program for American financial and moral support for a strong and, hopefully, united Europe that would no longer be a breeding ground for war. . . .

General Marshall invited all European countries except Spain to set up an organization that would coordinate the reconstruction efforts. Sixteen—Austria, Belgium, Britain, Denmark, France, Greece, Iceland, Ireland, Italy, Luxembourg, the Netherlands, Norway, Portugal, Sweden, Switzerland, and Turkey—responded. . . . They set up the Organization for European Economic Cooperation. . . .

Between 1948 and 1952 Congress voted grants and credits to Western Europe to the order of $13-billion, this atop the more than $9-billion already transferred since the war. The largest sums went to Britain and France, followed by Italy and Germany.

The Marshall Plan dollars started a process that has made Western Europe into one of the main economic power centers of the world and a competitor of the United States. Today, as Washington officials say repeatedly, "it's a new ball game." . . .

There was little doubt the food and raw materials the Marshall funds provided saved the Continent from economic collapse, but more than that they laid the foundation for spectacular growth in the 1950's and 1960's. . . .

The institutions created spurred the Europeans to think in terms of working together for mutual benefit. At first this took the form of the cautious but nevertheless important step of reducing monetary and trade barriers that took place in Paris negotiations in the late 1940's.

Then came the famous Schuman plan of June, 1950, in which the French Foreign Minister, Robert Schuman, and his chief aide, Jean Monnet, announced association with West Germany to form a single market for coal and steel—an association, or community, open to other European countries as well.

Ancient enemies forged a basic link that would help them work together for peace and higher standards of living. Four other countries—Italy, Belgium, the Netherlands and Luxembourg—joined what became the European Coal and Steel Community, and the six went on in 1957 to create the Economic Community, the customs and economic union that Britain is finally joining next January 1.

Two Economic Titans

The New York Times,
January 7, 1973, p. 3,
© 1973 by the New York
Times Company. Reprinted
by permission.

If one thinks of nations like rival heavyweights or football teams, the United States has acquired a formidable economic opponent in the expanded European Common Market. But at the same time, the two can be thought of basically as partners, with much to give each other.

The new European Economic Community, which grew from six members to nine last week with the official entry of Britain, Ireland and Denmark, ranks behind the United States in some respects, but outmatches it in others. . . .

The United States has a bigger resource base. Its land mass covers 3.54 million square miles compared to the Common Market's 587,000. The United States is four times as rich in primary energy sources—crude oil, natural gas, primary electricity, coal and lignite. But both blocs are short of energy, and this is likely to be a source of conflict between them—for access to Soviet or other energy resources.

How strong economically is the European Common Market compared to the United States and the Soviet Union?

COMPARATIVE STRENGTHS OF THE UNITED STATES, THE SOVIET UNION, AND THE EUROPEAN COMMON MARKET, 1970

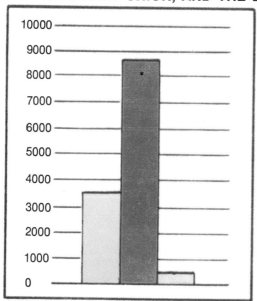

Total Area
(in millions of square miles)

* Total area does not include the
White Sea or the Sea of Azov

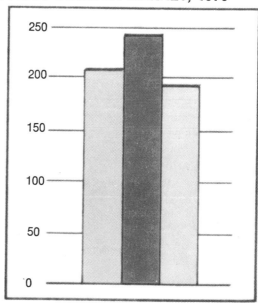

Population
(in millions)

370

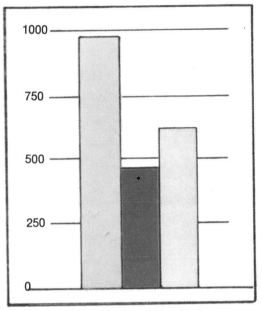

Gross National Product
(in billions)

* estimated

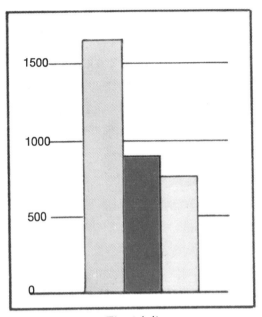

Electricity
(in billions of kilowatt hours)

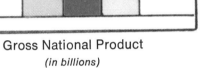 United States

Soviet Union

European
Common Market

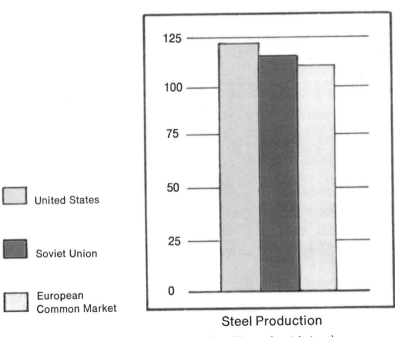

Steel Production
(in millions of metric tons)

America is deeper than Europe into the "post-industrial" age; more of its people have shifted from producing goods to services. The United States has over 60,000 computers in use—more than three times as many as Europe—and pours far bigger sums into scientific and technological research and development.

The European countries, with the major exception of Britain, have been growing faster economically than the United States. They have had lower rates of unemployment—but higher of inflation. . . .

The Nixon Administration accuses the Common Market of trying to stake out an unfair market claim over a much wider territory than its nine national members. Indeed, the European Community will in the next few years become a 16-nation, industrial, free-trade area; besides the nine full members of the Community, it will, according to an agreement already worked out, include Iceland, Finland, Norway, Sweden, Switzerland, Austria, and Portugal—the former members of the European Free Trade Association. The ex-E.F.T.A. members decided against full European Community membership and thus will be involved economically but not politically. . . .

With all the quarreling that has gone on over trade, investment, and monetary issues, many economists feel that there has been a tendency here to underrate the positive benefits for the United States of an expanding Common Market. They reject the analogy of contending heavyweights or football teams and stress the idea of partners with much to share. In 1971, for instance, the present Europe of Nine received $11.2-billion, or 25 percent, of all United States exports, while this country imported $10.4-billion of goods from the European Nine—or 22.8 percent of all United States imports.

As Europe grows, it becomes a bigger market for the United States, just as a growing America is a bigger market for the Europeans. Both become increasingly important areas for investment for each other's businesses. Although American investment in Europe has been much greater in the last two decades, the European rate of investment in the United States is growing faster now.

The two great blocs have a common, or at least similar, set of cultural and political traditions, and the flow of ideas—not only scientific and technological but also social, philosophical and moral—may in the long run be even more important than the flow of money.

FOR THOUGHT:

Do you think political, economic, and social progress can be made more rapidly by competing or cooperating nations?

Today the marks of western civilization appear in every area of the globe. In Tokyo, Japanese business people, dressed like business people in London and Chicago, hurry to work while neon signs advertise the wares sold in the city's shops. In Nairobi, Kenya, and in Lagos, Nigeria, skyscrapers rise into the sky. In Accra, Ghana, a parliament of Africans assembles in a manner reminiscent of Great Britain's Parliament. In India, a university scholar conducts experiments using the specific method developed by Galileo, Newton, and the scientists who followed them. In North Vietnam, a political leader broadcasts a speech to his people, explaining the principles of Karl Marx and then urging his followers to devote themselves to the nation. In the Republic of South Africa, the African majority hungers for equality.

Beginning in the 1400's and continuing through the present, western culture has been diffused to most of the nonwestern world. Diffusion means the spreading of traits, ideas, practices, institutions, products, and technological developments from one culture to another. Western culture has pushed its way into hidden villages and metropolitan centers. The impact of western diffusion has meant change—not always welcome—in the lives of most of the world's nonwestern peoples. And no one can truly understand the twentieth century without understanding this process and its results.

Diffusion began with the first civilizations that developed in the fertile river valleys of Mesopotamia. (See map, page 26.) At first, the diffusion was confined to its neighbors in the Tigris and Euphrates valleys. Gradually other civilizations formed, and, as they expanded, they spread their cultural achievements over longer distances. The ancient Greeks used the Mediterranean Sea as an avenue of commerce and ideas, and so transported their civilization from one end of the sea to the other. The Macedonian conqueror, Alexander the Great, spread Greek ideas farther eastward as he forged his giant empire in the Middle East. Later, the Romans who captured the remnants of Alexander's empire carried their ideas and institutions with them. As they moved into northern and western Europe, they brought with them the Greek values they had learned.

Until the late Middle Ages, diffusion had followed the natural highways through the river valleys and across the Mediterranean, and so was geographically limited. As a result, the civilizations of China, India, the Middle East, Africa, Latin America, and Europe had flourished while relatively ignorant of one another. When diffusion did begin to leap across geographical barriers, it traveled mostly from East to West. The agricultural revolution in late medieval Europe used the stirrup, the horse collar, and a heavy wheeled plow, all of which were imported from Russia. Gunpowder was originally a Chinese invention, as was the silk that the Crusaders introduced to Europe. The Crusades also reestablished western contact with Alexander's former empire where the works of great Greek thinkers had been preserved by Arab scholars. But with the Renaissance, the flow of diffusion reversed, traveling from West to East with rapidly increasing strength and speed.

Of all the aspects of western society that have been transplanted, perhaps the most obvious is the technological. The industrial changes that Great Britain experienced in the late 1700's spread to the European continent and to North America. Today, nearly all the wonders of western technology have been reproduced throughout the nonwestern world.

The West has also exported its democratic political institutions. In the legal courts of Ghana, organized when the nation was a British colony, the judges wear white wigs like their British predecessors. Similarly, the Philippine republic modeled its government after that of the United States. In addition to such political institutions, western ways of business management, of organizing universities, and even of family life have spread throughout the world.

Western ideologies have also passed into nonwestern thought. The ideal of equality was carried in the hearts of Americans and Europeans across the world's oceans. This ideal, and the democratic institutions that protect and stimulate it, has appealed to people everywhere. At the same time, the ideologies of Communism have been carried into much of Asia and parts of Africa and Latin America.

The early civilizations of China, India, North Africa, Sub-Saharan Africa, and the Middle East had all undergone highly innovative periods. Yet by the time the Renaissance had taken hold in Italy and the rest of Europe was beginning to throw off the traditions of the Middle Ages, these areas were moving closer to tradition. Finally, held back by tradition, they became open to the strong new ideas of the West. Their traditional ways could not hold out against the powerful western technology and social organizations. During the past five hundred years, the West has gradually come to dominate these other cultures.

One of the most obvious means of diffusing western culture has been conquest. During the sixteenth and seventeenth centuries, England,

▶ Do you think children should follow the ways of their parents, the ways of their own generation, or a combination of both?

France, Spain, Portugal, and the Netherlands conquered most of North and South America as well as India. After 1870, nearly all of Africa and much more of Asia came under western control. The conquering armies and the traders who followed them diffused western ideas and institutions throughout these continents.

The spreading of western culture into other nonwestern areas came with colonization. The British colonized Australia, bringing their language and institutions with them. Similarly, the Dutch colonized South Africa, to be followed two hundred years later by the British. The original colonists of the United States were mainly British, and they rerooted their ideas and institutions in the new land. The British were followed by millions of immigrants from nearly every nation, each group injecting some of its own culture.

The West has also diffused its culture by trade. Conquerors, colonists, and merchants set up a network of trade routes throughout the world. Over these routes moved all the products of western factories; back came the products of the non-West: tea, spices, rubber, art, philosophy, and many other things.

Education, both formal and informal, has also helped to spread western ideas and institutions. Thousands of nonwestern leaders have studied in western schools and colleges, both in their own lands and in Europe, the United States, and Canada. Books, movies, television shows, and radio broadcasts from the West are shaping the minds of people all over the world.

What happens when a modern western culture with an advanced technology and sophisticated political and social systems comes into contact with a land gripped by tradition? There is no one answer. The North American Indians rejected the culture of the white people except for their horses and guns. The Hottentots in South Africa acted similarly. On the other hand, some people have made a nearly total adoption of western ways. The Japanese have within a century made themselves into a western-style nation. But most nations lie midway between the extremes, having adopted some ideas and rejected other ideas.

What happens when two cultures meet depends on numerous factors. The sizes of the groups has some effect on the results of such contact. The Hottentots lived in tiny tribes centered around waterholes, and they had no large-scale political organizations to pull them together. Hence, they were easily exterminated when the Dutch, with an advanced technology, took their waterholes. On the other hand, because of the millions of Chinese, the Europeans could only establish a tiny foothold in China. Eventually, the Chinese were able to push the Europeans out entirely.

Another important factor is the way in which two cultures come into contact. Conquered peoples sometimes must accept ways of life they would not adopt willingly. Wars can prevent diffusion. The Bantu of South Africa who fought fiercely for their lands against the white invaders were not likely to accept European institutions willingly. On the other hand, nonwestern people who are eager to benefit from western technology and have something valuable to trade often find diffusion mutually advantageous. Japan's experience is a case in point.

Geographic environment also plays a role in the process of diffusion. It is difficult to transplant European civilization to the Arctic and Antarctic because farming, the basis of the civilization, cannot be carried on there. But Europeans quickly adapted to the North American continent where the physical environment is similar to the one they had known.

The points of cultural contact between two peoples must also be considered. It is easier for diffusion to take place if two societies have some common elements. But if they have very different political institutions, ways of making a living, family structures, values, and religions, then the members of the two societies are more likely to become enemies rather than learn from each other.

No matter how the diffusion of western culture takes place, it brings problems to nonwestern peoples. Living for many centuries according to the same ways, nonwesterners are suddenly forced to leave their small villages to work in factories. To adjust to city living, they have had to change the structure of their families. The extended families, in which relatives of three and four generations have lived under the same roof, have given way to the western family pattern of mother, father, and children. Their religions have been challenged by Christian missionaries. Their leaders have been conquered. Their values and their political institutions have been weakened.

Rapidly rising standards of living in many parts of the world are one of the benefits of western diffusion. Western medicines have wiped out many diseases. The western system of justice has improved the criminal codes· in some countries. Western conquest has sometimes ended tribal wars of many years.

However, the good has been mixed with some bad. The West has led some nations to adopt an extreme nationalism that encourages them to use many of their resources for the development of weapons rather than the goods their people need. The West has also exported totalitarianism. And Western institutions, inventions, techniques, and ideas have thrown some value systems into conflict. Many nonwestern people doubt that the cost of western culture has always been worth the gains it has brought.

65 THE DIFFUSION
OF THE WEST:
A PICTURE ESSAY

The pictures on the following pages have all been taken in nonwestern countries. Examine them carefully to answer the following questions:

1. What is being diffused?
2. What is the major agency of diffusion in each case?

Presidential campaign in Chile, 1971

Vietnam

Tokyo, Japan

Ghana

China

Uganda

Republic Day in Malawi

Soccer match in Ghana

Agricultural library in Nigeria

380

Tokyo, Japan

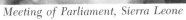
Meeting of Parliament, Sierra Leone

Egypt

Republic of the Congo

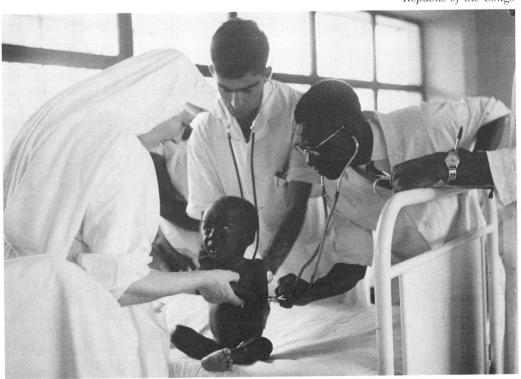

Boy Scout parade in Ghana

Japan

Sao Paulo, Brazil

For full descriptions of these activities, turn to the **Student Book of Activities and Readings** included among the materials for individual and group activities.

Activity 15A: Collage or bulletin board display of the spread of western influence throughout the world (individual or group)
Collect a number of pictures from magazines and newspapers that show evidence of western influence in different parts of the world today. Arrange them in a collage or bulletin board display.

Activity 15B: Examination of the role of the United States in the western world after World War II through the use of contemporary newspaper articles (individual)
Go to the library and read newspaper accounts of events in the western world during the years 1945–1960. Use your local newspaper as your source. Then write an essay on the role of the United States in the western world following World War II, based on the evidence you have found.

INDEX

C

Calvin, John, 100-101, 113; and Calvinist economic ideas, 191, 194, 204-205

capitalism, 323

capital resources: in eighteenth-century Europe, *p 202*, 205-206; in medieval Europe, 42-43; Soviet, 332

Catholic Church, Roman, 86, 89, 96; and Italian independence, 267-268; Council of Trent, 101-102, 106, 113-114; English Parliament and, 253, 260; Sacrament of the Eucharist, 102, *p 103*, 104; sale of indulgences, *p 84*, 101, 108, 113

Catholic Emancipation Act, 253

Cavour, Count Camillo di, 268, 270, 280

Cellini, Benvenuto, 70-75, 86

centralized planning, 335

Chamberlain, Houston Stewart, 344, 356

Chamberlin, Neville, 349

Charlemagne, 37-42; government of, 37-38, 57, 58; laws of, 39, 42; life of, 38-41

Charles I, King of England, 128-129, 136-137

Charles II, King of England, 129, 137

China, 312, 360, 365-366, 374, 375

China, Nationalist, 365

China, People's Republic of, 365

Chinese Communist Party, 365

Christianity: and equality, 235-236; before the Reformation, 89-91, 107; contribution to western values, 15, 29-31, 34, 36; in the Roman Empire, 57, 58

Church: Anglican, 129; Catholic, 86, 89, 96, 101-102, 106, 113-114; Orthodox, 315, 332; Reformed, 89, 92-93, 97-105, 108-114

citizenship, 221-222, 226, 228, 250; civil rights and, 235-239; movement for full, 233; political rights and, 233, 237, 238, 239, 240; social rights and, 245-250

city-states: in ancient Greece, 21, 258, 276; in Renaissance Italy, 64, 65-69, 72, 82, 83, 267

civil rights, 221-222, 223, 226; and citizenship, 235-239; and freedom, 233, 250, 252; in England, U.S., and France, 239, 251, 252, 253; in Soviet Union, 256, 333-334

classification system, 14; example of, 2

Code: Justinian, 27-28; Napoleonic, 232

Colbert, Jean-Baptiste, 153-159, 190-191

Cold War, 362-366, 367

collective farms, 325, 326, 332

collective security, 309-313

colonies, 244-245, 360, 362, 366, 374-375; English, 11, 114, 138, 218, 252, 290, 292, 307; French, 285, 287, 289; German, 288, 304, 306; Italian, 312

command economy, 38, 43, 334-335; economic growth in a, 195; *See also* absolutism, authoritarianism, autocracy, communism, Nazism

Common Market, 366, 369-372

communism, 280, 312, 343, 355; and equality, 237-238; and social rights, 256; in China, 365; in eastern Europe, 360, 365; in Germany, 338, 339, 341

communist ideology, 320-325

Communist Manifesto, 237-238, 321-322

Communist Party, 332-333, 334; achievements of, 330, 332; Twentieth Congress of, 323-325; under Stalin's control, 323

Communist Revolution: in China, 365; in Russia, 300, 314, 320, 325, 330, 360

computers, 6, 372

Confucius, 234

Congress of Vienna, 282, 287, 307-308

Constitution: British, see Magna Carta, Parliament; German, 338, 350, 356-357; Soviet, 329, 333, 334; U.S., 252

Copernicus, Nicholas, 172, 173, 176, 181-182

Council of Trent, 101-102, 106, 113-114

Crimean War, 316

Cromwell, Oliver, 129, 136-137

Crusades, 34, 58-59, *p 60*, 64, 82, 90, 108; and trade, 204, 374

Czechoslovakia, 304, 306, 312, 349, 357-358, 365

D

Daladier, Edouard, 349

Dante Alighieri, 75

Danzig, 304, 306, 342

Dardanelles, 285, 302

data, role of, in historical investigation, 14

decision-making, 38, 43, 188, 221, 293; in a market economy, 187, 194-195, 205, 209;

ART ACKNOWLEDGMENTS

ART ACKNOWLEDGMENTS

Chapter 8: p. 192 (top and bottom) The British Museum. p. 193 (top and bottom left) The British Museum; (bottom right) Staats Archiv, Hamburg. p. 199 The Royal Society for the Encouragement of Arts, Manufactures and Commerce. p. 202 (top) The Granger Collection; (center right) The Bettmann Archive; (bottom) New York Public Library. p. 208, National Gallery, London.

Chapter 9: p. 214 (top and bottom) New York Public Library. p. 220 (top) Culver Pictures; (bottom) The Bettmann Archive. p. 224 New York Public Library, Prints Division, Astor, Lenox, and Tilden Foundations. p. 225 (top and bottom) New York Public Library. p. 229 (left and right) New York Public Library.

Chapter 10: p. 236 P. Gunther, Shostal Associates. p. 241 Bill Strowe, Black Star. p. 249 (top) Mimi Forsyth, Monkmeyer; (bottom left) Roger Lubin, Jeroboam; (bottom right) H.R.& W. Photo. p. 254 U.P.I. p. 255 (top) Wide World Photos. p. 256, Michael Abramson, Black Star.

Chapter 11: p. 263 Brown Brothers. p. 269 (bottom) W.D. Murphy, Shostal Associates; (center left) H.R.& W. Photo; (top left) The Port of New York Authority; (top right) West Point Museum Collections, U.S. Military Academy. p. 274 United Nations Photo. p. 278 (top) N.A.S.A.; (bottom) courtesy, French Government Tourist Office. p. 279 (left) Brown Brothers; (top right) The West Point Museum Collections, U.S. Military Academy; (bottom right) H.R.& W. Photo by Russell Dian.

Chapter 12: p. 286 (top) Wide World Photos; (bottom left and right) Alan Mercer. p. 294 The Bettmann Archive. p. 295 (top, center, and bottom) The Bettmann Archive. p. 298 George Grosz, *Fit for Active Service*, The Museum of Modern Art, Conger Goodyear Fund. p. 310 (top left) Culver Pictures; (top right) H. Roger Viollet, Paris; (bottom) Imperial War Museum, London. p. 311 (top) Pictorial Parade; (bottom) Imperial War Museum, London.

Chapter 13: p. 318 (top and bottom) Culver Pictures. p. 322 The Forbes Magazine Fabrege Collection, courtesy, A La Vieille Russie, New York. p. 327 *The New York Times.*

Chapter 14: p. 347 (top and bottom right) Wide World Photos; (bottom left) U.P.I. p. 352 (top) Wide World Photo; (bottom) courtesy, YIVO, Institute for Jewish Research.

Chapter 15: p. 377 Ingeborg Lippmann, Magnum. p. 378 (top) Bruno Barbey, Magnum; (bottom left) Rene Burri, Magnum; (bottom right) Halperin, Monkmeyer. p. 379 (top left) Marc Riboud, Magnum; (top right) Unicef photo by George Holton; (bottom) Monkmeyer Press Photo. p. 380 (top) William Mares, Monkmeyer; (bottom left) Halperin, Monkmeyer; (bottom right) Rene Burri, Magnum. p. 381 (top left) Halperin, Monkmeyer; (top right) Bessim, Monkmeyer; (bottom) UNations. p. 382 (top left) Halperin, Monkmeyer; (top right) Paul Fusco, Magnum; (bottom) Bruno Barbey, Magnum.